THUG CRIMINOLOGY

A Call to Action

Edited by Adam Ellis, Olga Marques, and Anthony Gunter

Thug Criminology combines the urgent and as yet silenced voices of former gang/street-involved peoples turned academics, alongside their allies, in order to challenge and disrupt mainstream and academic knowledge about urban youth gangs specifically, and the "streets" more broadly.

The book questions how the "streets" – and the racialized and marginalized urban communities who inhabit them – are researched, taught, and subsequently politicized. It looks at who gets to produce such knowledge, who benefits from such knowledge, and whose voices are privileged within dominant academic and public policy discourses. Drawing on decolonizing methodologies, the book seeks to give voice to scholars with lived experience of a "street" or gang life. Adam Ellis, Olga Marques, and Anthony Gunter reclaim the terms *thug* and *gang* to reconstruct the narrative around street-involved youth, seeing them not as criminals but rather as survivors of historical oppression and trauma. Challenging the colonial structure of criminology and other disciplines that focus on street crime, *Thug Criminology* aims to disrupt and disentangle the knowledge that has been produced on gangs and urban violence.

ADAM ELLIS is an assistant professor of criminology at the University of Waterloo and the founder of The Street Institute.

OLGA MARQUES is an associate professor of criminology and justice at Ontario Tech University.

ANTHONY GUNTER is a senior lecturer and program lead for childhood and youth studies at The Open University.

Thug Criminology

A Call to Action

EDITED BY ADAM ELLIS, OLGA MARQUES,
AND ANTHONY GUNTER

UNIVERSITY OF TORONTO PRESS
Toronto Buffalo London

© University of Toronto Press 2023
Toronto Buffalo London
utorontopress.com
Printed in the USA

ISBN 978-1-4875-4557-4 (cloth)   ISBN 978-1-4875-4921-3 (EPUB)
ISBN 978-1-4875-4723-3 (paper)   ISBN 978-1-4875-4765-3 (PDF)

Library and Archives Canada Cataloguing in Publication

Title: Thug criminology : a call to action / edited by Adam Ellis, Olga Marques, and Anthony Gunter.
Names: Ellis, Adam (Lecturer in criminology), editor. | Marques, Olga, editor. | Gunter, Anthony, editor.
Description: Includes bibliographical references and index.
Identifiers: Canadiana (print) 20230207103 | Canadiana (ebook) 20230207197 | ISBN 9781487545574 (cloth) | ISBN 9781487547233 (paper) | ISBN 9781487547653 (PDF) | ISBN 9781487549213 (EPUB)
Subjects: LCSH: Gangs. | LCSH: Gang members. | LCSH: Hoodlums. | LCSH: Urban violence. | LCSH: Crime – Sociological aspects. | LCSH: Crime and race. | LCSH: Criminology.
Classification: LCC HV6437.T48 2023 | DDC 364.106/6–dc23

Cover design: Val Cooke
Cover illustration: iStock.com/chingraph

We wish to acknowledge the land on which the University of Toronto Press operates. This land is the traditional territory of the Wendat, the Anishnaabeg, the Haudenosaunee, the Métis, and the Mississaugas of the Credit First Nation.

University of Toronto Press acknowledges the financial support of the Government of Canada, the Canada Council for the Arts, and the Ontario Arts Council, an agency of the Government of Ontario, for its publishing activities.

Canada Council for the Arts   Conseil des Arts du Canada

I Couldn't Find My Smile in the Mirror

I couldn't find my smile in the mirror
Through trials tribulations n terror
I'm from the crow we fly high
Birds of a feather
We not a gang, we a family
At least that's what I thought
Till the wheels fall off
If you ever had a problem
I wouldn't think twice
I wouldn't blink twice
Right or wrong I'm skating on thin ice
We was going through it
This is more than music
Introduced to the game
I was just a student
Tryna find a way out
Feds did a shakedown
Almost had a breakdown
Times in my life, I been wanted
Making plays like the '96 Jordan
Whatchu know about payin mortgage
Whatchu know late night early mornings
Whatchu know about makin headlines
Can't find a job cause u x con
I been faced with jail time, house arrest then probation, interrogation
P.O. wanna know ya location
5-0 building new cases
The schools, the systems, police all racist.

Smirk. G

Contents

Introduction 3
ADAM ELLIS, OLGA MARQUES, AND ANTHONY GUNTER

Part One: They Don't Give a F**k about Us! Defanging and Decolonizing the Criminological Enterprise

1 Problematizing Traditional Criminological Perspectives on Thugs and Gangs 13
OLGA MARQUES

2 The White Male Criminological Gaze as Pornography: The Quasi-sexual Academic Obsession with Black "Gang Bangers" 27
ANTHONY GUNTER

3 Writing Themselves Out of Research: "Whitemaleness" and the Study of "Gang" Active Young Women 42
CLARE CHOAK

4 Somethin' Doesn't Seem Right: A Commentary on the "Scientific Method" and "Gang" Research 57
ADAM ELLIS AND ANTHONY GUNTER

Part Two: "Getting Over" and Inside the Ivory Tower

5 I Am (Not) What You Say I Am: Disrupting the Colonizers' "Gang" 75
GREGORY BROWN

6 A Black Scholar's Intellectual Journey and Subsequent Perspective on the White Colonial "Gang" Project 85
IAN JOSEPH

7 Good Trouble: Creating Spaces for Criminalized Populations in the Ivory Tower   93
LILY GONZALEZ, JAVIER RODRIGUEZ, AND ROBERT WEIDE

Part Three: Word on the Street

8 Shook Ones: An Insider's Perspective on Trauma, PTSD, and the Re-enactment of Street-Related Violence   111
ADAM ELLIS, STEPHANIE BÉLANGER, AND LUCA BERARDI

9 (De)Criminalizing the "Code of Silence": Reflections of a Former "Gang Banger" Turned Academic   131
ANTHONY HUTCHINSON AND JARED MILLICAN

10 The Raid: State Violence and Traumatic Responses in the Lives of Black Women   142
MELISSA P. McLETCHIE

11a Letter from the Streetz: Growing Up in the Gutter   153
TURK

11b Letter from the Streetz: Don't Interrupt Me   155
TG

11c Letter from the Penitentiary: The Change in Me   157
ALEJANDRO VIVAR

11d Letter from the Streetz: Dear Hip Hop   161
MARCUS SINGLETON

Part Four: Decolonizing the "Gang Industry"

12 Crime as Disease Contagion and Control: The Public Health Perspective and Implications for Black and Other Ethnic Minority Communities   167
ANTHONY GUNTER

13 A Violent Cure? Problematizing the "Cure Violence" Initiative   185
MALTE RIEMANN

14 When the System Harms: An Insider's Perspective on the Negative Socio-psychological Impact of "Gang Intervention"   198
TAMMY TINNEY

15 Fight Poverty, Fight Crime: A Justice-Focused Approach for Toronto/Canada   212
   YAFET TEWELDE AND JULET ALLEN

16 We Make the Path by Walking It: Repairing, Restoring, and Constructing Pathways   235
   RICK KELLY

Epilogue: Reflection   251
   ADAM ELLIS AND ANTHONY GUNTER

Contributors   255

Index   263

THUG CRIMINOLOGY

Introduction

ADAM ELLIS, OLGA MARQUES, AND ANTHONY GUNTER

Gaventa writes, "Fundamental questions must be raised about what knowledge is produced, by whom, for whose interests, and toward what end. Such arguments begin to demand the creation of a new paradigm and organization of science – one that is not only for the people but is created with them and by them as well" (1993, 40).

Following from Howard Becker (1963), scholars such as Liebling (2001) ask, Whose side are criminologists on? Who owns the discipline of criminology? Who polices its borders? Since the time of classical theorists such as Beccaria and Lombroso, the intellectual foundation of criminology has sought to understand why crime occurs. Although criminology has developed several schools of thought to answer this question (i.e., classical, positivist, Chicago school, etc.), these early classical theorists have recently been confronted by a "new criminology" that challenges the knowledge produced on crime and criminal behaviour. Since tis genesis, criminology has been a space where white males of privilege have written about the criminal "Other." Classical theorists such as Merton (1938), Shaw and McKay (1942), and others produced a vast body of criminological knowledge that largely focused on the "criminal behaviour" of lower-class minority youth. While these theorists have been celebrated for transforming our understanding of crime, including shifting intellectual ideas of criminal behaviour from that of individual pathology to environmental risks factors, the discourse of crime and youth delinquency has largely been framed from a white Euro-American-centred perspective.

More recently, the hegemonic racist patriarchy of traditional/mainstream criminology has been challenged by, for example, critical/convict/feminist/Black perspectives. However, these vital and urgent dissenting scholarly voices are still forced to speak from the margins of the discipline, and questions of who is "expert" and who is "spectacle" persist. Even more unremitting are questions of who belongs in those spaces. Such queries are prescient, considering that while new and more critical criminologies have emerged as a counterpoint to traditional criminological frameworks, they still repeat the unchallenged languages, perspectives and positions of privilege while still talking about being inclusive, intersectional, and liberating. In talking about "crime," the "criminal," and the "victim," criminological frameworks still use the language and knowledge of the hegemonic, the mainstream, and the status quo. Convict criminology, as a case in point, has tried to circumvent this positional dilemma by starting with the voices from within the penal system. However, while convict criminologists are not an exclusive group encourage[ing] "dialogue across the ex-con/non-con divide" (Ross et al. 2016, 494), do scholars who have been in conflict with the law, but never incarcerated, feel connected to a sub-discipline rooted in understanding and effecting change in incarceration? Is incarceration the starting point of importance for all insider-insider academics?

In reinvigorating debates about experts, knowledge, the spectacle, and insider/outsider status (that is mainstream academics with no ties to the streets and/or formerly street-involved people who are now scholars but do not hold an academic position), we noted a gap within criminology – which focused on the insider/insider researcher (that is formerly street-involved people who now hold academic positions). Within this context, we argue that the space of "traditional criminology" (and in some respects critical criminology) has become problematic, as those with the power to construct knowledge on crime and criminal behaviour continue to use the language *about* the "gangster," "thug," and "offender." With specific reference to violent crime and gangs, this is highly problematic because a small but influential number of criminologists in the United States – and an equally small but growing cadre of gang scholars based in countries such as the United Kingdom, Canada, and Australia – have dangerously and misleadingly conflated these two contested terms. Moreover, drawing uncritically on law enforcement statistics and agendas, these self-anointed "gang experts" provide the academic legitimacy, couched in scientific fact, as well as the language that is used outside the walls of academia to pathologize, criminalize, and disproportionately punish Black and other racialized minority communities.

"Thug" turned Criminologist

As an ex–gang member turned academic, I (the first author) remember what it was like growing up in poverty, within a subculture of violence, and what it felt like to be labelled a gang member or "thug." Years ago, I was sitting in a courtroom awaiting sentencing with my co-d's (co-defendants), arrested for fighting and possession of marijuana, all of us facing jail time as young offenders. While the events and sentencing did not bother me it is what the judge said in court that day that has affected me throughout my life. After handing down his sentence the judge stood up and said, "You are nothing but a menace to society

... thugs, criminals and delinquents." While the physical violence of gang war did not hurt, nor did the prospect of incarceration, it was the labels and words this white-privileged man used to describe us that destroyed my sense of humanity and hope. I recall how he reaffirmed that I was not part of "his" society or world, and as a result for the next several years I never saw myself as a citizen or participant within "normal'" Canadian society. Although his words sealed the fate of several young men just trying to survive, the narrative of the gang had far-reaching implications. As we moved through the criminal justice system, our police records, institutional documents, and probation reports continued to label us "delinquent" and gang-involved. Once we were back in our communities these labels of gang/gang member justified the police/courts' hyper-surveillance and punitive policing practices to control the "threat." For over a decade I watched my friends become targets of arbitrary frisks/searches, raids, and arrests. Young lives were ruined and families were dismantled because of criminal justice interventions.

Why and What Is Thug Criminology?

We are concerned about how the discourse on urban violence and gangs/gang members has been constructed within academia, and whether criminology has perpetuated stereotypes about the "othered" and racialized minority gang bangers/violent "super predators" / thugs. The criminological literature gangs is/has largely focused on the US context with comparatively little research conducted in other jurisdictions of the world. However, international scholars who study the gang phenomena rely heavily on US concepts, models, and methodologies to inform their own understandings about, the problem and prevalence of gangs, defining gangs, suppressing gang activity, and preventing lethal youth violence. We believe that the current literature on gangs and urban violence causes more harm than good and is helping to create a bloated gang industry comprising academia, law enforcement, and other state agencies, alongside community groups enticed by government funding to tackle gun violence and gang crime.

Thug criminology is a way to disrupt and disentangle the knowledge produced on gangs and urban violence. We hope to reimagine not only how marginalized urban youth and their communities are researched, but also how this information is shared through the education system and the media, and amongst policymakers. Thug criminology is driven partly by the frustration of ex-street-involved academics with the current knowledge on gangs and urban violence. However, thug criminology is not only about gangs and violent crime. Those with tangential experiences who start from perspectives that challenge normative criminological, psychological, legal, and law enforcement boundaries surrounding "thug," "gang," "gang member," and violent offender also have an important space within thug criminology. In this space we can dismantle the discursive languages, frameworks, and spaces used by crime and criminology experts that target and pathologize vulnerable groups, such as the *DSM* and political and media buzzwords, and the encroachment of police/legal positional standpoints onto the discipline of criminology.

Thug criminology centres on beginning the analysis with the voices from "below," that is, from those with lived experiences. In doing so, it is attentive to how labels of "thug," "gang member," "deviant," etc. are applied to the "Other" and how these labels originate from, and are the language of, privilege. While their personal backgrounds might not be described as such, academics occupy privileged spaces, who, through their work, invade marginalized spaces to unearth "their" truth. Within the voyeuristic research/academic enterprise, research subjects as *spectacle, outsider, other* are afforded limited spaces to speak. They are called upon for their knowledge but fail to be integrated as "expert." Their lived experiences are rewritten through the words and perspectives of the status quo, as "thugs," "gang members," and "criminals'" despite our best intentions, mainly because there are no other words. Thug criminology seeks to provide a platform to start these discussions and understandings.

This edited volume is more than a book, it is a movement – *A Call to Action*. We have gathered a community of scholar/activists, former "gang members" turned academics (and others who have worked with gang populations) to stand in solidarity, who not only provide a fresh – critical lens – on the topic, they also seek to challenge the status quo policies and practices constructed to dismantle the "gang problem." We conceive of this book as an invitation. It is a starting point. We hope that each chapter challenges readers to think about and through their own "knowledge" of gangs, gang membership, and gang members, particularly since there is much debate amongst scholars and practitioners about the definitions of these terms. Urban violence in the United States, Canada, and the United Kingdom, and specifically critiques of the misinformed and dangerous responses by law enforcement, policymakers, and the academy to these "street problems" are the main foci of this book. Moreover, while this volume includes a wide array of contributors, we are aware of key omissions and silences; for example, the voices and perspectives of street-involved young women and Indigenous youth are not included in this collection. This is an oversight we will endeavour to rectify in future thug criminology book projects.

Part One: They Don't Give a F**k about Us! Defanging and Decolonizing the Criminological Enterprise

The aim of this section and of the collection is to challenge and dismantle the criminologists' gang. Olga Marques's chapter problematizes the gaze of privilege that has framed criminology (and the other social science disciplines) and from which all knowledge about "crime," "the criminal," and most importantly "the gang member" and "thug" has been produced, repeated, and maintained. Mainstream lay and disciplinary-specific theorizing and understandings continue to incorrectly and dangerously reproduce articulations of what is a gang and who is a thug that originate from state institutions, and enforcers, of social control. Anthony Gunter moves on to look at race/racism and the question of gangs, provocatively comparing the white male academic's voyeuristic obsession with urban Black "gang bangers" to that of consumers of pornography seeking cheap thrills and sexual gratification. However, when one considers colonialism, slavery, and a 500-year history of the criminalization and violent oppression of Black bodies – and the role of the Euro-American academy – it is glaringly obvious that the quasi-sexual obsession of white males (not only scholars but also law enforcement, politicians, and journalists) goes far beyond gangs, back to the slave ships and plantations of the New World.

Clare Choak provides a long overdue gendered intersectional analysis rooted in her own positionality and lived experience. The chapter explores the representations and misrepresentations of young women in gangs from the perspective of academics and policymakers who have constructed them primarily as sexual victims and/or on the periphery. Last, it critiques the gang enthusiasts who have produced a body of academic research that fails to reflect on their own positionality in terms of age, class, gender, and race and adopt a positivist stance on the collection of empirical data. Adam Ellis and Anthony Gunter provide a critique (drawing on the first author's direct experience as a student criminologist) of the social-"scientific" research methodologies utilized by gang scholars for more than a century. During this period, largely privileged white Euro-American academic "colonizers" have created knowledge that has problematized, criminalized and "othered" Indigenous, non-white, and poor communities. Consequently, only one side of the story is/has ever been told; as such the chapter concludes by asserting the need for a new criminology that recognizes its privilege and one is open to transformation.

Part Two: "Getting Over" and Inside the Ivory Tower

Gregory Brown's chapter "I Am (Not) What You Say I Am" uses his own unique positionality – borne out of his experience as an insider to academia and an insider to the gang life – to deconstruct, rearticulate and "disrupt the colonizer's gang." Although he never claimed to be a gang member, the fact that he grew up in a poor and predominantly Black neighbourhood with an emerging Latinx population meant that he and his male peers were automatically identified and treated as a "gang member" by the police and wider society – bait for the "school-to-prison pipeline." Meanwhile, Ian Joseph provides a first-hand biographical account of the difficult personal journey that a young Black man, born and raised in a deprived urban community, bucked the "pipeline." Along the way, he provides an up close and personal discussion and critique chronicling how the present day UK "gang crisis" and its associated "industry" came to be. Lily Gonzalez, Javier Rodriguez, and Robert Weide make an important distinction between "bad trouble" and "good trouble." Bad trouble occurs when one is punished for doing wrong by others, but good trouble is when one is punished for doing right by others. In this chapter, these scholars provide biographical narratives that illustrate the challenges faced and personal price be paid by criminalized student and faculty populations for standing up for oneself in the oppressive environment of the neoliberal corporate university.

Part Three: Word on the Street

Adam Ellis, Stephanie Bélanger, and Luca Berardi's "Shook Ones" draws on an "insider's" knowledge of PTSD and street-related violence to explore several questions: Can the concepts of PTSD and the re-enactment of trauma be used to understand the violence espoused by street-involved populations? Can (and should) members of street organizations be seen and treated as trauma victims/survivors? Can their behaviours and actions (including violence) be understood as the result of trauma? Most important, do street-involved youth deserve our (society's) help? Anthony Hutchinson and Jared Millican set out to "decriminalize" the code of silence which – from normative societal viewpoints – is largely associated with racialized poor communities. Reflecting on the code of silence from the first author's insider experience, the chapter details a pervasive and perpetual "code of silence" that vulnerable and traumatized children experience in adult/societal abuse and their involvement in street gang behaviour. Then, continuing into adulthood and their experiences as employees, they encounter the institutional "code of silence" of the powerful, which protects alleged transgressors of human rights at the expense of victims.

Melissa P. McLetchie's chapter provides a raced and gendered first-hand experience of the psychosocial impact of police violence and other state-sanctioned systems of racial oppression. She argues that law enforcement systems, reproductive systems, and child welfare systems in North America have weaponized their "rights" and privilege against Black people for decades, particularly Black women. It is important therefore, as a Black woman, "for me to use my experiences (regardless of how they may be perceived) to challenge narratives about Black womanhood" while encouraging and empowering other Black women to do the same. This section concludes with four brief "Letters from the Streetz": Turk's "Growing Up in the Gutter," TG's "Don't Interrupt Me," Alejandro Vivar's "The Change in Me," and Marc Singleton's "Dear Hip Hop."

Part Four: Decolonizing the Gang Industry

Anthony Gunter outlines how in response to England's "violent crime epidemic" there is now an upsurge of media-driven political interest in this perspective – specifically, the Violence Reduction Unit of Police Scotland. He maintains that the public health approach fails to resolve fundamental questions about structural inequality, criminalization, and state racism. Instead of being a panacea, the chapter concludes by asserting that the crime as contagious virus perspective risks further stigmatizing already problematized Black and minority communities. Malte Remann's chapter critiques the cure violence model (CV): a public health approach to prevent gun violence pioneered in Chicago by Dr. Gary Slutkin. The premise of this model is that violence is a contagious disease that can be controlled and contained through epidemiological methods and strategies. Projects based on the CV model have been implemented in over 100 communities across sixteen countries. However, beneath its philanthropic innocence and anti-violence message, according to Reimann, CV produces violent practices and effects.

Tammy Tinney, a health care provider, voices frustration at the constant persecution and negative labels that people she works with are subjected to, because of repressive government policies that fixate on tackling crime and gang violence. Meanwhile, politicians refuse to address the systemic root causes for why those who are labelled and "othered" as "bad," "a criminal," "no good," and "a throw away" end up living the life they do. Tinney argues that until more attention is given to the systemic causes of inequality (poverty, discrimination, and marginalization) with this population, "I feel as though I'm helping them put bandages over open wounds, only for them to be thrown back into the same system that created the wounds in the first place."

Yafet Tewelde and Julet Allen argue that to better understand and address crime within Black, racially marginalized, and low-income communities, it is necessary to first examine how systemic violence – specifically racism and colonialism – in Canada has been directed towards the Black community. The authors also assert that in place of hard policing and racial profiling, true crime fighting is rooted in prevention and intervention via fighting poverty, exclusion, and racism. Rick Kelly's intervention makes clear that the label of "gang" does not reflect the underlying needs of individuals involved in street crime. His chapter draws on the voices and lived experiences of individuals who have experienced, seen, or participated in violence in their communities, incarceration, weapons charges, and the tragic loss of loved ones. The author applies a restorative lens focus on the reparative, restorative, and preventive approaches that lead to transformation for individuals and their communities.

REFERENCES

Becker, H.S. 1963. *Outsiders: Studies in the Sociology of Deviance*. New York: Free Press.

Gaventa, J. 1993. "The Powerful, the Powerless, and the Experts: Knowledge Struggles in an Information Age." in *Voices of Change: Participatory Research in the United States and Canada*, edited by P. Park, M. Brydon-Miller, B. Hall, and T. Jackson, 21–40. Toronto: OISE Press.

Liebling, A. 2001. "Whose Side Are We On? Theory, Practice and Allegiances in Prison Research." *British Journal of Criminology* 43 (3): 472–84. https://doi.org/10.1093/bjc/41.3.472.

Merton, R.K. 1938. "Social Structure and Anomie." *American Sociological Review* 3 (5): 672–82. https://doi.org/10.2307/2084686.

Ross, J.I., R.S. Jones, M. Lenza, and S.C. Richards. 2016. "Convict Criminology and the Struggle for Inclusion." *Critical Criminology* 24 (4): 489–501. https://doi.org/10.1007/s10612-016-9332-9.

Shaw, C.R., and H.D. McKay. 1942. *Juvenile Delinquency and Urban Areas*. Chicago: University of Chicago Press.

PART ONE

They Don't Give a F**k about Us! Defanging and Decolonizing the Criminological Enterprise

1 Problematizing Traditional Criminological Perspectives on Thugs and Gangs

OLGA MARQUES

Gangs are a survival unit that happens in the neighbourhood because people are tough. Young men decide: If we clique up, we're safer. That's all a gang starts out being. A protection unit. Then we decide, if three of us are tough, five of us are tougher. Meanwhile none of us has anything. Take the gangbangers' outfit. It is the least expensive clothing: A white tee shirt, some Converses, pressed jeans, a carefully folded rag. That's not by choice. That's the cheapest shit at the swap meet. So what the ghetto kids have done is take nothing and turned it into something by turning it into power. The kids in the suburbs, the rich kids, have their cars, computers, designer clothing. But here comes the gang. They can be scared of us. We get a little fun out of that. It's a way of balancing. (Ice T 2005, xviii)

How do we know what we know? *Why* do we know what we know? And most important, *who* (that is, from whose eyes/perspectives) do we know what we know? These questions are of central importance yet are rarely given critical thought. As scholars or practitioners who study or work with marginalized, stigmatized, and/or criminalized populations, we must seriously consider the call to question and understand where our own knowledges have come from, and most important, how our own work contributes to the cadre of scholarship that keeps social institutions and societal structures intact. Even the most critical of scholars and practitioners among us need to take heed. Much of our work, while chipping away at social institutions and structures, leaves them in place. Tweaking prison programming or policing practices, adjusting availability or accessibility of community services and supports, etc., does not challenge *why* the system exists the way it does. Nor does it dismantle these systems and structures that are designed as "othering" institutions. They remain intact, just covered with new wallpaper.

In April 2019, Critical Criminology, a working group that publishes *Radical Criminology* and *Thought|Crimes Press*, tweeted, "Too many 'criminologists' are committed to reproducing systems of repression, maintaining structures of oppression rather than understanding and thus ending them. Uncritically accepting the legitimacy of repressive institutions. Benefitting from careerist arrangements."

To be clear, this is not an indictment of criminology alone. In fact, many disciplines – criminology, psychology, anthropology, social work, etc. – were designed to explain, identify, and even "fix" or return the "other" to "normal." The issue is even more pronounced in disciplines such as biology, economics, business, etc. that take up some of these topics and issues without the disciplinary theoretical frameworks and understandings to do so, rendering their starting points as always already beginning from the privileged lens of "othering."

The production of knowledge is exclusionary. While the internet has democratized access to platforms, voice, and abilities to create and co-define common language, the authority to officially designate words, concepts, meanings, and perspectives as "official" or "accurate" has not been granted equally to all people or groups. As Janack (1997, 130) notes, "Epistemic authority is conferred on persons or groups through social, political, and economic practices, as well as through sexist, racist, and classist assumptions about reliability, intelligence, and sincerity." It has been the *privilege* of a select group of people to define, describe, and order the social world – to create the knowledge through which we come to understand as "common sense" and as the "baseline" of reality. In this sense, the questions I started this chapter with are fundamentally important. From *whose* eyes/standpoint do we know? Janack (1997, 132) elaborates:

> It is generally the case that people who are perceived to be non-European, female, or lower than middle class generally do not enjoy epistemic authority of any degree. This is true not only in the realm of public policy; it is often true with respect to the interpretation of social conditions and personal experience. People who appear to be white, male, upper middle or middle class, and well educated generally carry more epistemic authority on their shirtsleeves. While those of us who are not upper-middle-class white men may be epistemic authorities in some circumstances (with respect to our children for example), our authority is usually trumped by "experts" – who are often upper-middle-class white men. Many women find that in telling the story of their own experiences, their interpretations are given less credibility than those offered by husbands, doctors, or other authorities.

As a criminologist, I often think about epistemic authority, particularly as it relates to my teaching of incarceration from the perspective of those previously or presently incarcerated. When I present the words of prisoners speaking about or against the conditions of confinement, why is there backlash sometimes? Why are many people inclined to automatically believe the standpoints of those in uniform as "true" and "accurate"? When a person of colour, a woman, a former prisoner, or a former gang member speaks about their experiences, why is one main critique that the speaker is *biased*? Why is the first thought, "Of course they would say that," or that they are *indoctrinated*? The responses are usually different to the "facts" and figures given by governments, authority figures, and those wearing uniforms of social control. That knowledge is not readily questioned. The fact that knowledge production is not neutral is concealed. The utmost privilege of knowledge is that the standpoints creating and sustaining *what, how,* and *who* we know are invisible – never disclosed or revealed. It is also the central cause of oppression.

While they accord epistemic authority to themselves, the status quo withholds it from others. They do so by containing the knowledge produced by – and about – groups they consider subordinate. The discourses dominantly used to refer to such groups are rife with stereotypes – of incompetence, inferiority, deviancy, criminality, stigma, etc. These become the only ways society learns to refer to particular groups of people with similar characteristics. We speak about Black-on-Black crime, and not the more common and more pressing white-on-white crime. Many commentators have noted the discursive change between how the war on drugs effectively criminalized hordes of "dangerous" Black and Latino men and women, but the opioid crisis has rendered mostly white men and women as "victims" (Alexander 2010). The narrative of thug "has become a way to describe Black males who reject or do not rise to the standard of White America … the platform to dismiss Black life as less valuable and perpetuates a negative and criminal connotation" (Smiley and Fakunle 2016, 351). These discourses are not accidental, nor incidental to the power of knowledge production, but are structured by them. They also result in oppression. Fricker (1999, 191) writes that while "we are perhaps used to the idea that there are various species of oppression: political, economic, or sexual, for instance," we rarely consider that the very ways knowledge, understanding, and the world are structured also falls into this categorization. "Epistemic oppression," according to Fricker "arises from a situation in which the social experiences of the powerless are not properly integrated into understandings of the social world" (208). We come to know about gangs, for instance, not from the experiences of involved men and women themselves, but from the experiences of the agents of social control, of news reports, and of the state. Discussion of epistemic privilege has not remained ensconced only within the social sciences. For example, Nogueira (2018) writes, "Despite the growing public recognition of its incompleteness and its need to make dialogue with other knowledges, biomedicine continues to figure as a metanarrative, as an epistemologically superior medical model, defining and regulating what is meant by 'medical knowledge'" (1019). The chapters in this collection all challenge how we know – or think that we know – about gangs, gang members, and gang prevention/desistance.

The surveillance, criminalization, and broader social narrative of, and on, gangs has focused on the figure of the "gang member" as deviant, dangerous, and societal scourge. That they were never included in defining themselves is based on narratives of "thug" that cast these (mostly racialized) men as unredeemable and as a threat to the dominant social order and the status quo. Gang scholarship in Canada suffers another fate: "Much of what is known about the history of gangs comes from other countries – the USA, Britain, and France, among others" (Totten 2012, 17). This means that what we know about – and how we define – gangs and gang members is prescribed only from the perspective of law enforcement and lay opinions (and fears), and is never contextualized to the specific historical, economic, geographical, demographic, and social layers of the Canadian fabric.

This aim of this chapter – and the entire project of thug criminology – is to problematize the gaze of privilege that has framed the discipline of criminology (and *all* disciplines) and from which all knowledge about "crime" "the criminal," and most importantly "the gang member" and "thug" has been produced, repeated, and maintained. That mainstream lay and disciplinary-specific theorizing and understandings continue to reproduce articulations of what is *gang*, and who is *thug*, that originate from state institutions and enforcers of social control – despite claims to be "from below" – should be a provocative assertion to many.

Rewriting the Spectacle "Other"

Biko Agozino (2003) writes of the popular silence within criminology on the raced and classed history of criminological research and the racist foundations of European systems of justice that legalized institutions of colonialism and slavery. To Agozino we can add that there is also silence on the classed and gendered/sexed history of criminological research. Despite feminist scholarship to this point (Cook 2016; Naffine 1997), the study of gender and criminology is still treated in separate and clearly identifiable courses, usually relegated to the obligatory one or two courses on women and crime, as if men were genderless (Marques 2017). These realities continue to repeat the message that "feminism is about women, while criminology is about men" (Naffine 1997, 2). Again, this is not an indictment against criminology, but against the disciplines generally. In designing an "effective" curriculum on any topic, in any subject, we often present disciplinary theories, explanations, and research as if they were uncontested and without debate, as if historicizing was objective and that research and knowledge were neutral.

Critical, feminist, Indigenous, qualitative methodologists have long written about the colonizing effects and impacts of research. As much as research liberates and emancipates, it also silences. I am using silence/silencing here as the process of rendering the speech of others meaningless or unintelligible, in which privileged voices are used to create knowledge of and about the "other." Historically, the voices silenced or dismissed have usually belonged to individuals or groups outside normative boundaries. Appearing as quotations in written reports, research participants are often relegated to snippets of their accounts with no reference to them as complex individuals – and this is only if they are not disembodied completely and reduced to a mere number/statistic. Research silences the participants whose words are rewritten and analysed by an "expert" researcher, who is given authority over someone else's accounts (Fonow and Cook 2005). Statistical research involves complete erasure of individual participants, whose opinions, beliefs, and experiences are distilled into a quantifiable and generalizable numerical output. It also silences engagement by the audience who read research as though it indicates static scientific "truth," written by an "expert," validated with "objectivity," thus without room for academic debate and contrasting scholarly accounts. As bell hooks (1990, 153) poignantly articulates it, "No need to hear your voice when I can talk about you better than you can speak about yourself ... only tell me about your pain. I want to know your story. And then I will tell it back to you in a new way. Tell it back to you in a way that it has become mine, my own. Re-writing you, I write myself anew. I am still the author, authority. I am still the colonizer, the speak subject, and you are not the centre of my talk."

I often wonder why so many of us are averse to understanding social issues, phenomena, "problems," from the perspectives and standpoints of the people we are talking about – why so many are unwilling to hear about "gang" life from those who were or are involved, instead favouring media tropes, the accounts of non-involved individuals, and/or law enforcement.

Despite our best intentions, there is tacit failure within criminology to acknowledge why the discipline emerged in the first place, whose lens criminology is from, and whose lens criminologists keep repeating through research. Criminology is "primarily a science of 'others' than offenders ... not so much a history of offenders, as a history of the reactions of those in power" (Hoefnagels 1973, 11). At its base, it begins from privileged eyes – from the world of the dominant status quo. It is about understanding why those "others" – – those "them over there" – – do not follow "our" rules. Criminology – like other disciplines – has always been about colonizing the behaviours and languages of the "other" and making them palatable and understandable to "us." This is why much criminological research focuses on the crimes of the poor, of lower socio-economic status and ranking, and of racialized populations. What has been labelled deviant and/or crime has itself been based on the actions (whether real or perceived) of these groups of people. As Hoefnagels (11) notes, "Crime belongs to society also in the sense that society labels, or designates, certain behavior as criminal. The *principle of designation* is essential to the concept of crime."

Within the discipline of criminology, however, several criminologies have developed that challenge and nuance understandings of deviance, criminality, victimization, strategies of surveillance and capture, punishment, etc. There is robust and critical scholarship within, for example, Indigenous criminology, Black criminology, convict criminology. We hope to add thug criminology to that list.

A Gang Member by Any Other Name

Who is this invisible "us" that the entire social world is evaluated against and that entire disciplines are framed around? Who is this "us" that mass media creates films and television for, and that news reports are speaking to? Who is this "us" that history and geography begins from? Who is this "us"? This line of questioning is not meant to be pedantic. Rather it draws our attention to the underlying processes that structure how we come to know and that shape what we know and why.

As Totten (2012) so aptly highlights,

> Many people believe that the gang problem can be best understood by examining the individual characteristics of members. Statements like "he came from a good family," "she was trouble from day one," and "he always hung out with a bad crowd" abound. Why are these "explanations" so popular? Could it be because *they let us off of the hook*? When the focus is on individual agency or pathology, social factors such as poverty, racism, and the impacts of cultural violence are ignored. Families, schools, communities, and governments are not held accountable. Deplorable social conditions are ignored. Instead, we can lull ourselves by saying, "He was a bad seed." If only it were so simple. There are far too many gangs and gang members to explain away the phenomenon in such a simplistic way. The gang problem does have an individual aspect, but social factors are just as important. (20–21; emphasis added)

Despite media (news and pop culture) coverage, there is a pervasive cultural silence around gangs. This silence is due to the association of gangs with criminal behaviour which always already has discussions and policies in this realm. We talk about gangs – a lot – but most of what we say is filtered and shaped through discourse of fear, societal decay, criminality, urban culture, and racialized risk. There is silence about the genesis, operation, and function of gangs, particularly from the perspective of the youth and young adults we are speaking about. Insiders (those who belong to the group/category discussion and own the terms of that group/category) are rarely given the opportunity to speak to their own involvement. Even when allowed, understandings of "the gang" as about criminality, violence, and dehumanization envelope their experiences and rewrite them in ways palpable to outsiders and do not subvert dominant world views.

One thing that struck and disappointed me during my work in the federal correctional sector was how much and how completely carceral practices, policies, and principles were inscribed by a neoliberal individualism and psychology. The insistence that every action was an *individual* action, an *individual* choice, and *individual* issue, underscores therapeutic instantiations of responsibilization and accountability. I would support prisoners through the design of their own individual crime cycles (a timeline of their lives six months before and after the offence, to help them visualize where they could have made different choices), and never once was discussion of their social, economic, gendered, sexed, classed, or geographic location in society considered as something that should shape, constrain, and/or completely envelop their *individual* choice towards criminality. In the complete valuation of individual over society, we forget that society is made of individuals and individuals made society. We. Made. Society.

Adams et al. (2019) highlight a growing body of research on impacts of neoliberalism and psychology, noting that "psychological science is not just an observer of neoliberalism and its impact on mind and behaviour. Instead, knowledge products and practices of psychological science reproduce, legitimize, and bolster the authority of neoliberalism and its colonization of everyday life" (190). Nevertheless, carceral psychology depends on pathologizing the individual and individual choices, rendering society's role invisible. Speaking to the example of racism, Adams et al. explain that "besides constructing racism as a problem of individual prejudice, mainstream psychological theory and research amplifies neoliberal individualism by pathologizing racism perception" (199). I heard clinical conversations in which the normative (if conducted outside the prison setting) behaviours and responses of prisoners were reread as pathological. I was subjected to training that began with the question "What are natural gender differences between men and women?" and then later saw how prisoners who did not conform to stereotypical gendered behaviour were penalized with more talks, more worksheets to complete, more cynicism from staff. This does not even account for the Supreme Court critique (in Ewert v Canada [SCC, 2018]) that Correctional Service of Canada psychological assessments unfairly target and mistreat Indigenous prisoners, through their cultural bias, leading to higher rates of parole and rehabilitation program denial for these prisoners (Fine 2018). That the federal correctional sector does not use a criminologist as part of its front-line staff to provide broader societal contextualizing and support to prisoners is itself indicative of our compulsion to "other," individualize, classify, and pathologize particular groups of (predominantly marginalized) people while letting ourselves "off the hook."

Criminologists have long written about the impacts and pains of imprisonment. Prison changes people emotionally, psychologically, socially, physically, and economically. While I appreciate that the disdain for and visceral reaction to offenders as one of retribution and extreme punishment results from individualizing our own – or our loved ones' – potential victimization, we need to consider whether or not the status quo creates conditions that enable a healthy society to flourish. It does us a disservice to be punishing and moralistic about individual choices, without considering the social context that rendered certain decisions more easily accessible than others. This is not to laud, accept, or tolerate criminality, but to be genuine in our longing to understand it, and to our collective goal of creating an equitable and prosperous society. Moore (2014) argues that "prison is not somewhere vulnerable people are occasionally erroneously placed. They are places that are full of damaged and vulnerable people." However, this is not to say that the central issue – or the solution – lives with the individual prisoners, but that "we need to start with questioning their very imprisonment. By focusing on the reality of prisons it becomes obvious that the solutions are not located inside but beyond prisons" (17). Although Moore focuses specifically on deaths in custody, the sentiment applies to what we (think we) know about offenders and imprisonment broadly. The impacts of incarceration are interesting when applied to the topic at hand, as both correctional and scholarly accounts have found that it plays a significant role in gang recruitment, geographic spread, and upward mobility within the ranks of gang leadership (Totten 2012). Prisons breed gangs. Not only does imprisoning "gang" members not deter future "gang" involvement, it also furthers the reach and spread of what were once localized groups. Against a backdrop of increasing racialized, gendered, and classed inequalities, more punitive law enforcement and sentencing measures, and the continued mistreatment of prisoners, prisons also generate collectives of individuals, or "gangs." As Grekul and LaBoucane-Benson (2006, 1) highlight, these collectives "exist because they serve a purpose."

The data we have on prisoners continue to confirm that many have experienced childhood maltreatment and abuse. Most come from conditions of socio-economic precarity and lower educational attainment. Some have mental health issues, and others have had contact with the institutions set up to "help" them – the child welfare system, social help, etc. Most incarcerated women have histories marked by sexual violence. The lives of many gang-involved boys and men are similarly marked by "the structural violence that [leads] to marginality and feelings of hopelessness; the toxic masculinity that fuel[s] street warfare; the trauma of experiencing/witnessing violence" (Ellis 2019). These are all instantiations of trauma that occurs within a social context. Trauma leaves an indelible mark. This is not about being proverbially *soft* on crime, but about being *intellectually honest* about crime. It is about thinking about *why*, *how*, and from *whom* we know. It is about not equating entire individuals to singular acts (or series of acts) and to understand them as complex and whole social beings.

As Totten (2012, 16) describes it, "Gang members are not born bad. Instead, they are trained by the adults around them. Each gang member in Canada has a human face. Each is someone's son or daughter, sister or brother, nephew or niece.... They arrive in this world innocent and sweet, just children themselves. They leave in body bags, or are incarcerated deep in the bowels of correctional centres for most of their adult lives; they are outcasts. Given their traumatic lives, it is hardly surprising that they become involved in gangs. Not surprisingly, when they kill others, or die violent deaths themselves." It is by acknowledging and rethinking what we know, rather than silencing perspectives, experiences, and individuals we have been taught are "other" that we will be led towards encountering creative and constructive avenues for truly meaningful change.

The Path towards Democratizing Knowledge

How do the discourses that circulate in society; that frame our very thinking, understandings, perceptions, and opinions; that are the building blocks of social reality render one version of *reality* and *truth* visible, concealing another? What happens when confronted with alternate visions or versions of those things we think we know, or we think we know how to know? Do we recoil in discomfort and anger that our social reality and existence as we know it are being challenged? Or do we welcome the unveiling of realities unthought of?

In 2015, Adam Ellis and I went to a conference on critical criminologies. At this conference we introduced the term "thug criminology," wrapping it around broader discussions of experts and knowledge – and who can own and occupy these positions. While our presentation generated robust interest and discussion from the audience, one comment from a (woman) senior/tenured academic led us to much introspection about ourselves, our careers, and the ivory tower in general. Adam and I arrived at thug criminology from different upbringings. Our intellectual awakenings – and friendship – were forged over hours-long discussions and debates in hallways as we crossed paths between classes, in my office, and over working lunches. Although we have challenged each other, argued, and debated over many topics, we have also laughed, shared, and come to compromises and agreements. My admiration for Adam's tenacity and intellectual prowess runs deep. So when, in response to our critiquing of the strongly policed disciplinary boundaries of "expert," this senior/tenured academic suggested that we just do away with notions of experts and expertise and that upcoming scholars eschew these labels, Adam responded something to the effect of "Why is it that when marginalized groups start making inroads into the echelons of academia, we decide to render the road meaningless?"

I paused.

During my PhD one of the teaching assistantships I held was with a professor, who, lecturing on systemic gender biases and structural inequalities in education and work, asked, "Why is it, that at the moment when more women are entering and graduating from university programs, a university degree has been deemed worthless – likened to a high school diploma?" Women are populating Canadian universities. Recent data suggests that "with the exception of pure and applied sciences (where 43 percent of students are women) and engineering (where 20 percent of students are women), 60 percent of university graduates in Canada are women" (Civitella 2018). And narratives such as "There is no way in hell I'm going into thousands of dollars in debt just to get *a stupid piece of paper*" (Maddingly 2019; emphasis added) abound. While a connection that merits more interrogation, this intellectual detour was not accidental nor incidental to the topic at hand.

> We change the bar.
> The metrics change.
> They become unattainable – or if attainable, undesirable.
> Once lofty accomplishments, now have lowered perceived value.
> Achievements are downplayed.

There is much debate about gendered gaps in pay, particularly since common "sense" dictates that as women earn university degrees they too will pursue high-paying careers once occupied only by men. Yet, despite narrowing, pay gaps persist (Davis 2015; Faulk et al. 2013; Muench et al. 2015; Statistics Canada 2018). Rather than the often-touted rationalization that women are simply less qualified or less ambitious, the devaluation perspective suggests that work traditionally occupied by women is simply valued less by society and is afforded lower wages. For example, that computer programming is often touted as a lucrative career is much indebted to the fact that technology has been re-envisioned as a masculine profession, as it was not considered a prestigious or high-paying job historically when computer programming was seen as a menial job performed by women (Oldenziel 2004). Levanon, England, and Allison (2009) also found the opposite: that when women enter previously male-dominated occupations, the salary associated with these professions declines. Examining data across several occupations in the United States between 1950 and 2000, they found that "a 10 percent increase in proportion female is associated with a .5 to 5 percent decrease in hourly wage in each decade" (876). Their results showed that "wage rates are negatively associated with the proportion of females in each decade," even after "controlling for lagged log of median hourly wage, occupational levels of educational requirements, potential experience, returns to experience, proportion of each racial group and proportion in each region" (878). Entire occupations become less lucrative – more devalued – once women entered them en masse. Suggestions are made to revoke designations of knowledge, the university – once a bastion of stable and well-remunerated work – is slowly fragmenting, and precarious labour characterizes most employment offerings.

> We change the bar.
> The metrics change.
> They become unattainable – or if attainable, undesirable.
> Once lofty accomplishments, now have lowered perceived value.
> Achievements are downplayed.

Thug criminology was born out of discussions between Adam and me about the devaluing of experts and knowledge once the people who were traditionally viewed only as the researched enter into the realm of researcher. We call on certain people – in this case those who are gang-involved – to be our spectacles. Their words, thoughts, reactions, etc., line our journal articles and research reports. Their experiences and realities are displayed through invitations for special talks and lectures. Distilled to its most crude reality, academics build their careers and research identities on the backs of groupings of people or socio-economic-geographical segments of society. Ideally (and most often) this is done out of true care and concern for the populations of interest. We take their words, their experiences, their responses to surveys, their reactions in experiments, etc., we write them up in our own words, and we hope that our words – read by practitioners in the field – leave these people/communities better. But *better* is subjective. Better for *whom*? As there are many scholars who research and write from critical perspectives, there are many more who research and write from positions that repeat, maintain, and sustain current (privileged) iterations of "the norm" and "normal." That a criminology student, for example, can complete an entire undergraduate degree and never significantly cover cultural criminology, convict criminology, or penal abolitionism, or that the entire carceral system is underpinned by psychological (individualist) explanations and "treatment" of criminality and deviance is telling of – to evoke Howard Becker – whose side we are really on. I stand by Hoefnagel's (1973, 12) assertion: "A criminology which fails to ask whether criminalization is right or wrong, is not guided by science but by the legislators and the police."

Thug criminology is about hearing the sides and nuancing (if not completely dismantling) "common sense" narratives of gangs and gang members that are buttressed by police accounts, moral panic–induced news reports, and stylized stereotypical fictional representations. It is about talking *to* – not *about* – and actually hearing the voices of the involved men and women as they narrate their life experiences. It is about acknowledging the trauma lived. It is about designing meaningful and transformative programs, policies, services guided from the experience of those who are the experts in their lives and lived realities. It is about engaging in thought-provoking discussion about how we frame and label "gangs" and questioning what our conversations would/could like if we began from lived experience.

As Tobin (2008, 16) notes, "Definitions are often constricted within a social and cultural context that changes over time," with the label "gang" being most often "applied to youth groups in low socio-economic areas." What makes a "gang" or a "gang member" is contested. Many characteristics we assign to gangs, gang membership, and gang culture are not distinct and apply to many other groupings of youth (e.g., fraternities) and legitimate occupation-related subcultures. There is also the question of defines who is a gang member and what groupings are gangs. Is it the police? The public? Are involved individuals themselves ever permitted to define their own involvement? Is it "possible that groups that we identify as gangs today never sought the label?" (16). The primacy of a singular voice, a singular version, and a singular truth silences. However, the conversations we don't have are the stories we don't hear. The stories we don't hear are the narratives we can't change. The narratives we can't change are the realities that remain as they are. I envision thug criminology as a space to create noise.

REFERENCES

Adams, G., S. Estrada-Villalta, D. Sullivan, and H.R. Markus. 2019. "The Psychology of Neoliberalism and the Neoliberalism of Psychology." *Journal of Social Issues* 75 (1): 189–216. https://doi.org/10.1111/josi.12305.

Agozino, B. 2003. *Counter-Colonial Criminology: A Critique of Imperialist Reason.* Chicago: University of Chicago Press.

Alexander, M. 2010. *The New Jim Crow: Mass Incarceration in the Age of Colourblindness.* New York: New Press.

Civitella, A.C. 2018. "Women Academics Are Still Outnumbered at the Higher Ranks." *University Affairs*, 13 June. https://www.universityaffairs.ca/news/news-article/women-academics-are-still-outnumbered-at-the-higher-ranks/.

Cook, K.J. 2016. "Has Criminology Awakened from Its 'Androcentric Slumber'?" *Feminist Criminology* 11 (4): 334–53. https://doi.org/10.1177/1557085116660437.

Davis, A. 2015. "Women Still Earn Less Than Men across the Board." Economic Policy Institute, 7 April. https://www.epi.org/publication/women-still-earn-less-than-men-across-the-board/.

Ellis, A. 2019. "Will a Public Health Approach Reduce Gun Violence? No." *Toronto Star*, 7 January. https://www.thestar.com/opinion/contributors/thebigdebate/2019/01/08/will-a-public-health-approach-reduce-gun-violence-no.html.

Faulk, L., L.H. Edwards, G.B. Lewis, and J. McGinnis 2013. "An Analysis of Gender Pay Disparity in the Nonprofit Sector: An Outcome of Labor Motivation or Gendered Jobs?" *Nonprofit and Voluntary Sector Quarterly* 42 (6): 1268–87. https://doi.org/10.1177/0899764012455951.

Fine, S. 2018. "Correctional Services' Psychological Tests Fail Indigenous Prisoners, Supreme Court Rules." *Globe and Mail*, 13 June. https://www.theglobeandmail.com/canada/article-correctional-services-psychological-tests-fail-indigenous-prisoners/.

Fonow, M.M., and J.A. Cook. 2005. "Feminist Methodology: New Applications in the Academy and Public Policy." *Signs* 30 (4): 2211–36. https://doi.org/10.1086/428417.

Fricker, M. 1999. "Epistemic Oppression and Epistemic Privilege." In "Civilization and Oppression." Supplement, *Canadian Journal of Philosophy*, 25:191–210. https://doi.org/10.1080/00455091.1999.10716836.

Grekul, J., and P. LaBoucane-Benson. 2006. *An Investigation into the Formation and Recruitment Processes of Aboriginal Gangs in Western Canada: "When You Have Nothing to Live For, You Have Nothing to Die For."* https://www.publicsafety.gc.ca/cnt/rsrcs/pblctns/brgnl-gngs-nvstgtn-2006/brgnl-gngs-nvstgtn-2006-eng.pdf.

Hoefnagels, G.P. 1973. *The Other Side of Criminology: An Inversion of the Concept of Crime*. New York: Springer Science+Business Media.

hooks, b. 1990. *Yearning: Race, Gender, and Cultural Politics*. Boston: South End.

Ice T. 2005. "Foreword." In *Inside the Crips: Life Inside L.A.'s Most Notorious Gang*, edited by C. Simpson and A. Pearlman, xv–xxiii. New York: St. Martin's Griffin.

Janack, M. 1997. "Standpoint Epistemology without the 'Standpoint'? An Examination of Epistemic Privilege and Epistemic Authority." *Hypatia* 12 (2): 125–39. https://doi.org/10.1111/j.1527-2001.1997.tb00022.x.

Levanon, A., P. England, and P. Allison. 2009. "Occupational Feminization and Pay: Assessing Causal Dynamics Using 1950–2000 U.S. Census Data." *Social Forces* 88 (2): 865–91. https://doi.org/10.1353/sof.0.0264.

Maddingly, S. 2019. "Bachelor's Degree: The New High School Diploma." *Medium*, 26 May. https://medium.com/@seramaddingly/bachelors-degree-the-new-high-school-diploma-c76c65214e2a.

Marques, O. 2017. "Navigating Gendered Expectations at the Margins of Feminism and Criminology." In *Being an Early Career Feminist Academic: Global Perspectives, Experiences and Challenges*, edited by R. Thwaites and A. Pressland, 51–69. London: Palgrave Macmillan.

Moore, J.M. 2014. "Vulnerable Individuals or Harmful Institutions?" *Criminal Justice Matters* 98: 6–17. https://doi.org/10.1080/09627251.2014.984537.

Muench, U., J. Sindelar, S.H. Busch, and P.I. Buerhaus. 2015. "Salary Differences between Male and Female Registered Nurses." *Journal of the American Medical Association* 313 (12): 1265–7. https://doi.org/10.1001/jama.2015.1487.

Naffine, N. 1997. *Feminism and Criminology*. Oxford: Polity.

Nogueira, C. 2019. "A Sociological View on the Epistemic Privilege of Biomedicine: Deconstructing the Metanarrative." *Saúde e Sociedade* 27 (4): 1019–32. https://doi.org/10.1590/s0104-12902018180590.

Oldenziel, R. 2004. *Making Technology Masculine: Men, Women, and Modern Machines in America, 1870–1945*. Amsterdam: Amsterdam University Press.

Smiley, C.J., and D. Fakunle. 2016. "From 'Brute' to 'Thug': The Demonization and Criminalization of Unarmed Black Male Victims in America." *Journal of Human Behaviour in the Social Environment* 26 (3–4): 350–66. https://doi.org/10.1080/10911359.2015.1129256.

Statistics Canada. 2018. "The Gender Wage Gap and Equal Pay Day, 2018." https://www150.statcan.gc.ca/n1/pub/89-28-0001/2018001/article/00010-eng.htm.

Tobin, K. 2008. *Gangs: An Individual and Group Perspective*. New Jersey: Pearson.

Totten, M. 2012. *Nasty, Brutish, and Short: The Lives of Gang Members in Canada*. Toronto: James Lorimer.

2 The White Male Criminological Gaze as Pornography: The Quasi-sexual Academic Obsession with Black "Gang Bangers"[1]

ANTHONY GUNTER

In the acknowledgment section of my completed PhD thesis (and later published monograph) I noted, "This has been a long, eventful but very rewarding journey which began some twenty odd years ago ... when this [at the time] disaffected young black male left school" with virtually no formal qualifications (Gunter 2010, vii). When I was growing up in a decaying inner-city neighbourhood with limited opportunities and aspirations, the seductions of crime (Katz 1988) and the appeal of badness (Gray 2003; Gunter 2008) were too much to resist. My own commitment, and that of my peer group, to criminality and badness can be interpreted in hindsight as reflexive – a response to alienation and injustice; you subconsciously buy into, and creatively reappropriate, the negative imagery you constantly see reflected back to you from your earliest memory, by the media, police, and other state authorities. And contrary to Tupac Shakur's poetic musings, roses cannot grow in a concrete jungle where there is no topsoil, water, or sunlight to nourish its development and potential beauty.

As a working-class Black male turned academic, I find the debates about expert and insider/outsider knowledge irrelevant – I am an outsider/outsider. Ever since entering the white world of academia, which for me started when I began my undergraduate degree program at the end of the 1980s, I have been gripped by three themes and feelings: rage at the injustice of and inherent privilege within the system; survivor's guilt; and isolation. The world I came from, and the people who still inhabit that world, has been maligned, pathologized, and criminalized in equal measure: the academic depictions and examinations of Black British Caribbean life, from the 1950s to the present day, have focused on dysfunctional families, inter-generational conflict, and the four-decade-long recurring theme of youth violence and criminality. These Black (and Muslim Asian) communities have always been "othered," written about by sociologists, criminologists, social theorists, social workers, and educational psychologists. However, it is simplistic to add that these experts are also invariably white and middle class, as they have occasionally co-opted working-class, Black, Asian, and female conspirators into their ranks. These early career academics are aware of their novel position in the system and are the "bridge between" and/or "authentic voice" of the communities under scrutiny. The British colonial project has always worked in this way; an unholy alliance involving the dispossessed white working classes, alongside a select number of Indigenous "chiefs," and both are employed in their own differing ways to oppress and suppress the dark-skinned masses on behalf of the "white massa."

The United States as the home of the "gang" has its own unique history: its internal colonial subjects have endured annihilation (Native Americans) and subjugation, brutalization, and oppression (African Americans) throughout its five-hundred-year existence. More generally, Euro-American academia owes its lifeblood to colonialism, racism, and oppression, and much of this knowledge sustained and justified "white-supremacist-capitalist-patriarchy" (hooks 2004). Many of the "great seats" of learning (universities) in Europe and North America were financed by slave traders, plantation owners, and pirates (European explorers). Fast forward to 2020, and looking back through the historical post-colonial lens (Fannon 1986; Said [1978] 2003; Rodney 1973) the question soon becomes not Why are white male gang criminologists obsessed with urban Black youth, but Why wouldn't they be?

Colonialism, Anti-Blackness and (Criminal) Injustice

Criminology, more than the other discipline within the social sciences, has best served the interests of colonialism and postcolonialism (including neocolonialism). It emerged as a new area of academic enquiry – obsessed with new ideas and thinking about disciplining and controlling the "Other" – in a period of history when Indigenous peoples around the world were experiencing genocide and the violent appropriation of their ancestral lands, and African slaves were being tortured and dehumanized. Biko Agozino (2003) argues that criminology and the other social and natural sciences have colluded with colonialist white supremacist capitalist patriarchy and provided "scientific" justification for their atrocities and crimes against humanity. Criminology, by its preoccupation with the pathologies and law-breaking activities of the individual in the service of the dominant classes, largely ignores the crimes of the powerful and specifically has turned, and continues to turn, a blind eye to imperialism, which "is the basic form of all criminality since every criminal act implies the violation of the spaces of others and tries to colonize the spaces of the other and yet imperialism poses as the moral policeman of the world. My equation of imperialism with criminality means that the rapist, the pickpocket, the robber, the murderer, the arsonist, the bank fraudster, the dictator, all share the qualities of the criminal state that commits violence against the people: the abuse of power – physical, fiscal and or farcical" (Agozino 2010, ii–iii).

In the Age of Reason, "enlightened" thinkers and philosophers in Europe challenged the divine despotic tyranny of monarchs and only the absolute "truths" of positivism and scientific knowledge reigned supreme. However, the Enlightenment movement coincided with the codification of pseudo-scientific racism – whereby white Europeans were at the top of a new racial hierarchy, with Black and Indigenous peoples at the bottom – which acted as a principal handmaiden to white colonialist expansion, the transatlantic slave trade, and chattel slavery (Fryer 1984). Because of their skin colour, people of African descent were denied human rights, and those who had been kidnapped to toil on the plantations of the "New World," to become the property of their white masters, were treated not just as animals but also as imprisoned criminals.

By the late 1800s, Britain's burgeoning classes of industrialists, merchants, bankers, and planters were entwined in a devilishly ingenious and exponentially profitable economic system built literally on the backs of enslaved Africans. Britain became the first industrialized nation of the world – as the result of the vast fortunes obtained from its slave colonies in the Caribbean and its servicing of ships that sailed from London, Bristol, and Liverpool to the coast of West Africa, full to the brim with manufactured goods and textiles – to be bartered for human flesh. From here these ships sailed across the Atlantic to such islands as Jamaica, Barbados, and St. Kitts, where wretched Black souls who had survived the middle passage were off-loaded and exchanged for rum, sugar, tobacco, and spices, which were brought to Britain and sold. And so the vast fortunes and profits built up by this triangular trade based on human misery were ploughed into key industries and became a significant factor in the accumulation of capital that substantively financed Britain's Industrial Revolution (Williams 1944; Davidson 1980).

According to Baptist (2014, xxiii), the impact of slavery on the US economy was no less monumental, as from the late 1700s to 1861 the South "grew from a narrow coastal strip of worn-out plantations to a subcontinental empire." The huge financial returns from the southern states' global cotton monopoly (mass harvested by enslaved Africans, cotton was the most important traded raw material during the first hundred years of the Industrial Revolution) "powered the modernization of the rest of the American economy," so much so that at the dawn of the Civil War the United States became the second nation after Britain to undergo large-scale industrialization. Slavery's rapid expansion affected every part of the economy and politics of the United States and ultimately resulted in the development of this powerful new nation.

The expansion and the de jure reality of the social, economic, and legal system of racial slavery in the New World established by European colonizers was more than two hundred years in the making. Slavery in North America, through the 1600s to the early 1800s, did not evolve uniformly but was shaped piecemeal across time, region, and according to the diktats of Spain, Britain,

Portugal, Holland, and France. However, during the 1700s these colonial powers institutionalized the system of slavery by creating legal structures that would ensure Blacks remained irrevocably in bondage. New slave codes were enacted that prohibited their movements, manumission, social gatherings, playing of instruments, speaking to each other in their own languages, and miscegenation. These laws, further driven by the rampant fears about the contagion of violent insurrection on the plantations, became even more comprehensive and brutally repressive to control and discipline the slave population.

Racism, Crime, and the New Slavery

During the period following the abolition of slavery in the United States, and Britain's Caribbean island colonies, we see the codification and institutionalization of second-class Black citizenry via racist laws and practices. At this point racist social Darwinists and political leaders in the United States decry the end of slavery and the social control it had on tempering the inherent criminality of Blacks. They tried to evidence these beliefs by drawing on social data highlighting the disproportionately high numbers of Black people being charged, convicted, and imprisoned for committing a crime compared to whites. During his lifetime W.E.B. Dubois, the much-neglected African American pioneer of sociological and criminological thought, also significantly contributed to history, race relations, and civil rights activism. Through his earliest key writings, he was one of the first US scholars to examine the causes, consequences, and solutions of Black criminality. According to Du Bois (1901), it was only after Emancipation that African Americans in the South committed crime. Before the Civil War, the crime rate was low because under the law slaves could become criminals only in very exceptional circumstances, in addition to the fact that the master's role also extended to that of judge, jury, and executioner. The social and legal order established during slavery meant that Black slaves had no rights under the law, but rather the law could be utilized only by whites to maintain dominance and control of their human property. If slaves were murdered by a white person, whites' only punishment might be to pay financial compensation to the legal owner. Likewise, while white masters raped female slaves with impunity, if a male slave so much as looked at a white woman (who was considered the property of her father/husband) the punishment was guaranteed to be a painful and very public death.

The Civil War and Emancipation was supposed to sound the death knell for racial slavery, but the Southern economy's overdependence on slave-based agriculture meant that whites were determined that the system continued in all but name. "Elaborate and ingenious apprentice and vagrancy laws were passed, designed to make the freedmen and their children work for their former masters at practically no wages" (Du Bois 1901, 739). Federal government attempts, helped by the army, to uphold the newly established free system of waged labour were quickly undermined by judicial decisions made in the state courts, which effectively reduced "freedmen to serfdom.... The result of this was a sudden large increase in the apparent criminal population of the Southern states an increase so large that there was no way for the state to house it or watch it.... Throughout the South laws were immediately passed allowing public officials to lease the labor of convicts to the highest bidder. The lessee then took charge of the convicts – worked them as he wished under the nominal control of the state. Thus, a new slavery and slave-trade was established" (Du Bois 1901, 740).

For Du Bois ([1899] 2007, 1904), the growing problem of crime amongst Blacks was not a natural by-product of their biological makeup. Rather, it was directly linked to racial oppression, socio-economic deprivation, and the legacy of slavery. These same key arguments have "resounded in the literature on race and crime for nearly a century" and included them are analyses of (1) the differences in offending rates between Blacks and whites, (2) the impact of urban life upon criminality, (3) Black crime and the legacy of slavery, and (4) the link between crime and poverty (Hawkins 1995, 16). Du Bois was not concerned to assess the veracity of the data upon which his (and racist scholars' and politicians') summations about why crime rates of Blacks, and of those recently arrived white ethnic immigrant groups from Europe, in the cities of the North, were so high. Similarly, those scholars who followed from him in the liberal race relations and criminology tradition, while acknowledging the limitations of official crime data, sought to use evidence of Black disproportionality to support their arguments about the negative effects of inequality and systemic racism.

Ethnicity, Gangs, and the City

Monroe Work was another pioneering African American social scientist whose research set about holistically documenting and analysing the African American experience, in the late nineteenth and early twentieth century. His scholarly contributions to our understanding of Black crime, justice, and racist terror (lynching) encompassed the theories and data collection/analysis methodologies of sociology, economics, politics, history, and law. Work was also the first African American to obtain an undergraduate and a master's degree in sociology from the University of Chicago (Greene and Gabbidon 2000). Founded in 1891, as a Baptist school with funds donated by the philanthropist John Rockefeller, the University of Chicago established its Sociology Department in 1892. Over a short period, and helped by a considerable budget, the department brought together emerging scholars (theorists and field researchers), social workers and students who documented the city of Chicago's rapidly changing social ecology.

During the earlier decades of the twentieth century, Northern US cities like Chicago were at the vanguard of this new nation's rapid transformation into an industrial powerhouse, attracting large numbers of poor Black migrants from the Southern states and white immigrants from Europe. As already noted, during this period racist biological explanations about criminal behaviour in the United States also extended to incorporate discussions about the high levels of crime amongst white ethnic immigrant groups and their delinquent offspring. In response to the public debate about the problems caused by increasing arrivals from Eastern and Southern Europe, social scientists like Edwin Sutherland and Clifford Shaw, both from the Chicago school, provided evidence refuting claims about the inherent criminality of foreign-born whites. Shaw's (1929) *Delinquency Areas* along with his later work (see Shaw and McKay 1942) introduced the key concept of social disorganization as a way to explain the differing rates of crime amongst and between white ethnic groups and Blacks within urban contexts.

Du Bois and Work noted the peculiar historical context that underlined Black criminality, while other liberal criminologists like Sutherland argued there was more of a correlation between socioeconomic status and offending behaviour than with race and ethnicity. Still, all were concerned with trying to explain the higher rates of Black crime compared to that of whites. In contrast, Shaw's study found that delinquency, school truancy, and adult criminality – rather than being evenly spread throughout Chicago – was concentrated within particular neighbourhoods. Noting that these areas are inhabited by Blacks from the South and white immigrants from Europe, both groups were having to make major social and cultural changes to their new urban environment, which resulted in continued social disorganization, crime, and other manifestations of social deviance.

Frederic Thrasher ([1927] 1963) was also part of the Chicago school and his monograph was another early area study that contributed to understandings of social disorganization theory. Emerging in run-down urban neighbourhoods with transient high-density migrant populations, the gang was an interstitial group that developed organically and spontaneously, and then integrated through conflict. Living in the repellent shadows of the slum, the children of foreign-born white immigrants and Black migrants sought to create an exciting world that had meaning: "The gang touches in a vital way almost every problem in the life of the community. Delinquencies among its members all the way from truancy to serious crimes, disturbances of the peace from street brawls to race riots, and close alliance with beer running, labor slugging and corrupt politics – all are attributed to the gang" (Thrasher [1927] 1963, 3).

Interestingly, Thrasher viewed the African American experience in Chicago as ostensibly the same as that of the other white ethnic groups in the city, such as the Irish, Jews, and Italians. Gangs, delinquency, and the sociopathology of the wider adult community was, for him, "an ecological and class question, a problem of urbanization and immigration, of ethnic succession, and *not* one of race" (Hagedorn 2008, 16).

The Black Ghetto

It was not only Thrasher, but also his Chicago school colleagues who downplayed race[2] and the impact of street-level and systemic racism on the city's Black population. While white ethnic groups transitioned from the bottom of the socio-economic pile and into the middle class within one or two generations, African Americans were not afforded these same opportunities and instead found their pathway out of the ghetto deliberately blocked. It is ironic that, in the early part of the twentieth century, Blacks had arrived in the promised land of the North to escape poverty and Jim Crow in the South. This institutionalized system of racist oppression was enacted through the application of many laws and procedures barring African Americans from whites-only restaurants, hotels, schools, universities, rest rooms, and other public facilities.

White supremacy in the South was further augmented through the enforcement of repressive laws that in theory were colour-blind – like those relating to voter registration – but disproportionately targeted Blacks compared to whites. In addition to all these forms of legally sanctioned oppression, Black Americans were also the victims of "widespread legal and extra-legal violence" meted out under the auspices of racist organizations like the Ku Klux Klan, who were "tacitly supported by the state" and given free rein to murder and terrorize (Wright and Rogers 2015, 320). The Great Migration saw an estimated exodus of five million African Americans from the South to the cities of the North between 1915 and 1960. By the 1950s and 1960s, the promised land of hope and economic opportunity had for many blacks turned out to be an urban nightmare. Daily they were forced to confront everyday racism and discrimination in the workplace, police brutality on the streets, substandard schools, and deliberate spatial/residential segregation policies and practices which resulted in creating dense Black ghettos (Massey and Denton 1993).

Notwithstanding the considerable gains of the Civil Rights movement, the past fifty years has been catastrophic for many low-income African American urban neighbourhoods destroyed by poverty and violent crime. Deindustrialization and hyper-ghettoization transformed the Black ghetto – which housed the working poor and a small middle class – into a dilapidated urban enclave of worklessness and extreme poverty. Between 1970 and 1980, nearly 40 per cent "of all poor blacks in the 10 largest American cities" were living in extreme poverty, in comparison with just over 20 per cent "a decade before and with only 6 per cent of poor non-Hispanic whites" (Wacquant and Wilson 1993, 27). According to US census data, during the 1970s blue collar and clerical jobs disappeared while higher occupational range opportunities increased significantly. These labour market shifts had a profound impact on Black Americans, many of whom had not completed their high school education. Between 1950 and 1970, large numbers of African Americans working in the urban industrial sector did not hold any formal qualifications. But as the 1970s progressed, it became exceptionally difficult to obtain high-skilled, managerial, and professional job opportunities without a college degree (Kasarda 1993).

The Racialized Gang Problem

Thrasher's (1927) study described white ethnic and African American gangs emerging from the shadows of the slums of Chicago in the early decades of the twentieth century. By the 1950s and 1960s gang researchers, working within a new Civil Rights struggle, informed social policy climate and, using new survey research methodologies, became focused on the problem of disenfranchised Black and minority youth in urban ghettos[3] of the United States. This new academic social policy–oriented focus on street gangs soon collided with new political and media-driven moral panics decrying the triple threats posed by immigration, race, and violent urban crime. It is in the late 1980s that we see the problem of gangs in the United States transformed into a full-scale national law-and-order crisis blamed on an unprecedented proliferation of violent street gangs in poor Black and Latino neighbourhoods. Ironically, "just as gangs have proliferated across the nation – appearing in over eight hundred cities and towns – so has gang literature," and anti-gang policies and programs (Klein 1995, 8).

Federal law enforcement agencies were similarly making hysterical pronouncements about the serious threats posed by violent street gangs – imported from Central America, via illegal immigration and illicit drug trafficking – to national security. The real headline story during the past forty years is not the social havoc wrought by African American and Latino youth gangs, but the hyper-ghettoization and entrenched impoverishment of the neighbourhoods they live in. Loic Wacquant (2009) notes that, instead of tackling racial and socioeconomic justice, the neoliberal post-industrial state has focused its ire on criminalizing poverty and punishing its poor and surplus populations. According to Danny Dorling (2015), there are five beliefs that uphold injustice in its contemporary form: elitism is efficient, exclusion is necessary, prejudice is natural, greed is good, and despair is inevitable. Each belief also creates a distinct set of victims – the delinquents, the debarred, the discarded, the debtors and the depressed Drawing on the reflexive humanist insights of Howard Becker and C. Wright Mills, as researchers whose side are we on?

Administrative criminologists – whose academic interests are more closely aligned to the agendas of law enforcement and the punitive juvenile justice system than with the victims of systemic oppression – maintain that youth gangs pose the most risk to other young people in the same racial and class position, as well to their own wider communities. Gang scholars like Malcolm Klein assert there is a substantive difference between the work they do and the gang suppression of the police and other statutory agencies. But the truth is that these gang studies academically justify the neoliberal state's racialized war on crime and drugs in poor urban neighbourhoods. Since the 1980s, local, state, and federal laws focusing on drug-related criminal offences linked to street gangs has led to a prison crisis, resulting in several generations of African Americans being incarcerated. In 1965, the US prison population numbered about 200,000, by the early 2000s this figure had mushroomed to 2 million, and almost 50 per cent of those imprisoned were black (Kitwana 2002).

The war drugs, or what Michelle Alexander (2012, 49) describes as "he new Jim Crow," introduced by President Reagan in 1982, "from the outset had little to do with public concern about drugs and much to do with public concern about race." This new public policy focus on the inner city drugs menace resulted in Reagan delivering on his election promises – which employed racially coded tropes about the "welfare queen," the "food stamp program," and fighting "street crime" – about welfare reform and tackling crime. This new national punitive turn resulted in federal law enforcement agencies being given larger roles and bigger budgets in the fight against drug dealers in cities across the United States. Between 1980 and 1991 the FBI's drug enforcement budget rose from $8 million to $181 million, the Department of Defense's drug control funding pot ballooned from $33 million to $1 billion, and the DEA drug-fighting budget skyrocketed from $86 million to $1 billion. In comparison, federal agencies that were delivering drug treatment and prevention education programs had to contend with haemorrhaging core budgets. The National Institute on Drug Abuse's budget was slashed from $274 million in 1981 to $57 million in 1984, and funding for the Department of Education's drugs programs were reduced from $14 million to $3 million (Alexander 2012).

The decade between the Comprehensive Crime Control Act (1984) and the Crime Bill (1994) resulted in an extra $50 billion in federal funding for building new state prisons and expanding state and local law enforcement personnel. In addition to the extra financial resources, these new pieces of legislation included draconian penalties: mandatory minimum sentences for possession of a firearm and for dealing or trafficking crack cocaine – compared to the distribution of powder cocaine. Of particular significance, it was President Bill Clinton and Senator Joe Biden's $30 billion crime bill that introduced the federal "three strikes and you're out" law targeting gang members and "created dozens of new federal capital crimes, mandated life sentences for some three-time offenders" (Alexander 2012, 56).

Apart from the intergenerational catastrophe of the African American prison crisis, another legacy of the US war on drugs is the corrupt and lethal style of policing associated with it. The law enforcement tactics employed in poor African American neighbourhoods is deliberately "war-like in appearance, not by coincidence but by design." Leading the charge are paramilitary and tactical units "that in reality are specialist divisions of police departments trained to deal with hostage situations, bomb threats, suicide attempts, and the apprehension of murder suspects." However, using military equipment and tactics they are deployed "primarily in urban communities to serve drug warrants, carry out raids" and sometimes to "conduct street patrols, stopping mostly young citizens for minor offenses and arresting them for drug possession or outstanding warrants" (Kitwana 2002, 62–3).

In addition to national laws, throughout the 1990s many local jurisdictions passed legislation that criminalized the behaviour and activities of Black youth. Gang loitering initiatives prohibiting two or more young people from hanging around in public areas, simply congregating outside their own homes, could result in convictions, imprisonment, and heavy fines. In Chicago, the enforcement of anti-gang legislation resulted in up to 40,000 young people being arrested in the two years between 1992 and 1994. Other local and federal legislative gang-suppression laws led to the criminalization of African American youth styles and fashions, such as wearing bandanas and hair in braids, for being gang insignia, resulting in culprits being banned from shopping malls and schools. During this same period law enforcement agencies across the nation, from smaller cities like Milwaukee to metropolises like Los Angeles, produced "gang profiling" databases: "These databases consist of suspected gang members and their family, friends, and associates.... Most of those found in these databases are young Blacks and Latinos, as some of the characteristics of the profiling include being a member of a racial minority, graffiti writing, and dressing in a particular manner. In Los Angeles, the sheriff's department stores information on at least 140,000 individuals, many of whom have not committed any crime. Across the country, policies like these have become common in the 1990s" (Kitwana 2002, 16).

A Gang – in Name Only!

Notwithstanding the proliferation of laws and rapid growth of the US gangs industry – an alliance of gang scholars, law enforcement agencies, and juvenile justice system personnel – during the past four decades there is still no consensus on what a gang is (Greene and Pranis 2007, 9; see also, for example, Miller 1975; Ball and Curry 1995; Esbensen et al. 2001; Klein and Maxson 2006). Julie Barrows and Ronald Huff's review of federal and state gang policies found that only two of the fifty US states used the same gang definitions. In their research summary, the authors clarified that although the gang problem is garnering increasing attention across the United States, "researchers, police officers, and lawmakers have yet to agree on definitions used to characterize and understand the problem" (Barrows and Huff 2009, 675).

Randall Shelden et al. (2013, 23) assert that too many US gang researchers have "confused the term *group* with the term *gang* and have proceeded to expand the definition" to where it becomes a catchall that includes "every group of youths that commit offences together." What is the difference between drugs gangs, street gangs, and youth gangs? Why are many other white ethnic groups – whose identities are closely aligned with collective lawbreaking, like "stoners," skinheads, organized crime cartels, and biker gangs (see Sanday 1990; Spergel 1995; Venkatesh 2003) – largely excluded from the academic literature and popular discourses about gangs? Unsurprisingly, even though there has been no agreement about gang definitions and typologies, the racist agendas of politicians, administrative criminologists, and law enforcement have resulted in the de facto conflation of the term *street gangs* with Black and Latino urban youth. However, "the correlation between minorities and gangs may well be an artefact of definitional boundaries" rather than a true "measure of actual gang membership" (Coughlin and Venkatesh 2003, 51).

These definitional contestations, white ethnic group omissions, and racist conflations have not stopped the preoccupations of US street gang scholars from being imported and applied to other urban contexts around the globe. According to John Hagedorn (2008, xxiv) "a world of gangs" is the result, in which institutionalized groups of "armed young men have become permanent fixtures in many ghettos, barrios, and favelas across the globe." This explosion of gangs – taking over cities in Australia, Europe, Central America, and Southern Africa – is due to rapid urbanization, poverty, immigration, and failing states. Similarly, after surveying the research data on the gang problem across the globe, Malcolm Klein asserted that many countries had developed their own variants on the gang regarding typology and structure. However, others "have given birth to genuine street gangs" like those in the United States (Klein 1995, 228).

Notwithstanding the claims of Klein and Hagedorn, this obsession with street gangs (marginalized Black, brown, and Indigenous youth) by white male academics, politicians, and journalists is racist and dangerous: first, because it has led to the disproportionate targeting and punishment of Black and other racialized minority youth by law enforcement and other criminal justice agencies; and second, because there is no "social scientific evidence" that supports the assumption that gangs cause crime. Jack Katz and Curtis Jackson-Jacobs (2004, 93) argue that the principal problem with gang research, although rarely acknowledged, is "that we never have a good basis for thinking that gangs cause crime." Mercer L. Sullivan highlights the inherent dangers of linking youth violence with gangs too closely: "Much of what youth gangs do is expressive activity.... The complex intertwining of cultural symbolism and on-the-ground patterns of behaviour poses a serious problem for research. If we mistake symbols for behaviour, we commit errors of reification. Mass society and mass media feed on and reinforce the tendency to reify gangs" (Sullivan 2006, 16).

Conclusion

The pernicious legacy of colonialist white supremacy, where Black people are still lethally over-policed and de facto (rather than de jure) under-protected by the law, has continued through slavery and Emancipation through to the present day. Hiding under the guise of positivist social scientific truth, the street gang narrative that fixates upon Black youth violence and crime is the latest manifestation of the five-hundred-year history of blood and lies. Racial slavery was justified and premised on denying captured Africans their humanity, so that the amassed profits and fortunes derived from it would continue fuelling the capitalist empires of Britain and the United States. It is noteworthy that the supposed problem of inherent Black criminality, which has endured for over a century, began to be propagated by racist social Darwinists and political leaders only in the immediate period after Emancipation in the United States. Although biological determinist arguments about the links between race and crime also encompassed foreign-born white ethnic groups in the early decades of the twentieth century, by the 1950s and 1960s they no longer did so.

Informed by survey research methodologies and questions posed by the Civil Rights movement, a new generation of gang scholars began focusing their attention on the Black and brown ghettos of the United States. By the early 1980s this fixation on urban youth of colour, and specifically the continuing obsession with and fear of the inherently violent and criminal Black "Other," had metamorphosed into Reagan's wars on drugs, crime, and welfare. By the 1990s Clinton and Senator Biden's $30 billion crime bill essentially sealed the fate of generations of African Americans, who fell victim to the "new slavery 2.0" under the federal and local gang suppression laws, feeding the prison crisis and its associated lucrative industrial complex. In response to the punitive turn of the neoliberal state, rather than highlight the worsening socio-economic position of African Americans in poor urban neighbourhoods, gang scholars have provided the pseudo-scientific evidence to support their continuing racial oppression by law enforcement agencies and the criminal justice system.

NOTES

1 As well as being a popular description for gang members in the United States, ironically a "gang bang" is a colloquial British English term for a sexual orgy involving large groups of individuals.

2 The Chicago school also ignored the work and key sociological and criminological contributions made by pioneering African American scholars like W.E.B. Du Bois and Munroe Work.
3 See, for example, Cohen (1955), Bloch and Niederhoffer (1958), Cloward and Ohlin (1961), Yablonsky (1962), and Klein (1967)

REFERENCES

Agozino, B. 2003. *Counter Colonial Criminology: A Critique of Imperialist Reason*. London: Pluto.

– 2010. "Editorial: What Is Criminology? A Control-Freak Discipline!" *African Journal of Criminology and Justice Studies* 4 (1): i–xx.

Alexander, M. 2012. *The New Jim Crow: Mass Incarceration in the Age of Colorblindness*. New York: New Press.

Ball, R.A., and G.D. Curry. 1995. "The Logic of Definition in Criminology: Purposes and Methods for Defining 'Gangs.'" *Criminology* 33 (2): 225–45. https://doi.org/10.1111/j.1745-9125.1995.tb01177.x.

Baptist, E.E. 2014. *The Half Has Never Been Told: Slavery and the Making of American Capitalism*. New York: Basic Books.

Barrows, J., and C.R. Huff. 2009. "Gangs and Public Policy." *Criminology & Public Policy* 8 (4): 675–703. https://doi.org/10.1111/j.1745-9133.2009.00585.x.

Bloch, H., & Niederhoffer, A. 1958. *The Gang*. New York: Philosophical Library.

Cloward, R., & Ohlin, L. 1961. *Delinquency and Opportunity: A Theory of Delinquent Gangs*. London: Routledge and Kegan Paul.

Cohen, S. 1955. *Delinquent Boys: The Culture of the Gang*. Chicago: Chicago Free Press.

Coughlin, B.C., and S.A. Venkatesh. 2003. "The Urban Street Gang after 1970." *Annual Review of Sociology* 29: 41–64. https://doi.org/10.1146/annurev.soc.29.101602.130751.

Davidson, B. 1980. *Black Mother: Africa and the Atlantic Slave Trade*. Harmondsworth, UK: Penguin Books.

Dorling, D. 2015. *Injustice: Why Social Inequality Persists*. Bristol, UK: Policy.

Du Bois, W.E.B. (1899) 2007. *The Philadelphia Negro: A Social Study* Oxford: Oxford University Press.

– 1901. "The Spawn of Slavery: The Convict-Lease System in the South." *Missionary Review of the World* 14 (1901): 737–45. https://babel.hathitrust.org/cgi/pt?id=hvd.hxppcy&view=1up&seq=766&q1=convictlease.

– , ed. 1904. *Some Notes on Negro Crime, Particularly in Georgia*. Atlanta, GA: Atlanta University Press.

Esbensen, F.-A., L.T. Winfree, N. He, and T.J. Taylor. 2001. "Youth Gangs and Definitional Issues: When Is a Gang a Gang, and Why Does It Matter?" *Crime & Delinquency* 47 (1): 105–30. https://doi.org/10.1177/0011128701047001005.

Fannon, F. 1986. *Black Skin, White Masks*. London: Pluto.

Fryer, P. 1984. *Staying Power: The History of Black People in Britain*. London: Pluto.
Gray, O. 2003. "Badness-Honour." In *Understanding Crime in Jamaica*, edited by A. Harriot, 13–47. Kingston: University West Indies Press.
Greene, H.T., and S.L. Gabbidon. 2000. *African American Criminological Thought*. Albany: State University of New York Press.
Greene, J., and K. Pranis. 2007. *Gang Wars: The Failure of Enforcement Tactics and the Need for Effective Public Safety Strategies*. Justice Policy Institute Washington, DC. http://www.justicestrategies.org/sites/default/files/publications/Gang_Wars_Full_Report_2007.pdf.
Gunter, A. 2008. "Growing Up Bad: Black Youth, Road Culture and Badness in an East London Neighbourhood. *Crime Media Culture* 4 (3): 349–65. https://doi.org/10.1177/1741659008096371.
– 2010. *Growing Up Bad: Black Youth, Road Culture and Badness in an East London Neighbourhood*. London: Tufnell.
Hagedorn, J. 2008. *A World of Gangs: Armed Young Men and Gangsta Culture*. Minneapolis: University of Minnesota Press.
Hawkins, D.F., ed. 1995. *Ethnicity, Race and Crime: Perspectives across tTme and Place*. Albany: State University of New York Press.
hooks, b. 2004. *We Real Cool: Black Men and Masculinity*. New York: Routledge.
Kasarda, J.D. 1993. "Urban Industrial Transition and the Underclass." In *The Ghetto Underclass*, edited by W.J. Wilson, 43–64. Newbury Park, CA: Sage.
Katz, J. 1988. *Seductions of Crime: Moral and Sensual Attractions of Doing Evil*. New York: Basic Books.
Katz, J., and C. Jackson-Jacobs 2004. "The Criminologists Gang." In *The Blackwell Companion to Criminology*, edited by C. Sumner, 91–124. Oxford: Blackwell.
Kitwana, B. 2002. *The Hip Hop Generation: Young Blacks and the Crisis in African-American Culture*. New York: BasicCivitas Books.
Klein, M.W., ed. 1967. *Juvenile Gangs in Context: Theory, Research, and Action*. New Jersey: Prentice-Hall.
Klein, M.W., and C. Maxson. 2006. *Street Gang Patterns and Policies*. Oxford: Oxford University Press.
Klein, W. 1995. *The American Street Gang: Its Nature, Prevalence, and Control*. Oxford: Oxford University Press.
Massey, D.S., and D.A. Denton. 1993. *American Apartheid: Segregation and the Making of the Underclass*. Cambridge, MA: Harvard University Press.
Miller, W.B. 1975. *Violence by Youth Gangs and Youth Groups as a Crime Problem in Major American cCties*. National Institute for Juvenile Justice and Delinquency Prevention. Washington, DC. https://www.ncjrs.gov/pdffiles1/Digitization/34497NCJRS.pdf.
Rodney, W. 1973. *How Europe Underdeveloped Africa*. London: Bogle-L'Ouverture Publications.
Said, E.W. (1978) 2003. *Orientalism*. London: Penguin Books.

Sanday, P.R. 1990. *Fraternity Gang Rape: Sex, Brotherhood, and Privilege on Campus.* New York: New York University Press.

Shaw, C.R. 1929. *Delinquency Areas.* Chicago: University of Chicago Press.

Shaw, C.R., and H.D. McKay. 1942. *Juvenile Delinquency in Urban Areas: A Study of Rates of Delinquency in Relation to Differential Characteristics of Local Communities in American Cities.* Chicago: University of Chicago Press.

Shelden, R.G., S.K., Tracy, and W.B. Brown. 2013. *Youth Gangs in American Society.* 4th ed. Belmont: Cengage Learning.

Spergel, I.A. 1995. *The Youth Gang Problem: A Community Approach.* New York: Oxford University Press.

Sullivan, M.L. 2006. "Are 'Gang' Studies Dangerous? Youth Violence, Local Context, and the Problem of Reification." In *Studying Youth Gangs*, edited by J.F. Short and L.A. Hughes, 15–36. Oxford: Altamira.

Thrasher, F.M. (1927) 1963. *The Gang: A Study of 1,313 Gangs in Chicago.* Chicago: University of Chicago Press.

Venkatesh, S. 2003. "A Note on Social Theory and the American Street Gang." In *Gangs and Society*, edited by L. Kontos, D. Brotherton, and L. Barrios, 3–11. New York: Columbia University Press.

Wacquant, L.J.D. 2009. *Punishing the Poor: The Neoliberal Government of Social Insecurity.* Durham, NC: Duke University Press.

Wacquant, L.J.D., and W.J. Wilson. 1993. "The Cost of Racial and Class Exclusion in the Inner City." In *The Ghetto Underclass*, edited by W.J. Wilson, 25–42. Newbury Park, CA: Sage.

Williams, E. 1944. *Capitalism and Slavery.* Chapel Hill: University of North Carolina Press.

Wright, E.O., and J. Rogers. 2015. *American Society: How It Really Works.* New York: W.W. Norton.

Yablonsky, L. 1962. *The Violent Gang.* London: Collier-MacMillan.

3 Writing Themselves Out of Research: "Whitemaleness" and the Study of "Gang" Active Young Women

CLARE CHOAK

Introduction

I had a decade-long interest in the lives of young people from deprived areas before conducting research on gangs. I started my career as a journalist at the British Broadcasting Corporation. After being seconded as BBC sport community officer I mentored young homeless people and coordinated a national literacy skills project working with premiership football and rugby clubs. This cemented my interest in the lives of marginalized young people, and my first research project was a three-year national ethnographic study that explored how youth practitioners build relationships with young people from deprived areas through sport and other activities. Then I secured my first permanent senior lecturer university position and taught on a Youth and Community program for youth workers seeking National Youth Agency accreditation.

Motivation to involve myself in the colonial gang agenda stemmed from anger and frustration about how young women were being ignored or constructed as a homogenous group. English gang enthusiasts and policymakers have created a monolithic discourse in which their dominant identity within the gang is of sexual object. Policymakers and those in the academy rarely mention young women, and if they do it tends to be in response to their mistreatment by young men, rather than a consideration of those who are just as entrenched in "badness"[1] (Gunter 2008) as their male counterparts. As will be demonstrated, young women tend to be regarded as an afterthought in this body of work, an add-on to the "real" problem of young men, if they are mentioned at all. As academics appeared unbothered by this discrepancy, somebody had to take responsibility to show what was going on to provide a platform for a wider range of young women's stories to be heard. I became tired of reading that they are on the periphery and exist only to be sexually exploited. I wasn't denying that sexual exploitation is a real problem and needed to be highlighted, but I felt obliged to show that there was more to young women in England than being passively led into gangs through coercion and forced into activities against their own will.

Academics and policymakers on English soil then continue to seem reluctant to admit that young women can be violent and criminal, because to do so would challenge normative femininity, in which being feminine is linked to passivity and compliance, while masculinity is associated with toughness and aggressiveness. In the United States, while gangs can't be compared as like for like, the literature shows a much more nuanced approach to their identities and possibilities for resistance that correlate with my own research. This chapter will consider the misrepresentations of young women, the important role of reflexivity within qualitative research, and how I am positioned as an insider/outsider when doing this work.

Writing Myself into the Research

Objecting to the "whitemaleness" of the gang enthusiasts stems from the intersection of my classed, gendered, and raced position as well as my desire for young people themselves to be the subject of enquiry rather than the gang alone. As a white female academic, who until recently had held a permanent senior academic post for fourteen years, left the toxic and sterile environment, having never felt comfortable in the academy. Women are viewed as outsiders within academia, and particularly within criminology my outsideness is constructed through my gendered positioning coupled with a working-class background. Patricia Hill Collins (1986, 14) talks about the "outsider within" in relation to Black women in the academy, but she also argues that this can be linked to women more generally and to those from working-class backgrounds.

Being in academia feels like being between two worlds of marginality and privilege. My parents were both born poor and working class, at different ends of England, in the north-east and the south-west. They met when they lived in London, and this was where I grew up. While I was brought up with working-class values, my parents financially provided elements of a childhood that was more reminiscent with a middle-class, rather than a traditional working-class one as they had experienced. We lived in a nice house on a well-to-do street and took regular holidays. As a result I grew up thinking I was middle class until I got older and started to reflect upon my family's class background, core values, and the broad characteristics of working-class people, such as their warmth, honesty, and the banter which are essentially what make me who I am.

I excelled at school and loved learning. My parents offered to send me to a private girls school, but I was not interested in so I went to a local comprehensive. There was a large class divide in my year: typically the achieving students were middle class and the less achieving students were working class. Friendship groups tended to be divided by academic achievement, and children were labelled by clear binaries of "good" or "bad," even though things were more complex. I didn't limit my interactions to one set of peers and moved between both groups. As a young teenager I hung out with people who were a lot older than I, so I could party with them in spaces reserved for adults and had the opportunity to date older boys. My group of middle-class peers didn't accept this and no longer wanted me to be part of their circle. In their eyes I was not behaving respectably, I was too independent, and I was letting my academic talent go to waste. I have experienced this judgment in academia and in my previous career as journalist: somehow I didn't meet the standards of how an intelligent woman should be behave, I was too loud, too direct, and far too independent.

The rejection by my middle-class peers was a significant factor in whom I hung around with from that point onwards and encouraged me to be in and around "badness" for the next decade. It was also at about this time that I was making my own decisions about what I did, as my parents were not intervening, because they knew I couldn't be disciplined. I wasn't expected to report to anyone if I didn't come home for the weekend. I went to school, college, university, and by engaging in these traditional transitions, which were expected of me, I stayed under the radar of the authorities. I saw things that young people I have researched have experienced, or I know people who have. The knowledge of the underground economy, and the marginalization that can arise being working-class, have shaped the way I view young people and has helped my understanding of why they embark on alternative transitions to adulthood. I was often, but not always, the only female in spaces where badness was taking place and this also gave me a different perspective. It was a man's world as far as I could see, but even then the women I had dealings with were not simply peripheral to the activities. It became a normal part of life to earn money via the underground economy. As Choak notes (2021a), badness simply becomes a different form of work, which is normalized according to the spaces in which you move.

For Amanda Couture and colleagues (2012) it is possible to be an insider and an outsider simultaneously according to the differing positions and spaces you inhabit. One criticism of the insider/outsider binary is that our identities are shifting and complex and prone to change according to context. I am an outsider within criminology and I can also be viewed as an outsider by my research participants who see me only as a white privileged academic. At other times I can also be considered an insider, depending on whom I talk to. Some participants could tell I understood where they were coming from through my lived shared experiences of being in and around badness. Being viewed as an insider can result in participants sharing more than they would with somebody they feel is an outsider, in response to the connections within our social worlds. One participant said she couldn't believe she was revealing so much about her life to someone she had just met, but she was comfortable in doing so as she felt because of my past I wasn't judging her.

However, if you are seen as an insider, participants may not tell you everything because they assume you already know it. So I have experienced both sides of the insider and outsider binary when conducting research. Being an insider can help you develop greater rapport, which is particularly important if you are conducting interviews rather than ethnography. The credibility of my interviews with young women and practitioners in my research was validated by their being recommended through trusted contacts who then put me in touch with other young women and practitioners.

The Invisibility and Lazy Theorizing of Young Women[2]

At the beginning of the twentieth century the study of youth was called "boyology" (Griffin 2004, 30) and it is questionable to what extent has it has changed over the past century. Books and articles continue to be published about young people or youth that neglect to consider young women, as if they were not worthy of study or their continued absence didn't deserve an explanation. This also means that their experiences are racially undifferentiated. Criminality has been viewed as a rite of passage for young men. That explains the exclusion and misunderstandings about the extent to which young women are participating in badness. However, rather than being absent from street cultures, they have simply attracted less interest empirically than young men (Osgerby 1997). Young women in England continued to be invisible or positioned in certain ways, stereotyped as sexual victims or appendages to the action. This lack of empirical research made it problematic to satisfactorily rebuke claims of victimhood and a lack of agency in order to move away from the idea that a female's role is automatically one of second-class citizen.

There remain key similarities between the representations of contemporary English young women who are active gang members and those expressed almost a century ago from the Chicago school by Frederic Thrasher ([1927] 1963), such as the idea that females are not partial to the group dynamic and don't ascribe to collective resistance in the same ways as their male counterparts. Consequently impressions of female involvement that circulate have remained static and stagnant. The subcultural work from the post–Second World War era continued to ignore young women, and when they did feature were presented as sex objects, with interpersonal violence being an accepted part of the relationship. Young women fell into three categories: "somebody's tart" (a girlfriend), a "dirty ticket" (the promiscuous girl), or neither of these two and regarded as a waste of time (Parker 1974, 137–8). Where the contemporary English literature from this century differs and becomes more sinister is the representation of young women as sexually exploited victims in need of safeguarding from violent and over-sexualized male gang members. John Pitts (2008), for example, discusses how young women are sexually abused and experience high levels of intimidation from their peers. According to Allen Davis and James Densley (2011, 17) they have the "power to make the biggest difference in the lives of the boys," suggesting that young women don't have an innate propensity for criminality themselves and are regarded as a tool to extract young men from engaging in badness. The idea that women are a stabilizing influence can be traced back to the work of Cesare Lombroso (1911), who claimed that the savage group tendencies of the male who commits crime can be tamed only by females.

English policy and academic literature reveals a narrow focus on sexual exploitation: young women who have become victims of violence (Firmin 2010, 2011); the rise in young women joining gangs for sexual exploitation (Centre for Social Justice 2012); sexual exploitation and potential exit strategies (Beckett et al. 2012, 2013); a focus on multiple perpetrator rape (Densley, Davis, and Mason 2013); the vulnerabilities of young women and the risks they are susceptible to (Khan et al. 2013); sexual exploitation and abuse (HM Government 2013, 2015, 2016); as birds and sluts (Trickett 2016); gang-related sexual violence (Young and Trickett 2017); safeguarding gang-associated females (Pitts 2017); sexual exploitation within county lines (HM Government 2018). Females in these contexts then are positioned as "at risk" rather than being regarded as posing risks to others. As a result the US literature is adopted to support my findings, as it presents a range of complex and competing identities compared to the monolithic English context. As noted by Choak (2021b), although all young women bargain with patriarchy on road,[3] it still may not be acceptable for females to be sexually promiscuous, but they are encouraged to use badness to develop and sustain tough reputations in these spaces.

The dominant centring of the sexualization of young women feeds into the gang industry's sensationalist portrayal of young men (particularly Black youth) as hyper-violent gangstas (Gunter 2017; Choak 2020). Young Black men have been negatively labelled throughout the decades, with particular reference to crime and policing. In the 1970s they were muggers, in the 1980s they were the riot mob, and in the twenty-first century they are positioned as sinister gangstas. This is reinforced by the police, policymakers, media, and the music industry, given the limited opportunities for Black young men to express themselves creatively outside the glamorization of violence and misogyny. This then becomes a vicious circle of negative stereotyping entire populations of Black youth. The overwhelming focus on sexual exploitation also implies that this is not commonplace in wider society, but it "does not occur in a vacuum" (Beckett et al. 2013, 6). Furthermore, these discourses reinforce the position of young women as victims first and offenders second. Many young men are victims through their involvement in gangs but as a result of the clash with hegemonic masculinity and ideas of what it means to be a "man," their vulnerabilities tend not to highlighted as their identities are regarded as subordinate rather than hegemonic (Choak 2021b).

It is inappropriate to present these young women "exclusively as 'reluctant' participants lacking agency or as 'pure victims' in terms of their criminal activities" (Medina, Ralphs, and Aldridge 2012, 655). That they have the potential for violent and criminal behaviour, in the same ways as men, has been glossed over by focusing on their perceived natural passive state (Pollack and Davis 2005). This has resulted in a contradictory picture of young women in national policy, in which they are constructed as villains in their role as teenage mothers, and as victims regarding sexual exploitation by gang members. Davis and Densley (2011, 17) suggest that if a young woman can be persuaded that life on the street is a "fickle and dangerous world full of contradictions, and that they are second class citizens within it, the gang-involved boys will not get the plentiful supply of sex and adoration that makes the world seem so attractive in the first place." This statement negates the impact of structural and economic conditions that affect on the lives of working-class young women (in ways similar to and different from their male counterparts). Such an approach also fails to acknowledge respect and how some females work hard to create and maintain successful badass personas (Choak 2019b). Furthermore, if they aren't treated as equals and worthy of respect, there would be little motivation for them to be drawn into road culture. It is important that issues of place and economic background are not ignored in the discussion of young women engaging in badness, rather than simply explaining female behaviour only in terms of their sexual availability.

Many reasons for engaging in badness are shared by both young men and young women; however, involvement because of an attachment with a partner is predominantly associated with females. The assumption is that relationships with the opposite sex are their primary concern, while their male peers are not considered to be motivated by the same need for intimacy. Given that a sense of belonging can motivate young people to join groups, this requires further exploration. Anne Campbell (1990, 42) notes that young women have been portrayed as "isolated and inept pitiful figures trying to assuage their loneliness through brief, promiscuous liaisons with boys." Davis and Densley (2011, 2) note how females are "completely dependent on the boys" and can't gain respect in their own right, reducing them to a single stereotype when things are far more nuanced and complex. In contrast, females in Joan Moore's (1991) research did not agree that they were treated as possessions. This was the same finding as Choak (2019b).

Coercion can be viewed as a gendered pathway to crime, although it is important to move beyond the "he made me do it" hypothesis (Barlow 2016, 79). Coercion and agency should not be considered as binary opposites. Rather they are interwoven, as the reality of people's lives is far more complex. The relationship could be a mutually exploitative one wherein the young woman is manipulating the situation to achieve what she wants on the basis of her own ulterior motives, by using her partner as a stepping stone. Or it may be a relationship in which the woman is solely exploiting the man and she may view herself as an offender first and a girlfriend second (Barlow 2016). The fact that females can influence and coerce their male partners continues to be overlooked in terms of the power they can exert on road (Choak 2019b). Levels of coercion will vary according to the individual relationship and could ultimately result in providing young women the skills they need to survive without their partner. While their involvement in badness may start as they embark on a relationship, this does not mean they are forever defined by the relationship, and their role has the potential to change. Women have learned drug dealing skills from their boyfriends and then broke it off to set up their own businesses (Lauderback, Hansen, and Waldorf 1992).

As Peggy Giordano (1978, 69) suggests, it is not a "simple case of the girl adopting a passive role in going along with her boyfriend" or that he simply uses her as an accomplice while he gets on with the real work of criminality. However, what is lacking from English accounts is researchers challenging the peripheral and sexual roles that young women are presented as inhabiting. If the gang enthusiasts aren't committed to exploring other roles that young women perform, this a lost opportunity, as no group of young people is homogenous – in the same way not all young men are violent and aggressive. Isn't it time that a more complex view of both genders emerges that considers complex and competing identities, coupled with the recognition that identities are in continual shift?

It's not only white male criminologists who are guilty of this. Tara Young and Loretta Trickett (2017), for example, have exacerbated the stereotypical view of young women as one-sided. Given that Young has written more about gangs than any other female academic in England, her lack of attention of the complexities of what is actually happening on road (as opposed to the limitation of a sexual objectification focus) is a notable omission to the field. This is coupled with the exclusion of an analysis underpinned by an intersectional framework concerned with age, class, gender, and race. Trickett's (2016) article about birds and sluts draws exclusively on the views of young men to explore the experiences of young women. When researchers rely on the view of males, it tends to result in a picture of gang life that robs females of agency, as few men want to admit that they are equal to them and/or that they can be leaders in their own right.

To put forward a picture of what is happening we must hear from the young women themselves. Speaking to young men about young women is an outdated and deeply unsatisfactory approach to expanding the current discussions. It also raises the question of what has changed since the work of Parker (1974) in which girls were labelled sluts and prostitutes. Researcher's failure to challenge sexism makes them complicit. Harding (2014) included a small section on young women in his book, which showed a move away from the sexual victim diatribe. However, as Young and Trickett (2017) point out, it does not draw on any empirical data, so these points are not evidenced, and what is presented has been done so from the perspective of a white male researcher.

Qualitative Research Couched in Positivist Objectivity

Unfortunately the problems discussed so far within the English literature on young women active in gangs doesn't end here. A major criticism is its lack of reflexivity. Qualitative researchers are writing themselves out of the research, although they cannot escape reflecting on positionality, assumptions, and biases they brought to their work. This issue lies at the core of an interpretivist paradigm, and it is their responsibility to attend to these matters as part of their commitment to this kind of empirical study. This is particularly important, given that the gang agenda is dominated by white men who, as an influential group, are the ones who most need to adopt a reflexive stance.

The position of the researcher affects every single part of their work because each one brings values, assumptions, and bias to it. The interpretive paradigm, of which qualitative research belongs, demands an explanation of how we researchers interpret experiences. Reflexivity is more than reflecting. It is an "element of self-study ... and alerts researchers to the need to question the taken for granted knowledge they take into a study" (Richards 2005, 197). Positionality, acknowledgment of social identities and how they intersect, can be viewed as a part of reflexivity (Rourke 2014). Patricia Hill-Collins (1986) encourages researchers to reflect on their own subjectivity, positioning, and perspectives, as critical reflection on positionality "helps researchers to develop important insights into their research interests" (cited by Carstensen-Egwuom 2014, 270). Researchers cannot be a neutral part of the journey because qualitative research is characterized by researchers situating their own biographies and values within the research.

Transparency of positionality is key, as assumptions that researchers make during data collection and analysis are mediated, and made accountable, through discussions about their subjectivity and reflexivity. The social positioning of the researcher in age, class, gender, and race should be "placed within the frame of the picture that she/he attempts to paint" (Harding 1987, 9). As Brooke Ackerly and Jacqui True (2008, 696) contend, being a researcher demands a "commitment to a research process that requires being attentive to boundaries and their power to marginalise." It is remiss to assume that a male academic could write about young women and not reflect on his position because of the impact of power relations and patriarchy (in addition to age, class, and race). As Farhana Sultana (2007, 376) points out, "How one is inserted in grids of power relations" is a central concern of reflexivity.

Choak (2020) has highlighted what happens when researchers abuse their power. Simon Hallsworth and Tara Young (2004) have ruined lives of young people through their lack of reflection on the development of gang models that were adopted by police and policymakers. Although it is impossible to categorize peer groups because they differ so much, their creation of these models is a purely positivist venture. Whether a young person ends up on the gang matrix of the Metropolitan Police is key to being labelled as part of a gang, but the database is a racist tool because it presumes that the majority of gang members are Black young men (Gunter 2017). A postcolonial approach demands analysis of the research context through a lens of social injustice, with attention paid to those who are marginalized and disadvantaged (Chilisa 2012).

According to Inken Carstensen-Egwuom (2014, 273), "Aspects of privilege and power are often silenced and not recognised by those in hegemonic positions," and this is particularly pertinent for the English gang enthusiasts. The fact that researchers can't write themselves out of the research or stand outside the social world shows the need to decolonize social sciences research (Choak 2019a). This lack of reflection is not limited to England. For example Ross Deuchar (2020) and his English colleagues produced a paper on young women and gang involvement in Scotland – four white men presented research about young women with no reflection on their positionality or power differentials. The long-standing debate on men interviewing women considers the differences between their lived experiences against a backdrop of patriarchy and power relations. That is not to say that men cannot research women, but the potential implications need to be acknowledged of how the researcher is viewed by participants, and how data is collected and written up from a male perspective. A researcher need not be part of the cultural group under study. But it must be ensured that further subordination of marginalized groups doesn't occur by reflecting on one's own privilege as a white academic and how that may shape the research (Andersen 1993). If researchers' work is based on a reflection of their privilege and difference, it has the potential to lead to findings that couldn't have been discovered otherwise.

Sandra Harding (1991) contends that those who practise science are most likely to be white men in privileged positions, in the most dominant groups. Essentially then those who conduct qualitative research without attending to reflexivity are adopting a positivist approach within an interpretive paradigm. This then creates a methodological mismatch in how knowledge is produced. As Elizabeth Hordge-Freeman (2018, 1) argues, "Bringing your whole self to research" is necessary in order to make empirical contributions, and by doing so you are "empowered to make new theoretical findings and discoveries that can never be made in the same way as others." When they refuse to reflect on assumptions, bias, and positionality, researchers suggest that they have no influence on data collection or any part of the research, even though it is recognized widely that the researcher is part of the data and that reflexivity enhances the credibility and validity of the data (Richards 2005). "Weak notions of reflexivity" (Harding 1991, 162) are defined by lack of attention paid to cultural values of the researcher. Strong reflexivity demands that the researcher "gaze back at his own socially situated research project," as there needs to be "stronger standards of both objectivity and reflexivity" (163) as researchers move between marginality and privilege.

Reflexivity is an important part of any intersectional analysis, a "social justice project" that rejects an additive model, in which types of inequalities are tacked on, rather than considered as an interlocking process (Collins 2009, 43). Intersectionality interrogates how "power, ideology and the state intersect with subjectivity, identity and agency to maintain social injustice and universal patterns of gendered and racialised economic inequality" (Mirza 2015, 7). Particularly relevant are those who conduct research on marginalized young people and badness that is imbued with structural inequalities of age, class, gender, and race in addition to the ways in which potential forms of oppression intersect. Marcia Rice (1990) advocates for an intersectional approach that considers how social factors overlap and one that takes into account history, economics, and geographical location. More recently Parmar (2016) notes how British criminology as a discipline has barely been touched by intersectional ideas, with Coretta Phillips and colleagues (2019) arguing that the same applies to British feminist criminological research.

This lack of willingness to engage with the fundamental reflexive principles of qualitative research by the English gang enthusiasts, in addition to failing to challenge stereotypes and silences around young women, is part of what Hilary Potter (2015, 7) calls "whitemaleness." This perspective is not limited to white men. It is an attitude that crosses genders. As noted by Choak (2020), criminology urgently needs to be decolonized in order to address the gang agenda as a colonial project and stop centring whiteness as the norm from which other people are judged. Intersectionality can help to challenge "hegemonic imaginations in the field" (Carstensen-Egwuom 2014, 269). One strategy to achieve this is to adopt a Black and postcolonial feminist criminology that addresses the lack of attention paid to intersectionality and the role of Black women in the criminal justice system (Choak 2020). Cohn, Farrington, and Iratzoqui (2020) analysed the number of citations attributed to criminology scholars between 2011 and 2015, showing how white men continue to dominate the discipline. Of the top twenty most cited authors, all were white men except a Cuban American male and a white female. Despite this being the most obvious finding, the domination of white men did not merit a mention. David Farrington, who featured near the top of the list, is a key proponents of life-course criminology, which is a popular sub-discipline. This body of work continues to ignore gender and race, in addition to basing its findings on the experiences of white men (Choak 2021a). Travis Hirschi, another contributor in the top twenty list, was asked whether he considered the classed, gendered, and raced position of an offender to be significant, and he replied that "his image of a law breaker was someone *without* those identities ... the offender is everyone – they have no qualities of class, race or gender" (Potter 2015, 82). That the offender is faceless and undifferentiated indicates how far there is to go in decentring "whitemaleness" within criminology.

Conclusion

This chapter has evidenced that representations of female gang involvement in England have remained static and monolithic for the past half century. The gang may still be a male-dominated and patriarchal space, but it should be acknowledged there are young women who create and sustain successful identities in these contexts. On the other hand, the literature from the United States is far more nuanced and challenges the status quo, while the English gang enthusiasts have shown little interest in making young women visible or trying to change the dominant discourses through engaged and reflexive qualitative research. Instead we have a body of work that supports and informs, rather than resists, the flawed government colonial gang agenda. Those in the academy who adopt a position of "whitemaleness" should be engaging in the most rigorous forms of reflexivity on their values, assumptions, and biases. By refusing to adopt this necessary part of an interpretivist paradigm they are taking a positivist stance to objectivity by assuming they can somehow stand outside the social world they study. This distancing also ensures that they are locating their participants as "other." Refusal to adopt a intersectional stance, which centralizes the importance of age, class, gender, and race within the context of marginalization neglects to acknowledge the importance of social justice. Reflection, underpinned by an intersectional framework, is required to explore the identities of both participants and researchers. The attitude of "whitemaleness" indicates why the discipline of criminology is in urgent need of reform and decolonization.

NOTES

1 According to Gunter (2008, 352), "badness" refers to a social world characterized by "spectacular hyper-aggressive/hyper-masculine modes of behaviour, incorporating violent and petty crime, fraud/personal identity theft and ... drug dealing."
2 Please note that these observations on the literature were made in 2020.
3 Anthony Gunter (2008, 352) explains road culture as a "a small minority of young males or 'rude boys' – who immerse themselves into the world of 'badness' – taking

up the extreme margins." This takes place "on road," a UK term that allows researchers to "obtain a more holistic picture of them and situate their actions and behaviours within a wider neighbourhood context" (363).

REFERENCES

Ackerly, B., and J. True. 2008. "Reflexivity in Practice: Power and Ethics in Feminist Research on International Relations." *International Studies Review* 10 (4): 693–707. https://doi.org/10.1111/j.1468-2486.2008.00826.x.

Andersen, M.L. 1993. "Studying across Difference: Race, Class and Gender in Qualitative Research. In *Race and Ethnicity in Research Methods*, edited by J.H. Stanfield and R.M. Dennis, 39–52. London: Sage.

Barlow, C. 2016. *Coercion and Women Co-offenders: A Gendered Pathway into Crime*. Bristol, UK: Policy.

Beckett, H., with I. Brodie, F. Factor, M. Melrose, J. Pearce, J. Pitts, L. Shuker, and C. Warrington. 2012. *Research into Gang-Associated Sexual Exploitation and Sexual Violence: An Interim Report*. Office of the Children's Commissioner. https://www.basw.co.uk/system/files/resources/basw_90021-1_0.pdf.

– 2013. *"It's Wrong ... but You Get Used to It": A Qualitative Study of Gang Associated Violence towards, and Exploitation of, Young People in England*. Office of the Children's Commissioner. http://uobrep.openrepository.com/uobrep/handle/10547/305795.

Campbell, A. 1990. "On the Invisibility of the Female Delinquent Peer Group." *Women & Criminal Justice* 2 (1): 41–62. https://doi.org/10.1300/J012v02n01_04.

Carstensen-Egwuom, I. 2014. "Connecting Intersectionality and Reflexivity: Methodological Approaches to Social Positionalities. *Erdkunde* 68 (4): 265–76. https://doi.org/10.3112/erdkunde.2014.04.03.

Centre for Social Justice. 2012. *Time to Wake Up: Tackling Gangs One Year after the Riots*. CSJ. http://www.centreforsocialjustice.org.uk/library/time-wake-tackling-gangs-one-year-riots.

Chilisa, B. 2012. *Indigenous Research Methodologies*. London, UK: Sage.

Choak, C. 2019a. "Decolonising Power Relations within Social Science." Paper presented to the British Sociological Association, 25 October. London, UK.

– 2019b. "Young Women on Road: Femininities, Race and Gangs in London." PhD diss., University of East London, UK.

– 2020. "British Criminological Amnesia: Making the Case for a Black and Postcolonial Feminist Criminology." *Decolonization of Criminology & Justice* 2 (1): 37–58. https://doi.org/10.24135/dcj.v2i1.17.

– 2021a. "Alternative Post-16 Transitions: Examining the Career Pathways of Young Women 'On Road.'" *Journal of Youth Studies*.

– 2021b. "Hegemonic Masculinities and Badness: How Young Women Bargain with Patriarchy as Part of Road Culture." *Boyhood Studies*. Special edition.

Cohn, E.G., D.P. Farrington, and A. Iratzoqui. 2020. "Changes in the Most-Cited Scholars in 20 Criminology and Criminal Justice Journals between 1990 and 2015 and Comparisons with the Asian Journal of Criminology." *Asian Journal of Criminology* 16: 279–92. https://doi.org/10.1007/s11417-020-09328-x.

Collins, P.H. 1986. "Learning from the Outsider Within: The Sociological Significance of Black Feminist Thought." *Social Problems* 33 (6): S14–S32. https://doi.org/10.1525/sp.1986.33.6.03a00020.

Collins, P.H. 2009. *Black Feminist Thought: Knowledge, Consciousness, and the Politics of Empowerment*. 2nd ed. New York: Routledge.

Couture, A.L, A.U. Zaidi, and E. Maticka-Tyndale. 2012. "Reflexive Accounts: An Intersectional Approach to Exploring the Fluidity of Insider/Outsider Status and the Researcher's Impact on Culturally Sensitive Post-Positivist Qualitative Research." *Qualitative Sociology Review* 8 (1). https://doi.org/10.18778/1733-8077.8.1.05.

Davis, A., and J.A. Densley. 2011. "Gang Warfare." *Police Review* 119 (6145): 16–17.

Densley, J.A., A. Davis, and N. Mason. 2013. "Girls and Gangs: Preventing Multiple Perpetrator Rape." In *Handbook of the Study of Multiple Perpetrator Rape*, edited by M.A.H. Hovarth and J. Woodhams, 83–95. Oxon, UK: Routledge.

Deuchar, R., S. Harding, R. Mclean, and J.A. Densley. 2020 "Deficit or Credit? A Comparative, Qualitative Study of Gender Agency and Female Gang Membership in Los Angeles and Glasgow." *Crime & Delinquency* 66 (8): 1087–114. https://doi.org/10.1177/0011128718794192.

Firmin, C. 2010. *Female Voice in Violence Project: A Study into the Impact of Serious Youth and Gang Violence on Women and Girls*. London: Rota. https://www.rota.org.uk/sites/default/files/webfm/researchpublications/fvv_partnership_report_final_no_case_studies.pdf.

– 2011. *This Is It: This Is My Life. Female Voice in Violence Final Report: On the Impact of Serious Youth Violence and Criminal Gangs on Women and Girls across the Country*. London: Rota. https://www.rota.org.uk/sites/default/files/webfm/researchpublications/ROTA_FVV_FINALREPORT_2011_LR.pdf.

Giordano, P.C. 1978. "Girls, Guys and Gangs: The Changing Social Context of Female Delinquency." *Journal of Criminal Law and Criminology* 69 (1): 126–32. https://doi.org/10.2307/1142502.

Griffin, C. 2004. "Good Girls, Bad Girls: Anglo-Centrism and Diversity in the Constitution of Contemporary Girlhood." In *All about the Girl: Culture, Power and Identity*, edited by A. Harris, 29–44. London, UK: Routledge.

Gunter, A. 2008. "Growing Up Bad: Black Youth, 'Road' Culture and Badness in an East London Neighbourhood." *Crime, Media, Culture* 4 (3): 349–66. https://doi.org/10.1177/1741659008096371

Gunter, A. 2017. *Race, Gangs and Youth Violence: Policy, Prevention and Policing*. Bristol, UK: Policy.

Hallsworth, S., and T. Young. 2004. "Getting Real about Gangs." *Criminal Justice Matters* 55 (1): 12–13. https://doi.org/10.1080/09627250408553587.

Harding, S. 1987. *Feminism and Methodology: Social Science Issues*. Bloomington, IN: Indiana University Press.
— 1991. *Whose Science? Whose Knowledge?* Ithaca, NY: Cornell University Press.
— 2014. *The Street Casino: Survival in Violent Gangs*. Bristol, UK: Policy.
HM Government. 2013. *Ending Gang and Youth Violence: Annual Report 2013*. Home Office. https://www.gov.uk/government/publications/ending-gang-and-youth-violence-annual-report-2013.
— 2015. *Ending Gang and Youth Violence Programme: Annual Report 2014 to 2015*. Home Office. https://www.gov.uk/government/publications/ending-gang-and-youth-violence-programme-annual-report-2014-to-2015.
— 2016. *Ending Gang Violence and Exploitation*. Home Office. https://www.gov.uk/government/publications/ending-gang-violence-and-exploitation.
— 2018. *Criminal Exploitation of Children and Vulnerable Adults: County Lines Guidance*. Home Office. https://assets.publishing.service.gov.uk/government/uploads/system/uploads/attachment_data/file/863323/HOCountyLinesGuidance_-_Sept2018.pdf.
Hordge-Freeman, E. 2018. "'Bringing Your Whole Self to Research': The Power of the Researcher's Body, Emotions, and Identities in Ethnography." *International Journal of Qualitative Methods*, https://doi.org/10.1177/1609406918808862.
Khan, L., H. Brice, A. Saunders, and A. Plumtree. 2013. *A Need to Belong*. Centre for Mental Health. https://www.centreformentalhealth.org.uk/publications/need-belong.
Lauderback, D., I. Hansen, and D. Waldorf. 1992. "'Sisters Are Doin' It for Themselves': A Black Female Gang in San Francisco." *Gang Journal* 1:55–70.
Lombroso, C. 1911. *Criminal Man*. New York: Putnam's Sons.
Medina, J., R. Ralphs, and J. Aldridge. 2012. "Hidden behind the Gunfire: Young Women's Experiences of Gang-Related Violence. *Violence against Women* 18 (6): 653–61. https://doi.org/10.1177/1077801212453983.
Mirza, H.S. 2015. "'Harvesting Our Collective Intelligence': Black British Feminism in Post-Race Times." *Women's Studies International Forum* 51:1–9. https://doi.org/10.1016/j.wsif.2015.03.006.
Moore, J.W. 1991. *Going Down to the Barrio: Homeboys and Homegirls in Change*. Philadelphia, PA: Temple University Press.
Osgerby, B. 1997. *Youth in Britain since 1945*. Oxford: Wiley-Blackwell.
Parker, H. 1974. *View from the Boys*. London: David & Charles.
Parmar, A. 2016. "Intersectionality, British Criminology and Race: Are We There Yet?" *Theoretical Criminology* 21 (1): 1–11. https://doi.org/10.1177/1362480616677496.
Phillips, C., R. Earle, A. Parmar, and D. Smith. 2019. "Dear British Criminology: Where Has All the Racism Gone?" *Theoretical Criminology* 24 (3): 1–20. https://doi.org/10.1177/1362480619880345.
Pitts, J. 2008. *Reluctant Gangsters: The Changing Face of Youth Crime*. Cullompton, UK: Willan.

– 2017. "Whatever Happened to the Family? England's New Gang Strategy." *Safer Communities* 16 (1): 32–40. https://doi.org/10.1108/SC-11-2016-0020.

Pollock, J.M., and S.M. Davis. 2005. "The Continuing Myth of the Violent Female Offender." *Criminal Justice Review* 30 (1): 5–29. https://doi.org/10.1177/0734016805275378.

Potter, H. 2015. *Intersectionality and Criminology: Disrupting and Revolutionizing Studies of Crime*. Oxon, UK: Routledge.

Rice, M. 1990. "Challenging Orthodoxies in Feminist Theory: A Black Feminist Critique." In *Feminist Perspectives in Criminology*, edited by L. Gelsthorpe and A. Morris, 57–69. Buckingham, UK: Open University Press.

Richards, L. 2005. *Handling Qualitative Data: A Practical Guide*. London: Sage.

Rourke, B. 2014. "Positionality: Reflecting on the Research Process." *Qualitative Report* 19 (18): 1–9. https://doi.org/10.46743/2160-3715/2014.1026.

Sultana, F. 2007. "Reflexivity, Positionality and Participatory Ethics: Negotiating Fieldwork Dilemmas in International Research." *ACME: An International E-Journal for Critical Geographies* 6 (3): 374–85. https://acme-journal.org/index.php/acme/article/view/786.

Thrasher, F.M. (1927) 1963. *The Gang: A Study of 1313 Gangs in Chicago*. Chicago: University of Chicago Press.

Trickett, L. 2016. "Birds and Sluts: Views on Young Women from Boys in the Gang." *International Review of Victimology* 22 (1): 25–44. https://doi.org/10.1177/0269758015610850.

Young, T., and L. Trickett. 2017. "Gang Girls: Agency, Sexual Identity and Victimization 'on Road.'" In *Youth Culture and Social Change*, edited by K. Gildart, A. Gough-Yates, S. Lincoln, B. Osgerby, L. Robinson, J. Street, P. Webb, and M. Worley, 231–59. Basingstoke, UK: Palgrave Macmillan.

4 Somethin' Doesn't Seem Right: A Commentary on the "Scientific Method" and "Gang" Research

ADAM ELLIS[1] AND ANTHONY GUNTER

My Personal Experience with Orthodox (Traditional) Criminology

Not too long ago, I was an undergraduate in criminology, sitting in classes that ranged from 20 to 200 students. I was fresh off the streets, where I spent most of my life "surviving" the world of what orthodox scholars would reference as "gangs" and "organized crime." Within the grand halls of the ivory tower were lecture rooms designed for knowledge mobilization and pedagogy. At the front of the lecture hall was a stage, where professors pontificated on their "scientific truths."[2] As a new undergrad and a person who lived the "criminal" life that criminology spoke of, I was eager to move through the next four years of my life. I went to every class, participated regularly, and consistently received A's in my courses. However, by my second year, I started to question the authenticity of criminology.

First, everyone who was part of the Criminology Department (and more broadly the student body) did not talk like me nor look like me. In this context, my working-class "west-end" accent, tattoos, and gangster clothing made me feel like I was living in a different world. I found it difficult to fit into the middle- / upper-class framework of academia. I felt like I was being "pimped" by the system. Professors rarely celebrated my achievements, nor did they take the time to even acknowledge that I existed, but they certainly had time to take my money (as shown by my large student loan). The rare moments when I was able to get a meeting with "profs" and discuss my lived experience, they spent most of that time berating me for trying to have my own "criminological imagination" (however, I did have some great mentors during my graduate experience). My second issue with criminology was much more entrenched and emerged during my course work. For example, during one course, on gun crime, the professor provided grand –sterile – statistics that told us how many guns there were in Canada, whether these were lethal/non-lethal shootings, and how they seemed to magically appear across the border. Then, reciting from a

US textbook, he provided superficial and generalized data on the relationship between youth gang membership and gun violence (including the often-cited crime-oriented lens on gangs). While part of me was excited to be a part of a course that finally spoke to my lived experience, I was at deflated the same time as I came to realize that criminology, and its purveyors of knowledge, knew nothing about the world I came from (except from a distance). For instance, I asked the professor if he could name a gang from my city, and he could not. I asked if he knew how guns and crack got into my community, and he could not answer. I questioned him on whether he could tell me how it felt to shoot at someone or to be shot at, and he could not. I realized at that moment that so-called criminological knowledge was mostly ripe with misconceptions and disillusioned in its own incompleteness.

I recognized that some professors/researchers (both from a quantitative and qualitative orientation) were not Picassos painting detailed pictures of life "outside," and more like actors/marionettes performing and interpreting other people's reality on a stage (this is how I, as an insider to the streets and outsider to academia came to view pedagogy/research). These performers of "street culture" played roles, including story writer and storyteller (what I viewed as institutionalized marionettes). As a story writer, outsider academics can draw from the reality of other people's lived experience (i.e., data). As marionettes they can then use *their* voices and *their* bodies to interpret and tell other people's stories. However, those who have their voices abducted are rarely given the privilege to tell their own story from the same stage – academia. Professors like the one noted above have been able to use the space of academia and their positions of power (professors) to confirm their own version of "reality" (truths). Then these often-uncontested "truths" are passed down to students with little challenge and/or critique. Such pedagogical experiences are mirrored in the work of Freire (1970), who interprets the transmission of colonial knowledge/truths as the "banking system." Freire notes that "instead of communicating, the teacher issues communiques and makes deposits which the students patiently receive, memorize and repeat. This is the 'banking' concept of education, in which the scope of action allowed to students extends only as far as receiving, filing and storing the deposits" (58). Thus, docile students then digest these truths, unaware of the disconnect between the scholarship in front of them, and the social reality outside of the ivory tower (creating a perpetual incomplete narrative of the streets in particular and life in general).

Unfortunately, my initial negative experiences with criminology did not end with undergrad. In graduate school, including the all-encompassing PhD, these issues were compounded exponentially. The Criminology Department in graduate school also lacked diversity (not one academic came from the life/populations they were studying). Researchers/professors often lacked any "outside" experience (i.e., visiting the communities they study), but defined themselves as "experts" on youth crime (including gangs). The majority of criminologists in my department engaged in statistical-quantitative methods, which allowed them to absolve themselves from having to engage in "dirty" research. It became apparent that the quantitative method provided a "lifeline" to academics who lacked real connection to the culture/populations they wished to study. The quantitative method offered detached – outsider – researchers a pathway to create their own version of "truth" while staying relevant in the criminological field (amassing a portfolio of journal articles). These "quant" researchers also used the language of statistics to confirm their version of reality. I contend that, to maintain their "gatekeeper" status, "outsider researchers" appeared to use the quant-language/method to suppress critiques/challenges from the margins (few researchers who come from the street life are privileged to learn the mathematical language of the colonizers who have blocked them from social mobility). Although academics with lived experience may provide a better picture of reality (i.e., the Picassos), most have been denied access the academic stage, where they can perform their own version of social reality. So those who are privileged in society are positioned to write other people's history (often from a colonial-Eurocentric perspective).

So, like my undergrad experiences, my graduate experience also felt disconnected from reality. I tried to sign up for courses that could inform my lived experience, but there were few, except for one on youth crime and delinquency. The texts, journal articles, and scholarship for courses on youth crime were largely informed by US/Canadian quantitative research. While "scholars" (quantitative and qualitative) have made significant contributions to our knowledge about youth crime (gangs) (and that such research methods/knowledge is somewhat valuable), this scholarship has largely been dominated by those who come from privileged backgrounds (not those from the communities under study). Middle- /upper-class academics have been able to monopolize the knowledge on youth crime/gangs, leading to an often incomplete, distorted, and sterile picture of life in the streets.

Those from disadvantage (including a gang life) rarely make it to the ivory tower, so it is rare that the "outlines" of quantitative research are challenged. Thus, unchecked, the same knowledge about youth crime/gangs makes its rounds, informing the "blind" student body, while also confirming the professors who stand at the front of their stage, performing. Then through my own experience, I became gravely concerned about the "mistruths" that were perpetuated and circulated in the social fabric of my university. I worried about how this misinformation could harm the communities I grew up in. I still had family and friends outside academia who were being killed, going to jail/prison, experiencing mental health/addiction, and living a gang life. Thinking about my street family, I was deeply concerned that research studies (on gangs/gun crime) conducted by doctoral students/professors, that followed the status quo, would not only undermine the integrity of these projects but also the policies and practices that might be informed by such knowledge.

To disrupt the "truths" about gangs and gang violence (and youth crime in general), I sought to use graduate school to challenge the status quo. Having lived in a gang for over a decade I thought I could bring a fresh perspective to the incomplete narratives perpetuated by orthodox scholars. Who better to challenge the system than the ones who lived it? In the early stages of my doctoral work, I talked with my supervisor about how I could approach my research. I wanted to explore how macro-structural contexts led to the rise of "street warfare" (knowledge and experiences I acquired from over a decade in the streets). I wanted to understand how gang violence affected young people psychologically (e.g., thinking that aligned with C. Wright Mills, 1950, on sociological imagination). I was inspired by the work of Victor Rios (a former gang member) and Randol Contreras (a former drug dealer) who transcended the streets, became PhDs, and now wrote about their earlier lives from the ivory tower. These were my superheroes, my Picassos. I viewed them in a different light, because they could paint a more complete and more accurate picture of street life. I was fortunate to have Dr. Contreras as not only a mentor, but also a member of my doctoral committee. Through my relationship with him, I explored and experimented with "insider" research – or the methods of auto-ethnography/ethnography and Indigenous research. I struck gold, or so I thought.

Although I was excited by the potential to "tell my truth," my initial attempt to create a doctoral project out of my life experiences was shut down. I was stopped from committing "academic suicide." My life's work was disrupted by what Jock Young calls the "datasaurs" or the purveyors of quantitative research. I was being indoctrinated into a quasi-positivist criminology that went against my very being. As Young predicted, criminology has shifted from the personal knowing of the outside world. What has emerged is a monopolized, uncontested, orthodox criminology that lacks sociological imagination and a deeper understanding of the social worlds we study. Then during these initial discussions it was suggested that while my personal experience was interesting, it was not "scientific enough"! So I asked myself, How can someone who has never been to the "block," but studies it, be more scientific/knowledgeable, while those who lived and breathed it are dismissed? In further conversation, it was proposed early in my doctoral career that marginal methods such as auto-ethnography had no place in academia. I was warned by my supervisor that such an approach could seriously affect my doctoral defence and subsequent graduation. Pressure to conform was intense. Further, while I had a significant understanding of "gangs," my personal knowledge was often suppressed and/or undermined by more "experienced" researchers/academics who self-identified as experts. I felt I had reached a crossroads: Do I follow my instincts and become Picasso or do I fold and become part of the status quo – spending my career trying to become something someone else wants me to be!

The Barriers of Orthodox Criminology

The personal critiques of orthodox criminology while radical, are not new. Those conducting ethnographic research have long clashed with traditional criminologists (and sociologists) who have sought to monopolize the knowledge market, including scholarship on gangs. For authors such as Young (2011) the shift away from theoretical/soft criminology to one of positivism/statistical criminology has had a catastrophic impact on the field. The gatekeepers of orthodox criminology have been able to maintain the status quo. In this respect, a largely middle- /upper-class population of students/researchers and academics have become the "voice" of the streets. Comparatively, those who are the "researched" rarely have access or the opportunity to reach the halls of academia, where they can contextualize their own reality. Thus, from this perspective one must question the authenticity and completeness of traditional criminological research (including other disciplines such as sociology and psychology, that also research "gangs"). And with the lack of representation of people with lived experience in criminology, who then challenges these incomplete interpretations of street culture and gang life?

Numbers Can Lie Too: Critique of Quantitative Methods

Quantitative research methodologies suffer from the same problem as those within the qualitative framework: they derive from the Enlightenment belief in the divine truths of scientific knowledge. Drawing on the approaches of the natural sciences, Euro-American positivist social scientists, using and manipulating large numerical data sets, have religiously adhered to notions of reliability, objectivity, and generalizability. In contrast the interpretive branch of the social sciences, which became more popular in the early twentieth century, placed meaning-making at the heart of social enquiry and used the collection and analysis of qualitative data. However, both models clung to the false notions of scientific "truth" and "objectivity"; when they are in fact colonialist-derived instruments that allow the usually "white" privileged male (and some notable females, despite recent white feminist protestations) academic expert to appear front and centre of the research, going into the Heart of Darkness in order bring back new understandings about the phenomena under investigation: strange, exotic, and/or uncooperative natives. Even though the far-flung research fields of the empire have been replaced by the nearest faraway places in the back yards of their own decaying urban centres, the lies about objectively generated knowledge still dominate. How can we rely on numerical data sets constructed and informed by law-enforcement agencies to (1) inform us about the numbers and types of gangs, (2) gang membership, or (3) the nature and extent of crimes that gang members commit? By accepting data and the subsequent findings derived from such biased sources, we forego any claim that our research is objective, reliable, and generalizable.

A case in point is Walter B. Miller's monograph *Violence by Youth Gangs and Youth Groups as a Crime Problem in Major American Cities*[3] (1975, 3), which was based on the data and findings from a national survey on gangs undertaken across twelve large US cities. Site visits lasted two to four days and an interview guide was drawn up and served as an information-gathering tool rather than a questionnaire. "Staff members representing 81 different agencies participated in 64 interviews, with a total of 159 respondents contributing" (3). Of the 159 respondents interviewed, 50 were from police departments, 28 from municipal/county gang outreach programs, and 14 from private/agency gang outreach programs. The rest were from criminal justice agencies, with just two respondents from schools and one from academia. "In addition to interview data, approximately 225 pages of reports, statistical data, and other documents were obtained from agency representatives in the 12 cities" (3).

On the basis of the findings of his survey, Miller (1975) argued that while the gang problem was non-existent throughout the entire 1960s, the situation had changed by 1971 as gangs started cropping up in New York: in 1975 there were 275 police-verified gangs with 1,100 members. Allegedly these gangs were more heavily armed and lethal than their predecessors, and their violent activities were directed towards each other. However, it wasn't just New York that was seeing high levels of gang violence. It was a problem in Chicago, Los Angeles, San Francisco, Philadelphia, and Detroit. From his data, Miller estimated these cities had between 760 and 2,700 gangs, with membership ranging from 28,500 to 81,500, and there were also about 525 gang-related murders between 1972 and 1975. Although these claims were confidently proclaimed in the foreword to Miller's report by the assistant administrator of the Office of Juvenile Justice and Delinquency Prevention (OJJDP), "much of the base data from which conclusions are derived – single interviews with local respondents, press accounts of uneven detail, inhouse descriptions of agency operations, statistical tabulations compiled under less-than-ideal circumstances – fail to reach the level of quality necessary to sound research. Using such data clearly entails risks that conclusions derived from them may in varying degrees be inaccurate, incomplete, or biased" (Miller 1975, 4).

Perhaps the absence of gangs that Miller notes to from the late 1950s to early 1970s refers not to scientifically verified fact but is a better reflection of the ebbs and flows of academic interest in this issue. However, the sudden explosion of gangs and violence in the 1970s might be more accurately said to mirror the burgeoning law enforcement agenda – reaching maturity in the late 1980s – that viewed gangs as essentially criminal street-oriented conspiracies comprising hard-core sociopaths, and "the arrest and imprisonment of these individuals are required as a viable social policy" (Miller 1975, 4). This resulted in the implementation of state and federal laws[4] that used "almost identical wording in their definitions of 'criminal gangs.' Conveniently, omitting from 'these definitions are other groups [in fact there are no white groups] that technically may fit these standard definitions" (Shelden, Tracy, and Brown 2013, 24).

Miller, as an academic based in one of the world's most prestigious universities, was recruited by law enforcement and criminal justice agencies to provide a mirage of academic veracity to their racist gang agenda. This prototype model was fully formed in all its glory when the OJJDP launched its own National Youth Gang Center in 1995 to strengthen communities' abilities to tackle the youth gang problem. Between 1996 and 2012 the center conducted an annual survey of law enforcement agencies to assess the gang phenomena across the United States. The OJJDP (1998, 1), while acknowledging the "limitations in quality and uniformity," still maintained that data collected solely from law enforcement agencies "continue to be the best available resource for gauging the extent of youth gangs and their activities." The first of these surveys, conducted in 1996, was billed as comprehensive and statistically representative, in data collection and subsequent findings:

1. 3,024 police and sheriff departments were surveyed.
2. A youth gang was defined as "a group of youths in (the respondent's) jurisdiction that (the respondent) or other responsible persons in (the respondent's) agency are willing to identify or classify as a "gang." However, hate groups, prison gangs, adult gangs, as well as motorcycle gangs were all excluded from the survey.

On the basis of the data, the OJJDP reported that the United States had a substantial gang problem in 1996 (and in all the subsequent years up to 2012, as allegedly there were 31,000 street gangs and over 81,000 gang members spread across nearly 6,000 towns and cities, and about 80 per cent of gang members were African American or Latino).

Some might argue that law enforcement professionals are experts, and it is logical and ethically correct to use data derived from them and their criminal justice colleagues. However, the evidence is overwhelming on to how systemic racial bias and discrimination have resulted in decades of lethal police violence meted out against African Americans (Camp and Heatherton 2016). But quantitative methodologies that harp about the scientific truths and rigour of large (aw-enforcement-derived) data sets, random and representative sampling, objectivity, and reliability are flawed if they exclude data from certain key populations, and fail to consider the real lived "truths" and experiences of those communities, that are over-represented in the data and disproportionately targeted, surveilled, and punished by justice system actors.

The Sleight of Hand: Ethnography and Gang Research

While our understanding of gangs/gang behaviour has emerged largely from a positivist – orthodox – criminology, alternative intellectual spaces have challenged and resisted the status quo. Carving out their own spaces, feminist, Black-feminist, cultural, critical, Black, and Latinx criminologies have materialized in protest against the white orthodox criminology. While the work of these new critical scholars has drawn on both qualitative and quantitative methods/methodologies, others more interested in the stories/narratives of those on the margins have opted to use more exploratory tools such as the ethnographic approach. The ethnographic approach, in theory, seeks to provide researchers with an "insider's" lens, or an up-close personalized account of the populations under study. This access is supposed to demonstrate that researchers are accepted by the populations they study and this "access" somehow gives them privilege to be the voices of the voiceless. The profile of these ethnographers is often in stark contrast to the "insiders" or the populations being studied. However, in the search for scientific truth, ethnographers, like "quant" researchers, must also transform into quasi-marionettes. Here, seeking to construct "their" narrative, middle-/upper-class students/academics enter the universe of the "other," playing the role of the compassionate/caring research scientist, only to extrapolate the stories and identities of the people being studied. Some of these researchers spend a month in the community, while others spend years carefully building rapport and trust, hoping one day they can access the "secret map" that leads them to the communal treasure (i.e., data).

But whatever the length of time, insiders are always aware of their outsider status, their colonial gaze, and the sleight of hand that is the scientific method. So, like quant research, one must also be sceptical of the outsider-ethnographers' claims of "truth" – perhaps even more so. Are they not also intellectual marionettes devoid of personal reality/positionality, only to find it through other people's lived experience? And what impact does this have on truth and knowledge production? This, from my viewpoint, is one of social science's greatest illusions. As insiders (to the block, hood, bodega) we are led to believe, through the ethnographic "scientific" method, that the ethnographer is an extension of the community. We are led to believe that the research and the intrusion on our communities is for the greater good. We are led to believe that such intrusions are a social necessity to seek justice and to fight for our human rights. However, in the end, there is no justice, there is little change, and there is no solution to the core issues affecting many communities under study. And this is the sleight of hand. This is where the scholar becomes the magician. This is where the warriors for justice pull the wool over the eyes of those seeking to break free from the hands of oppression and structural violence. However, their truths are often given away, to researchers, who proclaim to be the "fighters" who will subsequently give voice to the voiceless. But what happens? Let's be real! The outsider-ethnographer finally gets inside, locates the map, takes the treasure (i.e., data) and escapes (although I recognize that there is a shift amongst some critical scholars/researchers seeking to include the community in the research process/project through decolonizing methods/methodologies).

Then with the treasure in hand (i.e., the data) they (orthodox scholars using ethnography) transpose this information into "codes" and "nodes" with which they can interpret and construct their own version of reality. Then qualitative researchers contend that they too, like their quant counterparts, have also found some vestige of truth about the social world. But have they? It is my experience, as demonstrated by contemporary ethnographies on gangs, that this research and scholarship must also be challenged and contested by those who have lived and breathed it. In this context, the insider/insider academic must then disrupt the research chain, whether qualitative or quantitative, and put to task the knowledge regimes that distribute misconceptions and distortions of *our* reality. This is not to say that some ethnographers have not come close to the truth (see Brotherton and Barrios 2004; Contreras 2013; Rios 2017). However, we must be deliberate and honest if we are to recast the way gang scholarship has been twisted and manipulated for over fifty years. We must recognize that even those with the best intentions to seek *our* truths may also lack the tools to become Picassos to paint the complexity of others' lived realities. And from my experience as a thug "insider" academic, we must be aware of the pitfalls of the most well-intentioned "scientific methods." In this light, and from an insider's standpoint, three primary contexts may challenge the authenticity and completeness of contemporary gang research: (1) true access to the populations under study, (2) the bias that researchers bring to participant observation and questioning and (3) the ethics of gang research.

"Real Recognize Real": Access to the Gang Population and "Their" Worlds

In the streets, we use the term "real recognize real" to denote that only a gang member can know the authenticity or "realness" of another gang member. This cannot be learned overnight. Our ability to sniff out bullshit and recognize real ones takes years to develop. One might call it a "Spidey sense" that allows us to look a man in the eye and know whether he has been through the "trenches" or not. It is well established within the sociological and criminological scholarship that gang members are a hard-to-reach population. For decades both quantitative and qualitative researchers have claimed that they have been able to not only infiltrate this hidden population, but also uproot the invisible truths that have lain dormant within the matrix of the "code of the street" (see Anderson 1999). As a former high-level member of a street organization (see Brotherton and Barrios 2004), I often questioned the authenticity of texts and journal articles that have made such claims. From my world, "real ones" do not cooperate with the "outside" world. Real ones move in the shadow. Real ones move in silence. This is not to say that former "gang" members have not broken the code and "talked." Quite the opposite. There have been influential literary testimonies by former street soldiers turned authors such as Monster Cody, Stanley Tookie Williams, Rick Ross, and Reymundo Sanchez. However, they made a choice to step out and break the code of silence, usually for self-fulfilling monetary gains. And fuck, who can blame them!

However, for many outsiders such texts lack the pedigree to be considered "scientific." The middle-class outsiders have dubiously fought to not only fill this scientific void, and they have also cornered the market on who is actually the "gang expert." In this context, the scientific world has created a regime of truth, in which the voices of those who come from gangs/street organizations and write about it are less genuine than the scientific experts. But if real ones stay silent, and the ones who talk seek to write their own scripts, who is actually being researched? I have long pondered this question. And I am rarely impressed by the superficial and detached texts of these so-called gang scholars. Sifting through hundreds of documents, I am often left scratching my head, questioning who these researchers actually spoke to, because I know, "on the real," that these folks did not actually get down with anyone from the "streets." While much of this fault can be found in the writing of quantitative researchers, the qualitative ethnographer is not safe from this critique either. Although real recognizes real, and real ones know real ones, I am always perplexed about who these "urban ethnographers" are actually "chopping it up with." Shit, criminologists and sociologists can't even define a gang/gang member, let alone find one.

The scientific method, including ethnography, teaches up-and-coming researchers that to access hard-to-reach populations, such as gang members, they need to use research tools such as recruitment posters, rapport/relationship building, and the snowball technique to acquire their "sample." While these are all fine and dandy, I know that these techniques rarely have traction. How do I know this? I know this because I was once knee deep in the streets, my life was encapsulated by drug markets and violence, and my day was relegated primarily to the monotony of getting high/drunk, sexing girls, evading the police, and staying alive. Sorry, I was not worried about somebody's fucking research project. The people I was around did not care about someone's research project. And my enemies did not care about a fucking research project. Get it!! So, what am I trying to say? In the plainest way possible, I, my crew, or my enemies would never, by any stretch of the imagination, allow an outsider researcher to hang, observe, take notes, or write about us! This is probably why there are no true studies of street culture in my city. This is why ethnographic studies rarely capture the real lives of street-involved youth/adults. Instead, we are offered a sleight of hand. Here, orthodox ethnographers are often "duped" by community organizations and community workers who proclaim that they can recruit "gang members" for their study and/or give them access to the community where the prolific and vile "gang" exists (similar to poachers showing game hunters where the golden tiger might be found). But believe me, these are not gang members or street soldiers. These are peripheral hang-arounds (i.e., not real ones) that we use as a diversion to get "you" away from "us." Furthermore, even if the middle-class researcher can find a "real one" who is will talk, trust me when I tell you, this is on our terms. You only get to see what we want you to see.

The inability of experts to access real ones raises serious questions about the authenticity and completeness of the stories being scripted. For example, in the streets, "gang members" must be vetted. This is done through informal tests that include proving family lineage to a gang and/or showing the individual is "down" on the basis of their street-performance (i.e., putting in work – drug selling, violence, etc.). While the streets might know who is real, it is a far stretch that community organizations working on behalf of researchers, or outsider researchers themselves, would be able to "vet" their sample (especially on the basis of arbitrary knowledge and definitions that become the orthodox scholars a priori of understanding about street life). It is unlikely that/orthodox ethnographers, know who they are really "getting down with." Contexts such as these raise significant ethical concerns and can lead to significant risks for the researched and researcher (see Venkatesh 2008). These issues can be found in some of the most highly acclaimed (orthodox) ethnographies of our time, such as Bourgois's (2003) seminal text *In Search of Respect*, in which the author set out to understand the relationship between structural violence, the emergence of crack markets, and street violence. However, not knowing the intricate geography of East Harlem and failing to properly vet his sample, he found himself immersed in a world of serial gang rapists – not "real" gang members – who in my world would be regulated and violated.

More problematic, Bourgois's (2003) work also reflects how outsider researchers fail to contextualize the experiences of those on the margins. In this respect his work fetishizes the violence of those on the margins without adequately exploring and understanding how structural violence bleeds into communities and how these stressors affect on a sociopsychological level (as an outsider it is impossible for the author to dispel the emotions and feelings that emerge with being a perpetrator and victim of violence). Thus, as an outsider's interpretation, or script of life in the "ghetto," one is left with only a superficial understanding of community/interpersonal violence and life in the streets.

Building on this critique, one must also question if other gang or "street" ethnographers have made similar fatal errors in their research. For example, how complete or accurate are the accounts found in Thrasher's (1927/1963) *The Gang*, Venkatesh's (2008) *Gang Leader for a Day*, Densley's (2013) *An Ethnography of Youth Violence*, and Rodgers's (2007) *Joining the Gang and Becoming a Broder*, to name a few. In this context, one must come to these readings with caution, as none of these texts have been vetted by those who were actually street-involved (this is not to say that some of these narratives are not true; however, without representation in academia from the street we will never know). As many of these researchers never came from the streets/community, let alone a street life, how can we trust they spoke with "validated" gang members. From my perspective, this issue holds significant weight.

As a former gang member, I can say without hesitation that ethnographers would never have access to "real ones," despite how some people on the block might self-identify. Of course, this is all subjective. While an outsider researcher might find someone who will talk and who identifies, for example, as a gang leader, this individual may be viewed as a low-level player amongst other peers in the community. However, outsiders would never know this, would they! They would never know to vet their sample, because they come to the "streets" blind. They are naive and have no understanding of how the streets work. While their arrogance informs their understanding, on a conscious level, that these issues can be resolved through their suave rapport-building skills and methodological toolbelt, they soon learn that the world they enter is not the one they scripted – it is messy, manipulative, and silent. Consequently, many of these researchers are duped or played. But again, they don't realize it, because they have no one to authenticate the people they are interviewing, or the information being telegraphed. Then one of my greatest fears is that outsider researchers swallow this information as "truth." Outsiders then craft a narrative about the "block" that is based on fallacies and untruths, only to be mobilized through articles/conferences and consumed by eager middle-class researchers seeking their own "street porn" from the safety of the academic bubble.

So failing to access "real ones" may subsequently lead to not only a false representation of the real world, but also a "street fetishization" and/or a sensationalized account of so-called gang life. What I have found in contemporary ethnographic accounts of gang life is a priori of bias, including sensationalist ideas of what the "other" gang world is and should look like (and when the "ugliness" of the streets does not match the researchers' preconceptions they often stretch and manipulate the data to mimic their hypothesis – thus leading to more distortions and untruths). For most middle-class sociology and criminology students, the other world is primarily a space of crime. Here students' biases are mapped onto conceptualizations of the "gangster world" that they see on TV or social media. Then even before they leave the classroom for the "block," they have already created a study that focuses primarily on the dysfunctions of the "other," rather than exploring the root causes and intersectionalities that lead to gangs/gang behaviour in the first place (or what Mills has sought to demonstrate through the sociological imagination – delineating between the public and personal).

When was the last time you heard of an ethnographic gang study that explored the lived realities of politicians, the police, or orthodox academics (the ones who create the knowledge and untruths that lead to structural violence – and gangs are groups that form to resist and protect against the harm delivered by the dominant group)? However, that is not sexy, is it! Subsequently middle-class researchers also seem to force themselves onto vulnerable populations such as gangs to gratify their pornographic fetishes of a street life. Then what are we intellectually left with? Mostly Through their lack of access to and knowledge about gang life, orthodox ethnographers may reproduce the same stereotypical scholarship they purport to stand against (the quantitative gang research). As a result, the street life is tokenized, where orthodox scholars/researchers extrapolate and reconstruct the lives of the "other." But even in this attempt, we must question what knowledge is being reproduced and whose lived reality is being scripted. In this context, with no one vetting the researchers before they step into a "gang world," with no one vetting who they recruited, and with no one vetting what was written, we are sure to repeat history, where the real lives of street-involved youth/adults are never truly documented in a meaningful and complete way.

Reflection and Looking Forward

This chapter has sought to raise and address key questions and concerns about the "scientific method" used by criminological/sociological researchers in general, and so-called gang research in particular (including the methods and methodologies deployed to understand "gang" or street populations). It is highly problematic that the colonial-orthodox criminological system has been allowed to thrive without critique or challenge from those who are all too often the subject of its gaze. Too often throughout history the dominant group has monopolized the institutions of power, such as that of academia, where "outsiders" are able to create, construct, and mobilize knowledge about those they deem to be "problematic." Consequently, one side of the story is told, and when those who are considered the "other" are asked about their lives, they are trivialized and tokenized, only to have their narratives interpreted from the perspective of the dominant group where their stories and lived experiences become the capital for the researchers' own social mobility, either academically or socially. Unfortunately, these orthodox knowledge regimes rarely provide an accurate picture of what is happening in the streets, thus increasing the risk that racist stereotypes are produced and reproduced about those on the margins (largely through the banking system of education). But what can we do to resist or change how researchers explore and interrogate "us"? For starters we need to provide more opportunities for young people to reach the halls of the ivory tower. Here, those who have been criminalized and harmed by the system may not only challenge what has been written about them but also become leaders themselves in creating a new dialogue about crime and criminal behaviour in society (one that may reposition the focus from the crimes of the poor to the crimes of the oppressors/dominant group).

Further, we must also push for a new "criminology" that recognizes its privilege and is open to transformation. As thug criminologists we do not seek to undermine the whole "scientific method." Quite the opposite: we do see value in some of the research tools that have been developed to understand social issues. Rather, we argue that "research" should not start within the institutions with a history of racism/colonization, nor should knowledge creation have its genesis in the hands of those who come from privilege. Comparatively knowledge creation and mobilization should be "FUBU" (For Us By Us). In this respect, thug criminology advocates for new criminological methods/methodologies that are not only sensitive to community needs (recruiting more young people from the margins into academia, providing them spaces to start and lead new discourses about social issues, and recognizing and positioning their "voices" as the primary sources of knowledge production/mobilization), but are also transformative (using methods that involve the community).

Conceptually then, and drawing on decolonizing/indigenous methods/methodologies (storytelling, participatory-action research, etc.), we seek to dismantle the orthodox-dominant criminological gaze by shifting the power of research away from the discursive space of academia and into the hands of the community. Thus, research should start and end in the community. In this context, we envision collaborative research projects that involve the community through each step of the knowledge building process. Such approaches (whether led by insider/insider or insider/outsider academics) should have the goal of community transformation, rather than the traditional "smash-and-grab" tactics of orthodox researchers. Through this shift in how we do research we can then ensure that youth on the margins are being recruited, trained, and mentored into academia where they can change the complexion and knowledge being produced within the halls of the ivory tower; and the "researched" gain from the knowledge building process, through training, employment opportunities, and/or co-authorship on projects.

NOTES

1 Sections of this chapter draw on and refer to the direct experiences of this author as presented in the first person.

2 These contexts are similar to what Paulo Feire (1970) denotes as the transmission model of education: knowledge is transmitted from teacher – the one in power – to students.
3 Walter B. Miller's (Center for Criminal Justice, Harvard Law School) research project was funded by the National Institute for Juvenile Justice and Delinquency Prevention, Law Enforcement Assistance Administration, and the U.S. Department of Justice under the Omnibus Crime Control and Safe Streets Act of 1968.
4 See, for example, California's Street Terrorism Enforcement and Prevention Act, 1988.

REFERENCES

Anderson, E. 1999. *Code of the Street: Decency, Violence, and the Moral Life of the Inner City.* New York: W. W. Norton.
Bourgois, P. 2003. *In Search of Respect: Selling Crack in El Barrio.* Cambridge, UK: Cambridge University Press.
Brotherton, D.C., and L. Barrios. 2004. *The Almighty Latin King and Queen Nation: Street Politics and the Transformation of a New York City Gang.* New York: Columbia University Press.
Camp, T., and Heatherton, C., eds. 2016. *Policing the Planet: Why the Policing Crisis Led to Black Lives Matter.* London: Verso.
Contreras, R. 2013. *Stick Up Kids.* Los Angeles: University of California Press.
Densley, J.A. 2013. *How Gangs Work: An Ethnography of Youth Violence.* New York: Palgrave Publishing.
Freire, P. 1970. *Pedagogy of the Oppressed.* New York: Herder and Herder.
Miller, W.B. 1975. *Violence by Youth Gangs and Youth Groups as a Crime Problem in Major American Cities.* Washington, DC: National Institute for Juvenile Justice and Delinquency Prevention. Accessed 19 May 2016, https://www.ncjrs.gov/pdffiles1/Digitization/34497NCJRS.pdf.
Mills, C.W. 1950. *The Sociological Imagination.* New York: Oxford University Press.
OJJDP. 1998. "Highlights of the 1996 National Youth Gang Survey." Fact sheet, Office for Juvenile Justice and Delinquency Prevention, Washington, DC: US Department of Justice, https://www.ncjrs.gov/pdffiles/fs-9886.pdf.
Rios, V. 2017. *Human Targets: Schools, Police and the Criminalization of Latino Youth.* Chicago: University of Chicago Press.
Rodgers, D. 2007. "Joining the Gang and Becoming a *Broder*: The Violence of Ethnography in Contemporary Nicaragua." *Journal of the Society for Latin American Studies* 26 (4): 444–61. https://doi.org/10.1111/j.1470-9856.2007.00234.x
Shelden, R. G., S.K. Tracy, and W.B. Brown. 2013. *Youth Gangs in American Society.* Belmont: Cengage Learning.
Thrasher, F.M. (1927) 1963. *The Gang: A Study of 1,313 Gangs in Chicago.* Chicago: University of Chicago Press.
Venkatesh, S. 2008. *Gang Leader for a Day: A Rogue Sociologist Takes to the Streets.* New York: Penguin.
Young, J. 2011. *The Criminological Imagination.* Cambridge: Polity.

PART TWO

"Getting Over" and Inside the Ivory Tower

5 I Am (Not) What You Say I Am: Disrupting the Colonizers' "Gang"

GREGORY BROWN

My Background as Insider/Insider Gang Researcher

Like many of my fellow thug criminologists, I am an insider to academia and an insider to the gang life. While I never claimed to be a gang member, I lived in a predominantly Black neighbourhood with a large and emerging Latinx population of mostly Mexicans. My neighbourhood and nearby neighbourhoods were called "hoods" by the local residents. These hoods were claimed by major Black and Mexican gangs. My neighbourhood would be described as poor and minority. It was a place where many males were prime targets of police, bait for the "school to prison pipeline." Many males would be incarcerated during their lifetimes and their mothers were receiving government assistance, often as food stamps, housing support, and programs like Families with Dependent Children. These social economic factors are important because they encapsulate the fact that I was the other/an outsider/a threat or potential threat/as a resident of a poor community filled with "gang members," drugs, violence, poor quality schools, and many mother-headed households.

While I have never claimed to be a gang member, that did not prevent the police from identifying me as a "gang member." Many times I was stopped by the police, and when they completed the Field Identification Card, they identified me as a "gang member." It did not matter if I was alone or with others. Growing up in my neighbourhood, gang members were present, but the vast majority did not participate in gang activity or claim gang involvement. Thus, if the police classified someone as gang member, it is likely that was *not* how the individual self-identified. Thus, I was classified and identified as a gang member because I lived in the same neighbourhood as my childhood friends and associated with them. Anyone interacting with them would be identified as "gang members" too.

Who Defines Gangs?

Understanding gang behaviour is tied to the definition of a gang and the methods used to study them (Bursik and Grasmick 2006). A commonly accepted definition of gangs is necessary to judge the extent and nature of gang behaviour and the changes that have occurred. Gang research in the United States has been dominated by mainstream "outsider" perspectives on gangs, including those in the criminal justice system, (law enforcement and prosecutors, and mainstream scholars studying the gang issue) (Bloch and Niederhoffer 1958; Cohen 1955; Esbensen et al. 2008; Klein 1971; Miller 1975, Thrasher (1927) 1963; Yablonsky 1962). These outsiders have defined gangs and the criteria that make a group a gang, specified how many individuals it takes to constitute a gang, and identified and described the activities (mostly criminal) in which a "gang" participates. Generally, these outsiders are white, middle- to upper-middle-class males who do not understand or look like the people they are studying. Since the existence of a "gang problem" can provide access to federal research and law-enforcement funding, law-enforcement agencies have a vested interest in identifying a gang problem in their communities (Bursik and Grasmick 2006) and academics have a vested interest in using those definitions as well. These financial incentives have led to a law-enforcement-driven definition of gangs in the United States.

Definitions of a gang are also related to theories about why gangs develop. From the beginning, the definition of "gang" in the United States developed from academic research influenced by white colonial knowledge, which focused on youth delinquency. One of the earliest research studies on gangs, originally published in 1927, was conducted by Frederick Thrasher from the Chicago school (Thrasher 1963). Thrasher sought to explain delinquency in white immigrant youth. He concluded that it is born out of the social disorganization of immigrant families, and the conflict they faced between "old country" and "new world" norms. He suggested that youth become disorganized by learning American values in school and old cultural values from their parents. For example, immigrant parents encouraged their children to beg, which developed into illicit activities and the beginning of gangs.

In Thrasher's studies, white immigrant youth were considered "minorities," since they came from cultures that varied from earlier Anglo-Saxon European immigrants. Their cultural behaviour was defined using a middle-class Protestant majority lens. Cohen (1955) called this the "middle-class yardstick." Thrasher's construct viewed immigrant groups as different from mainstream US society, as "others," establishing an "us" versus "them" mentality that has persisted throughout American gang research.

Other early theories developed primarily to explain delinquency and criminal behaviour in white immigrant groups also focused on the social process that give rise to gangs. From his study of delinquent subculture and its prominence among male, working-class youth in American society, Merton (1938) explained delinquent behaviour as a result of the pressure put on individuals to achieve socially accepted goals without the tools to do so. In Cohen's (1955) later version of strain theory, delinquency resulted from the "status frustration" lower-class youth felt when judged by middle-class values. As a result of their frustration, these youth acted out in non-utilitarian "negativistic" fashion through a gang. Cohen's premise that gangs were negativistic and rejected middle-class values was widely accepted.

Shaw and McKay's research (1931) also focused on the group nature of delinquency, following the finding that 90 per cent of delinquent events in Cook County juvenile court records involved at least two participants (Shaw 1929). Their social disorganization theory links delinquency and crime to neighbourhood characteristics. Sutherland's theory of differential association emphasized the roles of group dynamics and learned behaviour in delinquent behaviour and crime (McCarthy 1996).

Starting in the 1960s, the attention of the media, the public, and gang researchers turned from theory to crime. The focus of gang research shifted from the study of group dynamics to their delinquent and criminal behaviour (Hagedorn and Macon 1988). In 1962, Yablonsky documented the author's experiences with two gangs in New York City, focusing on their violent behaviour. In 1965 President Johnson declared a "War on Crime" and focused on increasing local law enforcement to serve as its soldiers. Gang researchers began to incorporate violent behaviour into their gang definitions. Under Klein's (1971) definition, involvement in a "sufficient" number of delinquent incidents was a requirement for a group to be a gang. According to Miller's (1980) definition, gang behaviour "generally includes" the conduct of criminal activity. According to Knox (2000, 1), "A gang is a group, informal or formal in nature, whose members recurrently commit crimes and where these crimes are known openly to the members, often conferring status or profit upon those members who commit the crime." According to Knox and other outsider gang experts, violence and/or criminality distinguishes a gang from a group. As insiders and from the thug criminological perspective, we reject this self-serving perspective.

These "outsider" gang researchers feed into the widely held public perception in the United States that gangs are a serious threat to society. Society focuses on street crime as opposed to white collar crime, despite the extraordinary social costs of the latter. Gangs represent people's worst fears about crime. The perception of street crime is that it is violent, even though the vast majority of crimes are property crimes. By including and even focusing on the violent aspects of gangs, the media capture the public interest. Including violence in the definition of gangs secures buy-in from academia, whose funding for research links them financially to definitions that support their research (Wood and Alleyne

2010). Outsider experts' focus on research that uses official statistics depends on the definition of gangs and gang-related incidents to bolster their agendas for more funding. This varies among police jurisdictions and the individual researchers, "outsider experts," who place gang status on a person or event (Curry and Spergel 1988).

The unidirectional, crime-centred definition of gangs fostered by the criminal justice system and mainstream academia does not help with considering how other factors contribute to why youth join gangs and participate in criminal behaviours. Many definitions and/or characterizations of gangs involve illegality, thus making law enforcement as the primary government agency tasked with controlling or suppressing them. Academic literature supports the "war on gangs," which in turn reinforces the image of gangs as a major crime and/or societal problem (Brown 2012, 2018; Miller 1975; Winfree et al. 1992).

Gang definitions have changed in part as a result of the specialization and professionalization of social science and criminology. Miller (1980) argues that police broaden or narrow the definition of gangs to meet their own needs and interests. Dichiara and Chabot (2003, 78) noted that "the crime-oriented view of gangs may be useful for getting federal funding for research but tends to omit from analysis other important aspects of the gangs – namely, their roots in a community that is wounded in one of several ways" and excludes the positive activities of some gangs. As an example, they describe the positive activities of Los Solidos, one of the largest gangs in Hartford, Connecticut. This research finding would not have been possible had they not taken an ethnographic approach that involved close interaction with gang members over several years, and active involvement helping the gang with political activities in the 1990s. Los Solidos considered itself a political organization, admittedly one that would use criminal means to achieve its goals. To outsiders, they were seen as a gang. Dichiara and Chabot (2003, 79) said, "The blanket indictment of gangs as criminal organizations is both intellectually dishonest and sociologically baseless. One cannot generalize about all gangs." Yet, generalizing about gangs had become commonplace because outsiders have dominated the discourse. This chapter attempts to change that.

> In addition to becoming criminalized, gang research has increasingly become racialized. During the 1980s and 1990s, the explosion of violence in major urban areas such as Los Angeles, Chicago, and New York was associated with gangs, as was the crack epidemic in minority communities. According to Valdez (2003, 12), "Most of these activities have been associated with African American, Latino and Asian youth gangs in large metropolitan areas in the United States." In the mid-1980s, California's Governor Wilson formed a task force comprising law enforcement personnel to study the gang problem. White gangs were mentioned in the task force's report, but the focus was on Chicano, African American, and Asian

gangs, and the gang problem in California was defined as a "youth of color" problem (López 2002). The state legislature's response to the "state of crisis" was to pass the Street Terrorist Enforcement and Prevention (STEP) Act in 1988, in Penal Code section 186.22 (California Penal Code 186.22, 1988). With Penal Code 186.22, California was one of the first states to codify the definition of gangs as "any organization, association or group of three or more persons, whether formal or informal, having as one of its primary activities the commission of criminal acts, having a common name or common identifying sign or symbol, and whose members individually or collectively engage in a pattern of criminal gang activity."

The STEP Act tried to help with the investigation and conviction of gang-related crimes. Under the STEP Act, more jail time could be added to a person's sentence for crimes committed for or in association with a gang. The law also extends to gang members not directly involved in the crimes, like Racketeering Influenced Corrupt Organizations laws. The outcome of the STEP Act was to label youth of colour as gang members while protecting white youth from becoming stigmatized as gang members (Lopez 2002; Hofwegen and Lynn 2008). It largely resulted in the incarceration of people of colour (Green and Pranis 2007; Lopez 2002), as the gang has come to symbolize the violence that occurs in Black and Brown communities. The STEP Act's definition of gang violence as the province of the ethnic gang has served as a model for other anti-gang legislation across the country. Forty-nine states and the District of Columbia have since enacted similar laws (Lopez 2002).

Some researchers have called out the problem of self-interest in gang definitions in gang research. As Brotherton notes, the people who study gangs "display widely disparate motivating interests and theoretical assumptions, which are at least in part, ideological in nature" (Brotherton 2008, vii). Their definitions serve their self-interests. Thug criminology provides an antidote to the serious limitations and narrow focus of gang research by widening our perspective on how we think about and define gangs.

How Do We Change the Language of Gangs?

Traditional definitions of gangs ignore the social environment that drives youth towards gang involvement. Some research in the late 1980s focused on new models of behaviour, questioning the extent to which youth make a rational choice to join a gang rather than being driven to join by the social and economic conditions in their lives. "Insider" research by those who grew up in, taught, or organized in gang neighbourhoods, and/or developed research relationships with former gang members (Moore et al. 1978; Hagedorn and Macon,1988; Vigil 1988; Fagan 1989; Brown, Vigil, and Taylor 2012) found that many views of the media and officials were distorted (Horowitz 1990). For example, gangs in suburban and rural areas were not extensions of big-city gangs as police and the news reported (Hagedorn and Macon 1988). Also, gang members are not the most common victims or perpetrators of homicides in all inner-city neighbourhoods (Curry and Spergel 1988; Spergel 1984).

Brotherton and Barrios (2004) point out the limitations of criminological and criminal-justice assessments of gangs. They argue that gangs and their members are "not simply the result of discrete processes of social adaptation or, worse still, of social and individual pathologies. Instead, they reflect a contradictory, misunderstood, and often ignored outcomes of sociohistorical agency" (xv–xvi). With outsiders in control of defining gangs and theories of delinquency, the objective research largely supported by the government has failed to provide a comprehensive understanding of the roles gangs play in their communities. There has been little research on the effects of the criminalization of gangs and its impact on poor urban communities of colour (Brotherton and Barrios 2004).

As a departure from the typical mainstream perspective, Vigil (1990) describes gang formation using the concept of "multiple marginality." Multiple marginality refers to macro-historical forces (racism, social and cultural oppression, and fragmented institutions) and macro-structural forces (immigration and migration, enclave settlement, and migrant poor barrio/ghetto) that prohibit youth from developing mainstream values and socialization. This results in youth holding values different from their parents', leading to a breakdown in the family. Youth are "street socialized" as they grow up in the hood, and eventually participate in gangs.

As a result of the intergenerational nature of gang involvement within families and communities, "most gang scholars agree that the urban youth street gang is the quintessential example of social reproduction at work" (Brotherton 2008, 55). Researchers also need to consider how gangs provide an avenue of individual and group resistance to hegemonic power. The open-ended views of earlier researchers such as Thrasher have been pushed aside to focus on the criminal behaviour of gangs. While the pathological view may apply to some gangs, it does not apply to them all.

Brotherton (2008) asks how gang research went from Thrasher's play group to the cause and agent of almost every urban social problem. The closest Thrasher comes to delinquency is his discussion of how play groups are unified through conflict. Forty years after Thrasher, Klein's definition of gangs is now probably the most widely used in gang research. The three elements in Klein's definition are (1) perceived as a gang by others in the neighbourhood; (2) recognize themselves as a gang; and (3) have been involved in enough delinquent acts to elicit a negative response from the neighbourhood and/or law enforcement. The concept of resistance is not new to gang research. Cohen (1955) described lower-class youth rejecting the middle-class requirements of school. Matza (1967) describes youth resisting the hypocrisy they hear from their teachers, parents, and law enforcement and trying to navigate their own way. Cloward and Ohlin (1960) describe youth resistance at their blocked opportunities to achieve the American Dream. Resistance is further grounded in the research of Moore et al. (1978), Quicker (1983), Campbell (1984), and Vigil (1988).

The nature of gangs in the United States is changing as gangs become global and transnational in a post-industrial world and with the merger of street gangs and prison gangs (Brotherton 2004). These groups are becoming "more open, innovative, purposive and layered" (65), creating fear involving "global cooperation among coercive social control networks and the ideologies of social exclusion, repression and cleansing" (66). Brotherton (2004) argues that the term "street organization" may be a better term for some groups. As examples of the globalization and legitimization of some gangs, Brotherton notes that the Latin Kings/Queens and the Netas gangs he studied in New York, with the help of local sociologists and anthropologists, became recognized as "cultural associations" in Barcelona and Genova, Spain.

While a key element in the transition from Thrasher's "play group" into a gang is contact with other groups of youth or adults that express opposition or disapproval of the group (Thrasher [1927] 1963), the concept of resistance is missing from most observations of gangs (Brotherton 2008). Hollander and Einwohner (2004) reviewed resistance literature and found that "its core conceptual elements were action, opposition, intent (by social actors) and recognition (by an audience)." They noted a lack in a unified definition of resistance, despite the increasingly popular use of this term (Brotherton 2008).

Bourgois (2003), a proponent of the social reproduction paradigm, conducted an ethnographic study of street-level drug dealers in East Harlem, gaining the trust and friendship of his subjects. When he returned to discover what happened to the gang members he had studied a decade earlier, he was surprised to find many had adapted to the socioeconomic opportunities of the mainstream by transitioning to legal occupations (Bourgois 2003). According to the complex process of "maturing out" of the gang, these gang members made a conscious decision to reject the gang life and/or to respond positively to new opportunities.

Traditional gang research ignores the roles of gang to absorb, mediate, produce, and reflect culture and struggle for representation (Brotherton, 2008). Critical gang scholars such as Bergin (2011) point out that most gang definitions have less to do with understanding the root causes of gang involvement and violence and more with justifying increased law enforcement budgets to deal with the problem. He argued that as these outsider experts became concerned with the "broad and increasingly criminalized definitions of gangs … the potential for these definitions to discriminate against disempowered poor and minority youth became a major fear in some circles" (121).

Thug criminology tries to counter traditional "outsider" theories on gangs with insights provided by insider perspectives, and to reclaim use of the terms "thug" and "gang" by redefining them. Thug criminology seeks to recognize the unique contributions that can be made by insider experts by expanding gang research beyond the current focus on gang crime and violence and to show the value of these contributions to mainstream researchers. Insider experts are best placed to conduct research on certain gang topics, such as understanding how to meet the needs of gang members trying to get out of gang life and in documenting the positive attributes of gang involvement. Now more than ever, considering what is happening in the United States, and around the world as it relates to defunding law enforcement, the heightened focus on police brutality, and the threat of law enforcement to communities of colour, this is the time for a thug criminological perspective/insider gang researchers to make our voices heard. This chapter attempts to achieve that.

REFERENCES

Bergin, T. 2011. "Style, Class, and Contradiction: Cultural Politics in *This Is England.*" *International Journal of Media and Cultural Politics* 7 (2): 241–8. https://doi.org/10.1386/macp.7.2.241_3.

Bloch, H.A., and A. Niederhoffer. 1958. *The Gang: A Study in Adolescent Behavior*. New York: Philosophical Library.

Bourgois, P. 2003. *In Search of Respect: Selling Crack in El Barrio*. Cambridge: Cambridge University Press.

Brotherton, D.C. 2004. "What Happened to the Pathological Gang? Notes from a Case Study of the Latin Kings and Queens in New York." In *Cultural Criminology Unleashed*, edited by J. Ferrel et al., 263–74. Oxfordshire, UK: Routledge-Cavendish.

– 2008. "Beyond Social Reproduction: Bringing Resistance Back in Gang Theory." *Theoretical Criminology* 12 (1): 55–77. https://doi.org/10.1177/1362480607085794.

Brotherton, D.C., and L. Barrios. 2004. *The Almighty Latin King and Queen Nation: Street Politics and the Transformation of a New York City Gang*. New York: Columbia University Press.

Brown, G.C. 2012. "Gangs and the California Criminal Justice System." In *California's Criminal Justice System*, edited by C.L. Gardiner and S.L. Mallicoat, 223–46. Durham, NC: Carolina Academic.

– 2018. "Gangs and the California Criminal Justice System." In *California's Criminal Justice System*, edited by C.L. Gardiner and G. Spiropoulos, 277–302. 3rd ed. Durham, NC: Carolina Academic.

Brown, G.C., J.D. Vigil, and E.R. Taylor. 2012. "The Ghettoization of Blacks in Los Angeles: The Emergence of Street Gangs. "*Journal of African American Studies* 16 (2): 209–25. https://doi.org/10.1007/s12111-012-9212-7.

Bursik, R.J., and H.G. Grasmick. 2006. "Defining and Researching Gangs." In *The Modern Gang Reader*, edited by A.E. Egley, C.L. Maxson, J. Miller, and M.W. Klein, 2–13. New York: Oxford University Press.

California Penal Code 186.21, Street Terrorism Enforcement Prevention Act, 1988.

Campbell, A. 1984. "The Girls in the Gang." *New Society* 69 (1135): 308–11.

Cloward, R.A., and L. Ohlin. 1960. *Delinquency and Opportunity*. New York: Free Press.

Cohen, A.K. 1955. *Delinquent Boys: The Culture of the Gang*. New York: Free Press.

Curry, G.D., and I.A. Spergel. 1988. "Gang Homicide, Delinquency, and Community." *Criminology* 26 (3): 381–406. https://doi.org/10.1111/j.1745-9125.1988.tb00847.x.

Dichiara, A., and R. Chabot. 2003. "Gangs and the Contemporary Urban Struggle: An Unappreciated Aspect of Gangs." In *Gangs and Society: Alternative Perspectives*, edited by L. Kontos, D.C. Brotherton, and L. Barrios, 77–94. New York: Columbia University Press.

Esbensen, F.A., B.T. Brick, C. Melde, K. Tusinski, and T.J. Taylor. 2008. "The Role of Race and Ethnicity in Gang Membership." In *Street Gangs, Migration and Ethnicity*, edited by F. van Gemert, D. Peterson, and I.-L. Lien, 117–39. Oxfordshire, UK: Taylor & Francis.

Fagan, J. 1989. "The Social Organization of Drug Use and Drug Dealing among Urban Gangs." *Criminology* 27 (4): 633–70. https://doi.org/10.1111/j.1745-9125.1989.tb01049.x.

Green, J., and K. Pranis. 2007. "Gang Wars: The Failure of Enforcement Tactics and the Need for Effective Public Safety Strategies." Justice Policy Institute. http://www.justicepolicy.org/uploads/justicepolicy/documents/07-07_rep_gangwars_gc-ps-ac-jj.pdf.

Hagedorn, J.M., and P. Macon. 1988. *People and Folks: Gangs, Crime and the Underclass in a Rustbelt City*. Chicago: Lake View.

Hofwegen, V., and S. Lynn. 2008. "Unjust and Ineffective: A Critical Look at California's Step Act." *Southern California Interdisciplinary Law Journal* 18 (3): 679–701. https://gould.usc.edu/why/students/orgs/ilj/assets/docs/18-3%20Van%20Hofwegen.pdf.

Hollander, J.A., and R.L. Einwohner. 2004. "Conceptualizing Resistance." *Sociological Forum* 19: 533–54.

Horowitz, R. 1990. "Sociological Perspectives on Gangs: Conflicting Definitions and Concepts." In *Gangs in America*, edited by C.R. Huff, 116–28. Newbury Park, CA: Sage Publications.

Klein, M.W. 1971. *Street Gangs and Street Workers*. Englewood Cliffs, NJ: Prentice-Hall.

Klein, M.W., and C.L. Maxson. 1989. "Street Gang Violence." In *Violent Crime, Violent Criminals*, edited by N.A. Weiner and M.E. Wolfgang, 198–234. Newbury Park, CA: Sage.

Knox, G.W. 2000. *Introduction to Gangs*. Peotone, IL: New Chicago.

López, J.M. 2002. *Gangs: Casualties in an Undeclared War*. Dubuque, IA: Kendall/Hunt.

Matza, D. 1967. *Delinquency and Drift*. Piscataway, NJ: Transaction Publishers.

McCarthy, B. 1996. "The Attitudes and Actions of Others: Tutelage and Sutherland's Theory of Differential Association." *British Journal of Criminology* 36 (1): 135–47. https://doi.org/10.1093/oxfordjournals.bjc.a014062.

Merton, R.K. 1938. "Social Structure and Anomie." *American Sociological Review* 3 (5): 672–82. https://doi.org/10.2307/2084686.

Miller, W.B. 1975. *Violence by Youth Gangs and Youth Groups as a Crime Problem in Major American Cities*. Department of Justice, Law Enforcement Assistance Administration, Office of Juvenile Justice and Delinquency Prevention, National Institute for Juvenile Justice and Delinquency Prevention.

– 1980. "Gangs, Groups, and Serious Youth Crime." In *Critical Issues in Juvenile Delinquency*, edited by D. Shichor and D.H. Kelly, 115–38. Lexington, MA: Lexington Books.

Moore, J.W., R. Garcia, J. W. Moore, and C. Garcia. 1978. *Homeboys: Gangs, Drugs, and Prison in the Barrios of Los Angeles*. Philadelphia: Temple University Press.

Quicker, J.C. 1983. *Homegirls: Characterizing Chicana Gangs*. Madison, CT: International Universities Press.

Shaw, C.R. 1929. "II Delinquency and the Social Situation." *Religious Education* 24 (5): 409–17.

Shaw, C.R., and H.D. McKay. 1931. *Social Factors in Juvenile Delinquency; A Study of the Community, the Family, and the Gang in Relation to Delinquent Behavior for the National Commission of Law Observance and Enforcement*. Washington, DC: US Government Printing Office.

Spergel, I.A. 1984. "Violent Gangs in Chicago: In Search of Social Policy." *Social Service Review* 58 (2): 199–226. https://doi.org/10.1086/644188.

Valdez, A. 2003. "Toward a Typology of Contemporary Mexican American Youth Gangs." In *Gangs and Society: Alternative Perspectives*, edited by L. Kontos, D. Brotherton, and L. Barrios, 12–40. New York: Columbia University Press. https://doi.org/10.7312/kont12140.

Vigil, J.D. 1988. *Barrio Gangs: Street Life and Identity in Southern California*. Austin: University of Texas Press.

– 1990. "Cholos and Gangs: Culture Change and Street Youth in Los Angeles." In *Gangs in America*, edited by C.R. Huff, 116–28. Newbury Park, CA: Sage Publications.

Winfree Jr, L.T., K. Fuller, T. Vigil, and G.L. Mays. 1992. "The Definition and Measurement of 'Gang Status': Policy Implications for Juvenile Justice." *Juvenile and Family Court Journal* 43 (1): 29–37. https://doi.org/10.1111/j.1755-6988.1992.tb00717.x.

Wood, J., and E. Alleyne. 2010. "Street Gang Theory and Research: Where Are We Now and Where Do We Go from Here?" *Aggression and Violent Behavior* 15: 100–11. https://doi.org/10.1016/j.avb.2009.08.005.

Yablonsky, L. 1962. *The Violent Gang*. New York: Macmillan.

6 A Black Scholar's Intellectual Journey and Subsequent Perspective on the White Colonial "Gang" Project

IAN JOSEPH

Towards the start of my doctoral research, while looking back over earlier policy notes and organizing the data I would include, I came across a journal I had kept since my teens. In it was an entry saying how the choice to do doctoral research had come full circle, reflecting a change in attitude to the academic research I had been openly critical of for many years. The ensuing months of going through drafts of documents, personal notes, and diary entries I had written, many of which had not been looked at for several years, as I once confided to my PhD supervisor, became much more than academic research. It was to be part of a painful catharsis through which I finally reconciled career, professional and personal dilemmas about racial disadvantage, and social exclusion. Without it, I doubt I would ever have had the time or energy to take a detached overview of the emotional conflict that came to a head over a thirteen-year period of my life, and that helped me connect the experience of growing up in a deprived inner-city area with personal conflicts that grew out of my later policy research.

The journey started with my family as the first non-white residents of an ordinary East London street coming to live in an ordinary terraced house in a normal working-class neighbourhood in the United Kingdom. Settlement in an area dominated by deep-seated cultural tradition and long-established kinship networks but largely typical of narratives developed out of the experience of Black workers as the "Windrush Generation" came from the Caribbean following an official invitation to help rebuild the economy of the "mother country" after the Second World War.

Born in the second generation of Black immigrants, I was simply too young to have a clear recollection of the major difficulties my parents and families like ours faced when trying to find work and somewhere to live. I mostly did not have to tolerate the stares of those who had not seen a Black person up close or any other intended or unintended racism: my generation grew up in a multiracial Britain and faced very different manifestations of individual, institutional, and systemic racial discrimination.

As a family, we had lived in several shared tenancies, and my memory is of large houses that smelled of damp and fumes from paraffin heaters. The excitement of arriving and exploring each room in our new home – a small three-bedroom terraced house – with my siblings, is still palpable. On that first evening we all had fish, chips, and even a pickled gherkin – a rare treat. Soon after, reality set in and my family quickly learned how our skin colour made sure we had not arrived at the promised land. While still in primary school I can still vividly recall the reaction of the class to a new pupil with a non-white face and non-English name. Other incidents involved physical violence. However, it however until my mother emerged deranged with fever from her sickbed to protect my sister from the racial slurs of a neighbour's child while their mother looked on, that open hostility towards our family stopped.

The part of London I grew up in provided every opportunity to engage in the stereotypical lifestyles foisted onto those who lived in the less than salubrious inner city. However, the milieu of working-class disadvantage, poor inner city conditions, and multiculturalism spurred a defiance in me and a group of friends (many of whom I am still in regular contact with after nearly fifty years) not to conform to the stereotypes conferred on us. What now are called "risk factors" drove this group of friends to exceed expectations and to achieve success in a way of repaying those who invested in and guided us during our childhood.

Social and economic change during the 1970s was the context to my formative teenage years. Huge economic restructuring accompanied technological change in a burgeoning globalized political economy, which imposed new demands on industrial relations. Heightened tensions between government, trade unions, and industry took place against the backdrop of declining economic prosperity. Mass Black immigration greatly helped rebuild the British economy but brought with it massive cultural change in many inner-city areas. Deadly IRA activity provided a climate for widespread racial discrimination and the rise of racialist violence from extremist groups like the National Front. The deepening social marginalization of Black communities gave rise to new forms of cultural awareness from which the "rasta" came as a symbol of disenfranchisement and a social focus for concerns about problematic second generation Black urban male youth.

The mix of changing cultural and socio-economic conditions and politics debate during my upbringing provoked personal questions about self-identity and belonging, but showed how collective action could help produce positive social change. The uncertainties of these adolescent years helped shape a lifelong search to understand the social processes responsible for my experiences of discrimination, racial inequality, and social exclusion. During these teenage years my search for answers to life's big questions was found not only in community activism but also religion: there was no contradiction between those of social transformation and spiritual salvation. So, in contrast to the normative social and personal development of many of my friends and family, and perhaps as a result of it, parts of my adolescent years were spent in church.

It was at this age I learned of individuals at school some of my brothers' friends "getting into trouble" and their involvement with "dodgy stuff." A post-pubescent world seemed to arrive overnight. I was suddenly aware of how popular and powerful wayward behaviour made individuals, a few local families and groups of young people that I knew. Some went to my school but others were at other local schools or, like the "snipers" (a group that as a result of their violence and geographic identity would be thought of today as a "gang"), lived in a particular part of East London. Despite popular images of the dangers of East London, to those who lived there it was common knowledge who and what areas you should stay clear of – particularly if you were a "blacky."

In the years after school, while some of my childhood friends went to university or on to worthwhile careers, others took advantage of opportunities with more immediate rewards – some of which resulted in criminal justice consequences. Much of the life I had growing up with, and many of those I shared it with, were part of a world that at an early age I determined to have no part of. However, these formative years became a key part of my later professional research, with much of it being carried out within a five-mile radius of my secondary school. I was an average pupil at school with unremarkable grades, but I passed my A-level exams. To the delight of my parents, this presented me with options for apprenticeships, trainee management positions, and a career in the armed forces – all of which would have been commendable for someone from my background, but it somehow felt as though it wasn't enough. Encouraged by a teacher at school, I was helped in applying for a university place and became the first in my family to be accepted for a degree course. I stayed closer to home and accepted a place in a Church of England ex-teacher-training college.

Although my college was merely in another part of London, the area and student life more generally were alien to anything I had known back home. I made friends with others I would have had nothing in common with and would have been intimidated by the privilege of their background; instead, some became life-long friends. Despite my being one of only a handful of working-class, non-white students, the friendly Christian ethos of the institution, fellow students, and lecturers did much to moderate the radicalism and activism of my earlier teenage years.

The importance I gave to social action was important in my decision to teach as a career, and teacher training was followed by few years as a secondary school teacher for what was then the Inner London Education Authority. Although it was highly rewarding, I quickly realized that education success depended on wider social pressures. This sparked a compulsion to engage with a broader range of issues and a change of career that soon found me working for a community organization, providing supplementary learning-support for African and Caribbean pupils in a borough close to where I lived. Along with a small team of full- and part-time staff and volunteers, the community project assisted parents, carers, and schools to better support pupils' learning and cultural needs. From small offices on a high street, the organization provided innovative and often tailor-made assistance to improve the academic attainment of those who were often "officially" assessed as having social, emotional, or psychological needs.

Part of the job was to go to formal meetings with council officers and elected councillors to represent community views on education policy and service needs of the Black community. However, part of this formal contact also often involved informal consultation, which introduced me to the world of community politics. The experience gave me greater understanding of local administration and policy procedures that proved helpful in a new job and move to a permanent local government post, managing a research team in the council's race relations unit in a borough I settled in for over twenty years. I was responsible for staff with either an Asian or Afro-Caribbean research focus to assess need, identify service gaps, and make recommendation to the council for improving service for local Black and minority ethnic residents. In support of statutory duties under race relations legislation, I was also responsible for formal consultation on the service department's policy developments carried out through a regular cycle of committee meetings. The team also worked closely with community organizations in the area to provide local activities and services through and oversee the allocation and tracking of annual grant-aiding.

Local government research was carried out in the 1980s during unparalleled advances in local government strategic policy and service developments. It provided opportunity for innovations that gave me great professional satisfaction and went a long way to addressing my questions about the role of policy research and social exclusion. The experience of working closely with members of Parliament, local councillors, community representatives, and council officers shaped my subsequent thinking I would return to in following years.

Although some issues investigated had national implications (e.g., service needs of refugees and asylum seekers) or international consequences (such changes to European trading arrangements with the Caribbean region), the research was most restricted to policy and practice for a local authority. Increasingly aware of broader policy and political issues, but also theoretical and methods debate connected to my work, I opened questions on the relevance and effectiveness of the policy research I carried out. As a way to address these growing questions and advance my professional development, I completed a master's degree in social research methods, followed soon after by three years of incomplete doctorate research. Both were equally enjoyable and rewarding, helping to develop critical theoretical analysis and broadening my understanding of research methods.

By this time, I was making steady progress up the career ladder. Better able to apply my knowledge and experience to the requirements of evaluation, intelligence gathering, policy analysis, and customer feedback, my work increasingly supported a broad array of strategic and corporate activity. This brought me into contact with an even wider range of stakeholders and decision makers and afforded me a more complex appreciation of competing governance and resource demands. However, I continued to live in a "deprived inner-city area," so I couldn't lose sight of the practical effects of policy/practice in tackling social exclusion from a local perspective. Although keeping up to date was part of my job, as so much related to my own interests, following research and policy debates also gave me a way to make better sense of growing tension between private and professional experience.

Questions about discrimination and social exclusion that had started in my teenage years now fed a widening gulf between what I knew from my professional/academic research and observation of everyday situations. I increasingly came to find the insights from policy research highly problematic. Much of it was conducted by "experts" who were "parachuted in" and expected to complete studies within a few months, allowing them little more than a snapshot of a constantly changing social reality. Further, a demand for "objective statistics" helped to distance many studies from the everyday circumstances in which problems took place and as a result was failing to capture the needs I routinely encountered. A consequence of inadequately accounting for the experiences of those living with the problem, and many findings and policy recommendations for the studies I carried out, were seen in some measure as detached from the people I knew and area I lived in.

Some research conducted by universities and private consultants helped confirm my creeping disillusion with more than a decade of policy research and evaluation. Changes to local government management and new duties to show efficiency, effectiveness, and value for money increased demand for studies that supported this policy objective. It culminated in the difficult decision to not complete my doctoral studies, nor pursue an academic teaching/research career, and to focus on furthering my policy research. By now my work more directly supported corporate decisions and strategic policy, particularly in best value, regeneration, and service planning. This meant that much of my daily activity was directed towards more mainstream concerns and even wider financial, service development, and political considerations. Even at this level, my work still could not address questions that occupied me on the purpose of policy research or support service developments addressing social inequality. Deepening frustration led to a career change in a direction that provided greater independence and the autonomy to develop the types of policy research I saw as important.

Happily, fifteen years of local government research provided me with useful practical knowledge of bureaucratic culture, the public administration of policy and procedure with specific experience of equality and diversity. I had also acquired substantive qualitative and quantitative policy research experience which alongside my post-graduate qualifications opened several opportunities. I made the bold decision to start a commercial research company. This let me bid for contracts and register with agencies that recruited experienced researchers, and through industry contacts I was able to directly pitch for work. All research as an independent consultant was subject to contractual terms, carried out for local authorities, universities, and public sector organizations on policing, street crime, violent youth crime, gangs, and street drugs. This was almost exclusively policy- or problem-orientated, aimed at developing a better understanding of local patterns in crime and more effective community safety interventions.

In each study in this period, I was employed for my specialist knowledge to give advice on race, but in also helping gain access to Black and minority ethnic communities for surveys and interviews. As their focus was on policy issues connected to policing, street crime, and street drugs, they also had implicit concerns about the perceived criminality of urban Black male youth. However, this was never intentionally openly examined. Despite their aims and my expected contribution, more senior decisions meant that, in practice, priority was given to using conventional forms of fieldwork, leaving little opportunity for more adventurous or time-consuming methods. I gradually came to the view these studies were not going far enough or deep enough. Their consequent failure to meaningfully explore mundane everyday experience in the communities I was familiar with and about which I was expected to provide specialist advice, resulted in many of their findings/recommendations inadequately representing particular perspectives on race and crime.

I developed a growing interest in the policy debates surrounding serious violence and services targeting youth crime and "gangs." However, the high-profile double homicide in Birmingham of Latisha Shakespeare and Carleen Ellis in a New Year's party had a profound and lasting effect on me. It sparked new political and public concerns about gun-related serious youth violence that helped to focus the direction of my research interests. On behalf of a community organization I carried out a small-scale study about drug-related violent conflict among African-Caribbean youth in a poor inner-city neighbourhood of an English city. It had an unexpectedly and very personalized impact. In ways not experienced before, I learned the people interviewed as part of the study and the working-class urban area in which it took place were not largely different from the community I had grown up in. The personal life stories and descriptions of events in the local community could have been given by many people I knew from home: my personal and research experience came together.

The study reaffirmed earlier differences between my private and professional experience that gave rise to often contrasting insights on race and crime but also created personal tensions and dilemmas. My increased involvement with crime and policing research and awareness of the issues and conversations often brought me into conflict with members of my family or my circle of friends. But individuals in my wider social network often provided invaluable insight or comments on a study being carried out. I also became circumspect about the potential of violence or criminal activity in social settings in ways that changed my behaviour and attitude. However, findings from this small ethnographic-based qualitative study even reached the media, receiving coverage in national newspapers and magazines but also interviews with the BBC, Sky News, and even Brazilian television! I also was an invited speaker to several conferences but most significantly, a member of a discussion panel at the annual convention for the Youth Justice Board of England and Wales discussing gangs and youth violence. This was to have a major impact on the direction of my future research.

At this time I began to question the ability of conventional approaches and methods to adequately understand race and crime in relation to the gang. Dismayed by public and political acceptance of assumptions, I developed an increasing scepticism about a growing call for particular types of evidence as the basis for developing gang policy. Growing tension between my personal social reality and professional research caused me to question official research and the academic pursuit of detachment and objectivity. What were argued as necessary conditions for a "scientific" approach merely narrowed, distorted, and distanced "gang" research from vital parts of lived experience and local social reality.

First-hand accounts of those with direct everyday contact with violence, drugs, and gangs became increasingly important to my own research. Only local knowledge could provide robust understandings of the causes, outcomes, and people involved. Although many studies asserted their authenticity and credibility, most failed to reflect local realities of youth crime, but more crucially, this had important implications for gang policy/practice in relation to race and urban Black male youth.

Despite the focus of my research, it continued to be dominated by the requirements of a particular approach and understanding of youth violence. I now started to assert the view that this not only failed to provide a detailed insight to the problem but in the areas such where I lived, it produced a disproportionate racialized criminal justice effect and damaging policy/practice consequences; many young people lived daily against a backdrop threat of violence while an adult world fumbled at taking effective preventive action to save lives.

Tensions grew from the inability of my academic knowledge and policy research to help make the change and provoked personal reflection. By now, many of the young people I researched had lost friends to serious violence, and I was now all too familiar with the grief of mothers, grandmothers, aunts, sisters, and close friends/family with first-hand experience. It triggered a dark critical introspection on the quality and relevance of my work, the role I had assumed as a Black researcher, the professional barriers I faced, and my competence. It caused me to turn in on myself, my personal and professional confidence draining away.

However, this crisis helped me make sense of my earlier local authority research and gain a perspective on the more recent race, crime, and gangs research. Accepting the limitations of some investigative methods and approach of official research provided a newfound appreciation of the benefits of qualitative methods for my research interests. This became the catalyst for the approach of my subsequent research that now gave a clear focus to developing community-based participative action research. Moreover, it reignited questions on the real-world problems I saw around me and how they might be tackled through policy research that led to reconsidering doctoral research.

Everyday mundane experience, such as my own or others' in my research from poor urban areas often gave perspectives about race, crime, and the gang that were markedly different from official sources. I was now firmly of the view that official statistics, crime metrics, and academic research drawn from "parachute interviews" (responses to predetermined themes/questions not growing from relationships built over time and based on trust) offered limited insight for helping develop effective gang policy and practice.

My research on race, crime, and the gang and its policy/practice implications brought new questions about conflicts between my professional and private experience. My everyday lived reality, identity politics, and social marginalization could not long be explored through further research but through academic study. More particularly, interest in auto-ethnographic methodology provided a way to explore my personal-professional tension about race and crime from a "bottom up" perspective. This came to support a PhD thesis that reflexively examined selected policy documents using everyday lived experience to analyse policy and practice tackling youth violence perpetrated by "gangs" with a focus on the implications for urban Black male youth.

7 Good Trouble: Creating Spaces for Criminalized Populations in the Ivory Tower

LILY GONZALEZ, JAVIER RODRIGUEZ, AND ROBERT WEIDE

When I was growing up, my mother and father and grandparents would tell me, "Don't get in trouble. This is the way it is." But then I heard Dr. King speak when I was 15. To hear him preach, to be in a discussion with him sitting on the floor, or in a car, or at a meeting in a restaurant or a church, or just walking together... He instilled something within us.

Dr. King and others inspired me to get in what I call good trouble, necessary trouble. And I think we're going to have generations for years to come that will be prepared to get in trouble, good trouble, necessary trouble. And lead us to higher heights. It's a struggle that doesn't last one day, one week, one month, one year. It is the struggle of a lifetime, or maybe many lifetimes. (Representative John Lewis, 2018)

A good friend, colleague, and accomplice of ours, Robert Hill, dean of Student Services at local Glendale Community College, recently brought to our attention a mantra often repeated by the late Congressman and civil rights icon John Lewis, which he calls "good trouble." Whenever Representative Lewis was asked how he felt about getting arrested and punished for his activism during the Civil Rights Movement, he distinguished between "bad trouble" and "good trouble." Bad trouble is when one is punished for doing wrong by others. Good trouble is when one is punished for doing right by others. It is the price to be paid for standing up for oneself in an oppressive environment. This is a useful framework for understanding the price we as criminalized students and faculty pay for daring to demand that we be afforded the respect and dignity in the academy that we deserve. We must thug our way into the ivory tower. No one will hold the door open for us.

More than three decades ago, when we were in our formative years, urban anthropologist James Diego Vigil recognized for the first time the multiple marginalizations that our communities have suffered for generations as native Angelenos (Vigil 1988). Perhaps most notable among the many intersections of our marginalization is that our generation has the unique experience of having been criminalized and incarcerated at a rate never experienced by any population in history. Our collective hyper-criminalization is no accident of history either. Rather, as Steven Spitzer (1975) suggested a generation before, we are the social dynamite, the surplus labour population in the Marxist sense, for whom the current economic and political system offers little material benefit and even less hope for the future. Without a stake in the system we are bound in, we represent an existential threat to that system. We are the thugs whose mere existence is a threat to the systems that marginalize us, and that is why we have been criminalized all our lives.

Whether we identify as formerly incarcerated, system impacted, or simply – as we call one another in common parlance – homies, we must recognize that this facet of our multiple overlapping intersectional identities is a primary source of our continued marginalization that is shared by a huge demographic of our generation. While many of us spent much of our younger lives divided among ourselves according to racial, territorial, and factional allegiances, we are increasingly realizing a revolutionary political consciousness and collective recognition of our shared experiences as the hyper-criminalized generation. No matter what we do, we will always be dismissed as nothing more than thugs by those in positions of authority, and we will always be treated as such.

Recognition of our collective hyper-criminalization has grown exponentially in the past few years, as students and faculty who have been criminalized throughout their lives have banded together, forming new student organizations and starting new programs on college campuses across the nation with which to serve and represent our interests as criminalized scholars within the academy. This upsurge has been met with alternating support and resistance from university administrations and the grant-funding institutions that provide resources for such endeavours. While university administrators have been quick to capitalize on the opportunity to earn diversity points (not to mention grant funding) by providing their patronage for programs and student organizations intended to support criminalized student populations, university administrators have also further marginalized us as members of this unique criminalized population. We are simultaneously exalted and marginalized in the academy because of how we carry ourselves and how we communicate ourselves. We are marginalized in the academy because when we are pressured to conform and assimilate to the cultural, behavioural, and communicative expectations of mainstream academia, we emphatically refuse. We are marginalized in the academy because of who we are.

We, the authors of this chapter, have been efforts at the forefront to establish student organizations and programs to serve and represent the interests of formerly incarcerated/system impacted students on our respective campuses. We write this chapter in collective solidarity to share our experiences to help those who walk in our footsteps to understand the academic politics we must navigate, the personal and professional sacrifices we must make, and to understand that they are not alone and they need not be afraid in the face of administrative authority in academic institutions. Each of us has a role to play and sacrifices to be made in carving out spaces for people like us to not just exist, but to thrive in the intellectually oppressive environment of the neoliberal university (Giroux 2014). We intend this chapter as a guide to those who share with us not only the experience of being criminalized, but also of being further marginalized within the academy because of who we are.

This chapter will begin with a brief discussion of the corporatization of the academy in the neoliberal era to provide a historical and theoretical foundation with which to understand our experiences. This will be followed by sections recounting each of our experiences at our respective universities written in the first person. The chapter will then conclude with analysis of how our experiences illustrate the challenge criminalized student and faculty populations face in the neoliberal university, and how others who share our experiences can do their part to carve out spaces for themselves and those who follow in our footsteps so that we can collectively thrive in the pursuit of our education and scholarship within the academy. We write this chapter alternating between the collective "we" in reference not just to us three co-authors, but in collective solidarity with all those who share the experience of criminalization, and the first person "I" when recounting our individual experiences.

The Neoliberal University

While the University of California (UC) and California State University (CSU) systems were established on the principle that every Californian should have access to tuition-free higher education, that principle has been gradually abandoned, beginning with the administration of Governor Ronald Reagan (1972–80). In the ensuing decades, student fees and tuition, as well as administrative bloat and compensation, have inflated dramatically. From the mid-1970s in-state student tuition fees at UC, for example, increased exponentially from $600 in 1975, to $4,139 in 1995, and $13,900 in 2018.

While public attention is commonly focused on these fiscal ramifications of the neoliberal war on higher education, other facets of the neoliberal project also adversely impact our experiences in the academy. Most significant for us criminalized scholars is the corporatization of the organizational structure of universities, which concentrates authority and decision making in corporate CEO-like administrators on our campuses (Giroux 2014). As authority and decision making have been consolidated in administrative positions that rule university campuses by virtual fiat, we as marginalized populations and criminalized scholars must understand the interests that drive administrative decisions affecting us if we are to have any hope of strategizing in solidarity with one another to contest our exploitation at the hands of neoliberal career administrators.

The first thing we need to come to terms with is that neoliberal administrators are essentially careerists, concerned foremost with advancing their own careers and not with our well-being. We need to understand why these people were chosen for these administrative positions. University administrators on our campuses are chosen by the board of trustees in the CSU system and by the UC regents in the UC system, but who are the regents and the trustees? According to Article IX, Section 9, of the California Constitution, "The University shall be entirely independent of all political or sectarian influences and kept free therefrom in the appointment of its regents and in the administration of its affairs." The UC regents comprise twenty-six members, eighteen of whom are appointed by the governor for twelve-year terms. The regents appoint a single student member, who serves a one-year appointment. There are two faculty members appointed for two-year terms, who do not have voting rights.

Perversely, given the above-cited section of the California Constitution, the regents are overwhelmingly representative of the corporate and political world, chosen for their political connections rather than their demonstrated commitment to representing the interests of marginalized student populations like us. Among the UC regents are corporate CEOs from the entertainment industry, a part owner of professional sports teams, an investment banker, corporate and politically connected attorneys, and former members of the California State Assembly, including one who dropped out of college. The remaining seven regents are ex officio members, serving as regents as a function of their holding political and executive offices including governor, lieutenant governor, assembly Speaker, superintendent of public Instruction, two executives of the UC Alumni Association, and the UC president who herself is the former secretary of homeland security. The CSU Board of Trustees – also appointed by the governor – is little better. However, they include two student members and a single voting faculty member, who is appointed. The CSU Board of Trustees include corporate and politically connected attorneys, an investment banker, presidents and CEOs from the media, entertainment, and real estate industries, and an equally impressive cadre of career politicos, including many of the same ex officio members of the UC regents.

It seems self-evident from their academic qualifications, or lack thereof, that these power brokers govern our public university systems according to the only framework they know. They choose university presidents, provosts, and administrators on the basis of their eagerness and effectiveness in executing the neoliberal agenda they are charged with, just as neoliberalism has penetrated every aspect of contemporary society (Harvey 2005). Senior administrators on our campuses are often former faculty members who earned their way up the chain of command by faithfully executing the neoliberal agenda as expected of them by the UC regents and CSU trustees, who represent the business and political worlds rather than the academic world, much less our own. Administrators do everything possible to aggrandize themselves with often tacky self-promotion to raise their stock and earn administrative positions even higher up the financial and status ladder of university administrative hierarchies. They are evaluated primarily on metrics, first of which is time to graduation, followed by fundraising, since the California State Budget has regressively redistributed resources from educational institutions to carceral institutions in the neoliberal era. They offer their patronage only where it is useful to their own career advancement, and not because they feel sincere affinity for us. They are not members of our communities or participants in our culture, they do not share our formative experiences, they cannot relate to us, and we cannot relate to them. Their mantras are professionalism and ambition, ours are solidarity and critical pedagogy (Giroux 2001, 2011, 2014).

We need to recognize that when they support us, they do so not out of the kindness of their hearts, but in the interest of their careers. They use us to pad their own curriculum vitae with accomplishments they can take credit for during their tenure in the positions of authority they hold. We are little more than diversity points for them, easily exploited and easily discarded should we dare to step out of line. Neoliberalism didn't spend decades criminalizing our generation, only to have a miraculous change of heart. As Marxist criminologists William Chambliss, Steven Spitzer, and Richard Quinney predicted at the onset of the neoliberal counter-revolution (Chambliss 1975; Spitzer 1975; Quinney 1980), in a tight labour market the carceral state loosens its reins under the guise of reform, incorporating the criminalized and excluded back into the workforce as needed. We must recognize that the neoliberal university is a primary vehicle for assimilating criminalized and excluded surplus labour populations like us back into the active labour market. The neoliberal university does this by disciplining both bodies and minds, policing the way we carry ourselves, what we may think, and how and when we may express ourselves. It does this via the simple carrot and stick strategy of social control.

When we are useful to administrators – when we are docile and acquiescent to their authority and ambitions, showing the servility they demand of us – we are rewarded with their patronage. They decide who among us receives a financial pittance out of the grant money they acquire under the pretence of serving our interests, and those who obediently offer themselves to be paraded for diversity points are privileged over those of us who dare to offer critique and will diverge from the cultural, behavioural, and communicative expectations administrators demand of us. Those of us who dare to be anything other than useful pawns for university administrators are punished by being promptly discarded and excluded from the programs we founded and advocated for. That is the logic of the neoliberal project: we are worthy of administrative patronage only if we are useful idiots who dare not step out of line.

Our own experiences on each of our campuses reflect this divergence of interests between us as students and faculty and them as administrators. However, before we share our narratives, we offer a further qualification. For several reasons, we consciously choose not to name the administrators who have manipulated, mistreated, discarded, and excluded us. We are not motivated by a vengeance that seeks to embarrass any administrator(s) individually. We recognize that they are merely performing the role they are charged with fulfilling. If not they, then it would be another who fulfils the same role and treats us the same way. To shame them individually would suggest that the way they treat us is due to their own personal lack of character and integrity. We recognize and appreciate that the way we have been treated by administrators is not due to the idiosyncrasies of individuals; rather it is a function of the neoliberal agenda that seeks to corporatize our universities and co-opt us into the neoliberal project by indoctrinating us into docile labour roles and servile career paths. We recognize that we are discarded and excluded simply because we refuse to abide by those expectations. We are the "good trouble" that Representative Lewis spoke of. These are our stories.

From One Brick Wall to Another

In my first year at California State University, Northridge (CSUN), after having transferred from East Los Angeles Community College, I was arrested and charged with murder and attempted murder as an accessory in my (ex)husband's case to pressure me into testifying against him (I refused) and him into taking a plea deal. While I was not involved in the murder and attempted murder my husband was charged in (he was also found innocent), I was sentenced to four years in prison on an unrelated forgery case I was charged with because I refused to testify against my husband.

When I left prison, I tossed my inmate ID card out the window of my brother's truck on the way home, wanting to forget the traumatic experience of having been incarcerated, to put it behind me and bury it forever. I imagined myself coming home, finding some creatively plausible explanation for the gap in my employment history, getting back to work, and moving on without ever having the discuss or acknowledge that part of my life experience – *La vida sigue*. In attempting to carry out the plan I had imagined for myself post-incarceration, reality hit me in the face like a rock in a sock. Every application I filled out for any job paying more than minimum wage had the felony box and I never got a call back. Eventually after two years of precarious and intermittent employment, I found my way to Homeboy Industries. When I was working at Homeboy Industries washing windows, sweeping floors, and chopping chiles in Homegirl Café, I didn't think I had many other options. Higher education was never a part of my plan or what I even could imagine for myself after my incarceration – my sole focus was day-to-day survival. After learning of my past enrolment at CSUN when I had been arrested, Brittany Morton, the educational services coordinator at Homeboy Industries encouraged me to resume my education.

The first administrative obstacle I was confronted with was that I could not simply re-enrol in classes. After my arrest I had no way of completing the courses I was enrolled in and, being too embarrassed to write my professors to explain my sudden absence, they failed me from the courses I was enrolled in and my matriculation was terminated by the university. To resume my education, I had to completely re-apply for admittance to the university as if I had never been a student in good standing. The experience made the prospect of resuming my education only that much more intimidating. Only with the support and encouragement I had received at Homeboy I found the courage to follow through with the application and was readmitted in the fall semester of 2015 as an undergraduate student in Chicanx studies.

The second administrative obstacle I confronted upon returning to campus was finding a way to pay my student fees. Even though I was making minimum wage at Homegirl Café I was denied financial aid by the university because of my low GPA before being incarcerated, which resulted from having been failed in all the courses I was taking when I was taken into custody – a classic "Catch 22." I appealed the decision and was denied on appeal. In the email thread going back and forth on the future of my academic career, the director of financial aid argued that my narrative wasn't convincing, as if I had fabricated my incarceration, and that I was unlikely to succeed academically, both of which the Provost's Office division of Hispanic Serving Institution & Diversity Initiatives agreed with. Only after mobilizing support from Father Gregory Boyle at Homeboy Industries, and sympathetic faculty and staff on and off campus, including Gabriel Gutierrez, chair of Chicanx Studies at CSUN, the late Jose Louis Vargas, director of the Equal Opportunity Program at CSUN, Doris J. Clark, director of EOP Admissions and Partnership Programs, and Dennis Lopez, professor of ethnic and women's studies at California Polytechnic State University, Pomona, the Provost Office finally relented and agreed to reinstate my eligibility for financial aid. I was honoured to be the first Homegirl from Homeboy Industries to graduate with my bachelor's degree in 2016.

After finally starting classes for the first time in over half a dozen years, I encountered yet another administrative brick wall. When I applied for a clerical position with the Office of Alumni Relations to simplify my daily commute from South Central Los Angeles, I was encouraged to be offered the position despite my felony conviction. My euphoria was short-lived. Senior administration in the Office of Human Resources vetoed my eligibility for the position because

I represented a potential liability to the university. To make matters worse, I was denied child care on campus for my four-year-old son, making it even more difficult to juggle my simultaneous roles of student, bread winner, and mother. All this in my first month back on campus, while trying to reacclimate myself to what had become an unfamiliar and unwelcoming environment – the ivory tower of academia.

In 2015, the Opportunity Institute, a non-profit that supports social mobility and equity through education, offered a grant of up to twelve million dollars for each campus to provide funds to expand the Project Rebound program throughout the California State University (CS) system. Presidents of CSU campuses around the state were asked to send a representative from their campus if they wanted their campus to participate in the program. Unfortunately, the president of CSUN declined. When a group of us formerly incarcerated students on campus asked why CSUN had demurred, we were informed by an administrator that the university "doesn't have the infrastructure to do so at this time." This was a disingenuous response to placate and pacify us, and we interpreted it as such. A more candid administrator informed us informally that senior administration was simply cold to recruiting and supporting formerly incarcerated students on campus. Faced with a brick wall of obstruction from administration, a circumstance that has defined my experience with administrators at CSUN, we established our own ASI student organization to support each other, since university administration had refused to even acknowledge the relevance of our existence on campus. With the support and solidarity of formerly incarcerated student members of the Underground Scholars Initiative and Project Rebound programs around the state, we inaugurated our new student organization Revolutionary Scholars in the spring semester of 2016.

The following academic year, senior administrators apparently realized that formerly incarcerated students were a marketable commodity for the university to be exploited for diversity points, and potentially grant funding. In 2017 I was selected by the president of the university to be awarded the Newman Civic Fellowship for 2018, which brought a modest grant from a non-profit organization based in Boston called Campus Compact and some significant diversity points for the university. My photograph and narrative were exploited on the university website's homepage, and I was featured in a much more generous light than my experiences would belie in a corresponding university press release to announce the fellowship I had been awarded. At least I got a weekend trip to Boston out of it.

In the fall semester of 2018 the new interim provost and the vice president of Student Affairs solicited us the students to write a grant proposal ourselves to expand the Project Rebound program onto campus finally at CSUN. We are composing the proposal. None of us have ever written a grant proposal before. This is a convenient arrangement for administration, because if we succeed, they get the grant money and the diversity points, but if we fail it's on us.

A House Divided

The Underground Scholars Initiative is a student group founded in 2013 by formerly incarcerated students Danny Murrillo and Steven Czifra and their accomplices at the University of California, Berkeley. After successfully demonstrating its capacity to support and advocate for formerly incarcerated students on the campus of UC Berkeley, formerly incarcerated students at the University of California, Los Angeles (UCLA), expanded the organization onto their campus. In 2016, five students at UCLA founded a chapter of the Underground Scholars Initiative on campus to support and advocate for formerly incarcerated students at UCLA.

Jose Ortega, a founding member, died from a heart attack the following year, mere weeks before his graduation with a bachelor's degree in history. After his death, Jose was dropped from all of his classes (which he was passing) in the spring quarter of 2017 and posthumously denied recognition for the degree he had earned. Administrators had decided that Jose did not meet the posthumous degree criterion of 160 units completed, lacking the 16 units he was enrolled in at the time of his death. USI at UCLA students, along with Jose's surviving brother, Daniel Ortega PhD, himself a formerly incarcerated UCLA alumnus, lobbied California State Senator Ben Allen and State Assembly Member Reginald Jones Sawyer, UC Regents Student Representative Paul Monge, and UCLA faculty members Leobardo Estrada, former UCLA academic chair, and Russell Thornton-Current, Faculty Executive Committee representative, for support to have Jose posthumously awarded the bachelor's degree he had earned at the time of his death. After over a year and a half of lobbying and advocating for Jose, UCLA administrators finally caved in and agreed to posthumously award Jose with the bachelor's degree he deserved, providing USI at UCLA students and his family with the closure they had been denied, with the honour and achievement Jose merited.

While USI at UCLA matured, having been forced to advocate Jose's academic accomplishments in its infancy, administrative impediments continue to plague the organization. Most notably, and in stark contrast to USI at UC Berkeley, where the organization was quickly adopted by the Center for Education, Equity and Excellence in 2015, student affairs administration at UCLA denied USI at UCLA a space to flourish in the Bruin Resource Center. Conversely, student affairs administration at UCLA co-opted an initiative introduced by USI students at UCLA called Reforming Education to Diminish Incarceration (aka REDI), which was placed under the administrative umbrella of the Community Programs Office (CPO hereafter) at UCLA. Regrettably, this co-optation was done with the collaboration of a single formerly incarcerated student on campus who saw an opportunity to privilege himself at the expense of other formerly incarcerated students who have chosen USI as the vehicle to pursue our interests at UCLA. Unfortunately, this individual filled the role of poster boy for administrative efforts to co-opt formerly incarcerated student interests, while refusing to acknowledge that we, the formerly incarcerated students at UCLA, have chosen USI as the primary support and advocacy organization for formerly incarcerated students at UCLA. While USI at UC Berkeley has enjoyed administrative and financial support, USI at UCLA has been denied institutional, administrative, and financial support for the organization at the time of this writing.

Unfortunately, student affairs administration at UCLA invested their support in the REDI program, which was founded by only a single formerly incarcerated student on campus in collaboration with senior administrators. This policy has resulted in a mutual enmity between formerly incarcerated students at UCLA between USI and the REDI project, who have been alienated from one another by the lack of administrative support for USI and the manipulative co-optation of the REDI project by the student affairs administration. The CPO exploited the REDI project for its own propaganda in its promotional literature distributed on campus called "Formerly Incarcerated Externship," featuring a photo with the single formerly incarcerated student, and eighteen other students, none of whom are formerly incarcerated, but has discarded the rest of us in refusing to support USI at UCLA.

As a result of the challenges we have faced with the administration, we have must recognize that there is lack of formal institutional support for the USI program that serves and represents formerly incarcerated students at UCLA. Nevertheless we have continued to serve formerly incarcerated students through recruitment, retention, and advocacy at UCLA, using policy and limited funding to conduct our own student development, peer support, and campus programming. USI at UCLA has hosted three graduation ceremonies for formerly incarcerated students honouring over forty students in three years. We successfully advocated for airfare and lodging for USI members to conduct panel discussions at Columbia University Beyond the Bars annual conference since 2016. USI at UCLA founded the first ever Just Culture festival, which included a lowrider car exhibit, live graffiti, cultural vendors, and community performers that centred on radical expression, making it the most successful festival on campus led by a student organization in recent years. In addition, USI on-campus programming includes quarterly film screenings, transfer workshops, panel discussions, an annual wellness retreat, weekly gatherings, and graduate-undergraduate peer mentorship. All this organizing has happened at UCLA while USI continues to use temporary spaces and is pushed around endlessly without a formal space on campus to operate. The way we have been treated by administrators at UCLA is a shame and embarrassment for the university, yet the arrogance of administrators committed to the neoliberal model of higher education doesn't surprise us. Rather it proves that serving marginalized student populations is worth it for administrators only if they can co-opt and divide us, while capitalizing on diversity points and identity politics.

The Castaway

After working as an adjunct instructor while completing my dissertation in Los Angeles, I was hired for a tenure track position at the assistant professor level in sociology at California State University, Los Angeles (Cal State LA), and began in the fall of 2015. Before being hired I had been organizing and advocating to expand the successful Project Rebound program for formerly incarcerated students at San Francisco State University (SFSU) onto our campus. My efforts were a principal point of praise I had received during the hiring process.

During my first academic year as an assistant professor, the Opportunity Institute, a non-profit that supports social mobility and equity through education, offered a grant of up to twelve million dollars for each campus to provide funds to expand the Project Rebound program throughout the CSU system. Presidents of CSU campuses around the state were asked to send a representative if they wanted their campus to participate. The president of Cal State LA sent the director of a new entity on campus he created with the self-explanatory name, the Center for Service, Engagement and the Public Good. Several CSU campuses declined to participate, and even after the size of the grant was decreased considerably after the initial call from up to twelve million to only half a million dollars per campus, Cal State LA was among eight CSU campuses committed to starting a Project Rebound program on campus, but with a catch.

I was told by an administrator that the president of Cal State LA has a mantra: "First, Best and Only," meaning that if Cal State LA isn't the first to do something, the best at it, and/or the only campus doing it, it is not worth doing. Since SFSU started the Project Rebound program over fifty years ago, was well experienced in administering it, and Cal State LA would not be the only CSU to have the program, the president wasn't interested. Thus, Cal State LA proposed an alternative, to start a bachelor's program at our local Lancaster State Prison, building on the work done with inmates there by a faculty member in the Department of English. The Cal State LA BA program at Lancaster State Prison is the first, best, and only BA program in the State of California where inmate students take face-to-face courses with Cal State LA faculty. However, the Opportunity Institute required that to fund the BA program at Lancaster State Prison, Cal State LA also had to simultaneously start a Project Rebound program on campus. The director of the Center for Engagement, Service and the Public Good was appointed the director of Project Rebound at Cal State LA by the president of the university, and I have served as faculty advisor since its establishment on our campus.

In my role as faculty advisor for Project Rebound I agreed to step in as interim program coordinator over the summer of 2018. I tried to go to any engagement related to the project that the director requested of me. One that he asked me to was to visit a new faculty member's service-learning class during the summer semester. The curriculum was to create an art project from one of dozens of mock county jail beds fabricated by a new social justice organization called Justice LA, for a publicity stunt they carried out in downtown Los Angeles. The mock county jail bed was to be installed in the University Library on campus to draw attention to incarceration. I also went to the installation of the mock jail bed at the University Library a few weeks later and made brief comments about Project Rebound at both engagements. Next to the jail bed installation was a computer screen playing a promotional video for Project Rebound that features me and several students. It was obvious from the start that no formerly incarcerated people were consulted in this project, as was laughably apparent: the mock "County Jail bed" had a ladder on the side like a child's bunk bed. Anyone who has ever been to County knows there are no ladders on the bunks in LA County Jail, or in any other jurisdiction I know of, and I've had the honour of gracing the cells of jail facilities from Los Angeles to San Francisco to Miami-Dade to New York City. During both the class visit and the installation, the faculty member who taught the course introduced as the artistic advisor an individual whom I recognized from somewhere, but I could not recall.

I learned who he was only after a local community coalition that organizes against gentrification in Boyle Heights with whom I and my students collaborate, collectively known as Defend Boyle Heights (DBH hereafter), posted a story on their Facebook page that the artistic advisor had been terminated from Self-Help Graphics, print shop and art space with historical ties to the Chicano Movement of the Civil Rights Movement era. He and the DBH coalition had long been adversaries. During his time at Self-Help Graphics, members of the community, including the DBH coalition, regarded him as a divisive figure who had regularly collaborated with and defended the art-washing and gentrification of the Boyle Heights community that the DBH coalition opposes. Concerned that his reputation would reflect poorly on us, I made a hasty comment on the DBH Facebook post in a reflexive attempt to defend my reputation and credibility, and that of my students and Project Rebound by assuring our friends, comrades, and community partners that we would disassociate ourselves from the installation for which he was artistic advisor. The text reads, "I knew this guy was no good, I just had a spider sense about him. He was the 'artistic advisor' for a 'Justice LA' installation in the name of formerly incarcerated populations at Cal State LA Library this summer. We will be mobilizing formerly incarcerated students to demand the faculty who invited him on the project denounce him and issue an apology. We have an obligation to look into this. We're hyper-vigilant about our population being used by people for the wrong reasons, as we should be."

The faculty member and the artistic advisor sent screenshots of my comments to administrators on campus, demanding I be punished. Administrators were not convinced that my comments were an attack on the faculty member because our director of faculty affairs took no disciplinary action against me. Although I was not found guilty of violating campus rules or regulations, the director of project rebound tried to terminate me as faculty advisor for Project Rebound at Cal State LA. I never received a letter of termination and was never informed of rules or regulations I had violated. When I asked what rule or policy I had violated that led to my termination, I was told that I had not been terminated, only that the new program coordinator whom I had introduced for the job had been chosen in my place. None of our formerly incarcerated students, nor any in the wider formerly incarcerated student, faculty, and alumni community in California, including the regional director from SFSU, were consulted or even informed that administrators had removed me. Not one of them thinks that I should resign or be terminated. However, with disregard for formerly incarcerated students and by administrative fiat alone, administrators decided that I would be relieved of my role as faculty advisor and that they alone would make that decision. The director instructed staff to exclude me from Project Rebound wherever possible.

"Wherever possible" is perhaps too generous, because I am woven into the fabric of Project Rebound. I am the primary faculty member with whom formerly incarcerated and gang-involved students bond on our campus. As a person with a long history of criminalization as a result of my participation in gang and graffiti street cultures, I am the faculty member students who share these experiences can relate to the most on our campus. I'm a homie like them, and I carry myself as such. I am also the faculty advisor for the student group auxiliary to Project Rebound at Cal State LA, the Student Homie Union. I personally connect to students and staff at most Project Rebound programs on other CSU campuses and student groups on University of California and Community College campuses throughout the state. I also personally connect to staff at the major non-profit organizations that serve our population in Los Angeles, including Homeboy Industries, the Anti-Recidivism Coalition, and a panoply of grassroots gang intervention and prisoner re-entry programs throughout Los Angeles County.

When our Project Rebound staff and the statewide regional director of Project Rebound met with our director, their attempts to communicate the depth of opposition to any attempt to remove me as faculty advisor were rebuffed. Soon after, I was denied the opportunity to teach a course in the BA program at Lancaster State Prison, for which the chair of my department had nominated me, given my knowledge in the course being offered and that I was not only the most qualified but also the only faculty member willing to take on the course on top of my contracted teaching load. When my chair asked why I was denied the opportunity to teach in the prison, she was informed that senior administrators were not happy with my politics or how I carry and communicate myself, which is unapologetically hood. Rather than accept their attempts to exclude me, we have simply ignored administrators and I have continued in my role as faculty advisor for Project Rebound.

Conclusion: Looking for Trouble

The effect of the neoliberal project in the university is apparent in our experiences. When administrators are reticent to support programs for formerly incarcerated students, it's because they see no advantage to their own careers in offering their patronage. When they realize that grant money and diversity points are to be claimed by having programs for formerly incarcerated students on our campuses, they seize administrative control of our programs, publicize our struggles as if they have helped rather than hindered us at every step of the way, while they soak up the grant money and diversity points, and hang us out to dry. When we step out of line, they discard and exclude us, as if they can erase our very existence. We see this cycle repeatedly in our experiences.

When treated with disregard it is because administrators expect us to fail and don't want our failure to hurt their metrics. When we instead succeed, we are featured in university propaganda as if the university has been supporting rather than hindering formerly incarcerated students, while we have surmounted possible administrative hurdle along the way. When we try to bring successful programs like Project Rebound and Underground Scholars to our campuses, administrators are not inclined to offer their patronage and support, simply because they can't take credit for something already working on another campus. They would much rather have their own program they can take credit for, and when they lend their patronage to such a program, they rule it by fiat with no input from us as formerly incarcerated students and faculty. When we are no longer useful to their optics, they discard and exclude us from the very programs we advocated for, founded, and established on our campuses.

How can we practise a pedagogy of resistance in the face of administrative authority in the neoliberal university? First, we need to maintain solidarity with one another on our individual campuses and between campuses. We cannot allow ourselves to be divided and conquered by administrators praising and privileging those who offer themselves as pawns for administrative ambitions, while discarding and excluding those of us with the dignity and integrity not to sell ourselves out. We must maintain a state of constant vigilance, collectively and individually, that we not be exploited by administrators for their interests and not ours, and where administrative machinations aim to co-opt and exploit us, we must stand fast and refuse to acquiesce. That is not to say we should not take advantage of substantive, particularly financial, support we can squeeze out of administrators. Rather, we should take advantage of every opportunity we can extract from administrators, unless doing so undermines our solidarity.

However, our solidarity cannot be limited to individual praxis. We must practise solidarity across and between our campuses. We advocate the formation of a statewide – or even nationwide – organization to advocate for and support criminalized and formerly incarcerated students, alumni, and faculty, that is not under the authority of campus administrators on our individual campuses. We need an organization to act as a vehicle for our interests under our control. We can then use that organization to apply for the grant money that otherwise ends up under the control of administrators, so we can control the financial resources supposed to be used for us, but all to often have been used by administrators against us to manipulate us against one another instead.

We also need to reject administrative attempts to co-opt and assimilate us according to their cultural, behavioural, and communicative expectations. We need to stop playing *pocho*. When we change our appearance and the way we carry ourselves, when we change the culture that our presentation of self reflects and the way we communicate ourselves, we are implicitly acceding there is something wrong with the way we dress, carry, and communicate ourselves. We are perpetuating the myth that there is something wrong with our cultural identities and our own marginalization. If we and those who follow in our footsteps are to feel social comfort in the halls of the ivory tower, we must demand that we be respected and valued for who we are, as we are. Every time we try to dress up, tone down, and speak in the passive demure voice authority demands of us, we debase ourselves by pandering to the behavioural, cultural, and communicative expectations of administrative patrons. Instead, we need to carve out a space for ourselves and for those who follow in our footsteps, by dressing, acting, walking, and talking as we always have in our own communities, like we do with one another in our own cultural milieu.

Finally, when despite all the machinations of authority arrayed against us, we thrive and succeed because of our own tenacity, perseverance, and solidarity, when we find ourselves in positions as faculty, graduate, and undergraduate students, we must use whatever position we find ourselves in to benefit all. We cannot let ourselves be trapped in careerism, sacrificing the collective interests of all those who like us have experienced a lifetime of criminalization at the altar of our own ambitions. We must use our presence, our praxis, and our very existence in the academy to carve out space for ourselves and those who follow in our footsteps. We must be willing to get in trouble, because the doors of opportunity will not open for us unless we kick them open ourselves, whatever the consequences.

We must recognize that administrators will not accept us for who we are. We cannot thrive and succeed in the academy by pleading for administrative patronage. We must take advantage of whatever resources trickle down to us, but we must keep our critical edge sharp. It is incumbent upon those of us who have made it this far to practise a critical pedagogy of resistance. We must expect that we will be discarded and excluded by administrators for our refusal to be conform to their expectations. It takes courage and tenacity to stand strong in the face of authority, but most of all it takes solidarity. We must support one another. We cannot let ourselves be divided and conquered. We must all make sacrifices individually and collectively to prevent our collective co-optation. We know we will get in trouble when we step out of line, and we embrace it. We are proud to be good trouble.

REFERENCES

Chambliss, W.J. 1975. "Toward a Political Economy of Crime." *Theory & Society* 2: 145–70. https://doi.org/10.1007/BF00212732.

Giroux, H.A. 2001. *Theory and Resistance in Education.* Westport, CT: Bergin & Garvey.

– 2011. *On Critical Pedagogy.* New York: Bloomsbury.

– 2014. *Neoliberalism's War on Higher Education.* Chicago: Haymarket Books.

Harvey, D. 2005. *A Brief History of Neoliberalism.* Oxford: Oxford University Press.

Lewis, J. 2018. "Why Getting in Trouble Is Necessary to Make Change." *Time*, 4 January. http://time.com/5087349/why-getting-into-trouble-is-necessary-to-make-change/.

Quinney, R. 1980. *Class, State, and Crime.* New York: Longman.

Spitzer, S. 1975. "Toward a Marxian Theory of Deviance." *Social Problems* 22 (5): 638–51. https://doi.org/10.2307/799696.

Vigil, J.D. 1988. *Barrio Gangs: Street Life and Identity in Southern California.* Austin: University of Texas Press.

PART THREE

Word on the Street

Iomos Marad

    Living in foul environments
is evident when death polls from gun pulls rise around a resident
No cheese for rent 'cause it was spent on gettin bent off a chemical design to snatch
balance from the mind of nation who created civilization
Frustration of whole generation now we facin
murder theft rape abortion addiction and unwed parents is above average
    proportion
welfare checks cut just for projects reduced from a human to a wanted suspect
trained to handle beef with a hot loaded tech
war among the youth societies in the threat Clockers clock non-stop while the
    government collect narcotics and politricks is part
of Lucifer's tricks
Evil ways last days displays how life pays burdened down with sadness this world
    gone
to madness
Killin one another so we can't progress
Rat infested homes occupied by young mothers
liquor stores flooded with spiritual dead brothers
encounters turn deadly when influence runs heavy
Steps are never steady when we walkin in strife
we can all get lost up in the sands of life

Marcus Singleton

8 Shook Ones: An Insider's Perspective on Trauma, PTSD, and the Re-enactment of Street-Related Violence

ADAM ELLIS, STEPHANIE BÉLANGER, AND LUCA BERARDI

I[1] grew up in a community with a long history of violence. In my neighbourhood the "war" (at least how we viewed it) was started by the state, meted out by its agents of control, and proliferated by the street soldiers on the "block." In the street, you were raised to be a "real one" (willing to do anything for the streets, the "gang," and the community) or a "shook one" (someone who pretended to be down for the streets, but ran when the risks became too real). I would like to think that I kept it "real" or 100. Growing up, we all knew the war was constructed by those in power – the outsiders to the block. We didn't manufacture guns or crack. We didn't create poverty, nor were we the harvesters of racism and hate. However, the perception from outside the block was that we created and propagated the war – and the government would send in their "specialized" agents of control (i.e., gang cops) to police and control our bodies and behaviours. We had our own specialized groups and members who resisted and challenged the "colonizers" who smiled at our demise, and the systems of oppression that penetrated our lives. On one end of the block, we had old-timers – the OGs (original gangsters) and Italian "families" who controlled the street-level soccer and social clubs. On the other end, we had biker clubs (or biker gangs, according to the police), who sought to rise to the power position of the mob. In the middle, where poverty and marginalization were most entrenched, the streets gave birth to what we viewed as families/protection groups, but what the police and dominant society framed as criminal street gangs.[2]

Through family lineage, I already had a lifeline to the streets. I connected to both sides of the underworld. I wasn't the toughest kid on the block, but I held a power position through my family's roots in the community. During my time on the streets, I was exposed to small, protracted conflicts. I was the product of the War on Drugs (the crack era) and the War on Gangs (the state's over-policing and mass incarceration of non-white, lower-income youth). I not only saw the proliferation of crack, but also the heavy hand of the law, and how the War on Drugs destroyed my community. At the community level, I also witnessed the rise of street organizations, who were trying to survive the structures that sought to destroy them. I was there, I felt the pain, and I had a front seat to the suffering. I watched my community become an epicentre for drug use, where street corners became drug markets, and the competition for financial success and social mobility fuelled turf wars that led to bloodshed and loss of life. I had seen more in my childhood than most civilians (i.e., the non-street-involved) see in their lifetime. I grew up fast amidst the realities of street combat – seeing people murdered, experiencing the cold hands of the criminal justice system, witnessing drug addiction, the detrimental effects of the underworld, and the "ops" who sought to dissolve it.

These combined stressors and pressures led me to what law enforcement officials, media pundits, and politicians call the "gang life." But for me, it was not a gang. It was my family. My family protected me, loved me unconditionally, and treated me with respect I gave my life to my brothers and sisters, and out of a sense of "loyalty" (and a need for protection from structural, community, and interpersonal violence). I was willing to put my life in harm's way to protect theirs. I did this to be real, not a "shook one."

Criminology's Point of View

The criminological literature is ripe with theories on criminal behaviour and punishment. The classical school, which emerged from the writing of Cesare Beccaria (1738–1794), Jeremy Bentham (1748–1832), and John Howard (1726–1790), introduced the concepts of free will, utilitarianism, rationality, and deterrence to the emerging field of criminology. These scholars argued that individuals have free will and can calculate the costs and benefits of behaviour – including criminal behaviour. Crime, they argued, could be explained through the "hedonistic calculus" (or the "pleasure principle"), with individuals seeking to maximize pleasure and minimize pain (Lilly, Cullen, and Ball 2015). Nearly two centuries later, these ideas gave rise to rational choice theory, which argues that although criminals carry a host of predispositions (e.g., intelligence, family background, neighbourhood context, and gender, to name a few) and motivations (i.e., entrenched inclinations towards criminality), crime remains a *choice* that is "committed with the intention of benefiting the offender" (Clarke and Cornish 2001, 24).

It was not until the 1920s that scholars began looking beyond the offender and individual pathology, towards social structural factors, for insights into why people engage in crime. This rejection of individualism was championed predominantly by two major traditions: the Chicago School of Sociology and strain theory. The Chicago School argued that the city itself had criminogenic forces that propelled people towards crime, so that "growing up in the city, particularly in the slums, made a difference in people's lives" (Lilly, Cullen, and

Ball 2015, 37). Burgess's concentric zone theory, Shaw and McKay's theory of juvenile delinquency, Sutherland's theory of differential association, and others provided important counter-narratives to pathological explanations of criminal behaviour, demonstrating that criminality "could be understood only by considering the social context in which [people] lived – a context that itself was a product of major societal transformations wrought by rapid urbanization, unbridled industrialization, and massive population shifts" (43).

The strain theories introduced by Merton (1938) and Agnew (1992) equally contributed to this shift from pathological theories of crime – locating the seeds of criminality within the social and structural fabric of American society. Merton, for example, did not directly reject the ideas emerging from the Chicago School, but proposed a different set of social processes leading to crime: the disjunction between culturally prescribed goals (economic success and the "American Dream") and access to the legitimate means of attaining them (e.g., family connections, higher education, employment, etc.). This disconnect "places large segments of the American population in the strain-engendering position of desiring a goal that they cannot reach through conventional means" (Lilly, Cullen, and Ball 2015, 68), which ultimately "produces intense pressure for deviation" (Merton 1968, 199). Merton presented four "modes of adaptation" that individuals rely upon to deal with this strain: conformity, innovation, ritualism, and retreatism. He argued that most criminal behaviour falls into the category of "innovation," with this group pursuing culturally prescribed goals, but, in response to blocked access to legitimate opportunities, ultimately turn to *illegitimate* (i.e., criminal) means to achieve them.

Building on the work of Merton, Agnew's (1992) general strain theory argues that people experience more than one source of criminogenic strain. In addition to the strain caused by failing to achieve culturally valued goals, individuals can also experience strain through removal of positively valued stimuli (by losing something they valued) and the presentation of negative stimuli (by being treated poorly by others). To cope, some people might engage in drug use, turn to crime to replace what was taken away (e.g., stealing a cellphone to compensate for one taken away by a parent), and/or engage in violence in response to the negative stimuli (e.g., assaulting an abusive family member) or to get revenge on those causing the strain (e.g., shooting at a rival gang or gang member). Agnew suggested that, "in general, the higher the dose of strain that a person experiences, the greater the likelihood of the person becoming engaged in crime or in some form of deviance" (Lilly, Cullen, and Ball 2015, 79).

While these approaches offer insights into the criminal behaviour of marginalized youth, they remain largely silent on the state's role in propagating structural violence – and how macro-level forces, such as poverty, systemic racism, marginalization, and social exclusion affect youth on a micro, social-psychological level. This chapter aims to redress these issues by integrating structural understandings of crime and criminal behaviour (including knowledge of "gangs") with the psychological literature on trauma. We argue that membership in a gang, street organization, or youth subculture results from the interplay between overlapping factors at the macro, meso, and micro level, and contend that trauma experienced within and across these levels may propel young people towards street organizations – which can serve as escape and protection from, and coping mechanism for, past trauma. We do not deploy the language of trauma as a neocolonial model to pathologize or criminalize minority youth; rather, we draw on the nosology of trauma to humanize their experiences – showing how structural violence can lead to community and individual trauma conducive to membership in a street organization.

An Alternative Perspective: Drawing from the Literature on Post-Traumatic Stress Disorder

Trauma has always been represented in the body of heroic literature. There are myriad examples of ancient combatants experiencing war-related trauma, such as Gilgamesh's terrible dreams after the loss of his best friend Umbaba, Ajax's epic disappointment for not receiving Achilles's armour, Plutarch's accounting of Zopir in terror when killing the horrifying Pyrrhus, to name a few. Loss of comrades, anger at leaders, and fear of the enemy are emotions, among so many others, that depict a warrior's experience of trauma (Ustinova and Cardeña 2014). More recently, in the last century, the science of psychiatry evolved with the emergence of war. What was then called "war neurosis" started to be treated in the war theatre itself, allowing soldiers to stay with their comrades, which seems to have increased the rate of immediate recovery (Crocq et al. 2000). It is during the "total war" that the relationship between physiology and psychology was established and that the psychiatric approach to "war neurosis" adopted a terminology closer to the current science of trauma: symptoms such as operational fatigue, psychosomatic states, guilt, depression, aggressive reactions, avoidance of emotions, recurrent dreams about the trauma, etc., were identified and treated (Crocq and Crocq 2000). In psychiatry, like in many other medical approaches, the experience of war always helped to propel the science and treatments for the wounded. What scientists and clinicians discovered and experienced about their patients during the two great wars was then used to treat individuals who suffered from other traumatic experiences related to severe stressors. If diagnoses and treatments can have similarities across all populations, the main distinction of the medical approach of war is that military medicine, including military psychiatry and even more so, forward psychiatry, always focused on the operation – the return of the patient to combat readiness (English 2016). Today, focus is also on long-term care for military personnel in service or who have transitioned to civilian life.

The *Diagnostic and Statistical Manual of Mental Disorder* (*DSM-V*) is now used for the diagnosis of post-traumatic stress disorder (PTSD), a cluster of symptoms (intrusive thoughts, avoidance, negative alterations in cognition and mood and alterations in arousal and activity) that may affect military and civilians suffering from an exposure to actual or threatened death, serious injury, or sexual violation. The PTSD construct was developed primarily to acknowledge and confirm the psychological damage incurred by combat soldiers because of war, whereby much-needed compensation and benefits could support them in their recovery. Similar efforts were introduced by feminist therapists such as Herman (1992), who saw the conceptualization of post-traumatic stress as relating to "survivors of childhood sexual abuse, women who were battered, and others routinely traumatized in a patriarchal society.... [T]herapists wanted their clients to get the benefits that *DSM* legitimization would bring: the harm being taken more seriously, coverage in insurance policies, and women being able to sue for damages" (cited in Burstow 2005, 430).

Disrupting the traditional thinking about trauma and PTSD, including the deficit-based "disorder" narrative, other scholars have begun to explore the transformative power of trauma through the lens of "post-traumatic growth" (Calhoun, Cann, and Tedeschi 2010). Further, new potential diagnoses are emerging within the literature on combat trauma – e.g., "moral injury" (Nash and Litz 2013), which has yet to be scaled and better defined as a subset of PTSD or a diagnosis in itself (Bélanger et al. 2018). For instance, regretting doing something one should not have done according to one's own personal, core values, or regretting not having acted when one thinks one should have can bring feelings of guilt and shame, sometimes mixed with many other emotions, such as anger, that can be found on the PTSD diagnosis scale. Further, these experiences are often lived in a potentially traumatic environment where the natural fear for survival is aggravated by the overwhelming danger surrounding the concerned individuals. Returning "home," to a "civilian" or "legitimate" life, can be challenging for some who experienced the extreme. Overall, throughout history, trauma in all its forms is often exacerbated by exposure (*DSM-5*).

The PTSD construct developed and deployed in reaction to the psychological needs of combat veterans, women fleeing abuse, and victims of childhood abuse may also apply to street-involved youth (especially those who participate in street organizations). Adam's narration of a glimpse of his childhood, and life as a teenager, is an excellent example of this phenomenon. His testimony of a "street life" shows a parallel world that sometimes crosses over into the "legitimate" sphere, but that is typically hidden and often ends in death or prison. Thus, the following account of Adam's life shows the complexity and "messiness" of "violence" in society, its intersectionality with mental health (trauma and PTSD), and how society might acknowledge and be attentive to the "cries for help" from those on the margins. His reaction, like that of so many other young people, is one of survival; his response to violence is violence – or more precisely, was violence. Whether it is at the service of good or bad, whether it is for a cause related to the nation or to democracy, or to ensure a delivery of crack cocaine, violence ultimately produces the same consequences on individuals. Anyone experiencing overwhelming violence – whether a soldier, a refugee, a child born and raised in a violent family, a teacher terrified in a school surrounded by violence, or a "gang" member – is likely to experience trauma. The point, here, is that while the causes may differ, all experience a shared suffering.

Giving Voice to the Past: The Re-enactment of Trauma

To enhance our understanding of the impact that trauma/PTSD has on life outcomes, scholars such as Van der Kolk (1989), Bloom (2010), and Herman (1992) have identified that past memories of trauma may be relived and/or re-enacted in contemporary life – what has been coined "the re-enactment of trauma and/or the compulsion to repeat." Scholars have outlined that trauma survivors who experience serious forms of trauma, such as violence, may in effect come to relive or re-enact the past in the present as an attempt to resolve what had happened to them. For survivors of violence, such re-enactments may become a mechanism by which individuals can communicate or give voice to the silenced trauma of the past. As a result, for some individuals, the intrusion of memories of the past, correlated with their need to resolve what happened to them in the present, leads to a desire or compulsion to "fix" their trauma through an alternative form of communication – "action." For some, this "action" may be positive behaviours such as engaging in sports, working out, or becoming a motorcycle enthusiast, while for others (especially those deprived of resources to cope with trauma), the drive to give voice to their past trauma may be negative behaviours such as self-harm, drug/alcohol use, and even violence. However, while the use of violence may seem to resolve the past in the present, these attempts are futile, as the survivor now becomes the perpetrator, who then adds to the cycle of violence in society that leads to more trauma and victims in its wake.

Thus, drawing on the knowledge on PTSD, and the re-enactment of trauma, our chapter seeks to explore several questions, including: Can the concepts of PTSD and the re-enactment of trauma be used to understand the violence espoused by street-involved populations? Can (and should) members of street organizations be seen and treated as trauma victims/survivors? Can their behaviours and actions (including violence) be understood through the lens of trauma, whereby one must consider both the macro and meso contexts that drive a person to join a street organization and engage in violent behaviour? Do street-involved youth deserve our (society's) help? Answering such questions, conceptually, disrupts long-held beliefs about minority youth, their "otherness," and their proclivity to crime and criminal behaviour, including that of so-called gang membership. As we will learn from Adam's testimony, street-involved youth/adults, like other traumatized individuals in society, cannot (and should not) be understood through a unidirectional or pathological lens; rather, through the prism of trauma, we must note how marginalized and racialized youth navigate systems of oppression and harm, often resulting in overlapping and/or comorbid psychological stressors that may lead to "gang" formation (or a street life) and the expression of trauma through violence (the re-enactment of trauma).

Adam's Story: First-Hand Perspective from Inside a Gang Life

Narrative 1: School Trauma and My Introduction to Community/ Interpersonal Violence

Until the age of fourteen or fifteen, I experienced significant bullying. The kids were relentless. The intense bullying I experienced was rooted in the entrenched subculture of violence that was almost like a cloud floating over our community (contexts related to structural factors that affect the family and children's well-being and development). We lived our lives in a never-ending competition where we strived to gain respect, to be "real," and to never be "shook." As early as I can remember, the kids I was surrounded by saw violence as the main way to prove that they were strong, brave, and tough – hallmarks of being a "real one" or a "real man." Perhaps this was their way to show they had value and could succeed in a world that had robbed them of every other way to move up the social ladder. We were the children of the mobsters, bikers, and gangsters. The only role models in our lives, and who gave a fuck about us, were the OGs who hung out in the shadows of the street corner, dive bars, and social clubs in our area. From an early age, the pimps, hustlers, and gangsters became our fathers, teaching us the ways of the streets (teaching us ways to combat the deficits left behind by deindustrialization/globalization and neoliberalism). While we were forbidden from joining street organizations in childhood, we exploited the spaces on the block to test the limits of our masculinities and express our trauma. Whether it was breaking collar bones during a session of British bulldog, getting black eyes and broken ribs in a "friendly" game of kick-the-can, or having to face the threats and attacks of the older and tougher kids at school, these were the origins of a communal experiment to "test" our pedigree for a street life.

While violence exposure during childhood prepared us for the "realness" of a street life, it was not until high school that this experiment accelerated and established its roots. While much of my socialization to violence came from my upbringing on the block, it was the social milieu of the school system (or the lack thereof) that solidified my transcendence into what civilian society would call a "gang." For young people, secondary school is supposed to be a safe space for learning and personal (positive) growth. But this was not my experience. Rather, my school was a conduit for street socialization and violence. Having been kicked out of my first high school for resisting the status quo (not wearing my Catholic uniform, skipping class, fighting, etc.), I was sent to "gladiator school." This new institution was set up to capture the failures, delinquents, and those who lacked the social capital to gain social mobility through the legitimate opportunity structure. Gladiator school was a dumping ground (or warehouse) for children who would become the next generation of surplus labour. Here, what the system considered "hopeless" children, those who society gave up on, were housed within "tech" schools where we were more likely to die, become drug addicts, and/or go to jail than graduate. Ostracized from the "legitimate world," the marginal school system became a fertile space for resistance groups and their illegitimate opportunity structure.

My first day of school was likely very different from that of children of "civilians." It was a beautiful fall day as I walked towards what was supposed to be the first day of the rest of my life. I approached the concrete steps at the entrance of the school, which looked like a gothic church. Cigarette butts lay like rose pedals leading to a lover's bed. From the corners of the gothic arches, the fall air was taken over by the stench of urine left behind by students with no desire to follow the school's rules and regulations. As I approached, I heard someone "holla" at me: "What up dog?" I turned and replied, "What up, B?" As a cloud covered the sun, I was surrounded by five "ops" (or "opposition") – guys from other neighbourhoods I might have beef with or might know. I heard another person yell, "What up, B, where you from?" Having been raised in the street, I knew I was being challenged or tested (in the streets we called this getting g-checked (see Garot 2010), I just did not know why.

Like Jason Bourne calculating his escape, my mind explored possible outcomes. I saw a garbage can I could use to smash the first guy in the face with. But it was chained to the pole. Fuck! I looked in the corner and saw a bottle left from a recent "bot" session (youth using a bottle to smoke hashish). I could break it in half and cut someone's face or throat. Okay, that's the move. Hopefully the blood from the one guy will scare the others and I can escape. Everything seemed to turn into slow motion. Voices became muffled as I prepared my move. I felt focused and prepared, to win and escape or, at worst, lose and take a beating or maybe even get stabbed up. But before I could slip through and grab the bottle, I had a gun to my face. Shit escalated and I froze. I felt as if I was watching from outside of my body – everything turned blurry and went into slow motion. I was trying to think, but I couldn't. I heard my agent of persecution say, "What up motherfucker, where you from?" Through my street identity, I replied and said, "Nowhere, fuck you." The kid then cocked the gun, put it to my head, and told me to kneel. As my knees buckled, I felt someone grab my backpack and another rummage through my pockets. I was being robbed and shaken down. In the streets, we called this "getting jacked" – a serious affront to one's masculinity, respect, and street credibility (see Anderson 1999).

After the robbery, I dashed to the basketball courts. At the courts, I linked with homies from the neighbourhood. I told them what went down. I also knew a couple of the guys who jacked me up (they were rivals from my neighbourhood), so revenge fantasies were already percolating. One of my homies, RN, told me not to sweat it, and that I kind of fucked up. My new school was segregated along racial and neighbourhood lines that no one had told me about. Each exit was controlled and "owned" by a particular group, usually a street organization (i.e., the Latino Alliance, Skinheads/Rockers, Bloods/Crips, etc.). You either needed to be known at the school (where you had a "pass") or have permission to walk through. On the other side of the building, one exit was designated for those who were not involved in a street life and/or the school's illegitimate market. I did not know this, so my attempt to walk through the door on that first day (which was controlled by the Jamaican Shower Posse), without permission, was a form of "disrespect." While I learned the rules of the school landscape, I was still pissed off. As a high-ranking "street soldier," RN told me he would talk to those guys and tell them they couldn't touch me. Meanwhile, RN took me to his car and told me, "Hold this." In my hand lay my first gun (a .22 calibre). He said, "If anyone tries to fuck with you again, tell them to come see me. If you're stuck, well then you know what to do."

In the weeks after the robbery, I became depressed. I feared for my life. I was not safe at school or in the community, so where the fuck was I supposed to go? I questioned who I was. Was I a "real one" or a shook one? I had trouble sleeping, and when I did, I had revenge fantasies. I practised posturing with my gun in the mirror, thinking of what I would say and do (but struggled mentally to reach a place where I could actually do what I wanted to do in my fantasy – contexts that relate to most street-involved youth who never use lethal violence – our lives were more about posturing and looking hard than actually becoming the extreme or the 1 per cent). I dreamt about what it would feel like to regain the power they had robbed from me. Outside of school, I was also becoming more entrenched in the street life. As I could not go to my parents or the police for help (this would be snitching and breaking the street code), I became closer to my street family, the homies on the block. In the streets, we tested our loyalty through fighting and violence, risk taking (like running from the police, breaking into cars, etc.), and drug and alcohol use (which also helped us to cope with our silenced and suppressed trauma). Soon the innocence of our childhood group/clique wore off, and we had become what many in the community, including the police, classified as a "problem" (or in their eyes, a junior gang). At the same time, we developed a reputation for "holding our own" by showing our capacity to use non-lethal violence (i.e., fist fighting/small weapons that could harm but not be fatal). We took over a community park and neighbourhood 7-Eleven – spaces that we claimed to be our "turf" (spaces that police had historically banned us from).

We acquired drugs from higher-level street families (organized crime groups) and built a small illicit marketplace. With our newfound turf and market, we were also forced to defend our area and product. Then violence became our primary tool for control and acquiring respect (always pushing the line between non-lethal and lethal violence). These early years were a blur. They were filled with endless days of monotony, including drinking and smoking drugs in the park, having sex with girls, and fighting. The shadows of the alleyways and parks became our second home, where we transformed from being boys to "men" (see Fraser 2015). We didn't give a fuck about nothing because no one gave a fuck about us! The society that was supposed to show us love (providing a pathway for us to make it in the legitimate market and to acquire social mobility) gave up on us. The people supposed to keep us safe did not protect us. So we were on our own. It was just us. The bikers and the mob would not take us in, so we went rogue. Through this transition, many of us rocked flags (or bandanas) to show what set or clique we were down with. This also created a sense of "brotherhood" and communal bonding. Our neighbourhood, historically, was a Blood set, so we easily fell into the communal framework and developed a partnership between Euro, Black, and Latino street organizations. Unlike US street organizations, we had no OGs from the Blood nation to guide us, so we had to just figure it out on our own. As we took on a bigger role in the community, this drew the attention of competing street organizations and the police. Then competition over scarce resources (product/money/pathways to get out of our neighbourhood) led to increased use of violence. The more we fought and used violence the more I noticed that my identity, and that of my "brothers," began to shift – moving from primarily victims of violence to perpetrators (that weighed heavily on my soul as I received no gratification from using non-lethal violence – for me it was the only way I could protect myself). Thus, in the wake of the emergent street violence one-on-one fights turned into swarmings, swarmings turned into stabbings, and stabbings turned into shoot-outs.

The violence I experienced inside and outside school took a psychological toll. I lived every day in fear (the only way I can explain it to civilians is to imagine you are locked in a room with a person who wants to kill you – however, the community was our locked room – what would you do?). I did not know if I was going to get beaten down, stabbed, or shot to death because of who I was and where I was were from. I couldn't tell anyone because I would be seen as a snitch, weak, and a shook one. So I had to take it in stride and in silence. While a lot [of ho]meboys (including myself) used the space of a "street life" as a replac[ement for] the socio-economic stress we experienced growing up, for others it wa[s the cons]tant threat of the "war" that pushed them to "hang and bang." For me, every fight, war, and form of aggression could always be linked back to the early trauma I was exposed to in childhood and adolescence (marginalization, over-policing of my community, economic stress, emergence of drug markets in response to financial stress, exposure to community, and interpersonal violence). However, and more important, my outward expression of violence can be linked to the memories and feelings associated with the five guys who tried to rob me and take my life. From that day on, every enemy became those five guys who stole my innocence. Perhaps by the age of fifteen, I was arrested for having my first gun (a borrowed community gun). While I harmed no one with my weapon, I felt it necessary to have a gun because of the violent world I was being raised in. With the constant threat of physical injury and/or death I felt that the only way to survive my environment was to be strapped (or to seem dangerous to those who wanted to harm me).

Narrative 2: The Compounding Force of Traumatic Violence

In recent discussions with some of my old colleagues, we estimated that our crew (thirty to forty members) participated in over 700 fights per year, ranging from simple one-on-one battles to larger street wars that involved knives, bats, bottles, machetes, and, on rarer occasion, guns. Many of these street conflicts had their roots in the competition for drug markets, drug deals gone bad, revenge for victimization orchestrated by our enemies, and/or someone feeling disrespected. Serious assaults took place between warring factions, with individuals losing limbs, becoming permanently scarred (physically and emotionally), and losing their lives. Memories of some of these battles continue to haunt me. I recall one fight between our crew and some "g's" from the "Jane Strip." The fight was over a drug deal gone bad. We locked the doors to the school with chains and everyone engaged in all-out war – punching, shanking, stabbing, and chopping everything that came our way. I remember people losing their limbs (some lost fingers, others lost pieces of their ears, and someone lost a chunk of his forearm) and it became so bad that we were slipping on the floor because of the blood, but no one died. This did not occur within school. Others included wars between the White rockers (skinheads who eventually moved on and obtained social mobility and/or who were pushed out by other street organizations), Asian triads, Latinos, and Blacks.

The school then lost all control. Teachers got assaulted and property got heavily vandalized, with classrooms being lit (what seemed to be an outward expression of violence that let us strike back against the systems that had oppressed our families and harmed us, as pissed off kids suspended, expelled, and pushed out of the school system because we were "problem students"). Eventually the police were brought in to clear house or "cleanse the system" of the "disease." Two undercover police officers monitored the school's property, but this made little difference, because the street wars era had found a permanent home in the communities and institutions of Toronto's West End.

As the wars in the streets became more dangerous, our ability to live normal, adolescent lives became more and more difficult. Turf lines were drawn by blood, and the risk to life increased every time we crossed into someone else's "hood," building, or park. I experienced being "rushed" (i.e., several street youths attacking one person) by several street organizations (or "ops") at bus stops and subway stations as I was trying to get somewhere in the city. The beat-downs endured, and the threat of losing my life only pushed me and my friends to develop serious paranoia about navigating public spaces. This then led to anxiety and nightmares, which numbed us to life in general, and violence. As my nightmares turned to reality, I delved deeper into the street life for solace and protection. As street organizations became more lethal, hand-to-hand combat became a thing of the past. Knives and guns made their way into communities, and the risks associated with street warfare became more significant. I brought my own weapons to school (i.e., knives, a gun etc..) to protect myself from the constant threats (however at this point I was still unsure if I had the capability to participate in lethal violence). My street organization grew bigger and so did the stakes. As the mid-1990s approached, street organizations moved from slanging weed to a new drug that took over the North American drug scene – crack cocaine.

Within my community, I became a "real one," moving up the ranks as my family connections paved the way for my full-fledged adoption of a street life. I also became a leader in the hip hop community, with my status as one of the best DJs in the city helping to solidify my street "cred." My music let me escape the limits of my violent surroundings while helping me to discover and explore other people's stories of hardship and pain. Although music gave me an avenue to navigate away from the street life (and give voice to my trauma), it also had the unintended consequence of growing my "street network" across Toronto. I soon connected with other homies, and we built a music empire – ruling the underground music scene with the best breakers, MCs, graffiti artists, and DJs. As we moved across the city, from venue to venue, new illegitimate spaces opened up to us through "rap battling." However, these rap battles often ended up with someone feeling disrespected and fights popped off because of what seemed to be challenges to masculinity, respect, or honour. This not only solidified our reputations as underground rap music icons in the city, but also the "man's dem" not to fuck with. My unique position as a DJ opened pathways multiple street organizations to unite, as I had some of the largest hip-hop parties in the West End of Toronto. This music-to-street pipeline created an informal pathway where street organizations could coalesce and seize social and financial opportunities. For example, if one of theirs could hook us up with guns, then one of ours could link them with the best weed and coke. If one of ours could link them with stolen clothes, one of theirs could link someone with cars, and so on (this is not to blame hip hop for crime, but to demonstrate how these spaces provided the opportunity for business transactions and networking).

During these years, the streets were not the only problem, as the school system and police had now identified certain groups as "criminal gangs" and targeted operations were established to take us down. As we were dodging "beef" in the streets, we were also running from the police who we saw as the biggest and most dangerous gang. The police often kidnapped "gang members" and took them places to get beatdowns (and to try to turn them into informants). I remember the first time the police picked me up for no reason they had in actuality a lot of reasons – because of where I was from, how I dressed, that I was down with a neighbourhood family, my family's association with the streets etc.). They took me to Cherry Beach, notorious for police beatings. The cops dragged me out of the car, kicking and punching my torso, not leave bruises on my face. Police also followed and interrogated us daily, bullying and questioning us for kicks. They always tried to get people to inform on their crew by making someone's life a living hell; however, the real ones knew what was up – no snitching.

As the game got more dangerous and the risk of dying increased with every moment on the block, my mom got me out the "hood" for a bit. I moved to another section of the city, which I will call "Gaza." In Gaza, I learned a whole new level of violence from my street "cuz" or cousin (whose family had endured intergenerational oppression and trauma including marginalization, racialization, and criminalization). Gaza was going through its own transition as the old-school weed game changed to the crack game, opening up a war for the scarce resources of the underground drug trade – resources that became the primary mechanism for economic survival for many young people. The area was a mix of high-rise and low-rise buildings, where young "street soldiers" took over apartments and turned them into drug dens. Violence in Gaza was key to controlling internal street politics and issues, managing "custies" (or customers), and mitigating external threats from outside the area. I built my "rep" through my "cuz," a gunman (and leader of his own street organization). As the turf war increased, young "street soldiers" started to get shot up, killed, and incarcerated. As I travelled back and forth to the West End for school, I expanded the illegitimate market as I learned about the crack game and the new weapons of warfare.

As the sun began to set on the chaos of high school, young adulthood saw the West End underground markets explode. With turfs now drawn, the city was easier to navigate as I could identify my enemies and allies. One of the last wars of our high school days was the longest and had the most casualties. From what I heard, one of my homies had robbed young gangsters from another West End hood called PK. We had allied with the older Scotian and Jamaican g's from the hood, but we had no respect for these small-time crooks trying to cross into our area to buy drugs, so they got "jacked up." A number of things happened and these guys rushed one of ours with baseball bats, leaving him to die outside a nightclub we used to frequent. Homeboy almost died, but the payback was already being orchestrated. One by one, we hunted the "enemy" down, doing what we needed to do (in a controlled way, so as to not have to resort to lethal violence). The police addressed this "beef" by placing gang cops and undercovers in our neighbourhoods. We experienced constant pullovers, illegal searches and questioning, and threats to ourselves and our families. As we fought to avenge our brother and to maintain our "respect," the police perpetrated their own violence on us, arbitrarily arresting homies for anything and everything (except for gang-related charges, which they could not get us on). The fighting, violence, and pressure from police took a toll on everyone. I thought I was losing my mind. I slept even less than usual (three to four hours a night) and started to question everyone's loyalty to the group, as my brothers did not step up when needed, including posting bail or providing canteen money for homies who were locked down in prison.

I also discovered that my mom was dying of cancer. Stuck in a street war, correlated with her illness, drove me to the darkest place I had ever been. In the following months, I had to watch my mother lose a courageous battle with cancer. As she took her last breath, I held her close, as she could barely speak, promised her I would make her proud, and watched a tear roll down her cheek as she passed into the heavens. The days and months that followed were a blur, as I consumed the underworld for all of its demons, binge drinking regularly to numb the pain and to escape the chaos of the streets. I forget much from those days; however, I began to realize the importance of life, and I could no longer stand the man I was. Yet, I was still drawn to my crew, as these guys were my family. We fought wars and shed tears together, and I felt I could not waste the past on an unknown future. Although I saw more and more that the streets were fake (friends were willing to backstab you; enemies were more likely to use lethal violence; the code of the streets was breaking down), and the people I once called friends were now strangers, it was still difficult to walk away.

While police were knocking down my door or hunting me in the streets, I was also burying the best friend I ever had – my mother. I continued to use music to escape, but the days got darker and more hopeless, as the friends I thought were true homies started to appear in a different light. I am not sure if it was because we were getting older, or the wars had taken a toll on the crew, but shit just didn't look the same. As I transitioned out of adolescence, into young adulthood, my original crew and acquaintances fell apart from addiction, incarceration, and other life events. Big homies who were once kings and idolized on the streets were now customers of the underworld they helped create. Over the years a few of my friends branched off, taking what they had learned from the street hustle, and reconfigured their previous "criminal" experiences into a new operation of organized and high-level crime. For me, I followed along as I chased what we had growing up – comradery, loyalty, and trust. I tried my hand in the legitimate world, working odd factory jobs, living pay cheque to pay cheque, and living without a home. However, I made a promise, and no matter the pain and hardship, I would find success beyond the war. I did this to be a "real one not a shook one."

Reflection: Understanding Street-Related Violence through the Lens of PTSD and the Re-enactment of Trauma

In recent months I drove through my old "hood," circling around the blocks where blunts were rolled, forties were cracked, and blood was shed. As my mind dissociates to the "days of old," I reminisce about the forgotten lives that were lost to the streets – those who were killed, incarcerated, or continue to carry the battle scars of the war. I feel a resurgence of energy rush through my body, a feeling of euphoria, as the streets that made me are still part of me. There is a saying on the block that "you can take the cat out the hood, but not the hood out the cat." Although I have moved away from my old street life, there is something about the comradery, the love, and the bond we had as street soldiers that makes me want it all back. However, underneath the guise of nostalgia, I also remember the pain and suffering that came with the "wars." The emotional and psychological exhaustion of having to navigate the streets (Berardi 2020), the constant running from the police and street rivals, and the sorrow of losing homies before they had time to reach their own potential all remind me of why I left (i.e., moral injuries).

Upon reflection, I have now come to realize how my past experiences in street life (including personal victimization) led me to use violence to cope (what may be understood as the re-enactment of street-related violence). Here, my personal identity and beliefs during my formative years shifted from that of survivor to one who perpetrates violence. This had a significant impact on who I was and how I came to view the world (as a place of danger). However, much of my violence was for self-preservation, and while the community and state criminalized my behaviour, I came to understand it as a necessary part of my survival (contexts that may be different for others who may find gratification in violence). However, I also came to realize through my street tenure that even those who sought to harm me, and/or those who appeared to use violence for self-gratification (both enemies and those who were part of my street family) were battling with their own "demons" and silenced trauma. Thus, through the lens of trauma, I recognize that we were not criminals, super-predators, or gangsters – labels that the media, law enforcement, and politicians applied to us to justify their cleansing of our community. Rather, we were all trauma survivors, both allies/friends and enemies. We all carried with us a history of trauma that was subsequently relived and/or re-enacted though the vestige of a street life (including violence).

However, not all was doom and gloom on the block. The dichotomy between positive and negative expressions of trauma was not linear either (in this context street-involved youth may use violence as a coping strategy, but they may also engage in positive behaviours such as playing basketball, rapping, and participating in the arts, to name a few). For example, within the vortex of street warfare, the strength and resilience of young people also emerges, demonstrating a will and ferocity to fight back against the oppression, poverty, and violence that encapsulates many of our communities. For me, pathways such as music and art played an important role in my ability to understand, reflect, and deal with the trauma of street violence. Some people found solace in sports, others in drugs, but for me it was hip-hop culture. My room was my sanctuary, where turntables and milk crates full of records became my escape away the horrors of life. In this space, I was talented, I had skills, and my identity was known and respected. Unlike the "real" world where I was labelled and viewed as an outcast, within the space of hip-hop culture I regained a sense of self that was stolen from me. The art of DJ'ing became my ritual, which allowed me to not only escape from the physical war zone outside, but it also provided a space where I could explore and understand the complex issues that were part and parcel of my lived reality. I created mixes as if they were pieces of life's complex puzzle, crafting and unpacking the narratives of young "g's" who were just like me.

Although the war had taken its toll on my body and mind over the years, music became my epicentre, which allowed me to attach myself to an alternative world that understood my pain. Looking back, however, I now realize that music was a Band Aid solution to much larger and more complex social, economic, and political issues. Life in street organizations and young people's subsequent use of street violence needs to be understood through multiple theoretical lenses, which not only look at the structural contexts or "root causes" of crime (systemic racism, poverty, etc.), but also incorporate an understanding of the psychological effects of marginalization and social exclusion on individuals living in disadvantaged communities, where subcultures of violence often emerge (Wilson 1987). I hope this chapter contributes to the development of knowledge on the psychological sequelae of street-related violence, providing a platform for further discussions on the development of policies and practices that may support youth in their transition out of street organizations and a street life. Although there have been great strides in our understanding of people's trauma, the focus of research, policy, and practices has been politicized. Only certain populations are able to have their trauma acknowledged and compensated through financial and therapeutic supports (although even these supports have been critiqued).

The construct of PTSD has been justifiably used to garner political, legal, social and economic responses to a diverse array of groups affected by traumatic violence (refugees, veterans, and women fleeing abuse). Many members of these groups have been correctly identified as "survivors" of trauma and thus have been able to draw on the medico-legal language of PTSD to acquire services and funding that support them in their physical and psychological recovery. The diagnosis of PTSD has also been used to affect legal outcomes (homicide cases involving combat veterans and women fleeing abuse who may have also used violence to re-enact and cope with their trauma) and/or influence decisions about cases involving refugees fleeing persecution.

However, the construct of PTSD appears to lack the breadth and reach to provide other, less favourable groups (criminalized and racialized youth/adults) with similar forms of access. As for street organizations (more specifically, minority youth groups), it is apparent that the suffering found in the urban enclaves of North American cities is less worthy of our attention, empathy, and support (as seen in our treatment of minority youth/adults where society has dealt with the trauma experienced by these individuals through the criminal justice rather than the public health system). This may be due to the emergence of white-colonial knowledge during the late 1800s and early 1900s that viewed minority populations as "backwards" and a threat to the dominant class. Within this context, race and crime were conflated to demonize and dehumanize the lives of those on the margins, thus justifying the control and oppression of minority populations in society (Alexander 2012). One can argue that there has been an erosion of empathy and understanding for those who are most disadvantaged in our society. Consequently, from my perspective, the racial constructs of "criminal," "thug," "offender," and "gangster" have disallowed those from the "streets" or "margins" to legitimize (or justify) their behaviours/actions through psychological vernacular, such as the PTSD category. Without the ability to demonstrate that street-based behaviours/actions result from pre-existing traumatic experiences (systemic racism, poverty etc.), youth/adults on the margins are pathologized, criminalized and funnelled into the hands of the criminal justice system rather than those of the public health system (where it is not about what they did, but why they did it).

In this context, I question whether youth involved in street organizations can ever be seen as trauma survivors rather than "criminals" and offenders. Can they access the label of trauma/PTSD and receive public health support instead of having their lives thrown away by a punitive justice system? Can the courts ever view street-involved youth as "survivors" rather than only as criminals? Can society understand that street-related violence is not just predatory, but is also a reflection of life-course trauma? Can society understand street-related violence through the lens of self-defence and protection – contexts that we afford other groups seeking to escape traumatic violence? These are pressing issues for state officials and policymakers and deserve a broader academic discussion that explores community trauma as a piece of the macro socio-economic contexts that proliferate violence in society.

Today, I not only suffer from the memories of street-related violence, I am also constantly reminded of the past through the scars on my body. I now experience a physiological and psychological symptoms, such as gastrointestinal complications, joint issues, and pain from the physical experiences of street combat. I am often asked at conferences and workshops what would have changed my life trajectory, and I am not sure if there is a simple answer. I am not sure what could have stopped the violence of street warfare, as many issues that contribute to a gang and/or street life are beyond the control of individuals, including complex socio-economic and cultural variables that intersect with race, class, gender, and crime.

Unfortunately, much of the policy and programming to combat street-related violence is punitive and reactive (where young minority men and women are often re-traumatized repeatedly). Future research needs to explore proactive solutions that target and support young people traumatized and harmed by multiple systems of oppression. Systemic racism, poverty, marginalization, and access to education need to be discussed in order to reduce the reliance on illegitimate opportunity structures and violence as mechanisms that resist and protect against oppression. In short, and reflecting on my own life, with the right people and resources, post-traumatic growth can be achieved. There is opportunity, through our collective pain and suffering, to turn negative situations into positive ones.

Keep yo head up my g's!

NOTES

1 Sections of this chapter draw on and refer to the direct experiences of this author (Adam Ellis) as presented in the first person. I have called on my colleagues, Luca Berardi and Stephanie Bélanger to speak to the theoretical components of the chapter.
2 Hereafter I have taken caution not to use the colonizers' term "gang." Rather, I will refer to street families/groups as street organizations – a term popularized by Brotherton and Barrios 2004

REFERENCES

Agnew, R. 1992. "Foundation for a General Strain Theory of Crime and Delinquency." *Criminology* 30 (1): 47–88. https://doi.org/10.1111/j.1745-9125.1992.tb01093.x.

Alexander, M. 2010. *The New Jim Crow: Mass Incarceration in the Age of Colorblindness*. New York: New Press.

Anderson, E. 1999. *Code of the Street: Decency, Violence, and the Moral Life of the Inner City*. New York: W.W. Norton.

Bélanger, S., H. Cramm, K. Fletcher, and J-S. Demers. 2018. "PTSD vs. Moral Injury: A Scoping Review." *Journal of Military, Veteran and Family Health* 4 (1): 2–4. https://doi.org/10.3138/jmvfh.4.1.002.

Berardi, L. 2020. "Neighborhood Wisdom: An Ethnographic Study of Localized Street Knowledge." *Qualitative Sociology* 44:103–24. https://doi.org/10.1007/s11133-020-09454-z.

Bloom, S.L. 2010. "Reenactment." Community Works. https://pdf4pro.com/cdn/reenactment-sanctuaryweb-com-43cd67.pdf.

Brotherton, D.C., and L. Barrios. 2004. *The Almighty Latin King and Queen Nation: Street Politics and the Transformation of a New York City Gang*. New York: Columbia University Press.

Burstow, B. 2005. "A Critique of Posttraumatic Stress Disorder and the DSM." *Journal of Humanistic Psychology* 45 (4): 429–45. https://doi.org/10.1177/0022167805280265.

Calhoun, L.G., A. Cann, and R.G. Tedeschi. 2010. "The Posttraumatic Growth Model: Sociocultural Considerations." In *Posttraumatic Growth and Culturally Competent Practice: Lessons Learned from around the Globe*, edited by T. Weiss and R. Berger, 1–14. John Wiley & Sons.

Clarke, R.V., and D.B. Cornish. 2001. "Rational Choice." In *Explaining Criminals and Crime: Essays in Contemporary Criminological Theory*, edited by R. Paternoster and R. Bachman, 23–42. Los Angeles: Roxbury.

Crocq, M.A., and L. Crocq. 2000. "From Shell Shock and War Neurosis to Posttraumatic Stress Disorder: A History of Psychotraumatology." *Dialogues in Clinical Neuroscience* 2 (1): 47–55. https://doi.org/10.31887/DCNS.2000.2.1/macrocq.

English, A. 2016. "Sex and the Soldier: The Effect of Competing Ethical Value Systems on the Health and Well Being of Canadian Military Personnel and Veterans." In *Military Operations and the Mind: War Ethics and Soldiers' Well-Being*, edited by S.A.H. Bélanger and D. Lagacé-Ro, 219–66. Montreal and Kingston: McGill-Queen's University Press.

Fraser, A. 2015. *Urban Legends*. Oxford: Oxford University Press.

Garot, R. 2010. *Who You Claim: Performing Gang Identity in School and on the Streets*. Vol. 3. New York: NYU Press.

Herman, J.L. 1992. *Trauma and Recovery*. New York: Basic Books.

Lilly, J.R., F.T. Cullen, and R.A. Ball. 2015. *Criminological Theory: Context and Consequences*. Thousand Oaks, CA: Sage.

Merton, R.K. 1938. "Social Structure and Anomie." *American Sociological Review* 3 (5), 672–82. https://doi.org/10.2307/2084686.
– 1968. *Social Theory and Social Structure*. New York: Free Press.
Nash, W.P., and B.T. Litz. 2013. "Moral Injury: A Mechanism for War-Related Psychological Trauma in Military Family Members." *Clinical Child and Family Psychology Review* 16: 365–75. https://doi.org/10.1007/s10567-013-0146-y.
Ustinova, Y., and E. Cardeña. 2014. "Combat Stress Disorders and Their Treatment in Ancient Greece." *Psychological Trauma Theory Research Practice and Policy* 6 (6): 739–48. https://doi.org/10.1037/a0036461.
Van der Kolk, B.A. 1989. "The Compulsion to Repeat the Trauma: Re-enactment, Revictimization, and Masochism." *Psychiatric Clinics of North America* 2 (2): 389–411. https://doi.org/10.1016/S0193-953X(18)30439-8.
Wilson, W.J. 1987) *The Truly Disadvantaged: The Inner City, the Underclass, and Public Policy*. Chicago: University of Chicago Press.

9 (De)Criminalizing the "Code of Silence": Reflections of a Former "Gang Banger" Turned Academic

ANTHONY HUTCHINSON[1] AND JARED MILLICAN

Introduction

What is honour? What is loyalty? What is trust? For as long as I can remember, I could never decipher or embrace what these concepts have truly ever meant in the core of my being. Growing up as a fragmented, mixed-race "Heinz 57" "hodgepodge" individual of Indo-Afro-Latin, European, and Caribbean backgrounds but born and raised on the west coast of Canada, I could never fully reflectively actualize any strong sense of ethnic let alone functional psychological or psycho-social identity. Despite my being born as a first-generation "Canadian," I entered the world in a dominant Caucasian society, and it was made very clear from my earliest years that I did not belong. The social exclusion I faced from the time I was a young lad even to this very day (over a half a century later) has changed little. Then moving from my being a severely challenged, anxiety-ridden young child (across a range of adverse psycho-social domains) to being a criminalized teenaged street gang member, I grew to become an "esteemed" university professor and a doctor of health-care services to the public. Despite the magnitude of such a broad life transition or "evolution," I never fully corrected the experiences of exclusion and demoralization that affected me as a marginalized child or criminalized youth.

From the time I was three or four years old, I lived a life of racism, sexual abuse, and social exclusion. It was a life that never approximated economic affluence. I grew up in a household of violence. The abuse I experienced throughout my elementary and high school years was relentless. Through much of it, I generally learned to keep things to myself, and it was never a good choice to utter a word that could mitigate the injury caused to me from the time I was a young child, not to mention the next five decades of my life (which I shall address shortly). As a teenager, I came to learn that acquiring and having (illegal) handguns gained a certain sense of "empowerment" in that when you pointed a loaded handgun at a person making fun of you, the teasing immediately stopped.

I came to learn that taking strategic shortcuts to securing money through gang-involved thievery was a valid and safer option, compared to my securing a reasonable job as a teenager. Consider that I was making next to nothing delivering thousands of advertising flyers door-to-door only to be attacked by an unleashed Doberman Pinscher that nearly severed my left thumb. On the other hand, from my perspective, my gang-involved economic-equity opportunity secured ways for me to buy things I wanted and needed to make my life more meaningful (especially drugs, alcohol, and cigarettes). In short, accessing drugs, alcohol, and cigarettes provided more affirming street credit than my being attacked by free-range vicious neighbourhood dogs while I was delivering papers. Moreover, my providing community peers with drugs, alcohol, and cigarettes gained through my illegal activities also provided surrogate forms of "respect" in terms of my being a "supplier" to other neighbourhood youth. Perhaps, however, most notably, having my (illegal) handguns in each palm reinforced my credibility as a "power broker" to mitigate my experiences of exclusion.

Notwithstanding such "successes" in my attempts to gain respect and empowerment, I never uttered a word to people in authority (such as parents, teachers, or members of law enforcement – consider that as a young child I was conditioned to seek the police if I ever needed help). Furthermore, once I entered my youth gang peer relationships, matters of codes of silence became increasingly pronounced for me, to never "rat out" my community peers or gang "colleagues," because ultimately "they had my back" far beyond anyone in "mainstream society," including my parents, my schoolteachers, and most certainly police.

I secured my first (illegal) handguns around the age of fourteen. I used my "metal friends" to harm people and/or to gain a sense of "respect" (if not stimulate fear and intimidation). Honour and loyalty were given to my guns – and truth was only to me, myself, and I. However, honour and loyalty were eventually expanded to some of my peer (gang) co-members of the C – *Bloods Crew* with whom I associated through my teenage years. My "snakes and ladders" adolescent development involved a plethora of "conflict with the law" scenarios involving me and my criminal gang behaviours that would follows. Within such contexts, no one, from my vantage point, could ever be trusted. If I could not trust my own parents, who was anyone else? Lies became the basis for existence, and maintaining codes of silence was the core method of ensuring self-preservation and credibility at the street level. The less said, the more power.

Hence I started off my life as a child troubled and rocked by adverse social, racist, and economic forces. I then tried to resist such forces through teenage gang-involved relationships and activities. Yet, a mere twenty-five years later, I was recognized as an award-winning university professor and a court-certified, judicially qualified forensic assessment expert witness in matters of street gang analysis, urban street language (psycho-social linguistics), and the code of silence manifested amongst criminal youth gang members. Notwithstanding my expert roles within the courts of Ontario as an academic-based, so-called expert witness, however, the disparity between how the justice system values the lived experiences of the manifestations of codes of Silence with a criminal street gang societal subculture versus pedagogically informed "authoritative/expert" perspectives became resoundingly pronounced for me.

Within such disparities, I eventually asked myself, What do loyalty, honour, and trust mean at this point in my life? Where does the code of silence begin and end within society as a "legitimate" phenomenon? Perhaps an even more intriguing question is, What defines whether or not a code of silence is criminal? Spending my last twenty years as an instructor and professor in post-secondary education in the province of Ontario, I can sadly state that I have witnessed a plethora of cover-ups of adverse social phenomena such as sexual harassment, sexual discrimination, administrative bullying, and harassment, disability, and racial discrimination, as well as other horrifying adverse acts and behaviours within the "hallowed halls of academia." Moreover, as a Doctor of Psycho-Social Clinical Practice, I have also provided clinical intervention to self-confessed "dirty cops" during which I found that the hypocrisy of demonizing the engagement of codes of silence by so-called criminal street gang members paled in comparison to the pervasiveness of codes of silence within "blue walls of silence" amongst the police officers I treated in my clinical health-care practice. In this chapter I suggest that criminalized codes of silence exist where resources and societal influence are absent, but codes of silence amongst criminalized street gang members are no more dysfunctional than those in supposed legitimate and/or respected societal structures such as university and/or police institutions. Further, I suggest that codes of silence are simply necessary parameters of survival for any member of a social group seeking to secure their sense of functional identity within that group. Such codes are a fundamental factor in human nature and codes of silence should not themselves be criminalized. Rather the underlying negative actions that such codes seek to cover need to be addressed. Referring to codes of silence in referencing criminalized youth gang members and not referencing such codes within post-secondary academic institutions and/or police conduct in similar ways seems to be a significant double-standard in treating deleterious behaviour differently on the basis of whether such behaviour occurs in "illegitimate" or "legitimate" social groups.

Code of Silence Defined

Codes of silence have been broadly defined as unwritten, unspoken, and/or implicit understandings/agreements between individuals and/or groups to withhold information from authorities (Dunham and Alpert 2015) or to remain a bystander rather than speak out as a witness (Rothwell and Baldwin 2007; Syversten, Flanagan, and Stout 2009). Such manifestations have also been present in arrangements where certain subgroup members (regardless of their place in a hierarchy) wish to circumvent or be camouflaged within situations where there are oversight structures/institutional hierarchies (Westmarland,2005). For example, Kelner (1970) explored the pervasiveness of codes of silence amongst practising doctors. Citing a Boston University Law Medical Research Institute survey, it was reported that from 214 doctors surveyed, 31 per cent of specialists and 27 per cent of general practitioners expressed a willingness to appear in court as expert witnesses for patients who underwent surgical procedures to remove a diseased kidney whereby the wrong kidney was removed by mistake. Despite an egregious error committed by a hypothetical surgeon, amongst these doctors there was a desire to maintain silence on the potential malpractice of their fellow medical practitioners.

Pervasiveness and Sub-dimensions of Codes of Silence within Society

Based on the code of silence definition and example discussed above, codes of silence within socio-subcultural groups can be seen and/or understood along four dimensions: (1) code of silence as formal versus informal construct; (2) code of silence as micro- versus macro-level phenomenon; (3) code of silence as implicit versus explicit manifestation; and (4) code of silence as criminal versus non-criminal element. In conceptualizing each dimension there are two important points to consider. One, each continuum is not mutually exclusive from another, and each continuum should not be viewed as static but may allow for fluidity in each parameter as society adapts and changes within socio-cultural-political terminology, language, and so on. Finally, each dimension illustrates the pervasiveness of the code of silence throughout various aspects, professions, and cultural norms throughout society.

THE CODE OF SILENCE AS A FORMAL VERSUS INFORMAL CONSTRUCT

Examples of formal structures of a code of silence can be seen within organized crime arrangements such as the omertà within mafia or similar criminal organizations (Raab 2016). The omertà has "been traced back to the 16th century of opposition to Spanish rule.... [It] stipulates that even if one is convicted of a crime he has not committed, he is supposed to serve the sentence without giving the police any information about the real criminal, even if that criminal has nothing to do with the Mafia himself" (Gutierrez and McLaren 2012, 310). Simply stated, such formal norms or mores are created, monitored, and enforced within such organizations in the contexts of accepted formal hierarchies and structures.

More informal manifestations of a code of silence can be found within North American hip-hop culture. For example, as identified by a United States Department of Justice report (USDOJ 2009) as a result of a DVD titled "Stop Fuckin' Snitching," much attention and antagonism within the socio-subcultural hip-hop community was directed to group members who might consider cooperating or who actively cooperated with police. In Baltimore, Philadelphia, and other major American cities, "Stop Snitching" T-shirts were worn and encouraged to be worn by many influential hip-hop celebrities (Woldoff and Weiss 2010). The purpose in wearing such T-shirts was reportedly focused on discouraging dialogue and cooperation with police. While many hip-hop artists perpetuated this idea, their actual motives in promoting such anti-authority or anti-institution practice(s) are unclear. Perhaps they were not to incite people to not cooperate with police but rather to simply generate income for the hip-hop artists through T-shirt sales, to perpetuate an overall anti-authority attitude for their own mischievous or self-indulgent purposes, or with overt criminal intent interest (Woldoff Weiss 2010). Whatever the case, hip-hop culture is a far less formally structured, cohesive subcultural grouping compared to more formal criminal arrangements such as organized crime arrangements (i.e., the Mafia).

THE CODE OF SILENCE AS A MICRO VS. MACRO-LEVEL PHENOMENON

Codes of silence are easily seen in micro, day-to-day interactions with one another. Examples could be a small group of childhood friends who agree not to tell others of a shared embarrassing event. Or men hiding extramarital affairs from their wives. Or the dystopian cult-classic book and film *Fight Club*, which yielded the epitaph "The first rule of Fight Club is don't talk about Fight Club" (Palahniuk 2005). Another example may come from North American tourism advertising and marketing: "What happens in Vegas, stays in Vegas" (Shankman 2013). Such codes of silence are more related to specific micro-oriented contexts and not necessarily institutionalized within more macro-level contexts.

The code of silence was also evident in a macro-level context, in the US Armed Forces' (now repealed) "Don't Ask Don't Tell" practice introduced by President Bill Clinton to address gay service men and women. More specifically the notion of "Don't Ask, Don't Tell" has become code for "business as usual" in the United States. In other words, so as long as "you" do not rock the boat, "I" will not ask "you" to be honest and "I" will not require "you" to be transparent about anything that may clash with the status quo. For example, bosses will not "ask" if you are a legal citizen, so as long as you "don't tell" them that you are undocumented. "It is these normative prescriptions that dictate and determine the relationships and practices of accountability in today's neoliberal capitalist state" (Gutierrez and McLaren 2012, 313). On an even broader level, a macro-level code of silence can be seen in the now defunct Operation TIPS program, which was implemented shortly after the terror attacks on the World Trade Centers to provide a platform for everyday citizens to report suspicious activities of their neighbours to authorities. The program was dismantled over concerns about civil liberties (Hentoff 2002). Both "Don't Ask, Don't Tell" and Operation TIPS were institutionalized programs, started on macro-level – vis-à-vis, national – scales, evidencing the wide degree to which codes of silence could be normalized.

THE CODE OF SILENCE AS AN IMPLICIT VS. EXPLICIT MANIFESTATION

The code of silence can be understood as implicit in context. For example, in lower-income urban Black communities, the code of silence and/or "no-snitching ethos" are more exaggerated and pronounced (Woldoff and Weiss 2010; Kubrin and Weitzer 2003), despite evidence that codes of silence are manifested outside of urban Black communities. For example, the now infamous sexual abuse scandal and cover-up at Penn State University (Gutierrez and McLaren 2012) or the well-documented and researched "Blue Wall of Silence" in and across police institutional arrangements (USDOJ 2009; Crank 2014; Rothwell and Baldwin 2007) both demonstrate implicit manifestations of codes of silence.

Explicit manifestations of codes of silence can be exemplified within non-disclosure agreements in which individuals sign documents stating that the signer may or may not discuss directly or indirectly with others in any content as bound within the context of such agreements. Another example of explicit manifestations of codes of silence can be found within the US Naval Academy, which requires midshipmen (students) to "monitor both their own behavior and the behavior of their peers through a system of self-regulation called the Honor Concept, because the Naval Academy is an organization that requires peers to monitor one another's behavior and because systems of social control that rely on self-regulation create the ethical dilemma of whether to betray the organization or one's peers" (Pershing 2003, 150).

THE CODE OF SILENCE AS A CRIMINAL VS. NON-CRIMINAL ELEMENT

A final important distinction regarding the code of silence pertains to the part of the concept of being a criminal versus non-criminal element. Examples of criminal conduct such as obstructing justice or a childcare worker who fails to disclose the abuse of a child (where an alleged abuser may be a fellow childcare worker) may demonstrate acceptable applications of the code of silence as dovetailing with criminal intent. Again, reconsidering non-disclosure agreements as discussed in the code of silence as a formal versus informal construct above, such agreements may likewise be viewed as a non-criminal example of a code of silence understanding between business prospects and/or macro-level government policies such as the United States Naval Academy Policy above, and the more widespread US military undertaking "Don't Ask, Don't Tell."

Differentiating Honour, Loyalty, and Codes of Silence

Despite evidence of codes of silence pervading nearly every realm and stratum of society, a distinction is made as to if such code of silence norms exists as by-products of honour and loyalty or if they are a concerted effort to undermine law enforcement through criminal conspiracy. These lines of distinction are drawn partially based on culture groups. In considering parts that differentiate one culture group from another, considerations of moral development arise, as culture plays a formative role in the development of morality (Graham et al. 2013). In psychology, moral foundations theory posits that morality consists of components similar to taste receptors. These "moral taste receptors" consist of care, fairness, loyalty, authority, and sanctity (Graham et al. 2018). Different cultures will develop different moral foundations and focus on and perceive each of these taste receptors differently. For instance, social-psychologist Jonathan Haidt has found variances in moral foundations between political liberals and conservatives in the United States (cf. Haidt 2012).

These differences of moral foundations that derive from differences in culture often serve as antecedents to social divisions and moral pronouncements and/or judgments. Dominant perceptions and attributions of acceptable versus non-acceptable standards of morality are generally forced upon marginalized communities by parties consistent with having dominant economic power and/or dominant political influence. In other words, a morally upright system of loyalty and/or honour such as a code of silence within a marginalized community could be criminalized if defined or thought to be so by those who wield the balance of economic and/or political control.

When reflections as noted above are prevalent in society, it is reasonable to surmise that subservient societal structures such as law enforcement and/or the justice system are empowered to make moral pronouncements on marginalized groups that take the form of oppression and/or criminalization. Simply because the powerless are socially, economically, and/or politically excluded from any meaningful or substantive considerations in such relevant moral discourses, such populations are subjected to rules, interpretations of law, and/or socially acceptable standards that may or may not be consistent with their own intrinsic (but not necessarily criminal or offensive) realities. However, when "suspicious actors" or those outside of police culture are not perceived to cooperate with law enforcement, a view of contempt by law enforcement may be developed (Asbury 2010), creating a false dichotomy that "if these communities do not cooperate, they are against us" and therefore part of a criminal element.

The Paradox of Community Desire and Distrust for Police Engagement

As Asbury (2010) noted, "Refusal to cooperate with police investigations should be viewed as neither ethically condemnable nor inexplicable, but rather as a natural extension of the innate human aspiration to be loyal" (1258). These loyalties are not predicated on a disposition to oppose law enforcement generally, but upon general distrust. This is clear in 2018 Gallup poll data that show 54 per cent of "fragile community residents' desire greater police presence and time within their community, 40 per cent desire the same level of police involvement, whereas only 5 per cent indicate a desire for lesser involvement (Center for Advancing Opportunity, 2019). Conversely, the same report found only 8 per cent of "fragile community" residents have "very positive" views of their local police force and 48 per cent hold "positive" views, compared to 36 per cent who hold "negative" views and 8 who hold "very negative" views of local police. The disparity between these communities' expressed desires and current perceptions of their local law enforcement illustrates this cultural and moral divide that underlines the boundary between honour and loyalty from so-called codes of silence.

Reflection

In my reflections of the code of silence from my insider experiences, (1) I maintained a pervasive "code of silence" as a child who grew up experiencing chronically abusive and debilitating treatment; (2) I then maintained a sustained "code of silence" as a youth involved in criminal street gang behaviour; (3) I was seemingly forced to maintain a "code of silence" after being falsely accused (with criminal allegations) as an adult while I was employed as an academic professional and health-care provider (or risk losing my job for being "guilty," despite the presumption of innocence); and (4), I witnessed/observed how a "code of silence" seemingly protected alleged transgressors of human rights in the halls of higher learning while self-reported victims of such reported transgressors seemed to fade into realities of pain, anguish, and/or desolation.

These reflections on honour, loyalty, and the code of silence raise several implications for future research from thug criminology perspectives. These authors highlight four implications for further enquiry. First, to offset the propensity of societal institutions to resort to moral judgments, engage with community stakeholders to develop solutions to redress social divisions and the moral conflict that arises from the marginalization of youth and members of these communities. Thug criminology approaches are ideal to explore solutions, as they rely upon the lived experience of individuals who have found themselves on "both sides of the tracks," regarding these issues. Insider thug criminology perspectives should help illuminate and provide context to these moral conflicts.

Second, future research should further examine accountability structures for codes of silence in other areas of society compared to alleged criminal street gang subcultures. As noted, codes of silence pervade nearly every corner of society. The primary difference between many aspects and dimensions of the codes of silence in other cultures and in so-called criminal subcultures is based upon social acceptance. Further, consistent standards and definitions should be applied to institutions and cultures that maintain codes of silence. Future research should more extensively examine the code of silence in more comparative contexts and determine the extent to which it differs from other manifestations, dimensions, and contexts outlined within this examination. Then benchmarks can be established on how to categorically redress codes of silence, so that objective and consistent standards can be applied. Perhaps then more effective progress could be made towards equity on issues between marginalized communities and prevailing institutions and structures.

Third, further research should examine moral conflict between law enforcement and communities. Given that Gallup data show a disparity between current felt levels of trust for local police and the desire for the police to be active in the community, it is imperative for future research to examine antecedents to this distrust, further exploring how relationships can be strengthened and nurtured between law enforcement and community. This apparent disparity is surprising and antithetical to the common perceptions of current social movements to reduce police presence within marginalized communities. Future research should more extensively explore and examine the disparity between desired presence and reported trust within current social movements against police brutality against minorities. It is clear that dominant society does not understand the needs of these communities. I hope future research can illuminate these outlined issues.

Fourth, future research should integrate the lived experience of thug criminologists to provide context and a lens by which to understand differing perspectives and nuance that arises from lived experience. Thug criminology perspectives can provide more context to current theoretical perspectives, paradigms, and applications. Mainstream dominant society has silenced insider viewpoints and the lived experience of experts for far too long. These perspectives and voices can provide more context and understanding to antecedents to social division within society. Finally, as they relate to codes of silence, thug criminologist insider perspectives can clarify the disparity in how codes of silence are perceived and addressed in the streets, as compared to the halls of academia and the rest of society as a whole.

NOTE

1 This chapter extensively draws on, and refers to, the direct experiences of this author as presented in the first person.

REFERENCES

Asbury, B. 2010. "Anti-Snitching Norms and Community Loyalty." *Oregon Law Review* 89 (4): 1257–312. https://doi.org/10.2139/ssrn.1491630.
Center for Advancing Opportunity. 2019. *The State of Opportunity in America: Understanding Barriers and Identifying Solutions*. Washington, DC: Thurgood Marshall College Fund. https://tacc.org/sites/default/files/documents/2018-07/gallup_the_state_of_opportunity.pdf.
Crank, J.P. 2014. *Understanding Police Culture*. New York: Routledge.
Dunham, R.G., and G.P. Alpert. 2015. *Critical Issues in Policing: Contemporary Readings*. Long Grove, IL: Waveland.
Graham, J., J. Haidt S. Koleva, M. Motyl, R. Iyer, S.P. Wojcik, and P.H. Ditto. 2013. "Moral Foundations Theory: The Pragmatic Validity of Moral Pluralism." In *Advances in Experimental Social Psychology*. Vol. 47, 55–130. Amsterdam: Academic Press.
Graham, J., J. Haidt M. Motyl, P. Meindl, C. Iskiwitch, and M. Mooijman. 2018. "Moral Foundations Theory." In *Atlas of Moral Psychology*, edited by K. Gray and J. Graham, 211. New York: Guilford Press.
Gutierrez, A.B., and P. McLaren. 2012. "To Be or Not To Be a Snitch or a Whistleblower: Years of Silence at Penn State." *Cultural Studies <—> Critical Methodologies* 12 (4): 309–16. https://doi.org/10.1177/1532708612446429.
Haidt, J. 2012. *The Righteous Mind: Why Good People Are Divided by Politics and Religion*. New York: Vintage.
Hentoff, N. 2002. "The Death of Operation TIPS." *Village Voice*, 17 December. http://www.villagevoice.com/news/the-death-of-operation-tips-6411861.
Kelner, J. 1970. "The Silent Doctors: The Conspiracy of Silence." *University of Richmond Law Review* 5 (1): 119–27.
Kubrin, C.E., and R. Weitzer. 2003. "Retaliatory Homicide: Concentrated Disadvantage and Neighborhood Crime." *Social Problems* 50 (2): 157–80. https://doi.org/10.1525/sp.2003.50.2.157.
Palahniuk, C. 2005. *Fight Club*. New York: W.W. Norton.
Pershing, J.L. 2003. "To Snitch or Not to Snitch? Applying the Concept of Neutralization Techniques to the Enforcement of Occupational Misconduct." *Sociological Perspectives* 46 (2): 149–78. https://doi.org/10.1525/sop.2003.46.2.149.
Raab, S. 2016. *Five Families: The Rise, Decline, and Resurgence of America's Most Powerful Mafia Empires*. New York: Macmillan.
Rothwell, G.R., and J.N. Baldwin. 2007. "Ethical Climate Theory, Whistle-blowing, and the Code of Silence in Police Agencies in the State of Georgia." *Journal of Business Ethics* 70 (4): 341–61. https://doi.org/10.1007/s10551-006-9114-5.
Shankman, S. 2013. "A Brief History of 'What Happens in Vegas Stays in Vegas.'" *Week*, 1 October. http://theweek.com/articles/459434/brief-history-what-happens-vegas-stays-vegas.
Syvertsen, A.K., C.A. Flanagan, and M.D. Stout. 2009. "Code of Silence: Students' Perceptions of School Climate and Willingness to Intervene in a Peer's Dangerous

Plan." *Journal of Educational Psychology* 101 (1): 219–32. https://doi.org/10.1037/a0013246.

US Department of Justice (USDOJ). 2009. *The Stop Snitching Phenomenon: Breaking the Code of Silence*. Washington DC: Office of Community-Oriented Policing Services (COPS).

Westmarland, L. 2005. "Police Ethics and Integrity: Breaking the Blue Code of Silence." *Policing and Society* 15 (2): 145–65. https://doi.org/10.1080/10439460500071721.

Woldoff, R.A., and K.G. Weiss. 2010. "Stop Snitchin': Exploring Definitions of the Snitch and Implications for Urban Black Communities." *Journal of Criminal Justice and Popular Culture* 17 (1): 184–223. https://www.researchgate.net/publication/228665131_Stop_Snitchin'_Exploring_Definitions_of_The_Snitch_and_Implications_for_Urban_Black_Communities/citation/download.

10 The Raid: State Violence and Traumatic Responses in the Lives of Black Women

MELISSA P. McLETCHIE

Introduction

It started with a loud bang, followed by a man's voice yelling, "Police!" I awoke feeling confused and afraid. I remember looking my partner in the eyes while holding our baby and saying, "I'm scared" and I meant it. It's probably the only time in my life I've been truly afraid. The fear where your breath catches in your throat and your heart feels as though it's beating through your chest. I felt like I was in a movie. "This can't really be happening," I thought to myself.

"Come down or we're coming up!" the voice yelled. I could hear windows being broken.

Slowly I made my way down the stairs towards the front door, my eyes taking in the destruction around me. As I stepped into the sunlight, I could see that the house was surrounded by black SUVs and police officers wearing helmets and bulletproof vests. Each held a large rifle. To my right my partner was face-down in the grass being handcuffed. Above me people on their balconies were watching the drama unfold. My emotions fluctuated between fear and shame.

I sat in the office of a police station in a city not my own, waiting for investigators to speak with me. My daughter was calm, but hungry and wet. About forty-five minutes later, three officers entered the room. They closed the door behind them and told me that upon their search of the home a firearm had been located. Because I was one of the only two adults in the house I would be charged with possession. I began to sob. I held my baby and just cried. One officer stepped forward and took my child from my arms, while another handcuffed me. I felt like my heart had been ripped out of my chest. Her innocent eyes looked back at me while I screamed her name and cried. I felt I had failed her. Why was this happening? I had done nothing wrong! What would happen to my child? Where were they taking her?

Finger-printed, photographed, shackled, and imprisoned, it was by far the lowest point of my life. I didn't know what to do or expect. One officer told me

I had the right to speak to an attorney and directed me to a list of lawyers beside a phone on the wall. There were close to forty names on the sheet. Which one should I choose? I decided to let fate decide. I closed my eyes, made a short prayer, and ran my index finger up and down the paper three times, and stopped on a name. The lawyer I spoke to was sympathetic to my situation and prepared me for my interrogation. He told me that the police wanted to speak with me to find out what I knew, and that I should tell them what I already told him. That's what I did.

After speaking with the officers, I was brought back to my cell. The bed was metal and cold, with no mattress. I began to cry. My breasts became so engorged with milk that I was in physical pain. I called out to the guards for help. A female officer came to my cell with a Styrofoam cup for me to empty my breastmilk into. I stared into the cup, crying and thinking about my baby. After the night in jail, I was released on my own recognizance and began the process of getting my child back. Three days later, after being emotionally tortured and degraded by a Children's Aid worker, I was finally reunited with my daughter.

Anyone who has been involved in a police raid or had a child in protective custody will know these are traumatic experiences. For years leading to the date it all began, I felt anxious. My anxiety moved into days of sobbing as I played out every moment of emotional and mental trauma I had experienced. Even as I write this eight years later, my heart beats faster and tears roll down my face. The emotions I grapple with every time I remember this experience have led me to explore how police raids and interactions with child welfare agencies serve as acts of violence contributing to memories of trauma in the lives of Black women. I hope that by using my own experience of "the raid" as the lens through which to look into this militarized practice, we can gain a better understanding of the unintended consequences that result.

Black Feminist Thought

It is hard to explore any phenomenon affecting Black women using traditional Eurocentric, masculinist bodies of knowledge, because they cannot grapple with the experiences and identities that govern Black women's lives. Black feminist theory (BFT) is unique and necessary here, because it "challenges the traditional body of knowledge about Black women and the ways it is produced and validated" (Richie 2012, 127). Constructed out of the need to not only identify the lived experiences of Black women and challenge dominant hegemonic European-guiding ideas of Black womanhood, BFT articulates the assumed knowledge of Black women and encourages the creation of new self-definitions that confirm a Black woman's standpoint (Collins 1989, 750).

I've found it difficult to find literature that speaks to the Black-Canadian woman's experience of state violence. There are several reasons this may be so, but the perspective I find most authentic argues that Black feminist perspectives are suppressed by more powerful groups because encouraging standpoints of oppressed groups can stimulate them to resist their oppression (Collins 1989, 749). In other words, Black feminist perspectives are empowering. It is precisely for this reason that I will use BFT in my exploration of the traumatic consequences of police raids and state-initiated child removal in the lives of Black women.

What Is Trauma?

Studies exploring trauma began with the works of Sigmund Freud and emerged from his works on hysteria. Trauma studies were closely linked to modernity, especially the new and dangerous machines of the Industrial Revolution and the rise and growth of the bourgeois family (Kaplan 2005, 25). Within early studies on "traumatic hysteria," clinicians hinted at the prolonged onset of symptoms of trauma, attributing this delay to the fact that "traumatic memories are not available to the patient in the way his commonplace ones are, but act 'as a kind of foreign body' in the psyche, 'an affective agent in the present even long after it first penetrated'" (26). As someone who has experienced a traumatic event, it took time to "forget" how frightening the experience was. However, it wasn't until my partner's recent arrest that I realized those memories were *not* "forgotten" or resolved because my knowledge of his arrest immediately triggered the exact feelings of eight years prior.

Post-traumatic stress disorder (PTSD) originated out of pressure from the US government for mental health experts to define the behaviour of Vietnam War veterans. The traditional definition of PTSD is "characterized by behaviours that fall into the symptom categories … with symptoms lasting at least one month" (Jenkins 2002, 33). The diagnosis of PTSD was "proposed to recognize that persistent psychological reactions to horrific events represented an illness requiring care and treatment" (Galatzer-Levy and Bryant 2013, 652), as opposed to ostracization or ridicule. The second version of the *Diagnostic and Statistical Manual of Mental Disorders* or *DSM-II* required four out of twelve symptoms from three criteria for PTSD diagnosis. It was amended in later versions to include the requirement of eight of nineteen symptoms, and expanded to include traumatic events outside of war or the Holocaust, such as "experiencing, witnessing, or being otherwise confronted with any event that involves actual or threatened physical harm to self or others" (653). Three criteria of the *DSM* are "experiencing symptoms such as intrusive thoughts or images of the event or 'flashbacks' when the individual feels as if he or she are back at the event (Galatzer-Levy and Bryant, 2013, 653). Avoidance and numbing symptoms include "efforts to avoid activities or situations associated with the traumatic event or diminished interest in activities overall," whereas arousal symptoms are characterized as "difficulty falling or staying asleep, irritability or outbursts" (653).

My partner's recent involvement with the criminal justice system triggered symptoms from each criterion. Upon hearing he had been arrested, I was mentally and emotionally transported back to 2012. I began having flashbacks of the police infiltrating the house, only this time it was happening at my current home. Whenever I went out, I visualized police cruisers racing down my street and blocking off my vehicle. I imagined every car that drove behind me was an undercover police officer and I hyperventilated so severely that I had to pull over. I became filled with so much fear at the thought of once again being arrested for a crime I had nothing to do with and losing my children that I packed up my daughters and brought them to my mother's home to keep them safe and with family should I be arrested again. I found it impossible to sleep because I experienced nightmares and persistent flashbacks of the initial "bang" that woke me up eight years ago. The trauma and fear of another raid became so real I went to stay at a friend's house, medicating myself to take brief naps on her couch for almost one week.

The Connection between Race and Trauma

To my knowledge, few scholars conduct research that looks at the way race-based discrimination encourages PTSD-like symptoms. When they examined the relationships between symptoms of trauma and race-based traumatic stress, Carter et al. administered the Race-Based Traumatic Stress Symptom Scale (RBTSSS) on 421 participants. The RSTSSS consists of a fifty-two-item questionnaire "with an open-ended format section, in which participants describe, in their own words, three memorable events of racism or racial discrimination they have experienced, and participants select the event that was the most memorable" (Carter, Kirkinis, and Johnson 2020, 12–13). This questionnaire helps to argue that trauma symptoms can result from experiences outside of those referenced in any version of the *DSM*. Some scholars have even argued that "the current definition of trauma in the *DSM-5* may be problematic, in that it limits the ability for people with other types of trauma to access appropriate diagnosis, medical care, and insurance reimbursement, and could also contribute to pathologizing misdiagnoses" (11).

Considering that Black people tend to score higher than other groups on PTSD scales, it highlights "the important role that racial and ethnic discrimination may play in the development of PTSD among these populations" (Carter, Kirkinis, and Johnson 2020, 12), and that interpersonal trauma are factors as significant in PTSD symptoms as life-event-related traumas such as natural disasters, car accidents, etc. (12). Under the *DSM-5*, my experience of being in a police raid along with the race-based stress I encountered while engaging with the Children's Aid Society would not classify as PTSD. However, the findings from the Carter study reveal that "race-based traumatic stress symptoms [are] significantly related to PTSD conceptualizations of trauma ... particularly dissociation, anxiety, depression, the mixed array of symptoms associated with trauma history, sleep disturbance, and sexual problems" (16). It would be beneficial for the American Psychiatric Association to expand its definition of PTSD to include experiences of racial discrimination.

Legacies of Trauma in the Lives of Black People

While everyone is vulnerable to trauma, the effects of traumatic events are not homogenous and are racially distinct. It wasn't until speaking with other Black women directly and indirectly affected by the criminal justice system through the arrest and incarceration of their male partners that I realized my trauma wasn't unique. Like me, these women experienced frequent anxiety, paranoia, and fear. Black women and our communities have been the victims of trauma for centuries, beginning with the theft of Africans from the continent, chattel slavery and Jim Crow laws, and contemporary apparatuses like the justice and child welfare systems that have persistently targeted and terrorized Black communities.

Some people would argue that Black people need to stop bringing slavery into our analysis of present-day phenomena, since Black folks have elevated socially, politically, and economically since the abolishment of chattel slavery. For these people, I will vehemently argue that "we cannot use the progress that a small, *exceptional* population of the [B]lack race has made to represent the progress of the entire race. This practice obfuscates the progress that has not yet been made" (214). It's important for us to address the fact that although Black communities have progressed socially and materially, psychological effects like generational trauma have yet to be resolved.

Law Enforcement Systems

When an all-white police tactical team intrudes on the homes of Black people, these encounters carry with them "rememories"[1] of strategies used during slavery and the Jim Crow and Civil Rights eras to dismantle and terrorize Black families. Koritha Mitchell explores how African American women routinely survived the physical attack and were left to face a forever-altered future (2017, 147). White vigilantes terrorized emancipated Africans in private spaces such as churches and schools, however "they often preferred invading their victims' households, and these intrusions lasted at times for hours and involved prolonged interaction and dialogue between assailants and victims" (148).

Contemporary law enforcement has its origins in slave patrols to keep enslaved Africans in their subordinated place. When police raid the homes of Black people, their actions are tied to a history of whites "invad[ing] Black households and forc[ing] occupants to perform their powerlessness – reveling in creating circumstances under which [B]lack fathers and husbands could not prevent the violence against their family members" (Mitchell 2017, 149). During the raid in 2012, I remember my partner yelling, "My family is here! My child is here!" as we descended the staircase to prevent the officers from enacting physical harm against us. Black folks have unresolved histories of interpersonal trauma connected to law enforcement. Contemporary issues of hyper-surveillance, police brutality, and murder exacerbate the fears and anxieties of Black people who come into contact with the police. In the past decades countless videos of Black folks being assaulted and/or killed by the police have gone viral, "for people of colour, frequent exposure to the shootings of [B]lack people can have long-term mental health effects" (Eaton 2019, 180). The terror that came over me during the raid stemmed from my understanding of how police officers interact with Black people, from what I had directly and indirectly seen.

Thinking back on the experience and the gaping hole in the literature that fails to deal with the consequences of police raids in the lives of Black women, I am encouraged by Black feminist scholars to tell my story. For it is through documenting these stories that Black women sharpen theoretical and praxes-based tools that contribute to Black women's studies– which is committed to disrupting, challenging, and radicalizing intellectual production by centring our voices, experiences, and standpoints (Lindsey 2015, 1).

Reproductive Control Systems

In addition to a history of state-sanctioned police violence, Black women have a strained relationship with systems of control that attack Black motherhood. Between 1939 and 1950 in the Jim Crow South, several state systems were put in place to restrict and eliminate the reproductive rights of Black women. These constraining and experimental systems were "developed within a framework of proper mothering that did not include poor Black women as ideal mothers" (144). Ironically enough, the perception of Black women as unfit mothers did not impede on their ability to be "mammies" or wet nurses to white women's children.

Planned Parenthood's "Negro Project" was established in 1939 with the goal of "providing birth control access for poor Blacks in the America South" (Edmonds-Cady 2017, 149). Although it was presented under the guise of offering obstetrical and infant care that would reduce infant mortality in Black communities, the Negro project was an elaborate state-supported plan to remove reproductive agency from Black women. The Negro Project infiltrated and influenced Black women to engage in birth control practices that were harmful to themselves and their children.

Voluntary and involuntary sterilization was another form of birth control promoted by Planned Parenthood, to control Black women's reproduction. If a woman requested sterilization "and her husband objected, regardless of the number of children she had, her petition would be denied" (Edmonds-Cady 2017, 158). Also, if a poor Black woman or girl had a baby out of wedlock, "she might be labeled feeble-minded and ordered to undergo forced sterilization" (158). And although Black peoples were being racially oppressed during this time, a Black man still had more rights than a Black woman. This highlights the significance of intersectionality to our understandings of the simultaneous discriminations (gender, race, class, etc.) experienced by Black women day-to-day. During the eugenics movement, sterilization was the popular choice in the "quest to eliminate or reduce births to those deemed undesirable" (158), and who at the time was more undesirable than Black folks?

Labelling has always been a long-standing strategy used to oppress Black women. Black women are constantly assaulted with negative images of mothering and womanhood that can initiate traumatic episodes. These practices negatively influence Black women's lives by acting as barriers to adequate health care due to our lack of trust in the system. Also the controlling images of Black women as "welfare mothers" limit our right to motherhood by labelling us as unnecessary and even dangerous to the values of the country. As Patricia Hill Collins (2000) writes, "Part of a generalized ideology of domination, stereotypical images of Black womanhood take on special meaning. Because the authority to define societal values is a major instrument of power, elite groups, in exercising power, manipulate ideas about Black womanhood" (69).

These stereotypes influence how state workers interact with Black women and can perpetuate experiences of interpersonal trauma. The first time I met with my Children's Aid worker after the raid I noticed right way she had a problem with me. She was a white woman who seemed to be in her late twenties or early thirties. Her demeanour was cold and arrogant, and she spoke down to me, accusing me of intentionally putting my child's life in danger by continuing to be in a relationship with her father knowing he had a criminal record. She made it clear that if I ever wanted to see my child again, I needed to "convince" *her* I had my daughter's best interests at heart and that I was a "fit mother." During my first interaction with her, she asked me if I did drugs and I told her "No, because I'm a Muslim." She laughed, telling me that being a Muslim meant nothing, given my current situation. She told me I had to "prove" I didn't use drugs by taking a urine test.

The officer who was brought in to assess the sample said that it was the ideal negative result, stating, "This is how everyone wants their test to look ... there isn't a trace of illegal substances in it." Yet this didn't satisfy the worker. She refused to release my child to me and demanded I get someone else to come into her office within two days with a police check or else my child would remain in custody. When I left her office, I was heartbroken. I felt as if the worker was judging and discriminating against me, but I had no one to complain to. After meeting with her I questioned myself as a mother. I felt physically sick and hopeless. I spent the rest of the day crying in my motel room, trying to figure out how to get my daughter back.

Child Welfare Systems

The fact that Black children are disproportionately represented in child welfare agencies in Canada and the United States (Clarke 2011; Gourdine 2019; Ontario Human Rights Commission 2018) has been a human rights issue for decades. However, the practice of removing Black children from their homes dates to as early as the eighteenth century. Legal principles served and protected white children while ignoring Black children and subjecting them to harsher treatment. In the United States early poor laws inherited from English colonies "provided that children from indigent parents be indentured as servants to others or be sent to the poor house" (889). Poor children were removed from their homes and forced to live and work in other people's homes or around their farms.

State agencies and private organizations like the Children's Aid Society were responsible for "taking" or "rescuing" these often immigrant children, sometimes without regard to parental rights or the best interest of the child (Jimenez 2006, 889). In the twentieth century, poor laws were reformed by "child savers" who sought more humanitarian solutions to child abuse and neglect, like foster care (890). The responsibility of parents for their children shifted, and greater emphasis was placed on the nurturing and development of the child as opposed to their labour value. However, these reformative practices did not extend to African American children, "as family life continued to be characterized by a struggle for economic survival" (890). Black children continued to be excluded from liberal reforms, and legal principles such as "parens patriae."[2] This legal contract came into effect in the 1960s and allowed the state to "step in and assert its rights over the disposition of the child by making the child a ward of the court, assigning temporary custody to biological or foster parents, pending further investigation" (891). While this legal contract protected many children from abuse and neglect, these rights still did not extend to African American children.

Instead of foster care, Black children "were sent to institutions for delinquent children as well as including adult prison when they needed care due to family breakdown or abandonment" (Jimenez 2006, 897). It wasn't until reformers concerned with the disproportionate number of Black children being sent to reformatories "lobbied to create a private program known as the Department of Child Placing for Negro Children" (897), that the rights of Black children started to be recognized. Since then, however, things have gone from bad to worse with child welfare agencies being weaponized against Black families. This state practice of control continues to have lasting effects on Black families in Canada and the United States.

In Canada, Black children continue to be disproportionately represented in protective care. In 2015, the Children's Aid Society (CAS) of Toronto examined their service data going back seven years and shared it with Black African-Caribbean Canadian stakeholders in community consultations across Toronto (Children's Aid Society 2015, 6). Their data show that in 2013 Black children and youth comprised 29 per cent of the ongoing 2084 family cases, and 31 per cent of the 1521 children and youth in care were Black (Addressing Disproportionality, Disparity and Discrimination in Child Welfare, 2015, 10). Black mothers were stereotyped as "angry Black women" unable to protect their children, and Black fathers as "dead-beat-dads" and "criminals" incapable of caring for their own children.

Poverty and class are once again key risk factors in the referral of Black families to CAS, and in the displacement of Black children and youth from their homes. Class biases in CAS delivery "occurs at various levels of the child welfare decision-making process (e.g., reporting, screening, investigation, substantiations, disposition, placement, and re-unification), which makes poor children and their families vulnerable to child welfare intervention" (Clarke 2011, 276). Given the state's history of removing Black children from their parents, we can see how being directly or indirectly connected to child welfare agencies can be a traumatic for Black women. The decision to move my daughters to my mother's home after the recent arrest of my partner stemmed from my fear of having them removed by the state. Research from Canada and the United States indicate that "child welfare workers with cultural biases are susceptible to discriminatory behaviour increasing the likelihood of removals" (Kokaliari, Roy, and Taylor 2019, 140). My traumatic reaction was triggered by the fear I would once again be judged and punished for staying with my partner by a white case worker who would evaluate my parenting abilities on the basis of their own parenting beliefs and stereotypes of Black people as dangerous and ill equipped to competently raise their children (140–1). In the study by Kokaliari et al. of African American community members who had been (or were) involved with child welfare services, "participants discussed the overwhelming trauma of removal. They repeatedly noted that child advocates rarely understood their compromised situations and failed to recognize the magnitude of trauma they experienced when their children were taken from them" (p. 143). In hindsight the likelihood of these things happening again was slim, but in the moment I kept thinking of how my previous involvement with CAS might complicate things, should I be arrested.

Conclusion

As a Black woman in an anti-Black society, my experiences of trauma do not fit neatly with the definitions of PTSD in medical literature like the *DSM*. My trauma is less related to life events and is triggered through interpersonal relations. When the house I was staying in was raided in 2012 and my daughter was captured by the Children's Aid Society, I knew that my race and social location wouldn't warrant me the same treatment and consideration it would a white middle-class woman in a similar situation, and that frightened me. Although I regained custody of my daughter and the charges against me were eventually stayed, the trauma of those encounters remains with me to this day. After my partner's recent arrest, I found myself in a state of paranoia, fear, hopelessness, and depression. I self-medicated with sleeping pills to calm my nerves and silence the terrorizing voices in my head that were telling me my house was about to be invaded by police and my children would be taken away forever.

Black families share a legacy of state-sanctioned violence against our communities. Law enforcement systems, reproductive systems, and child welfare systems in North America have weaponized their "rights" and privilege against Black people for decades, particularly Black women. As a Black woman it is important for me to use my experiences (regardless of how they may be perceived) to challenge narratives about Black womanhood, while encouraging and empowering other Black women to do the same.

NOTES

1 Toni Morrison's meditations on what she calls *rememory* clarify the ways in which memories become collective and how they exist even when not consciously remembered. I borrow the term as a way to think through how slavery's collective trauma, as experienced or imagined, informs a Black critical, political, and cultural conscience (Patterson 2020, 220).
2 Parens patriae is an English common law principle that established the state as the ultimate parent for children without parental oversight (Jimenez 2006, 890).

REFERENCES

Carter, R.T., K. Kirkinis, and V.E. Johnson. 2020. "Relationships between tTauma Symptoms and Race-Based Traumatic Stress." *Traumatology* 26 (1): 11–18. https://doi.org/10.1037/trm0000217.
Children's Aid Society of Toronto. 2015. "Addressing Disproportionality, Disparity and Discrimination in Child Welfare." https://www.torontocas.ca/sites/torontocas/files/baccc-final-website-posting.pdf

Clarke, J. 2011. "The Challenges of Child Welfare Involvement for Afro-Caribbean Families in Toronto." *Children and Youth Services Review* 33 (2): 274–83. https://doi.org/10.1016/j.childyouth.2010.09.010.

Collins, P.H. 1989. "The Social Construction of Black Feminist Thought." *Signs: Journal of Women in Culture and Society*, 14 (4): 745–73. https://doi.org/10.1086/494543.

Eaton, K. 2019. "'Lay Down Body, Lay Down': Mitigating Transgenerational Trauma through Spirituality in Jewell Parker Rhode's Magic City." In *Art from Trauma: Genocide and Healing beyond Rwanda*, edited by R.B. Gilmore and G. Herndon, 179–97). Lincoln, NB: University of Nebraska Press.

Edmonds-Cady, C. 2017. "A Right to Motherhood? Race, Class, and Reproductive Services in the Jim Crow South." *Journal of Sociology & Social Welfare* 44 (4): art. 8. https://scholarworks.wmich.edu/jssw/vol44/iss4/8/.

Galatzer-Levy, I.R., R.A. Bryant. 2013. "636,120 Ways to Have Posttraumatic Stress Disorder." *Perspectives on Psychological Science* 8 (6): 651–62. https://doi.org/10.1177/1745691613504115.

Gourdine, R.M. 2019. "We Treat Everybody the Same: Race Equity in Child Welfare." *Social Work in Public Health* 34 (1): 75–85. https://doi.org/10.1080/19371918.2018.1562400.

Jenkins, E.J. (2002). "Black Women and Community Violence: Trauma, Grief, and Coping." *Women & Therapy* 25 (3–4): 29–44. https://doi.org/10.1300/J015v25n03_03.

Jimenez, J. 2006. "The History of Child Protection in the African American Community: Implications for Current Child Welfare Policies." *Children and Youth Services Review* 28 (8): 888–905. https://doi.org/10.1016/j.childyouth.2005.10.004.

Kaplan, E.A. 2005. *Trauma Culture: The Politics of Terror and Loss in Media and Literature.* New Brunswick, NJ: Rutgers University Press.

Kokaliari, E.D., A.W. Roy, and J. Taylor. 2019. "African American Perspectives on Racial Disparities in Child Removals." *Child Abuse & Neglect* 90: 139–48. https://doi.org/10.1016/j.chiabu.2018.12.023.

Lindsey, T.B. 2015. "A Love Letter to Black Feminism." *Black Scholar* 45 (4): 1–6. https://doi.org/10.1080/00064246.2015.1080911.

Mitchell, K. 2017. *The Black Mother/Wife.* Vol. 1. Champagne: University of Illinois Press. https://doi.org/10.5406/illinois/9780252036491.003.0006.

Ontario Human Rights Commission. 2018, February. *Interrupted Childhoods: Over-representation of Indigenous and Black Children in Ontario Child Welfare.* https://www3.ohrc.on.ca/sites/default/files/Interrupted%20childhoods_Over-representation%20of%20Indigenous%20and%20Black%20children%20in%20Ontario%20child%20welfare_accessible.pdf.

Patterson, R.J. 2020. "Black Lives Matter, Except When They Don't: Why Slavery's Psychic Hold Matters." In *The Psychic Hold of Slavery*, edited by S.D. Colbert, R.J. Patterson, and A. Levy-Hussen, 212–20. New Brunswick, NJ: Rutgers University Press.

Richie, B. 2012. *Arrested Justice: Black Women, Violence, and America's Prison Nation.* New York: New York University Press.

11A Letter from the Streetz: Growing Up in the Gutter

TURK

When you grow up in a place like Regent Park in the heart of downtown Toronto, you already have the odds against you the day you were born. Every day after that is an uphill battle for you and your family as well as your neighbours and community. This however doesn't by any means give you an excuse to quit, or an excuse to cause destruction to the community although it is exactly what happens in many cases. It starts with small things like wanting a pair of shoes or something as essential as just wanting to fill your stomach with a meal. Other pressures can be things like rent and bills that you see your parents struggling with on a daily basis. I have seen twelve-year-old children resort to selling cocaine with hopes to help their parents pay the rent. This of course didn't end like that, the outcome being their parents spending the money they didn't have on lawyers to bail him out of jail. Making the decision to enter the street life is a million times easier than making the decision to exit the street life.

My personal story goes just like the above paragraph in too many ways. Coming out of our building in the morning time there wasn't much positive influence to look up to. Our environment seems set up as a dumping ground or wasteland metres away from the super-rich. Instead we were greeted by the gangsters and local drug dealers who would to a certain extent look out for us, give us a couple bucks here and there. They would also try to teach us how not to get caught by the police while making money and surviving at the same time. When you look around you and you see all of your friends, all of your peers, all of your classmates slowly one by one choosing this option it begins to feel normal, like this is how life works in this environment. Once it does start to feel normal, that's when the rest is downhill. Choices get worse and your crimes escalate as well as your need to survive because you're involved in a game with everybody from regular people to professional hustlers to known killers. You're also left with a choice of becoming the sheep or the lion. My decision was easy from day one. I decided I would never be the sheep and I would die a lion long before ever considering becoming a sheep or a lamb.

That decision has cost me almost eight years of my freedom from my adult life. But it possibly has kept me alive to do what I'm doing today. These are years that I can and never will get back due to choices I made, which in my case for the most part was protecting my life with a weapon by any means necessary. This is the same thing that police officers are trained and paid to do in our environment, which is to protect their life with a weapon by any means necessary if they are threatened or their life is in danger. The only difference with us is we are not registered firearm owners because we didn't know that this was an option so we just simply wanted to live and not to die. But what happens when those who are supposed to protect us, hurt us instead? The Us vs Them concept comes into play, as people in these communities are targeted and lives are ruined, while on the other side a person's life gets rewarded and they advance farther in life or chosen career.

I have personally lost over fifty close friends that I grew up with. Not acquaintances, these were my real friends who I called my brothers. The ones who didn't lose their lives to bullets have lost their life to the other side of the gun and are now serving large sentences. Some may not live to see their release dates and some will be old men by the time they come home, even though they went in as teenagers and or as young men.

When you read the newspapers and the news stories it looks bad, and it looks like these are people who just wake up and decide to be bad people. However, that is the farthest thing from the truth possible. Most of these young men are our fathers, sons, brothers, uncles, friends, and community members just like everybody else. The only difference is we were born in positions where every day ahead of us was going to be a battle to survive and also a battle to stay free. The people who are supposed to protect the neighbourhood, which are the police, wake up in the morning with goals to come into our community and lock us up. I'm not saying all police do this but I am definitely saying the police that were assigned to Regent Park in the years where I was active definitely had those goals on their agenda on a daily basis. I have personally seen people set up by the police, they have had drugs planted on them. I have seen people get beaten up by the police and I have seen a man get shot by the police. Again feeding into this Us vs Them mentality and forcing the community into a corner it doesn't know a way out of. The countless stories from friends and communities, things that we are able to see now due to the internet and cameras being introduced make it clear that there has to be a change in the way policing is done in Toronto. As well as the rest of North America, change with the environment is also desperately needed in order to have even a little chance of positive progress and growth. The more they lock us up the worse it will make us, because jails are gladiator camps, and if we didn't go in a gladiator you can bet your last dollar we will come out a gladiator. I will end this by breaking everything down into one sentence the best I can: "If the seeds aren't growing into prosperity, you need to change the soil."

11B Letter from the Streetz: Don't Interrupt Me

TG

As professionals we are guided by principles, morals, and ethics, especially in those institutions and systems we hold by the highest standards (i.e. health, judice, city council, police services, academics, etc.). They are asked to swear or affirm an oath to practise and act in a just and professional manner as to "do no harm" to those they serve. I ask then why within the realm of community and social service are these oaths, spoken or unspoken, not being upheld? We do more harm than good to our young people when self-proclaimed experts are at the helm of "new" programming that make false claims of violence prevention by addressing root causes. We continue to cause further damage by leaving older versions of these programs unchecked without evaluation. The destructive effects caused by their actions take years to undo and can actually lead to further violence within the community.

Take me, for example. I grew up in a neighbourhood that was deemed "at risk." The use of this language led to an oversaturation of programming led by those that believed we needed to be treated or fixed. "Fixed" implied that we were broken, "treated" implied we were sick or diseased; the cause of the increased violence that beset our community. Enter the "interrupters" with a "cure violence" approach to control the "contagion" and save the day. It's quite clear by the stats that they didn't stop the "virus." The majority of the programs did not look to address the roots of the problem but further victimized, racialized, and criminalized individuals, all while being validated by those that claimed to be able to relate. Unbeknownst to them, they had just singled us out for further discrimination and "treatment." We were "monitored" and "tracked" by over-zealous police, thrusted into poverty, "quarantined" from the rest of the world within social housing, diminished to nothing more than our postal codes. The perfect breeding ground for violence.

The introduction of former gang members into my life would have not interrupted any of this. They were institutionalized, which meant neither their logic nor loyalties could be trusted. They too were bounded by the invisible borders between blocks. Interruption was needed when at an early age training and conditioning to survive in a "war zone" began, when the fragmented health services left my mother's mental illness untreated and unrecognized simply because she couldn't afford it, when the breakdown in the household occurred which led to Children's Aid Services (another intervention) ripping us away from my parents. Interrupt the trauma I experienced at the hands of a foster parent, interrupt the injurious masculinity that taught men that the answer to all emotions was to hit, even if the target was a female, interrupt the day I tripped over a dead body near the park, interrupt the day my friend got shot in the face with a sawed off, interrupt the many incidents where bullets almost took my life, interrupt the conflict between communities that added members of my family to the ninety-six homicides of 2018.

You may doubt me, as I was not dragged before a judge, nor have I been shot or incarcerated. I am, though, without a doubt collateral damage of such an approach. The forced psychiatrist drugs treatments increased my trauma and left me numb. A time bomb waiting to explode. It wasn't I that needed to be fixed, but the systems that led me down a crooked path and many unfortunate others down a rabbit hole filled with trauma, racism, and injustice where "off with your head" is translated not only as a physical action but a mental one.

I'm not saying communities that live in constant crisis do not need assistance, nor am I saying that programming cannot work. I am simply saying programs need to be evaluated and backed by high-quality research to help us better understand the risks and benefits of applying and recommending such "treatment." There needs to be reminders that we should neither overestimate our capacity to heal others if we have not healed ourselves, nor underestimate our capacity to cause harm. We cannot continue to inject "placebos" into problems and put Band-Aids on bullet holes.

11C Letter from the Penitentiary: The Change in Me

ALEJANDRO VIVAR

The mattress I lay on was pancake-thin, the ceiling a maze of veiny cracks. The walls were thick concrete and cold to the touch. If a door hadn't been across from me, I would have been enveloped in walls. The nights – each indistinguishable from the last – left me alone with my thoughts. As they swirled faster and faster, they made me sick. I felt the millions of butterflies tickling the inside of my intestines as I turned the same question over and over. What would I do to him when I saw him? I was told that he just shy of twenty, six feet and over two hundred pounds – only a bit bigger than me. I didn't know much more than that. But in my excited mind, he was an ugly pimple-faced kid with greasy hair and a grin on his face that told me he didn't give a fuck.

My family hated him. "Did you find him yet?" "Do you know where he is?" they would ask. In the short time I had to be with them, he was valuable currency. Inquiries were launched at me like a volley of missiles – with little fear of damage.

I felt an enormous pressure to avenge the murder of my godson, Justice. Justice was a son to me. With his thick black hair pulled back, he dressed like me and used the same slang and hand gestures. He could have been anything he wanted – with his smile and laugh, the world was his. He loved girls and parties and was full of life. But then he was murdered. I remember listening to my family sob on the other end of a greasy prison pay phone as I was sat on a steel stool bolted to the ground, missing the funeral. As their bodies heaved over his stillness, I sat in concrete cell.

What would you do if you were about to be face-to-face with someone who stole the life of a member of your family, who murdered a piece of you with a knife in a drunken rage, plunging it once through his flesh and into his heart and then pulling out the serrated blade, throwing away his bottle of *Southern Comfort*, stumbling away as your family member lay in a patch of dirt in neighbourhood park, the darkness overtaking him as he bled to death?

It was my job, when I found him, to turn that smirk into a look of horror, to deflate his body into a pile of mush until he realized the pain and suffering he had inflicted on me and my family. The prescriptive code I'd lived by told me to take matters into my own hands. There was little room for protest; I was obliged. But deep inside, wedged past the swarm of butterflies, was the feeling that I didn't want to. Part of me silently prayed, in the quiet of my cell, that this would never happen.

It was only a matter of time until I would be face-to-face with him. I was three years "in" – going to court every two weeks. My life was reduced to a series of scheduled events, all of them out of my control. I would be summoned from my cell to court, and then returned. And then summoned once more. But as the machinery worked to wear me down through bureaucracy and rules, I learned other routines. I knew the courthouse was the place to bump into people from all of the jails in the city: Maplehurst, The Don, The East, and The West Detention Centres. This is where, with the right timing, past sins could, and often did, catch up. Despite the outward pretence of security, armed guards, steel, and concrete, the system was teeming with chaos. If you had a beef with someone, you could prepare beforehand. And I did. I had a four and a half inch shard of porcelain – blade that would rip through a pig's guts – hidden up my ass. It didn't set off the hand-held metal detectors at the courthouse as I was herded through. I also had a name: Cioppa. Last name, first name – it didn't matter. It was written all over the weapon I had concealed in my body.

Every time I landed in high court, I asked which jail Cioppa was in. I asked guys that I knew and I asked guys I didn't know. I asked guys with "Death Before Dishonour" tattoos on their necks and inked-in initials on the soft flesh of their hands. I asked guys in dark suits who were going through jury trials. I asked men in track suits on simple remands. Weeks before, I asked a pony-tailed South Asian with two missing front teeth. He whispered through the gap that Cioppa was in the Maplehurst, a jail west of the city. I was in the Toronto East Detention in Scarborough, Ontario. Our jails were about seventy-five kilometres apart, but our worlds would cross; our tangled lives were fated by the courts. Mine would be for sentencing on drug and gun-related offences and his for a bail hearing for the second degree murder of my godson.

Every two weeks, I went to court. The grinding routine had little effect. I knew that eventually Cioppa would be placed inside the same bullpen as me. The bullpen lived up to its name; men jostled around, nerves firing inside the steel and concrete-reinforced room. Some sat on the concrete benches along the wall, others stood. There was a single metal toilet in the bullpen that sounded like a rocket going off when it was flushed. An inch-and-a-half of Plexiglas wall lined with steel bars and a single door was the only way in and the only way out. I walked to the toilet, untied the makeshift belt made out of bed sheets, took off my shoes and placed them carefully on the metal toilet seat. I then sat down to push out the weapon I had wrapped in cellophane hidden in my darkest crevice. Every night, before I slept, I would sharpen the blade on a jailhouse floor. Soon, Cioppa and I would share this same room.

On the morning of 10 October 2010, I went up to court and was told that my sentencing would be delayed until the afternoon, giving my lawyers more time to negotiate. I was sent back into the bullpen, where two other inmates had arrived. I asked them what jail they were from. Maplehurst. I asked them if they knew an Italian kid, six-feet, 200 pounds, with glasses. They did. "He's upstairs," said one. My body was prepared for battle, my muscles were hard as stone, my pupils dilated. I felt energy coursing through me. I felt I was on a drug and could see everything. I had eyes in the back of my head. I was light, I could glide and touch the ceiling. I was fast. I was a predator. In an instant, without any of the eight other men in the bullpen noticing, a flash of white porcelain could cut him down. I clenched the knife in my pocket, and began to pace.

The elevator that connects the dungeon to the upper courthouse has a six-by-six prisoner cage tucked into the back – the sardine can – and has to be opened by the two guards escorting a prisoner to court. When it lands in the dungeon, we hear the distant rattle of keys, the sound of metal on metal, and then a click and a barred door sliding open. And then the footsteps. The guard will holler to other dungeon staff who it is returning. "Prisoner Cioppa back from bail court" and then another guard will say "Throw him in cage two." The footsteps got closer because that was the cage I was in. This was it. My heart pounded. I put my back against the wall and slowly pulled out the blade from my pocket. I held it behind my back, squeezing like a stress ball. My grip slipped, palms wet with sweat. But I held it tight and clenched my forearms. The world continue to unfold moments, unaware of what would soon happen. No one knew, except for me and God.

I came from a world where stabbing a person was nothing. I was used to violence – a language I could understand. I have survived shootouts, been stabbed, and accepted it as a part of my life. But when Cioppa approached and was about to be placed inside the cage with me, he was only a boy. He wasn't the monster I pictured, nothing like the man I had killed over and over again in my mind. He was a child. He had parents. And he didn't have the look that told me he didn't give a fuck. He was scared, an oversized boy with big glasses and a suit that draped over him as only a father's could. When I looked at him, I saw my nineteen-year-old self. I saw a boy who had made a horrible choice and that my godson, whom I loved with ferocity, was the victim. But now, with the knife in my hand, the fog of my rage burned away – leaving an unfamiliar feeling. I didn't want to kill him.

I would be taking life, destroying Cioppa's family, his parents. Just like we mourned over Justice, they too would see only dreams unfulfilled. I would be charged with murder and my life would be destroyed. I would come back to be a father to my children who needed me. And in my mind, I heard a quiet plea from Justice, not to do it. Replacing the anger, I felt sympathy. Before I made the choice to stand down, the lock turned and a guard shouted in the background that Cioppa had a lawyer visit. His hefty frame was escorted into an interview room and then led back up to court. The bullpen door was locked and I stood, the knife still in my hand. He was granted bail and walked out of the prisoner's box, the deflated body in an oversized suit, to his waiting mother and father.

Later that afternoon I was sent up to the courtroom. I pled guilty to weapon and drug-related offences and was sentenced to ten years and four months in a federal penitentiary. The bullpen was empty when I got back and the guard told me that the next wagon would arrive in about an hour. I took that time to think. I needed to convince myself that I was proud of the decision I had made. In the past, I dealt with all my problems through violence; I would act on impulse instead of reason. Maybe this, I thought, was the start of a new life for me. A month later, I would be in a federal prison, a place where they spoke my language fluently. It was the only way issues were resolved. With this new mentality, I wondered how I would survive.

11D Letter from the Streetz: Dear Hip Hop

MARCUS SINGLETON

Dear Hip Hop,

You have always been in my ear speaking to me and directing me toward having a *knowledge of self*, teaching me about my identity and how important it is for me to have self-awareness and strong self-esteem through countless rhymes and songs that I've listened to. I will never forget the time you were speaking to me through "The Message" by Grandmaster Flash and the Furious Five, as it was blasting out the boom box my moms bought me in '84; hanging out on my grandma's porch in my community (Englewood) on the South Side of Chicago. I was a young B-Boy trying to master all the moves I saw on movies like *Beat Street*, *Breakin'*, and *Wild Style*. Back then, I was too busy hunting for cardboard to practise my up rock and backspin with my friends to see how volatile my block and neighbourhood was until some older cats from outside my community came and snatched the life of a close friend. That's when I knew life was real and you can lose your life over nothing.

You were there, Hip Hop, when I realized that every step and decision I would make could be the difference between life or death. You were there when I wrote my first *real* rhyme entitled *the Steele*, lamenting and reflecting on the loss of my friend due to gun violence, and Black genocidal tendencies existing in my city, even back then. Like Common, I was a young prophet *"raised amongst Black Disciples and Black Stones who wasn't concerned about cardboards or mic cords."* To me, it seemed to be all about making money at the expense of your own people, which ultimately crumbled and destroyed strong Black communities on the South Side.

During the time I was growing up, the South Side of Chicago was primarily the home of the Black P Stone Rangers and Black Gangster Disciples, who were not gang members but members of two distinct organizations. If you weren't affiliated with either one, you were considered a *Neutron*. And as a Neutron, I learned how to navigate my neighbourhood and other communities that these organizations unofficially sectioned off, but we were well aware of. A few of the brothers I knew were Gangster Disciples, but the majority of the brothers I rotated with were Black Stones. These brothers would tell me that many of them were introduced to their specific organizations because of a family member or based on where they lived. Back in the day, you could identify Black Stones because they wore their hats to the left, and their colours were red, black, and yellow. Gangster Disciples wore their hats to the right, and their colours were black and (royal) blue. Depending on which neighbourhood you were in, you could lose your life if your hat was turned either to the left or the right. This is the world I grew up in. A world where you didn't think you would make it past your teens or even see your twenties, and if you did, it was only by the grace of God, and your God-given intuition, instincts, and discernment that helped you to survive. This was a world where you couldn't fake being something that you wasn't. Like my brother Blax once told me, "If you ain't solid, don't holla it." This meant that you had to know your *lit* (literature) and know yourself to be considered a member of these organizations, and if you didn't, you would catch a *violation* (get beaten up). Twenty to the eye no blinkin' which meant you take twenty punches to your eye and if you blink, the punches start over again from one until you reach twenty, so it was told.

Because of you, Hip Hop, I was able to navigate my world, discover who I was as a young Black man, and you gave me the tools and language to resist and fight against the marginalization and erasure of my people due to capitalist-colonial-white supremist ideals. Because of you, Hip Hop, I was introduced to artists and groups like *KRS-One, Rakim, Brand Nubians, Jungle Brothers, Poor Righteous Teachers, Public Enemy, X-Clan* and many more. These artists and groups provided me with those tools and language I needed to help me answer questions about my Blackness and Black identity as a young man growing up in Chicago, and they helped me navigate a so-called violent city where the invisible yet visible borders were constructed around gang culture and affiliations. I consider it a blessing that I grew up during a time when you thought consciousness and knowledge of self was popular. During the age of being self-aware and being proud to exhibit the highest form of *Black intellectualism and Black radicalism*. But it makes me sad to say, you're not the same anymore.

In 2009, at a Hip Hop Forum during a Nation of Islam event called "Saviour's Day," Wise Intelligent of the legendary group Poor Righteous Teachers said, "Hip Hop changing from positive to negative was not a consequence of history. It was nothing that just happened on its own. It had nothing to do with the changing of the times. It had nothin' to do with that. It had everything to do with the fact that there are people, in this particular society, who want to see us [Black people/youth] exactly where we are, and we cannot let that point elude us" (Wise Intelligent 2009).

What happened to you Hip Hop? Why did you switch from positive to negative? Why did you allow the powers that be to shift the paradigm from love, peace, unity, and having fun to money, power, respect, and bussin' uh gun? The music bearing your name today does not reflect the concern and care you once had for *the people. Your people.* You were once concerned about developing, strengthening, and changing your people's consciousness and mindset to make things better in our communities. Now consciousness or being critical thinkers is a bad word and an unpopular label/title for artists who claim to represent your name. I heard somebody say, "Rappers view consciousness as a bad word because materialism and the pursuit of money are the gods they worship now." Hip Hop, is this true? Is it true that you exchanged the well-being of the people, *your people*, for money and allowed capitalism to kill, steal, and destroy the conscious Hip Hop movement? Is it true that you went from *Fight the Power* to *We gon be alright?*

I interpret *"fighting" as* resistance against institutions and industries that want to see Black people/youth exactly where we are today, and I interpret *"we go be all right"* as settling for how things are and just hoping that things will change even if we don't. Are my interpretations and assessments correct? Am I off to think that you are content with leaving your people sleepwalking and passive? I learned from Nas on "N.Y. State of Mind," *"Sleep is the cousin to death."* For our people, to be asleep and not aware or conscious is leading to the premature death of young Black youth, and youth dying young is becoming normative. Do you think you played a part in how our youth view death? Do the music bearing your name today promote life and living or do it promote murder and death? I heard KRS-One ask, "What is the music of today producing?" Back in the day Conscious Hip Hop produced academics, educators, social workers, and community activists. What are you producing today, Hip Hop?

If you don't have an answer, let me bring you up to speed. The most popular forms of music bearing your name today are called Trap and Drill. Trap or The Trap is Atlanta slang for a place where people cook (produce) and sell drugs in the southern parts of the US. Drill music is a style of trap music that is dark and violent with nihilistic lyrics (Wikipedia). Both rap genres are created by Black youth. Both genres of rap fall under the umbrella of your name. The name of Hip Hop. Both are multi-million-dollar entities. Both entities that are invested and profiting off the message of Black death. According to an nbcchicago.com article entitled *Chicago Shootings, Homicides Are Up at Halfway Point of 2021: CPD Statistics*, "Chicago has seen at least 336 homicides for the first six months of the year, just two more than at this point in 2020 but 33 percent more than 2019's 252 homicides, according to an analysis by the Sun-Times. The city has recorded at least 1,892 shootings through June 28, [2021], the most recently available statistics, an increase of almost 12 percent compared to 2020s 1,692 and a 53 percent increase over 2019s 1,234 shootings during the same time."

I would argue that the statistics above are the result, or the fruit of the music being created in your name. Yes, it is true that gun violence existed during the conscious Hip Hop era, but I would argue that it is not to the extent that it is today. With that being said, my response to you, Hip Hop, is with the same energy and spirit of Malcolm X talking to Sam Cooke in the movie *One Night in Miami*, where Malcolm was saying, "I am trying to give [*you*] a wake-up call [Hip-Hip]! There is no more room for anyone! Not anyone! To be standing on the fence anymore! Our people are literally dying in the streets every day! Black people are dying! Every day! And a line must be drawn in the sand! A line that says, 'Either you stand on this side with us, or you stand over on that side against us!' [And] I believe in your potential too much [Hip Hop] to let you stay over on the other side."

As long as I am alive with air in my lungs, I will fight and continue to advocate for the potential I strongly believe you still have to lead our youth back in a positive direction. Back to the culture of critical consciousness and knowledge of self. I want you to know that I have personally drawn a line in the sand and taken the same vow as Jeru the Damja in the introduction of his song "Ya Playin' Ya Self." I'm not a pimp or a hustler but I am willing to stand alone like a man has to sometimes when he stands on what he believes. I am willing to save the lives of our youth, even if it means losing my own life. I learned this from you, Hip Hop.

I strongly believe the time has come for you to reclaim and live up to the meaning of your name. *Hip* means to know. *Hop* means to spring up and move into action. Your name means the more one becomes aware and conscious (Hip) the more one is moved and motivated to change things (Hop). It's time for you to return to your original mission of love, peace, unity, and having fun. People say things are supposed to evolve, but I always respond to that frail statement with the question, What are we evolving into? If we are evolving into an unconscious violent society where we are looking at each other as the enemy, what is our purpose for living?

After all these years, I still love and believe in you Hip Hop, because you gave me direction and guidance growing up. It's because of you that I realized that I was a descendent of Africa and that I wanted to be and educated Black man instead of becoming a gangster or a star. So now it's time for me to return the favour to you. I hope whoever reads this letter to you will join with me in the fight to transform our youth in Chicago, Detroit, Toronto, and beyond into community activists, agents for change, public intellectuals, and advocates for living and not dying. I am going to help (Black) youth rediscover the original purpose and mission you once stood for to change their communities for the better. I believe that you still have value, and I refuse to let the lessons I learned from you go and not passed on to the next generation. I refuse to let you go, Hip Hop. I still believe that you have the power to "play the resurrector, and give the dead some life."

In love, peace, unity, and having fun,\
Your brother,

marcus

PART FOUR

Decolonizing the "Gang Industry"

"The road to hell is paved with good intentions."

12 Crime as Disease Contagion and Control: The Public Health Perspective and Implications for Black and Other Ethnic Minority Communities

ANTHONY GUNTER

Introduction

Since the early 2000s the "growing problem" of gang-related violence in London and England has been extensively reported on in the news media (Alexander 2004; Sveinsson 2008; Gunter 2017; Williams 2015). Since 2010, government-led responses to gun and knife violence in England have tended to be formulated and implemented via a gang suppression and prevention lens (Cottrell-Boyce 2013; Smithson, Ralphs, and Williams 2013; Gunter 2017). In addition to national "Ending Gang and Youth Violence" programs (HM Government 2011, 2016) there are also a number of local anti-gang and youth violence initiatives. Examples include Manchester "Guns and Gangs" strategy (Manchester 2008), "Birmingham Reducing Gang Violence" (Birmingham City Council 2010), Waltham Forest Council's "Enough Is Enough" (LBWF 2012), and the London Crime Reduction Board's "Anti-Gangs Strategy" (MOPAC 2012).

Although there has been an upsurge in gang scholarship (cf. Pitts 2008; Densley 2013; Fraser 2013; Harding 2014) the evidential base for the existence of violent street gangs in Britain is "extremely threadbare and partial" (Hallsworth 2011; Williams 2015; Smithson and Ralphs 2016; Gunter 2017, 100;) much of it "distorted, London-centric and police-constructed" (Shute et al. 2012). Moreover, gang-related violent crime in England's urban centres has become synonymous with Black young males (Sveinsson 2008; Gunter 2010; Williams 2015) and can be within a longstanding police- and media-driven race and crime narrative about African-Caribbean muggers, rioters, and drug dealers that stretches back to the 1970s (Hall et al. 1978; Gilroy 1982; Keith 1993; Murji 1999).

However, in spite of this decade-long policy and law enforcement fixation on gang-related violent youth crime, according to official police statistics the problem of serious violence is reportedly getting worse. From October 2017 to year ending September 2018, recorded violent offences involving a knife or sharp instrument in England and Wales increased by 8 per cent to 39,818; and homicides increased by 14 per cent, from 649 to 739 offences (ONS 2019a). Also, the number of homicides with a knife or sharp instrument is at its highest since 1946; between April 2018 and year ending March 2018 there were 285 incidents (ONS 2019b).

In September 2018 and responding to the growing media-driven public concern about escalating violent crime in London, the mayor of London, Sadiq Khan, unveiled his plans for the creation of a new Violence Reduction Unit (LVRU). This new multi-agency partnership comprised professionals from health, law enforcement, and local government "to lead and deliver a long-term public health approach to tackling the causes of violent crime" (MOPAC, 2018). The LVRU's public health approach to violence prevention is based on the same model adopted by Police Scotland when it established the Scottish VRU in 2005 (SVRU 2019).

The political appeal of the public health approach to violence prevention is not limited to Scotland and London. In October 2018, Home Secretary Sajid Javid also announced new measures to address violent crime in the United Kingdom. This new package of announcements to be carried forward by the Conservative government included an additional £200 million early intervention fund aimed at ten- to fourteen-year-olds, an independent review of drug misuse, and consultation on new legal duty to underpin a "public health" approach to tackling serious violence. This last proposal would result in teachers, health professionals, police officers, and local government officers having a new legal duty to take action and prevent violent crime (HM Government 2018).

The public health perspective – which emerged in the United States more than forty years ago (Dahlberg and Mercy 2009) – views violence as a contagious disease that is preventable. Moreover, this approach uses epidemiologic methodologies to propose treatments and interventions by determining the different types of violence that exist, how they are transmitted, who is infected and risk and protective factors (IOM and NRC 2013). Drawing extensively on the US experience of the public health approach to violence during the past forty years, this chapter will discuss how this perspective – which has identified African Americans as the population group with the highest rates of interpersonal violence and homicide infection (Heckler 1985; CDC 1994, 2012) – has failed to acknowledge the inexorable link between concentrated poverty, inequality, and systemic racism to high levels of violent crime. Last, it will also look to highlight the potential implications of the problematic violence as disease model for many of the United Kingdom's already criminalized and over-policed Black and minority ethnic populations.

Public Health and Violence Prevention

As early as 1996, the Forty-Ninth World Health Assembly declared that violence was a major and growing public health problem globally and asked all member states to urgently address violence within their own borders. The assembly also requested that the World Health Organization set up public health activities to deal with the problem (Krug et al., 2002). The public health approach to violence prevention was developed in the United States and garnered increasing national recognition and acceptance from the late 1970s onwards (Mercy et al. 1993; Dahlberg and Mercy 2009). Published in 1979, the *Surgeon General's Report on Health Promotion and Disease Prevention* noted that many life-threatening and communicable diseases had almost been eradicated. In contrast, three-quarters of all deaths in the country were caused by degenerative diseases exacerbated by poor lifestyle choices. The report asserted that improving the health of the American people requires a commitment to prevent disease and promote health (USDHEW 1979). Violence is touched upon only briefly and forms part of a more significant discussion about the harmful consequences of stress, with the control of stress being identified as one of the 5five types of behaviour that affect health and are targets for health promotion programs (USDHEW 1979). By 1980, the US Public Health Service in its *Promoting Health/Preventing Disease* publication had established broad national goals for the prevention and control of fifteen health priority areas, one of which was the control of stress and violent behaviour (USDHHS 1980).

By the 1990s, this new public health vision became more focused upon identifying risk and protective factors (Kellerman et al. 1993; Bailey et al. 1997; Tjaden and Thoennes 2000) and with the aid of US national government support, the implementation and evaluation of violence prevention programs within schools and communities (USDHHS 1993, 2001). This more ambitious national approach came about during a period of unprecedented levels of violent crime, suicide, and homicide (ADAMHA 1989; Hammett et al. 1992; CDC 1994). During the 1980s nearly 220,000 people died and an additional 20 million suffered non-fatal physical injuries from violence (Mercy et al. 1993).

There is now a forty-year history of local, state, and federal government-supported public health initiatives in the United States aimed at understanding and preventing suicide, homicide, youth violence, sexual violence, physical child abuse, and domestic violence (Dahlberg and Mercy 2009). However, the public health approach is just one of several competing perspectives about the causes of violence and the potential solutions. Although the US Department of Health and Human Services (USDHHS) has pushed this health-focused agenda, other US government agencies, most notably those with criminal justice arena have pursued more punitive crime-control strategies (Tonry 1995; Garland 2001; Mauer 2004; Alexander 2012; Lerman and Weaver 2014) "focused primarily on deterrence through punishment and imprisonment" (Rosenberg and Mercy 1991, 17).

Tough Law and Order

The growing acceptance by the DHHS that violence could be addressed from a public health perspective in the 1980s and 1990s coincided with US domestic policy fixations of welfare reform and tough crime control (Garland 2001; Wacquant 2009; Alexander 2012). In 1979, the surgeon general declared that "further improvements in the health of the American people can and will be achieved," not through ever-increasing health-care expenditure, but "with better Federal, State, and local actions to foster more careful behaviour, and provide safer environments" (USDHEW 1979, 8–9). The streamlined role of the state envisioned by the surgeon general chimed with the broader neoliberal focus on cutting government spending; the notable exception was law-and-order expenditure.

During the past four decades, notwithstanding the USDHHS's recognition of violence as a major public health issue, tackling crime and violence in the United States has largely been considered the sole jurisdiction of law-makers, police, courts, and correctional agencies (Mercy and O'Carroll 1988; Gau and Brunson 2010; Haegerich and Dahlberg 2011; Potter and Rosky 2013). Nowhere is this more evident than in US illicit drug policy, which has focused largely on supply-side punitive measures – resulting in mass incarceration, police militarization, racial profiling, and criminalization/disenfranchisement of poor non-white communities (Lusane 1991; Tonry 1995; Small 2001; Chin 2002; Bobo and Thompson 2006; Alexander 2012; Block and Obioha 2012) – rather than demand-side harm-reduction strategies more in keeping with a public health model (Marlatt and Tapert 1993; Watters 1996; Tammi 2004; Eversman 2014).

In the United States, the public health perspective on violence prevention encompasses a broad range of harmful behaviours. Since the 1980s, the USDHHS funded many epidemiological research studies and preventive programs that have focused upon domestic violence, physical child abuse injuries and deaths, youth suicide, injury and deaths in the workplace, interpersonal violence and homicide within African American youth population, and adult homicide (ADAMHA 1989; Hammett et al. 1992; Kellerman et al. 1993; Bailey et al. 1997; CDC 1994; Tjaden and Thoennes 2000; USDHHS 2001). In comparison to the USDHHS approach, the criminal justice system has been concerned almost exclusively with tackling drug-related urban crime and violence. Although the academic study of gangs in the United States stretches back to the 1920s (Thrasher 1927), by the 1990s gangs had become synonymous with drug dealing within popular culture and was the reason put forward for the unprecedented proliferation of violent street gangs in poor Black and Latino neighbourhoods (Padilla 1992; Klein 1995; Curry 2001).

During this period, tackling street gangs came to be viewed as a national law-and-order priority and resulted in the creation of a large and rapidly expanding US gang industry comprising academics, law-enforcement professionals, and a plethora of anti-gang policies and programs (Greene and Pranis 2007). However, there is still no consensus, either among academic experts who study them or law-enforcement professionals who police them, on what a gang is or is not. The only common ground among this industry of experts is the fact that they have consistently been able to agree on only one thing: that "that there is no agreement" (Ball and Curry 1995; Esbensen et al. 2001; Klein and Maxon 2006; Greene and Pranis 2007, 9). In Barrows and Huff's (2009) review of federal and state gang policies, only two out of the fifty US states used the same gang definitions.

According to Shelden, Tracy, and Brown (2013), too many US gang researchers have confused the term "group" with the term "gang" and have proceeded to expanded the definition to the point where it becomes a catchall boundary that includes every group of youths who commit offences together. However, the boundary is "catchall" only in relation to African Americans and Latinos and of whom the term "gang" is largely synonymous. In contrast, white ethnic law-breaking groups – like biker gangs, skinheads, "stoners," organized crime cartels, or even college fraternities (see Sanday 1990; Spergel 1995; Venkatesh 2003) – are generally excluded from the research literature and popular discourses about gangs. Moreover, there is no available empirical evidence to support the commonly held view – which has guided US criminal justice policy for the past thirty years – that gangs cause violent crime (Katz and Jackson-Jacobs 2004; Sullivan 2006).

Inequality: Linking Violence and Health (and Racism)

Rather than viewing violence as a contagious disease that disproportionately infects specific population groups, there is a compelling body of international research evidence linking high levels of violent crime and homicides with social and economic inequality (Cronin 1991; Daly, Wilson, and Vasdev 2001; Fajnzylber, Lederman, and Loayza 2002; Neapolitan 1999; Wilkinson 2004). Moreover, what is most significant is that the greater the scale of inequality – income differentials between rich and poor – within a society, the higher are its rates of violence and murder. Societies that are more unequal are most likely to not just suffer from higher rates of violent crime, but will also be characterized by concentrated poverty, poor housing, low levels of social capital, racial/ethnic and class-based exclusion (Krivo and Peterson 1996; Parker and Pruitt 2000; Kubrin and Weitzer 2003; Strom and MacDonald 2007).

During the 1980s, the United States experienced alarming levels of violent crime and increasing levels of income inequality, whereby the average rate of poverty was 17 per cent higher than the average for the 1970s. The poverty rate for children and minority populations was even more startling; whereas the African American and Latino child poverty rates were 44 per cent and 38 per cent respectively, the poverty rate for white children was 16.2 per cent (Donziger 1996). In their study of poverty clustering and violent crime rates across 236 US cities, Stretesky, Schuck, and Hogan (2004) specifically found a direct relationship between homicide rates and high levels of poverty clustering. Similarly, MacDonald and Gover (2005) found that the unprecedented growth in youth homicides in US cities during the 1980s and 1990s was strongly linked to rising concentrated disadvantage brought about by urban restructuring and economic deprivation.

The multitude of stigmatized and impoverished urban neighbourhoods around the world are all typically depicted as hotbeds of violence, deprivation, crime, and social and cultural dysfunction (Davis 2006). However, the fabric of advanced urban marginality (Wacquant 2008) is not everywhere the same, and – as the US example amply illustrates – it is not even as simple as separating the Global South from the overdeveloped West. Reports of the gang violence crises affecting nations such as Brazil or South Africa and the news media portrayals of dramatic outbreaks of violence in France's suburbs illustrate that violent crime is not restricted to the world's poorer nations. Indeed, increasing outbreaks of violence and crime and the development of "lawless zones" and "no-go areas" is also occurring in the cities of rich Western nations with large disparities in wealth and opportunity. Between 2000 and 2012, homicide was the fourth leading cause of death for young adults aged ten to twenty-nine in every region, including high-income countries across the globe (WHO 2015). Societal inequality also has a direct causal relationship with a range of other social problems, including poor educational outcomes and alcohol/illicit-drug addiction, and is also a key determinant of ill health (Lynch et al. 2000; Wilkinson and Pickett 2009; Dorling 2013).

Since the early 1900s, the health of the American people had significantly improved to the point that by the early 1980s the average life expectancy had climbed to over seventy-five years, at least for white Americans. In contrast, and since official federal health records began, during this same period African Americans had persistently experienced much lower life expectancy and higher rates of ill health in comparison to the US population as a whole. From its analysis of mortality data between 1979 and 1981, the Task Force on Black and Minority Health found that six causes of death were responsible for more than 80 per cent of mortality observed among African Americans and other minority groups over the white majority population (Heckler 1985). The six leading causes of excess deaths in Black and minority communities, listed in alphabetical order, were cancer, cardiovascular disease and stroke, chemical dependency and cirrhosis, diabetes, homicides and accidents, and infant mortality. Significantly, homicide is firmly classed here as one of the six preventable diseases that result in excess deaths amongst African Americans and other minority groups.

Commissioned in 1984 by the secretary of state for health, the task force on Black and minority health was the first major health review of its kind, yet the fact that it was reporting to a key cabinet member in President Reagan's administration was also of particular significance. As the fortieth president of the United States, Reagan made good on his two major campaign trail themes/speeches about crime and welfare, both of which were presented in racially coded terms such as the "welfare queen," the "food stamp program" (Hancock 2004), and fighting "street crime." During his two terms in office, the FBI saw its anti-drug funding pot rise from under $10 million to nearly $200 million, while the drug enforcement agencies budget ballooned from $86 million to $1 billion (Alexander 2012). However, under his presidency the number of poor people in the country increased by 3 million, while the income of the top 1 per cent of earners increased by 135 per cent (O'Connor 1998).

Unsurprisingly, in its key recommendations the task force promotes the importance of health education programs undertaken within Black and minority communities targeting the six leading causes of excess deaths. There is no mention of public health spending in this 241-page document. Instead the report focuses on ways for the USDHHS "to exert leadership, influence and initiative to close the existing gap" (Heckler 1985, 3); evidently the onus is firmly on behavioural change by Black and other minority groups. Also, there is no acknowledgment of or discussion about the role and history of endemic racism in the United States – nor the disproportionate impact of Reagan's welfare reforms – on the persistent disparities in the burden of death and illness on African Americans and minorities.

Criminogenic BAME Communities

In the 1970s and 1980s race became synonymous in the United Kingdom with "crime" and "riots" and with Black British youth. The roots of Black, Asian, and Minority Ethnic (BAME) young people's ongoing criminalization can be traced back to the public anxieties and fears about the fact that since the 1950s, as the result of large numbers of "coloured" settlers, Britain was no longer the "white man's country" (Miles and Phizacklea 1984). By the 1970s the longstanding British preoccupation with the white working-class youth "problem" (Pearson 1983) had mutated, via the rearticulated lens of race/immigration and crime, into a moral panic about the inherent criminality of second-generation Black British youth. During the past forty years, BAME communities in the United Kingdom have been stigmatized by the news media and the forces of law and order as hotbeds of dysfunctionality and rampant criminality (Hall et al. 1978; Keith 1993; Kundnani 2014). Within this context, BAME populations, and in particular African Caribbean youth, have found their activities and behaviours on the streets and in other public settings scrutinized and violently targeted by the police.

The issue of BAME over-representation within every stage of the criminal justice system in England and Wales stretches back to the 1980s. However, concern about police racism and racial discrimination against BAME people can be traced back to the 1970s. Over the past four decades, research evidence has consistently highlighted that while BAME groups have been over-policed, they have also been under-protected; the police have generally failed to provide Black and Asian people with equal protection under the law (Bowling, Iyer, and Solanke 2015). Racial disparities in the use of stop-and-search by police has been a longstanding and contentious issue that has affected Britain's African Caribbean communities in particular. While the use of stop-and-search fell by 75 per cent between 2010/11 and 2016/17, Black people were still found to have been stopped and searched nearly nine times more often than white people, but Asian people were three times more likely to be stop-searched than whites (Shiner et al. 2018). Evidently, the ethnic penalties arising through stop-and-search and other police actions continues through to prosecution, conviction, and sentencing (Uhrig 2016; Lammy 2017).

Further evidence of the "ethnic penalty" is provided in the Institute of Race Relations" publication *Dying for Justice* (Athwal, Bourne, and Webber 2015), which reveals that at least 509 individuals from Black and minority backgrounds have died in suspicious circumstances while in state detention since 1991, with most deaths occurring in prison or police custody. According to the campaigning charity INQUEST, the disproportionate number of BAME deaths in custody have been due to lack of due care or excessive use of force, or as a result of fatal police shootings (INQUEST 2015).

Racialized police violence is not restricted to deaths in custody or fatal shootings. In May 2015, a national newspaper investigation uncovered the fact that more than 3,000 police officers, who were all still patrolling the streets at the time, were under investigation for alleged violent assault against members of the public. The Metropolitan and West Midlands Police forces accounted for the majority of these complaints, with BAME individuals representing more than 55 per cent of alleged victims of police brutality (Gallagher 2015). According to the London Campaign against Police and State Violence (LCAPSV), it is well known within BAME communities that "over 99% of complaints alleging racism are dismissed by the Met Police." However, the number of complaints that do become officially logged are "not representative of the actual level of police brutality. Such instances are regular occurrences … but are unreported and thus not recorded" (Kyerewaa 2015, 24).

While there is a wealth of research literature about police racism and stop-and-search, racial discrimination and BAME disproportionality in the criminal justice system post-arrest is less well evidenced. However, an analysis of management information data undertaken by the Ministry of Justice in 2016 found BAME disproportionality particularly pronounced in the following criminal justice system areas: being tried at Crown Court rather than magistrates' court, custodial remand and plea at Crown Court, custodial sentencing, and adjudications of prison discipline (Uhrig 2016). While BAME men and women make up just 14 per cent of the UK population, prison population data at 31 March 2018 showed that they represented 27 per cent of all prisoners.

Further analysis of prison population data by ethnicity, religion, and age reveals a diversity of experience of BAME disproportionality within the criminal justice system. There are 10,000 Black British individuals in prison, which represents 13 per cent of the total prison population and four times their number in the general population. Asian British people make up 8 per cent (6,691) of all prisoners, but 15 per cent of all prisoners in the United Kingdom self-identify as Muslims, compared with just 4 per cent in the general population (MoJ 2018). Between 2006 and 2016, the proportion of BAME young people, those aged eighteen and under, in prison rose from 25 per cent to just over 40 per cent (Lammy 2017); as of December 2018, half (51 per cent) of all male young offenders in the prison estate were from a BAME background (HMIP 2019).

Conclusion

According to the news-media, aided and corroborated by police crime statistics, London and other parts of urban England are in the midst of a violent crime epidemic, "reportedly" driven by street gangs engaged in post code wars and the illicit drug trade. As a response to the intense political and media criticism and calls for action, the mayor of London, Sadiq Khan, set up a Violence Reduction Unit (LVRU). Adopting a public health approach that treats violent crime as a disease that needs to be contained and then eradicated, before being prevented. The LVRU – which comprises professionals from health, education, police, and other criminal justice agencies – will largely focus on tackling serious youth violence and functions alongside tough law enforcement. The LVRU, just like the public health model that informs its thinking and practice, is race-neutral on the face of it, as it is concerned only with working to prevent violent youth crime. However, on closer inspection "race" is the elephant in the room, and this is before unpacking the contested and problematic crime-as-disease thesis.

The public health approach to violence prevention first gained acceptance and recognition in the United States in the 1980s, and by the late 1990s its sphere of influence had spread globally under the auspices of the World Health Organization. During the past forty years, public health initiatives in the United States have focused on understanding and preventing a broad range of harmful behaviours, including suicide, homicide, youth violence, sexual violence, physical child abuse, and domestic violence. However, while the Department of Health and Human Services has pursued its own public-health-focused violence-prevention agenda, tackling crime and violence in the United States has largely been considered the sole jurisdiction of the criminal justice system. As a consequence of the five-decade "war" on drugs and urban crime, criminal justice agencies have used punitive crime control strategies predicated on deterrence through punishment and imprisonment – rather than harm-reduction strategies more in keeping with a public health approach.

Evidently, the public health perspective on violence has yet to gain much traction within the criminal the justice system or mainstream criminology, even in the United States. The core premise of this model, of violence being a contagious disease that disproportionately infects specific population groups, is also very contentious, because there is a compelling body of research evidence linking high levels of violent crime and homicides with social and economic inequality. Those societies, whether in the poorer Global South or the over-developed West, that are more unequal will most likely suffer from higher rates of violent crime, concentrated poverty, poor housing, low levels of social capital, and racial/ethnic and class-based exclusion. The United States is a case in point: whereas the public health epidemiological approach has highlighted the fact that African Americans are most at risk from the contagious diseases of violent crime and homicide, this model fails to discuss the significant impact of concentrated poverty and systemic racism, or indeed propose solutions to tackle these macro structural issues.

When discussing the problem of violent crime, whether in the United States or the United Kingdom, it is almost impossible not to also address race and ethnicity. For more than four decades, Black-British and Muslim-Asian British youth and the communities they come from have been criminalized, scrutinized, and violently targeted by the police. BAME groups are over-represented at every stage of the criminal justice system, and this is played out against a longstanding backdrop of police racism around stop-and-search and the excessive use of force. The over-policing of BAME communities has been persistently justified on the basis that they are hotbeds of criminality and social dysfunction. In the 1970s, heavy-handed policing was required to deal with the mugging problem, and unfortunately this street crime narrative has continued until the present day. with the purported gang and knife-crime epidemic (Gunter 2017).

There are many fundamental questions that LVRU's violent-crime-as-disease perspective fails to address, not least its fixation on preventing youth violence and the centrality of tough law enforcement within its design. The public health perspective, as adopted by the LVRU, also fails to consider the macro structural determinants of violent crime and ill health, such as state racism and criminalization, and social and economic disadvantage. Instead of viewing all violence as social harms created by macro structural and psychosocial conditions, LVRU's police-driven approach can only further criminalize, target, and disproportionately punish BAME youth, but under the more neutral and "caring" banner of public health.

ACKNOWLEDGMENTS

I am grateful for feedback on earlier versions of this chapter from Coretta Phillips, Alpa Parmar, and Rod Earle.

REFERENCES

Alcohol, Drug Abuse, and Mental Health Administration (ADAMHA). 1989. *Report of the Secretary's Task Force on Youth Suicide*. Vol. 1. Washington, DC: ADAMHA. https://eric.ed.gov/?id=ED334501.

Alexander, C. 2004. "Imagining the Asian Gang: Ethnicity, Masculinity and Youth after 'the Riots.'" *Critical Social Policy* 24 (4): 526–49. https://doi.org/10.1177/0261018304046675.

Alexander, M. 2012. *The New Jim Crow: Mass Incarceration in the Age of Colorblindness*. New York: New Press.

Athwal, H., J. Bourne, and F. Webber. 2015. *Dying for Justice*. London: Institute of Race Relations. http://www.irr.org.uk/wp-content/uploads/2015/03/Dying_for_Justice_web.pdf.

Bailey, J.E., A.L. Kellermann G.W. Somes, J.G. Banton, F.P. Rivara, and N.P. Rushforth. 1997. "Risk Factors for Violent Death of Women in the Home." *Archives of Internal Medicine* 157 (7): 777–82. https://pubmed.ncbi.nlm.nih.gov/9125010/.

Ball, R.A., and G.D. Curry. 1995. "The Logic of Definition in Criminology: Purposes and Methods for Defining 'Gangs.'" *Criminology* 33 (2): 225–45. https://doi.org/10.1111/j.1745-9125.1995.tb01177.x.

Barrows, J., and C.R. Huff. 2009. "Gangs and Public Policy." *Criminology & Public Policy* 8 (4): 675–703. https://doi.org/10.1111/j.1745-9133.2009.00585.x.

Birmingham City Council. 2010. *Partnership Working to Tackle Gang Violence in Birmingham*. Birmingham, UK: Equalities and Human Resources Overview and Scrutiny Committee. https://www.birmingham.gov.uk/downloads/file/470/partnership_working_to_tackle_gang_violence_in_birmingham_scrutiny_report_april_2010.

Block, W.E., and V. Obioha. 2012. "War on Black Men: Arguments for the Legalization of Drugs." *Criminal Justice Ethics* 31 (2): 106–20. https://doi.org/10.1080/0731129X.2012.719671.

Bobo, L.D., and V. Thompson. 2006. "Unfair by Design: The War on Drugs, Race, and the Legitimacy of the Criminal Justice System." *Social Research* 73 (2): 445–72. https://doi.org/10.1353/sor.2006.0010.

Bowling B., S. Iyer, and I. Solanke. 2015. "Race, Law and the Police: Reflections on the Race Relations Act at 50." In *Justice, Resistance and Solidarity: Race and Policing in England and Wales*, edited by N. El-Enany and E. Bruce-Jones, 7–10. London: Runnymede.

Centers for Disease Control and Prevention (CDC). 1994. "Homicides among 15–19-Year-Old Males: United States, 1963–1991." CDC. https://www.cdc.gov/mmwr/PDF/wk/mm4340.pdf.
— 2012. "Youth Violence: Facts at a Glance." Atlanta: CDC, – Division of Violence Prevention, http://www.cdc.gov/ViolencePrevention/pdf/YV-DataSheet-a.pdf.
Chin, G.J. 2002. "Race, the War on Drugs, and the Collateral Consequences of Criminal Conviction." *Journal of Gender, Race & Justice* 6: 253–78. https://doi.org/10.2139/ssrn.390109.
Cottrell-Boyce, J. 2013. "*Ending Gang and Youth Violence*: A Critique." *Youth Justice* 13 (3): 193–206. https://doi.org/10.1177/1473225413505382.
Cronin, H. 1991. *The Ant and the Peacock* Cambridge: Cambridge University Press.
Curry, G.D. 2001. "The Proliferation of Gangs in the United States." In: *The Eurogang Paradox: Street Gangs and Youth Groups in the US and Europe*, edited by M. Klein, H.-J. Kerner, C. Maxson, and E. Weitekamp, 79–92. Boston: Kluwer/Plenum.
Dahlberg. L., and J. Mercy. 2009. "History of Violence as a Public Health Issue." *AMA Virtual Mentor* 11 (2): 167–72. https://doi.org/10.1001/virtualmentor.2009.11.2.mhst1-0902.
Daly, M., M. Wilson, and S. Vasdev. 2001. "Income Inequality and Homicide Rates in Canada and the United States." *Canadian Journal of Criminology* 43 (3): 219–36. https://doi.org/10.3138/cjcrim.43.2.219.
Davis, M. 2006. *Planet of Slums*. London: Verso.
Densley, J. 2013. *How Gangs Work: An Ethnography of Youth Violence*. London: Palgrave Macmillan.
Donziger, S.R. 1996. "Crime and Policy." In *The Real War on Crime: The Report of the National Criminal Justice Commission*, edited by S.R. Donziger, 1–44. New York: Harper Collins.
Dorling, D. 2013. *Unequal Health: The Scandal of Our Times*. Bristol, UK: Policy.
Esbensen, F.-A., L.T. Winfree, N. He, and T.J. Taylor. 2001. "Youth Gangs and Definitional Issues: When Is a Gang a Gang, and Why Does It Matter?" *Crime & Delinquency* 47 (1): 105–30. https://doi.org/10.1177/0011128701047001005.
Eversman, M.H. 2014. "'Trying to Find the Middle Ground': Drug Policy and Harm Reduction in Black Communities." *Race and Justice* 4 (1): 29–44. https://doi.org/10.1177/2153368713517395.
Fajnzylber, P., D. Lederman, and N. Loayza. 2002. "Inequality and Violent Crime." *Journal of Law and Economics* 45 (1): 1–40. https://doi.org/10.1086/338347.
Fraser, A. 2013. "Street Habitus: Gangs, Territorialism and Social Change in Glasgow." *Journal of Youth Studies* 16 (8): 970–85. https://doi.org/10.1080/13676261.2013.793791.
Gallagher, P. 2015. "Over 3,000 Police Officers Being Investigated for Alleged Assault – and Almost All of Them Are Still on the Beat." *Independent*, 2 May. http://www.independent.co.uk/news/uk/crime/over-3000-police-officers-being-investigated-for-alleged-assault-and-almost-all-of-them-are-still-on-10220091.html.

Garland, D. 2001. *The Culture of Control: Crime and Social Order in Contemporary Society.* Oxford: Oxford: Oxford University Press.

Gau, J.M., and R.K. Brunson. 2010. "Procedural Justice and Order Maintenance Policing: A Study of Inner-City Young Men's Perceptions of Police Legitimacy." *Justice Quarterly* 27 (2): 255–79. https://doi.org/10.1080/07418820902763889.

Gilroy, P. 1982. "The Myth of Black Criminality." In *The Socialist Register,* edited by Martin Eve and David Musson, 47–56. London: Merlin.

Greene, J., and K. Pranis. 2007. *Gang Wars: The Failure of Enforcement Tactics and the Need for Effective Public Safety Strategies.* Washington, DC: Justice Policy Institute. http://www.justicestrategies.org/sites/default/files/publications/Gang_Wars_Full_Report_2007.pdf.

Gunter, A. 2010. *Growing Up Bad: Black Youth, Road Culture and Badness in an East London Neighbourhood.* London: Tufnell.

– 2017. *Race, Gangs and Youth Violence: Policy, Prevention and Policing.* Bristol, UK: Policy.

Haegerich, T.M., and L.L. Dahlberg. 2011. "Violence as a Public Health Risk." *American Journal of Lifestyle Medicine* 5 (5): 392–406. https://doi.org/10.1177/1559827611409127.

Hall, S., C. Critcher, T. Jefferson, J. Clarke, and B. Roberts. 1978. *Policing the Crisis: Mugging, the State and Law and Order.* London: Macmillan.

Hallsworth, S. 2011. "Gangland Britain? Realities, Fantasies and Industry" In *Youth in Crisis? Gangs, Territoriality and Violence,* edited by B. Goldson, 183–97. London: Routledge.

Hammett, M., K.E. Powell, P.W. O'Carroll, P.W. O'Carroll, and S.T. Clanton. 1992. "Homicide Surveillance: United States, 1979–1988." *Morbility and Mortality Weekly Report,* 1–34. Atlanta, GA: Centers for Disease Control and Prevention. https://www.ncjrs.gov/pdffiles1/Digitization/149875NCJRS.pdf.

Hancock, A. 2004. *The Politics of Disgust: The Public Identity of the Welfare Queen.* New York: NYU Press.

Harding, S. 2014. *The Street Casino: Survival in Violent Street Gangs.* Bristol, UK: Policy.

Heckler, M.M. 1985. *Report of the Secretary's Task Force on Black and Minority Health.* Washington, DC: US Department of Health & Human Services. https://collections.nlm.nih.gov/catalog/nlm:nlmuid-8602912-mvset.

HM Government. 2011. *Ending Gang and Youth Violence: A Cross-Government Report i\Including Further Evidence and Good Practice Case Studies.* London: HM Government. https://www.gov.uk/government/uploads/system/uploads/attachment_data/file/97862/gang-violence-detailreport.pdf.

– 2016. *Ending Gang Violence and Exploitation.* London: HM Government. https://www.gov.uk/government/uploads/system/uploads/attachment_data/file/491699/Ending_gang_violence_and_Exploitation_FINAL.pdf.

- 2018. *Home Secretary Announces New Measures to Tackle Serious Violence*. London: Home Office. https://www.gov.uk/government/news/home-secretary-announces-new-measures-to-tackle-serious-violence.
HM Inspectorate of Prisons (HMIP). 2019. *Children in Custody 2017–18: An Analysis of 12–18-Year-Olds' Perceptions of Their Experiences in Secure Training Centres and Young Offender Institutions*. London: HMIP and Youth Justice Board (YJB): https://www.justiceinspectorates.gov.uk/hmiprisons/wp-content/uploads/sites/4/2019/01/6.5164_HMI_Children-in-Custody-2017-18_A4_v10_web.pdf.
INQUEST. 2015. *Deaths in Custody: Black and Minority Ethnic Deaths*. London: INQUEST.
Institute of Medicine (IOM) and National Research Council (NRC). 2013. *Contagion of Violence: Workshop Summary*. Washington, DC: National Academies.
Katz, J., and C. Jackson-Jacobs. 2004. "The Criminologists Gang." In *The Blackwell Companion to Criminology*, edited by C. Sumner, 91–124. Oxford: Blackwell.
Keith, M. 1993. *Race, Riots and Policing*. London: UCL.
Kellermann, A.L., F.P. Rivara, N.B. Rushforth, J.G. Banton, D.T. Reay, J.T. Francisco, A.B. Locci, H. Prodzinski, B.B. Hackman, and G. Somes. 1993. "Gun Ownership as a Risk Factor for Homicide in the Home." *New England Journal of Medicine* 329 (15): 1084–91. https://doi.org/10.1056/NEJM199310073291506.
Klein, M.W., and C. Maxson. 2006. *Street Gang Patterns and Policies*. Oxford: Oxford University Press.
Klein, W. 1995. *The American Street Gang: Its Nature, Prevalence, and Control*. Oxford: Oxford University Press.
Krivo, L.J., and R.D. Peterson. 1996. "Extremely Disadvantaged Neighborhoods and Urban Crime." *Social Forces* 75 (2): 619–48. https://doi.org/10.2307/2580416.
Krug, E.G., L.L. Dahlberg, and J.A. Mercy et al. 2002. *World Report on Violence and Health*. Geneva: World Health Organization. https://www.who.int/violence_injury_prevention/violence/world_report/en/.
Kubrin, C.E., and R. Weitzer. 2003. "Retaliatory Homicide: Concentrated Disadvantage and Neighborhood Culture." *Social Problems* 50 (2): 157–80. https://doi.org/10.1525/sp.2003.50.2.157.
Kundnani, A. 2014. *The Muslims Are Coming! Islamophobia, Extremism and the Domestic War on Terror*. London: Verso.
Kyerewaa, K. 2015. "Against Police Brutality." In *Justice, Resistance and Solidarity: Race and Policing in England and Wales*, edited by N. El-Enany and E. Bruce-Jones, 24–6. London: Runnymede.
Lammy, D. 2017. *The Lammy Review: An Independent Review into the Treatment of, and Outcomes for, Black, Asian and Minority Ethnic Individuals in the Criminal Justice System*. London: Lammy Review. https://assets.publishing.service.gov.uk/government/uploads/system/uploads/attachment_data/file/643001/lammy-review-final-report.pdf/.
Lerman, A.E., and V.M. Weaver. 2014. *Arresting Citizenship: The Democratic Consequences of American Crime Control*. London: University of Chicago Press.

London Borough of Waltham Forest (LBWF). 2012. *Enough Is Enough: The First Nine Months. Waltham Forest Council Gang Prevention Programme*. London: Waltham Forest Council.

Lusane, C. 1991. *Pipe Dream Blues: Racism and the War on Drugs*. Boston, MA: South End.

Lynch, J.W., G.D. Smith, G.A. Kaplan, and J.S. House. 2000. "Income Inequality and Mortality: Importance to Health of Individual Income, Psychosocial Environment, or Material Conditions." *BMJ* 320: 1200–4. https://doi.org/10.1136/bmj.320.7243.1200.

MacDonald, J.M. and A.R. Gover. 2005. "Concentrated Disadvantage and Youth-on-Youth Homicide: Assessing the Structural Covariates over Time." *Homicide Studies* 9 (1): 30–54. https://doi.org/10.1177/1088767904271433.

Manchester City Council. 2008. *Guns and Gangs*. Manchester: Children & Young People Overview and Scrutiny Committee. http://www.manchester.gov.uk/egov_downloads/Guns_and_Gangs.pdf.

Marlatt, G., and S. Tapert. 1993. "Harm Reduction: Reducing the Risks of Addictive Behaviors." In *Addictive Behaviors across the Lifespan: Prevention, Treatment, and Policy Issues*, edited by J.S. Baer, G.A. Marlatt, and R.J. Marlatt, 243–73. Newbury Park, CA: Sage.

Mauer, M. 2004. "Race, Class, and the Development of Criminal Justice Policy." *Review of Policy Research* 21 (1): 79–92. https://doi.org/10.1111/j.1541-1338.2004.00059.x.

Mayor's Office for Policing and Crime (MOPAC). 2012. *London Crime Reduction Board Partnership Anti-Gangs Strategy*. London: MOPAC.

– 2018. "Mayor Launches New Public Health Approach to Tackling Serious Violence." London: MOPAC. https://www.london.gov.uk/press-releases/mayoral/new-public-health-approach-to-tackling-violence.

Mercy, J.A., and P.W. O'Carroll. 1988. "New Directions in Violence Prediction: The Public Health Arena." *Violence and Victims* 3 (4): 285–301. https://doi.org/10.1891/0886-6708.3.4.285.

Mercy, J.A., M.L. Rosenberg, K.E. Powell, C.V. Broome, and W.L. Roper. 1993. "Public Health Policy for Preventing Violence." *Health Affairs* 12 (4): 7–29. https://doi.org/10.1377/hlthaff.12.4.7.

Miles, R., and A. Phizacklea. 1984. *White Man's Country*, London: Pluto.

Ministry of Justice (MoJ). 2018. *Her Majesty's Prison and Probation Service Offender Equalities Annual Report: 2017/18*. London, MoJ. https://assets.publishing.service.gov.uk/government/uploads/system/uploads/attachment_data/file/760093/hmpps-offender-equalities-2017-18.pdf.

Murji, K. 1999. "Wild Life: Constructions and Representations of Yardies." In *Making Trouble: Cultural Constructions of Crime, Deviance, and Control*, edited by J. Ferrell and N. Websdale, 179–202. New York: Aldine De Gruyter.

Neapolitan, J.L. 1999. "A Comparative Analysis of Nations with Low and High Levels of Violent Crime." *Journal of Criminal Justice* 27 (3): 259–74. https://doi.org/10.1016/S0047-2352(98)00064-6.

O'Connor, J. 1998. "US Social Welfare Policy: The Reagan Record and Legacy." *Journal of Social Policy* 27 (1): 37–61. https://doi.org/10.1017/S0047279497005187.

Office for National Statistics (ONS). 2019a. *Crime in England and Wales: Year Ending September 2018*. London.: ONS. https://www.ons.gov.uk/peoplepopulationandcommunity/crimeandjustice/bulletins/crimeinenglandandwales/yearendingseptember2018#main-points.

– 2019b. *Homicide in England and Wales: Year Ending March 2018*. London: ONS. https://www.ons.gov.uk/peoplepopulationandcommunity/crimeandjustice/articles/homicideinenglandandwales/yearendingmarch2018.

Padilla, F. 1992. *The Gang as an American Enterprise*. New Brunswick, NJ: Rutgers University Press.

Parker, K.F., and M.V. Pruitt. 2000. "Poverty, Poverty Concentration, and Homicide." *Social Science Quarterly (University of Texas Press)* 81 (2): 555–70. https://www.jstor.org/stable/42863975.

Pearson, G. 1983. *Hooligan: A History of Respectable Fears*. London: Macmillan.

Pitts, J. 2008. *Reluctant Gangsters: The Changing Face of Youth Crime*. Cullompton, UK: Willan Publishing.

Potter, R.H., and J.W. Rosky. 2013. "The Iron Fist in the Latex Glove: The Intersection of Public Health and Criminal Justice." *America Journal of Criminal Justice* 38 (2): 276–88. https://doi.org/10.1007/s12103-012-9173-3.

Rosenberg, M.L., and J. Mercy. 1991. "Violence Is a Public Health Problem." In *Violence in America: A Public Health Approach*, edited by M.L. Rosenberg and M.A. Fenley, 3–13. New York: Oxford University Press.

Sanday, P.R. 1990. *Fraternity Gang Rape: Sex, Brotherhood, and Privilege on Campus*. New York: New York University Press.

Scottish Violence Reduction Unit (SVRU). 2019. *Violence Is Preventable – Not Inevitable*. SCRVU). http://www.svru.co.uk/wp-content/uploads/2020/02/VRU_Report_Digital_Extra_Lightweight.pdf.

Shelden, R.G., S.K. Tracy, and W.B. Brown. 2013. *Youth Gangs in American Society*. Belmont: Cengage Learning.

Shiner, M., Z. Carre, R. Delsol, et al. 2018. *The Colour of Injustice: "Race," Drugs and Law Enforcement in England and Wales*. London: Stop Watch. http://www.stop-watch.org/uploads/documents/The_Colour_of_Injustice.pdf.

Shute, J., J. Aldridge, and J. Medina. 2012. Loading the Policy Blunderbuss. *Criminal Justice Matters* 87 (1): 40–1. https://www.tandfonline.com/doi/abs/10.1080/09627251.2012.671018?journalCode=rcjm20.

Small, D. 2001. "The War on Drugs Is a War on Racial Justice." *Social Research* 68: 896–903. https://www.jstor.org/stable/40971924.

Smithson, H., and R. Ralphs. 2016. "Youth in the UK: 99 Problems but the Gang Ain't One?" *Safer Communities* 15 (1): 11–23. https://doi.org/10.1108/SC-10-2015-0034.

Smithson, H., R. Ralphs, and P. Williams. 2013. "Used and Abused: The Problematic Usage of Gang Terminology in the United Kingdom and Its Implications for Ethnic

Minority Youth." *British Journal of Criminology* 53 (1): 113–28. https://doi.org/10.1093/bjc/azs046.

Spergel, I.A. 1995. *The Youth Gang Problem: A Community Approach*. New York: Oxford University Press.

Stretesky, P.B., A.M. Schuck, and M.J. Hogan. 2004. "Space Matters: An Analysis of Poverty, Poverty Clustering, and Violent Crime." *Justice Quarterly* 21 (4): 817–41. https://doi.org/10.1080/07418820400096001.

Strom, K.J., and J.M. MacDonald. 2007. "The Influence of Social and Economic Disadvantage on Racial Patterns in Youth Homicide over Time." *Homicide Studies* 11 (1): 50–69. https://doi.org/10.1177/1088767906296199.

Sullivan, M.L. 2006. "Are 'Gang' Studies Dangerous? Youth Violence, Local Context, and the Problem of Reification." In *Studying Youth Gangs*, edited by J.F. Short and L.A. Hughes, 15–36. Oxford: Altamira.

Sveinsson, K. 2008. *A Tale of Two Englands: 'Race' and Violent Crime in the Press*. London: Runnymede.

Tammi, T. 2004. "The Harm-Reduction School of Thought: Three Fractions." *Contemporary Drug Problems* 31 (3): 381–99. https://doi.org/10.1177/009145090403100301.

Thrasher, F.M. 1927. *The Gang: A Study of 1,313 Gangs in Chicago*. Chicago: University of Chicago Press.

Tjaden, P., and N. Thoennes. 2000. *Full Report of the Prevalence, Incidence, and Consequences of Violence against Women: Findings from the National Violence against Women Survey*. Washington, DC: National Institute of Justice, Office of Justice Programs, United States Department of Justice, Centers for Disease Control and Prevention. https://www.ncjrs.gov/pdffiles1/nij/183781.pdf.

Tonry, M.H. 1995. *Malign Neglect: Race, Crime, and Punishment in America*. New York: Oxford University Press.

Uhrig. N. 2016. *Black, Asian and Minority Ethnic Disproportionality in the Criminal Justice System in England and Wales*. London: Ministry of Justice. https://www.gov.uk/government/publications/black-asian-and-minority-ethnic-disproportionality-in-the-criminal-justice-system-in-england-and-wales.

US Department of Health, Education, and Welfare (USDHEW). 1979. *Healthy People: The Surgeon General's Report on Health Promotion and Disease Prevention*. Washington, DC: USDHESW. https://profiles.nlm.nih.gov/101584932X92.

US Department of Health & Human Services (USDHHS). 1980. *Promoting Health/Preventing Disease: Objectives for the Nation*. Washington, DC: USDHHS. https://files.eric.ed.gov/fulltext/ED209206.pdf.

– 1993. *The Prevention of Youth Violence: A Framework for Community Action*. Atlanta, GA: USDHHS, National Center for Environmental Health and Injury Control Division of Injury Control, Office of the Assistant Director for Minority Health. https://stacks.cdc.gov/view/cdc/27385/.

– 2001. *Youth Violence: A Report of the Surgeon General*. Washington, DC: USDHHS, Office of the Surgeon General. https://www.ncbi.nlm.nih.gov/books/NBK44294/.

Venkatesh, S. 2003. "A Note on Social Theory and the American Street Gang." In *Gangs and Society*, edited by L. Kontos, D. Brotherton., and L. Barrios, 3–11. New York: Columbia University Press.

Wacquant, L.J.D. 2008. *Urban Outcasts: A Comparative Sociology of Advanced Marginality*. Cambridge: Polity.

– 2009. *Punishing the Poor: The Neoliberal Government of Social Insecurity*. Durham, NC: Duke University Press.

Watters, J.K. 1996. "American and Syringe Exchange: Roots of Resistance." In *AIDS, Drugs, and Prevention: Perspectives on Individual and Community Action*, edited by T. Rhodes and R. Hartnoll, 22–41. London: Routledge.

Wilkinson, R. 2004. "Why Is Violence More Common Where Inequality Is Greater?" *Annals of the New York Academy of Science* 1036: 1–12. https://doi.org/10.1196/annals.1330.001.

Wilkinson, R., and K. Pickett. 2009. *The Spirit Level: Why More Equal Societies Almost Always Do Better*. London: Penguin.

Williams, P. 2015. "Criminalizing the Other: Challenging the Race-Gang Nexus." *Race & Class* 56 (3): 18–35. https://doi.org/10.1177/0306396814556221.

World Health Organization (WHO). 2015. *Preventing Youth Violence: An Overview of the Evidence*. Geneva: WHO. http://apps.who.int/iris/bitstream/10665/181008/1/9789241509251_eng.pdf?ua=1&ua=1&ua=1.

13 A Violent Cure? Problematizing the "Cure Violence" Initiative

MALTE RIEMANN

Neither primitive nor modern man has yet succeeded in identifying the microbe responsible for the dread disease of violence. (Girard 1979, 34)

Violence is a contagious disease. This is good news as this knowledge offers new strategies for control.... As we have done before – for plague, typhus, leprosy, and so many other diseases – we can now apply science-based strategies and, as we did for the great infectious diseases, similarly move violence into the past. (Slutkin 2012, 45)

Introduction

I am not a criminologist. Nor have I ever been in a gang. Growing up in a small village in rural Germany, my engagement with gangs and questions about crime was limited to Scorsese films, TV documentaries and the news. My horizon broadened while conducting PhD research in international relations. Exploring the contested nature of conceptualizing and criminalizing violent non-state actors, I was introduced to the works of Michel Foucault. His genealogy of the modern penal system (Foucault 1995) altered my perspective on the emergence of concepts and the creation of subjectivities, and opened my eyes to the power/knowledge dynamics at play within and constitutive of discourse. Still, my interest in crime, criminology, and gangs was still limited, as the focus of my research remained tied to problems of the international – as opposed to the "domestic" – problem of crime. This changed after I stumbled across a TED talk by former World Health Organization (WHO) epidemiologist Gary Slutkin. In his talk Slutkin outlined the Cure Violence (CV) model – a public health–based approach to prevent gun violence that drew on his experience of combatting infectious diseases. It operates on the premise that violence "is a contagious disease" (Slutkin 2012, 111), arguing that violence can be controlled and contained via epidemiological methods and strategies that are applied in infectious disease control. Projects based on the CV model have been implemented in over 100 communities across 16 countries, including Africa, Latin America, the Middle East, and Europe.

Listening to the ease with which the CV model bridged the question of violence with answers derived from medical knowledge generated a deep feeling of discomfort in me. Despite its compelling logic that violence spreads from host to host through learned behaviour and that introducing changes to such harmful behaviour interrupts transmission, it eerily reminded me of earlier medically informed attempts to regulate bodies and fix the normative codes for the management of populations of which Foucault's work so vividly speaks. It generated several questions in me. What assumptions underpin the conceptualization of violence as a disease? What discourses help to produce and shape this conceptualization? What kinds of subjectivities and practices does such an approach produce? And what forms of violence are involved in the politics of knowledge production that inform a public health approach to violence prevention?

To engage with these questions, I conduct a critical discourse analysis of Web-based content to investigate the social reality that CV constructs and the effects produced by understanding violence as a disease. I argue that CV's approach to reduce violence rests, paradoxically, on violent practices and effects. In exploring them, this chapter will first describe CV's "public health approach to lethal violence" (Ransford, Kane, and Slutkin 2014, 233); then outline the approach to discourse analysis upon which this article is methodologically based, and lastly conduct a critical discourse analysis to expose and problematize the violent effects that CV produces by approaching violence as a disease. CV has shown mixed results. Butts et al. have shown that CV significantly reduced gun violence in most communities within which the program was implemented, but in many instances there was no effect or the program was even linked to an increase in violence (Butts et al. 2015; Webster 2015). The US National Institute of Justice's CrimeSolutions.gov (2011) database labels CV "promising" rather than "effective." This chapter, however, does not aim to assess whether CV's public health approach to reduce violence is effective, but rather to critically examine what assumptions govern CV's policy approach, what it silences, and what effects it produces by understanding violence as a disease.

A Cure for Violence? Background to CV and the Medicalization of Violence

Research into violence has traditionally been divided into the domains of biology, psychology and sociology. Approaches based on biology focus on genetic and hormonally pre-determined dispositions towards violence; psychological approaches place violent behaviour within an individual's history of abuse and neglect; and sociology locates violence within the relationship between society and the individual (Matthews and Goodman 2013). Within all approaches we find studies that metaphorically equate violence with a contagious disease (Girard 1979). But what if violence is really an epidemic, a true disease? This is the promise of the CV program, as founder and director Slutkin (2011) explains: "In my presentations I often show several graphs side by side. One shows a cholera outbreak in Somalia, where I worked for three years trying to curb this terrible epidemic as it devastated refugee camps. Beside it, another graph shows a curve of a better-known tragedy – the 1994 mass killings in Rwanda, which claimed nearly 800,000 lives. A third graph shows killings in US cities, which appear like outbreaks of tuberculosis in Europe centuries ago. Side by side, they demonstrate how violence behaves like outbreaks of disease" (para. 6).

Hence violence is an epidemic that mimics other infections such as cholera and Ebola: "It has been said for a long time that violence begets violence, but it is just as tuberculosis begets tuberculosis, or flu begets flu, that violence begets violence" (Slutkin 2012, 104). Hence, "That violence is an epidemic is not a metaphor; it is a scientific fact" (Slutkin 2011, para. 7). Therefore, by analysing violence according to epidemiological findings, it can be cured via a "public health approach to lethal violence" (Ransford, Keane, and Slutkin 2014, 233).

The Aetiology of Violence: A "Public Health Approach"

The approach of CV is simple. If we establish that violence spreads like a disease, then we must be able to identify its behavioural patterns and interrupt it before it spreads. This is the logic of epidemiology and it is based on Slutkin's former experience as a WHO epidemiologist. The CV approach mimics an anti-epidemic strategy, which follows a three-phase system: identification, interruption, and change (Cure Violence n.d.) This system depends on a constant stream of data and a continuous assessment of it. "In today's data driven world, communities demand evidence-based programs that have been proven successful through rigorous, independent, scientific evaluations" (Cure Violence n.d.). With these data, Slutkin argues, it becomes possible to identify high-risk subjects that will commit violent acts.

The first step of the CV process – identification – identifies zones of contagion in which a high level of violent acts occurred over time. With these data it becomes possible to generate an epidemiological map, which then allows localization of high-risk subjects. The data by which CV identifies such high-risk subjects is based on an indeterminate list of "risk factors specific to a community" (Cure Violence n.d.). However, CV requires that subjects meet at least four of seven criteria for being at highest risk: "carries or has ready access to a weapon; has a key role in a gang; has a poor criminal history; is involved in high-risk street activity such as dealing in illegal drugs; is a recent victim of a shooting (in the past 90 days); being between 16 and 25 years of age; and finally, being recently released from prison or a juvenile facility for a criminal offense against a person" (Ransford, Keane, and Slutkin 2014, 237).

Following the identification process, the interruption phase begins. This phase is really the core of CV and aimed at interrupting the transmission of violence from person to person. To guarantee the success of this phase CV hires anti-violence health-care workers: "violence interrupters" (VIs). VIs are "culturally appropriate workers who live in the community, are known to high-risk people, and have possibly even been gang members or spent time in prison, but have made a change in their lives and turned away from crime" (Cure Violence n.d.). Their experience with violence enables VIs to localize "at-risk" subjects, as the VIs themselves had been "at-risk" subjects before and can appropriately deal with "at risk" subjects by intervening before violent behaviour develops. Also, as VIs are perceived as credible messengers, they can form relationships with high-risk and gang-involved individuals, track ongoing disputes and learn about future violent acts of retaliation before they occur. As Butts et al. (2015) describe this process, "When one person is injured or shot, the victim's friends and known associates are likely to seek revenge. The VI's from Cure Violence sites seek out those associates and try to 'talk them down,' or persuade them that there are other ways to negotiate the conflict without engaging in more violence that could risk their liberty and even their own lives" (p. 41)."

But to cure violence, the norms within the community, which accept and encourage violence, must change as well. This is the last phase of CV's anti-violence strategy, in which outreach workers (OWs) take on a specific role. OWs, much like VIs, need to be perceived as credible messengers to be able to create trusting relationships with high-risk individuals. Their tasks, however, "are not as focused as those of the VIs on monitoring threats of violence and intervening directly," but on using "their relationships with program participants to help connect high-risk individuals to positive opportunities and resources in the community, including employment, housing, recreational activities, and education" (Butts et al. 2015, 41). In additional to the individually focused work of OWs, CV engages in community-centred approaches to change the norms surrounding the acceptance of violence. The efforts that this phase includes are "special events such as rallies, marches, community barbeques where anti-violence messages are propagated, and community workshops and summits where high risk individuals are convened to discuss the use of violence. Additionally, a public education campaign, which has been shown to effectively change other behaviors such as smoking, is deployed to change group and community norms related to violence" (Ransford et al. 2016, 3).

Once the new anti-violence norm has become accepted by a critical mass of individuals living within zones contaminated by violence, it can begin to spread throughout the community like a contagion itself, a "positive epidemic" (Frazier 2010, 2).

A Violent Cure: The Effects of Diseasing Violence Prevention

The very core of the culture that fights the hypervirus ... is infected by it. (Bardini 2008, 153)

As I outlined above, I have no personal gang experience nor a research grounding in criminology. For this reason I am neither an insider/insider nor the typical outsider/insider. Policy analysis, however, forms a key concern in my research in international relations. To analyse CV and to acknowledge my own subject position, I develop my analysis via a specific form of discourse analysis focused on policies: the "What is the problem represented to be?" (WPR) approach developed by Carol Bacchi (2009). WPR facilitates the critical examination of public policies to analyse "how the 'problem' is represented within them and to subject this problem representation to critical scrutiny" (Bacchi 2012a, 21). Such an approach shifts the focus of analysis from policy as a "problem solving" exercise that is a technical and neutral process, towards an analysis that perceives of policy as an act that creates "problems" (Marshall 2012). Acknowledging that policies construct problems invites us to engage with the implicit assumptions that govern research (both our own and the research informing gang policies) and forces us to question the politics of knowledge production that informs "expert knowledge." WPR as an analytic method interrogates the representation of problems through six interrelated questions:

> 1) What's the "problem" represented to be in a specific policy or policy proposal?; 2) What presuppositions or assumptions underpin this representation of the "problem"?; 3) How has this representation of the "problem" come about?; 4) What is left unproblematic in this problem representation? Where are the silences? Can the "problem" be thought about differently?; 5) What effects are produced by this representation of the "problem"?; 6) How/where has this representation of the "problem" been produced, disseminated and defended? (Bacchi 2009, 2)

Posing these questions not only allows an interrogation of how policies produce problems, but it also reveals how subjects are produced through these very policy solutions with specific attention to marginalized and oppressed groups (Bacchi 2012b). The following section subjects the CV initiative to a WPR analysis with a focus on questions 1, 2, 4, and 5. Questions 3 and 6 are deliberately omitted out of practical considerations, as they would require a broader engagement with discourses beyond the scope of this chapter (see Riemann 2019).

A WPR analysis begins with the proposal of a specific program, policy, or initiative (Question 1) (Bacchi and Goodwin 2016). CV proposes that violence *is* a disease, and violence is an epidemic that mimics other infectious diseases such as cholera and Ebola (Slutkin 2012, 104). In the words of its founder, "That violence is an epidemic is not a metaphor; it is a scientific fact" (Slutkin 2011, para. 7). Hence, following the logic of WPR, if an epidemiological approach based on medical, scientific knowledge is the proposal, it is assumed that violence *is* a public health problem and that other "non-medical" solutions to violence, such as sociological, are problematic. As Slutkin makes clear, other solutions to violence "do not correctly understand the problem scientifically," leading "to ineffective and even counterproductive treatments and control strategies" (95).

What are the assumptions and presuppositions that underpin the CV initiative (Question 2)? First, CV presupposes the superiority of a quantitative, evidence-based epidemiology over other approaches to prevent violence. It argues that prior assessments of violence have failed because they were based "on moralistic or sociological diagnosis" and not "on proven scientific findings" (Cure Violence n.d.). Following CV, modern science however allows us to move away from analysing violence through incorrect, sociological, or moral lenses, thereby preventing us from making the wrong diagnosis. Second, in this the CV narrative displays a teleological outlook that is typical of modern society (Conrad and Schneider 1980). It argues that earlier assessments of violence have failed because "we did not know – did not *yet* know – what was really happening" (Slutkin 2012, 94–5). Like medieval people, who stigmatized those infected with an infectious disease such as the plague as "bad" people, we today share similar views about those who commit violent acts (Slutkin 2012). And as modern science dispelled the superstition of the Middle Ages by replacing it with scientific facts, CV argues that science can do the same for our concern with violence. CV therefore purports a progressive narrative in which medical progress is seen as promising a solution to the age-old human problem of violence. Third, insofar as CV focuses on identifying "high risk" individuals and stipulating individual pathology in its approach to reduce violence, it is firmly anchored in methodological individualism. As such CV is part of the wider shift of focus in epidemiological studies, away from methodological holism to methodological individualism (Yadavendu 2013). This has important implications for the presuppositions that guide CV, because it neglects wider determinants of risk that go beyond the individual. By placing the ideological marker of disease on the problem of violence, CV replaces political solutions with medical diagnosis and treatment models. As a result, violence becomes disentangled from socio-economic inequalities and explained by reference to individual pathology alone. As Rojas Durazo has argued, transposing a disease model "sets out to deflect attention away from social injustices, while highlighting individual pathology" (Rojas Durazo 2016, 181).

This leads us to the silences in CV's "violence as disease" narrative (Question 4). CV's reliance on an epidemiological approach to violence conceals any structural, political, and sociological factors that might underpin violence in the name of a value-free science. The conceptualization of violence as a disease, therefore, turns violence into a biological condition alone. CV thus constructs "regimes of truth" (Foucault 1980) that delegitimize alternative regimes that purport a disconfirming explanation, such as those based on "sociological diagnosis," and changes the terms of the debate from contingent sociological factors to the seemingly timeless forces of nature and biology. By moving the focus to biology, CV's "violence as disease" narrative displaces the conceptualization of violence as a social problem, obscuring any structural factors that might create the social conditions for violence. Penny Powers (2001) has captured this move in her analysis of the medicalization of social control: ""The medicalization of social control is visible when 'system' problems of order and deviance in a culture begin to be addressed in term of the medical model of disease and thereby bypass other discourses such as those of aesthetics and ethics. Human problems are not seen as social issues for discussion and critique but 'problems' to be solved in terms of diagnosis and treatment model" (21).

Hence, as the narrative of CV understands violence in terms of a disease that can be cured via a diagnosis and treatment model, social, political, and economic forms of violence are disguised. By making violence the object of natural science, CV explicitly excludes any sociologic analysis and engages in an epistemic violence (Spivak 1988) that purports that the medical gaze of a "science based," epidemiological framework is superior to mere "sociological analysis." In this, CV reveals a strong neoliberal narrative that lies hidden behind an "objective" and analytical scientific language. By making violence the object of natural science, it explicitly excludes any sociologic analysis. This implies that by treating violence as an epidemic, violence becomes reduced to biological concerns alone. If violence is only biological, structural factors that might underlie this violence become void. Through CV's "violence as disease" narrative, violence cannot be read as a response to inequalities generated by neoliberal policies, but rests within the infected individual alone. The neoliberal system thereby protects itself and reduces such violence to apolitical factors and actions. But this is exactly the aim of neoliberal practices: to empty politics of its meaning by reducing politics to statistically accessible numbers and surrender it to the superiority of the market (Brown 2015). The neoliberal message is expressed on the CV website: "All people deserve to live, learn, work, play, raise families, *and shop in safe places*" (Cure Violence n.d.).

Then what are the effects of CV's representation of the problem (Question 5)? By approaching violence as a disease that can be opposed by using the statistic-based techniques of modern epidemiology, perpetrators of violence are reduced to a statistical biomass that can be quantitatively assessed, and zones "contaminated" by violence are turned into "governable spaces" (Rose 1999, 31). Within these spaces, at-risk individuals are reduced to objects of knowledge that can be governed via techniques of behaviour change. These techniques, as Legget (2014) has pointed out, are a tool of neoliberal governmentality to direct human behaviour in a paternal fashion. CV does so via the "medical gaze" of OWs and VIs, which exposes at-risk individuals to the constant surveillance, regulation, and normalizing judgment of CV experts to restore at-risk individuals' capacity to serve as productive citizens that become "contributors to their local economies" (Cure Violence n.d.). CV therefore facilitates a public health–based social policy that leaves questions of inequality as a cause of violence relatively untouched, as its focus of intervention is the individual not the structure, while promoting neoliberal paternalism as a necessity to improve people's lives. CV's approach has thus a strong paternalist bent, despite its insistence on responsibilization and self-care. This is, however, not in opposition to neoliberal modes of governing, as Milton Friedman (1980), a key proponent of neoliberalism, made clear: "Freedom is a tenable objective only for responsible individuals.... We cannot categorically reject paternalism for those whom we consider as not responsible" (32–3). And here biology provides the scientific justification for CV's construction of irresponsible subjects. Although CV does not go so far as to invoke a violence microbe, it refers to biological mechanisms (mirror neurons, hormonal reward systems, dysregulation in the limbic system and prefrontal cortex) that are accountable for the infection (Slutkin 2012, 19, 107). In CV's "violence as disease" narrative, violent offenders are therefore not acting subjects, but biologically driven bearers of a mental deformation and therefore "irresponsible" subjects in need of paternal care. To identify "irresponsible," or in CV's language, "at-risk" individuals, statistical data provide CV with the scientific facts. In this, CV confirms Lupton's (1995) observation that "risk" is a moral technology used to identify specific targets for healthcare intervention. What is more, the construction of epidemiological "facts" produces the "normal" subject; that is, those who fall within the normal distribution of health determinants or status and the "at-risk" subject that falls outside this distribution (Petersen and Lupton 1996). Hence, the epidemiologist's activity of "naming, mapping [and] grouping" is not an innocent act (Nguyen 2010, 133). Although the use of statistical analysis to identify at-risk populations is treated as being purely descriptive, these groups are not "naturally" existing groups but created through the very process of their epidemiological identification (Nguyen 2010). Epidemiological research is therefore not merely a neutral, descriptive act, but "a productive process that has the potential to create social identities and realities" (Führer and Eichner 2015, 1). The epidemiological approach used by CV offers a compelling example of this productive process. Through its public health approach, CV defines the boundaries between the "normal" and the "pathological," thereby producing new identities of risky bodies and subjectivities in which the categories of identity and difference are derived from assumptions concerning biological infection or immunity resistance. As Slutkin (2012) makes clear, the marker for violence, as it is with any contagious disease, lies within the body itself: "An infectious disease begins with *exposure* to the infection by a susceptible person. *Susceptibility* refers to the level (or lack) of *resistance* to infection for an individual; this could be due to the immune system" (101). And here, judging from the pictures on the CV website, the colour of susceptibility and lack of biological/mental resistance is the non-white. Indeed, as Ransford, Kane, and Slutkin (2014) mention, "Although being part of a minority population is not a criterion, the majority of the CV clients are in fact either Hispanic or African American" (237). Hence, by classifying already marginalized groups as bodily unfit, white master-narratives reveal themselves. This is further enhanced as, within the narrative of CV, white people become not only subjects that are greatly immune to violence, but also those "gods in white" who are solely able to cure violence. The pictures on the CV website make this clear, as the men "in charge," whether scientist, doctor, or priest, are white only. CV therefore produces two sets of identities in which, on the one hand, white subjects are in charge and able to find a solution to violence, while on the other, Hispanic and African American individuals are perpetrators or passive victims of violence. On the CV website, the overwhelming majority of individuals portrayed (seventy-two) are non-white, while only white are white (Riemann 2019, 7). People of colour are overwhelmingly represented as victims, potential perpetrators, high-risk individuals, OWs, or VIs. In stark contrast, the health professionals "in charge," whether scientist, doctor, or state representative, are only white. This becomes particularly apparent in the website sections outlining CV's "health toolkits." Here the website images show a white doctor treating a non-white gunshot victim, a white scientist identifying a zone of contagion on a city map, and two white state representatives attending a meeting with a non-white VI blurred in the background (Cure Violence n.d.). By drawing the line between the "normal" and the "pathological" according to markers of "race," already marginalized individuals who happen to live within zones "contaminated" by violence are re-stigmatized. Hence, although Slutkin wants to free the perpetrators of violent acts from "moral" stigma, his project reinforces just that. CV therefore hides a violently racialized discourse behind the supposedly value-free scientific language it deploys.

Furthermore, liking violence to a contagious disease allows not only the stigmatizing of those who are "infected," but also calls for a violent suppression of those potentially infected by it, as the contagion narrative portrays individuals living within the contaminated zones as potentially dangerous and diseased. This racially inflected contagion narrative of violence is nothing new; on the contrary, its roots date back to, at least, colonial times. Donna Haraway (1991) has, for example, argued, "In the face of the disease genocides accompanying European 'penetration' of the globe, the 'colored' body of the colonized was constructed as the dark source of infection, pollution, disorder, and so on, that threatened to overwhelm white manhood (cities, civilization the family, the white personal body)" (223). CV's virus paradigm therefore allows the emergence of an infection paranoia that implies that not only the virus, but also those infected must be suppressed (Weinstock 1997, 83). In response to this colonial narrative, CV might be read in relation to a broader consideration of the violent implications that accompany globalization. Hardt and Negri (2000) have argued, "The age of globalization is the age of universal contagion" (136). It is a time "in which increased contact with the Other has rekindled anxieties concerning the spreading of disease and corruption since permeable boundaries of the nation-state can no longer function as a colonial hygiene shield" (Sampson 2012, 2). Hence, with the hygiene shield gone, contagion can be avoided only by vaccination. And here "culturally appropriate intervention workers" (Cure Violence n.d.) are used to protect the white body politic. These "culturally appropriate intervention workers … who have made a change in their lives" (Cure Violence n.d.), however, can only become transmitters of the cure, but are never cured, nor become the cure themselves. They are reduced to an epidemiological defence shield. Hidden within the scientific language of CV is therefore a racist colonial settler logic, a logic in which "the white West affirms its humanity by denying the full humanity of the nonwhites who most viscerally embody the threat of viral contagion" (Dougherty 2001, 5). Therefore, violence becomes classified as residing only within the uncivilized former "colonial" subjects. The contagious effects of violence are thereby inscribed within those very colonial subjects who now "colonize" the spaces of the former colonizer, bringing the violence prevalent in their "uncivilized" spaces with them. Through such an understanding, violence can then temporally and spatially be moved to the colonies itself. CV's "violence as disease" narrative is thus engaged in a purifying violence that externalizes pure, or direct, physical violence by making it a disease that comes from the "outside."

Conclusion

In this chapter I engaged with the CV initiative on its discursive level. Using the WPR approach helped me to engage with the unease that the CV initiative triggered in me, allowing me, a researcher from outside the field of criminology and with no personal gang experience, to illuminate the underlying assumptions that govern CV's representation of urban violence and to draw attention to the effects produced by representing violence as a disease. My analysis showed that beneath its philanthropic innocence and anti-violence message, CV produces violent practices and effects. First, by making violence the object of natural science, CV engages in an epistemic violence that devalues and silences sociological, political, and economic explanations of violence. Second, by endorsing a public health solution to violence prevention, CV replaces political solutions with medical diagnosis and treatment models. In doing so, violence becomes separated from structural factors and explained by individual pathology alone. Third, CV's epidemiological approach violently draws boundaries between the "normal" and the "pathological" according to markers of race. This produces new identities based on the value-free scientific language of biological infection or immunity resistance. Last, CV's contagion narrative portrays individuals living within the contaminated zones as potentially dangerous and diseased and as such calls for their violent suppression. Hence, in its quest to find a remedy for the dreaded disease of violence, CV is not immune to practising violence itself.

REFERENCES

Bacchi, C. 2009. *Analysing Policy: What's the Problem Represented to Be?* Sidney: Pearson Australia.

– 2012a. "Introducing the 'What's the Problem Represented to Be?' Approach." In *Engaging with Carol Bacchi: Strategic Interventions and Exchanges*, edited by A. Bletsas and C. Beasley, 21–4. Adelaide: University of Adelaide Press.

– 2012b. "Why Study Problematizations? Making Politics Visible." *Open Journal of Political Science* 2(1), 1–8. https://doi.org/10.4236/ojps.2012.21001.

Bacchi, C., and S. Goodwin. 2016. *Poststructural Policy Analysis: A Guide to Practice*. New York: Palgrave.

Bardini, T. 2008. "Hypervirus: A Clinical Report." In *Critical Digital Studies: A Reader*, edited by A. Kroker and M. Kroker, 143–57. Toronto: University of Toronto Press.

Brown, W. 2015. *Undoing the Demos: Neoliberalism's Stealth Revolution*. New York: Zone Books.

Butts, J.A., C. Gouvis Roman, L. Bostwick, and J. R. Porter. 2015. "Gun Violence: A Public Health Model to Reduce Gun Violence." *Annual Review of Public Health* 36: 39–53. https://doi.org/10.1146/annurev-publhealth-031914-122509.

Conrad, P., and J.W. Schneider. 1980. *Deviance and Medicalization: From Badness to Sickness*. St. Louis, MO: Mosby.

Dougherty, S. 2001. "The Biopolitics of the Killer Virus Novel." *Cultural Critique* 48 (1): 1–29. https://doi.org/10.1353/cul.2001.0032.

Foucault, M. 1980. "Truth and power." In *Power/Knowledge: Selected Interviews and Other Writings 1972–1977*, edited by C. Gordon, 109–33. New York: Random House.

– 1995. *Discipline and Punish: The Birth of the Prison*. New York: Vintage Books.

Frazier, J. 2010. "Using the Power of Networking and Video to Disrupt the Community Violence Epidemic." Cisco Internet Business Solutions Group. https://www.cisco.com/web/about/ac79/docs/pov/Cure_Violence_POV_081710_v16_Final.pdf.

Friedman, M., and R. Friedman. 1980. *Free to Choose: A Personal Statement*. New York: Harcourt.

Führer, A., and F. Eichner. 2015. "Statistics and Sovereignty: The Workings of Biopower in Epidemiology." *Global Health Action* 8 (1). https://doi.org/10.3402/gha.v8.28262.

Girard, R. 1979. *Violence and the Sacred*, translated by P. Gregory. Baltimore, MD: Johns Hopkins University Press.

Haraway, D.J. 1991. *Simians, Cyborgs and Women: The Reinvention of Nature*. New York: Routledge.

Hardt, M., and A. Negri. 2000. *Empire*. Cambridge,MA: Harvard University Press.

Leggett, W. 2014. "The Politics of Behaviour Change: Nudge, Neoliberalism and the State. *Policy & Politics* 42 (1): 3–19. https://doi.org/10.1332/030557312X655576.

Lupton, D. 1995. *The Imperative of Health: Public Health and the Regulated Body*. London. Sage.

Marshall, N. 2012. "Digging Deeper: The Challenge of Problematising 'Inclusive Development' and 'Disability Mainstreaming.'" In *Engaging with Carol Bacchi: Strategic Interventions and Exchanges*, edited by A. Bletsas and C. Beasley, 53–70. Adelaide: University of Adelaide Press.

Matthews, G., and S. Goodman. 2013. *Violence and the Limits of Representation*. New York: Palgrave MacMillan.

National Institute of Justice. 2011. "Program Profile: Cure Violence (Chicago, Ill.)." https://www.crimesolutions.gov/ProgramDetails.aspx?ID=205.

Nguyen, V. 2010. *The Republic of Therapy: Triage and Sovereignty in West Africa's Time of AIDS*. Durham, NC: Duke University Press.

Petersen, A.R., and D. Lupton. 1996. *The New Public Health: Health and Self in the Age of Risk*. London. Sage.

Powers, P. 2001. *The Methodology of Discourse Analysis*. Sudbury, MA: Jones and Bartlett Publishers.

Ransford, C., C. Kane, and G. Slutkin. 2014. "CV: A Disease Control Approach to Reduce Violence and Change Behaviour." In *Epidemiological Criminology: Theory to Practice*, edited by E. Valtermauer, and T.A. Aker, 232–42. New York: Routledge.

Ransford, C., T. Johnson, B. Decker, M. Payne, and G. Slutkin. 2016. *The Relationship between the Cure Violence Model and Citywide Increases and Decreases in Killings in Chicago (2000–2016)*. Chicago: Cure Violence.

Riemann, M. 2019. "Problematizing the Medicalization of Violence: A Critical Discourse Analysis of the 'Cure Violence' Initiative." *Critical Public Health* 29 (2): 146–55. https://doi.org/10.1080/09581596.2018.1535168.

Rojas Durazo, A. 2016. "Medical Violence against People of Color and the Medicalization of Domestic Violence." In *Color of Violence: The Incite! Anthology*, edited by INCITE!: Women of Color against Violence, 179–88. Durham, NC: Duke University Press.

Rose, N. 1999. *Powers of Freedom: Reframing Political Thought*. London: Cambridge University Press.

Sampson, T.D. 2012. *Virality: Contagion Theory in the Age of Networks*. Minneapolis: University of Minnesota Press.

Slutkin, G. 2011. "Rioting Is a Disease Spread from Person to Person – The Key Is to Stop the Infection. *Guardian*, 14 August.

—— 2012. "Violence Is a Contagious Disease." In *Contagion of Violence: Workshop Summary*, edited by D.M. Patel, M.A. Simon, and R.M. Taylor, 94–111. Washington, DC: National Academies.

Spivak, G. 1988. "Can the Subaltern Speak?" In *Marxism and the Interpretation of Culture*, edited by C. Nelson and L. Grossberg, 271–313. Urbana: University of Illinois Press.

Webster, D.W. 2015. "Commentary: Evidence to Guide Gun Violence Prevention in America." *Annual Review of Public Health* 36: 1–4. https://doi.org/10.1146/annurev-publhealth-031914-122542.

Weinstock, J.A. 1997. "Virus Culture." *Studies in Popular Culture* 20 (1): 83–97. https://scholarly.cmich.edu/?a=d&d=CMUFac1997-04.1.1&e=-------en-10--1--txt-txIN%7ctxAU%7ctxTI--------.

Yadavendu, V.K. 2005. "HIV/AIDS and Socio-Historical Inequality. *Health & Development* 1 (2&3): 89–99. https://www.academia.edu/4537241/HIV_AIDS_AND_SOCIO_HISTORICAL_INEQUALITY_AN_EXPLANATION.

—— 2013. *Shifting Paradigms in Public Health: From Holism to Individualism*. New Delhi: Springer.

14 When the System Harms: An Insider's Perspective on the Negative Socio-psychological Impact of "Gang Intervention"

TAMMY TINNEY

When I was a little girl, I was obsessed with those "choose your own adventure" stories. They were small stories where you could choose your own path a few pages in, and it would take you on a different adventure, depending on your choice, ultimately leading to a different ending. It wasn't until I was much older that I realized these small stories are a perfect metaphor for real life, with each small story representing chapters of our life and how our identity evolves. In life, every one of us has our own identity. We choose our own paths and we make decisions along the way that shift and mould our identity, ultimately shaping our life story. The problem is, not everyone has the same number of paths presented to choose from. Some paths are clear with easy strides until the next path is reached. Other paths have many roadblocks or are buried and have to be searched for, giving the perception to some people that they don't have the power to choose how their story unfolds at all. For those who have been oppressed their whole lives, this one path story is all that they know. They don't know to search for another path because it doesn't exist to them.

I have worked in mental health and the intersection of the criminal justice system for over ten years. It can be rewarding and extremely challenging. Unfortunately, I see the above metaphor play out in real life far too often. The men I work with often describe feeling as though they wear "invisible handcuffs" with no choice but to participate in the treatment mandated by the very systems that have oppressed and labelled them their whole lives. Individuals can be further traumatized by being forced to talk about their trauma and engage in treatment, especially within a system of their oppressors and with an outsider they feel will never understand their lives or the decisions they have faced. So how do I work within this system as an outsider without further perpetuating negative experiences? How do I connect in a meaningful way and provide unbiased support they might not have experienced before? I'm not sure I know the answer to this question and I certainly know the answer will not be the same for everyone and in every situation. I also recognize that ideally my job should be given to someone who is an insider/insider. I don't hesitate to say that many people with lived experiences would do a far better job in my field than I could ever provide as someone looking from the outside in. I understand that this isn't about me, but as an outsider/insider it involves me as I continue to work within a system I more often than not feel like I'm fighting against. In a lot of ways, I've hit the proverbial revolving door of white privilege while the individuals I work with have hit the revolving door of continued oppression, poverty, racism, and discrimination. My privilege has played a major role in why I'm even writing for this book.

I often get asked, "What made you get into this line of work?" For the longest time my answers would be "I like helping people," or "Everyone has a story and deserves unbiased support," etc. Frankly, although those answers are truthful, they are cop-out answers. I was using my desire to help people as a way to avoid reflecting on my own life experiences, especially the traumatic ones. Helping others gave me an outlet and a reason to not deal with my own trauma, because it "wasn't as bad as what other people have gone through or are going through." If my life experiences were not as traumatic as the stories of the individuals I was helping, I could just suck it up and move on with my life; or so I thought. I eventually realized how hypocritical it was of me to never sit down and critically reflect on my experiences and the paths I have chosen when I expect others to sit down in front of me and do the same. So why do I do what I do? Although I am still answering that question every day, below are a few of my experiences that have guided me to my current life path.

I grew up in a small predominantly white town in a nuclear, middle-class family. I went through elementary school, high school, two undergraduate degrees, and a master's degree with relative ease. I've had no criminal justice involvement, nor has anyone in my immediate family. I was as curious as a child as I am today, seeking answers to questions I had, despite the conversations never being brought to me about issues such as culture, diversity, racism, and discrimination. I remember how a few of my closest friends who were non-white were treated differently just because of their skin. I never understood why at the time, because I thought they were just like me. However, the naivety in that belief is telling. There was never much discussion about race, culture, and diversity where I came from. But I did recognize that something was wrong, and it led me to ask questions – a lot of questions. It also led me to specialize in social justice and diversity in my master of social work degree. I knew I had a lot to learn and that this specialization would be the most educational for the career path I intended.

Some of my earliest memories about noticing the way people were "othered" in society is from living next to two male halfway houses. I would hear different people in our neighbourhood saying mean things, alluding to these men being violent, and not wanting them around. I wanted to know why and my mother's humanistic responses and her compassion for others had a huge influence on who I am today and why I chose the paths I did. She told me that there was nothing to fear and that they had likely made mistakes in their life and were just starting new chapters of their lives. She told me that some people have more difficult life paths and fewer options presented to them in life. As I grew older, I sought to understand more about halfway houses, the criminal justice system, and why people were viewed as outsiders by pursuing my first undergrad degree in sociology and criminal justice.

Life was relatively simple for me until I was twelve years old. My father was diagnosed with Parkinson's disease at a very young age. By the time he was diagnosed, it had already progressed to a stage that prevented him from working. This had a severe negative effect on his mental health. A man who was once active and happy had his world come crashing down on him, and he quickly became a different person. Over time he became emotionally and verbally abusive towards me. Eventually the abuse turned physical. I still have flashbacks, one specifically of him breaking down our bathroom door and whipping me with his belt while I was curled up in the bathtub screaming. I tried to spend time outside my house, sleeping with friends, staying with family members, sleeping in a park. It was a difficult situation because my mother was a stay-at-home mom her whole life, and she had just recently started working night jobs. She couldn't afford to leave him, nor did I tell her the entire story of what was happening.

By the time I was eighteen and left home to start my first undergraduate degree, my parents were separating and I was no longer speaking to my father. The shame and the guilt I felt was insurmountable. I turned to alcohol to numb my pain. I partied far more than I should have, eventually losing the scholarships I had worked so hard to achieve. One night, after a night out, I woke up in an unknown bed, and when I realized I didn't know who the guy was beside me I tried to leave. However, he had other plans and so did his friend. I was punched and raped multiple times. I later explained my black eyes with a simple "I was drunk and fell" comment, which became a running joke with my roommates. I never reported it because I was too ashamed, and I thought it was my fault because I was intoxicated. I feel guilty about that to this day. These traumatic life experiences along with other traumatic experiences led me down a path where I couldn't see the light at the end of the tunnel. I didn't see another path. I felt more depressed and continued to have post-traumatic stress disorder symptoms as the days bled into one another. I didn't had no hope for the future and I just wanted the pain to stop. I planned to kill myself, gathering up pills, Drano, and alcohol, but halfway through I stopped myself when I started to think about my mom. I couldn't do it to her. Her life was hard enough, and I knew it would destroy her.

So, when I am asked why I do what I do, these are some of the difficult answers I don't tell. Through my pain I found a passion for helping others.

When I hit my lowest of lows, my saving grace was my mother. Some people don't even have that; they don't have anyone in their corner. Although my experiences are different and I can't relate as an outsider to the trauma experienced because of street and gang violence, I have experienced the lowest of lows through my own trauma. I know how hard it is to push and persevere to choose a new path when there doesn't seem to be one. I want to use my privilege to shine light on paths that don't seem to exist for others when they have hit their lowest of lows.

My career in the mental health and justice sector has let me work with individuals, who in many aspects have had life trajectories the opposite of mine. I've worked in the health-care system, criminal justice system and community organizations. I've seen the interweaving of these systems and the perpetual flaws within them, which often fail the individuals and communities they are supposed to support. These systems are often marketed to society as agents of social change, when in reality they are often agents of social control, furthering detrimental and disproportionate effects on the individuals and communities they are supposed to care for. The goal of this chapter is to provide an outsider/insider's perspective of the three systems noted above. I will discuss what is and isn't working and what changes need to be made. Although there will be some narratives of the experiences of individuals I have worked with, this chapter is not about speaking for these individuals. They are not voiceless, and they do not need me to speak for them.

The Health-Care System: First, Do No Harm?

One of the first obstacles I come across when treating individuals affected by gang and street violence is the fact that they are mandated to treatment in a health care setting. More often than not, it's not their decision to come in for treatment, and they have been ordered to come by the criminal justice system, their oppressor. That automatically connects me to a system they don't trust. Then when they walk through my door to see a young, white female who doesn't look like someone from their community or someone they can relate to, my job becomes that much harder. How would you feel if you were being forced to talk about traumatic life experiences you weren't ready to talk about, and with someone you feel will never understand you? A lot of you probably wouldn't do it. I wouldn't. It's not uncommon for the young men I work with to self-sabotage. Some recognize and openly admit that they need help, but they reject it and fight against it because they don't like being told to "change" by the criminal justice system, or anyone else, for that matter. Some individuals view resisting treatment as a way to regain their power, even if they identify that the treatment may be beneficial to them. Once a health-care provider acknowledges these power dynamics, it can be extremely difficult for them to be broken down in a way that allows for a strong therapeutic alliance to be built, but it is possible.

Unfortunately, often power dynamics are just not dealt with, for many reasons. Sometimes the power dynamics are not acknowledged by the health-care provider; the health-care provider doesn't care to shift the power balance; and/or doesn't have the time to build a strong therapeutic alliance with individuals with complex life experiences and needs. Health-care systems are quick to advertise their duty to patients and throw out the notion of patient- and family-centred care. "The patient comes first" is not an uncommon phrase heard in the health-care industry. But, as an insider to this system I can undoubtedly say this phrase should have an asterisk beside it followed by a list of exceptions like you'd hear in an infomercial. "The patient comes first," unless you come from neighbourhood X, Y, or Z; you have charges and you're a "criminal," "offender," "gangster," except if you're "a drug addict," you don't have money to donate to our foundation, etc. Patients are "othered" even in settings where their care is supposed to be of the utmost importance. Why does this happen? There's not one answer, but a big one is that health-care systems need money. They want to use the resources and funding they must filter into programs that will return their investment such as programs in cardiovascular, oncology, and children's departments. These programs get a lot of donations, and they also treat individuals whom society views as worthy of receiving support. The individuals I work with see this "othering," and their outlook on treatment becomes tainted by seeing the health-care system as just another institution that values the worth of other humans over themselves.

This feeling can be further perpetuated by the lack of knowledge and culture and diversity within health-care settings. The majority of individuals I work to treat are Black and individuals of colour, arguably because of the historical discrimination, oppression, and mistreatment of these populations in society and the criminal justice system. Health-care systems are historically rooted in dominant privileged, heteronormative, whitewashed practices. They seek to diversify their staff and organizational culture, and although there have been great ideas and changes within these systems, a lot of work remains. Racism and discrimination are prevalent in our health-care systems and experienced by patients, communities, and health-care providers. In my opinion, health-care systems are guilty of tokenism, often producing statements and "training" after events such as a patient's mistreatment receiving news coverage or the Black Lives Matter movement. Putting out a statement after a significant event and providing a few training sessions on culture and diversity will not fix historically rooted discriminatory practices. Education and training need to be happening consistently. Anti-racist/anti-oppressive practice cannot be taught in an eight-module "educational series" that takes thirty minutes to complete. It also needs to be provided by individuals/groups representative of these groups and communities. If I sit around a table and everyone looks like me and nobody has lived experience and knowledge of what we are learning, I will seriously question the validity of anything I'm being told. As should everyone else. I have had multiple patients tell me about experiences in health care where they felt they were being treated differently because of the colour of their skin or the neighbourhood they lived in. Even sometimes when there has been no mention of criminal charges, they felt as though they were treated as a criminal. This creates further distrust for the health-care system and the providers attached to it. It makes it even harder to break down walls to provide treatment. Experiences in the health-care system matter, and if someone comes to me who has had negative experiences with health-care providers, I know I will have be extra diligent in my approach. It's not uncommon for health-care providers to not want to work with patients when they see they have criminal charges against them. It's often assumed that they may be difficult or dangerous. The mix of mistrust and mistreatment often gets diagnosed as specific personality traits or disorders, particularly antisocial personality disorder. The labels these individuals have had applied to them at the hands of our government, our "justice" system, and others in society continue to follow them, even when they are supposed to be in a safe place where no harm will be done.

I believe strongly that therapy and psychiatric care can be extremely beneficial to individuals suffering from significant mental health challenges such as complex post-traumatic stress disorder, major depression disorder, anxiety disorders, substance use, and more. I've seen first-hand how life changing treatment can be. However, it takes a lot of time to build a meaningful relationship and trust with these individuals before you can get to the stage of starting this type of treatment. You have to be patient and innovative. Stagnant clinical counselling and assessments will not get you there, I promise. A common barrier I see in my practice is hypermasculinity. Hypermasculinity can be defined as the "exhibition of stereotypic gendered displays of power and consequent suppression of signs of vulnerability" (Spencer et al. 2004, 234). In some neighbourhoods hypermasculinity can be a source of protection and self-preservation that can help young men gain respect from other men in their community (Sullivan 2017). Stigma associated with mental illness can be counterproductive to a man's hypermasculine identity and can "diminish their reputations and status in the community and jeopardize their relationships with neighbors and the public" (16–17, as cited in Cunningham et al. 2013, 987). This often causes the young men I work with to reject mental health support because of the stigma attached to mental illness and their perception that they may be viewed as weak, which can be life-threatening in the streets. When I can finally break down those barriers, treatment becomes complex Breaking down the hypermasculinity is like asking them to remove their mask. I start to make progress when they trust me enough to tell their story and let themselves be vulnerable with me. However, as soon as they step out of my office, the mask must go back up to match their social identity in the streets. Having to deal with the complexity of shifting their identities, which depend on their social location, is often seen to be too difficult, especially when they cannot change the environment that promotes fear. In an environment where violence is used to address conflict, "the code teaches working-class youth that you can either survive the streets by fighting or become a punk where you will endure a lifetime of victimization" (Ellis 2017, 12). Although I believe that usually some treatment is better than none, if done by a qualified and knowledgeable professional, treatment could also lead to unintended consequences such as symptoms becoming worse as the result of constant exposure. The health-care provider also must be aware that some suggestions for treatment might be unrealistic or unsafe for some individuals because safety in the streets is a significant concern. Treatment should be thoroughly analysed and reflected on before being provided. Our health-care system continually ignores key issues that affect an individual's physical and mental well-being, such as affordable housing, poverty alleviation, rights to education, discrimination, racism, stigmatization of mental health, toxic masculinity/hyper-masculinity, and affordable and equitable access to health and wellness services that are culturally appropriate. All of these should be considered and included in a plan to address an individual's mental health. But they aren't, because it's not part of what's laid out in the program objectives. There's an underlying assumption that these services will be provided in the community. However, community services aren't the ones being funded enough to provide effective change and support. Habitual Band-Aid solutions are applied for wounds that need surgery. The health-care system continually sees these problems but doesn't step up to the plate to advocate for the root issues to be addressed. They don't want to bite the hand that feeds them.

Unfortunately, for a variety of reasons we rarely see innovation in healthcare programs that are not in those "golden programs" such as cardiovascular, oncology, and children's programs. First, many people working in mental health and justice programs aren't familiar enough with these individuals and communities to even know how to be creative in their approach to treatment. Throughout my career in this field I have rarely been asked about my lived experience. Although my work has been closely involved with the criminal justice system, a degree in criminology or criminal justice has never been a requirement for a job I have had or have applied for. Instead job qualifications are more likely to be educational achievements such as having a bachelor's or master's degree in a field that may or may not be applicable to the position. No degree will give anyone everything they need, but it does provide a foundation of knowledge that will help them do their job. Second, mental health and justice programs aren't provided with as much funding as other programs. Last, the red tape. I have tried many times to be innovative in my approach to treatment. I know from research and hands-on experience that incorporating things such as art, music, sports, and fitness into therapy approaches can have a significant positive effect on an individual's mental health treatment. However, such approaches don't fit within structured programs, which are laid out and dictated from the top down. You really have to question who is benefiting from these programs. Our government controls the narrative of the lives of my patients, often labelling them as "gangsters" and "criminals." The same government controls the funding and creates the programs designed to "rehabilitate" them, while further stigmatizing them by defining even health-care programs with justice labels. I am not aware of any non-criminal justice approaches that are publicly funded to support the health and well-being of the young men I work with. The government benefits from their agenda being met, the health-care systems benefit from the funding they receive, but how are the individuals and communities benefiting? It's hard to believe that these questions even want to be answered, because the answers will not fit into the desired narratives of those in power.

The "Criminal Justice" System: When Enforcement Trumps Rehabilitation and Prevention

It's impossible for me to focus on every flaw I see within the criminal justice system, and I know that a lot will be discussed throughout this book. However, I think it's important to draw attention to a few issues I've been continually confronted with throughout my career. Anyone that knows me wouldn't be surprised to hear that I think unfavourably of our current criminal justice system. I believe that it's entrenched in oppressive colonial practices that advantage the elites in our society. It isn't broken, because it's working exactly the way it was designed – to oppress. From the perspective of an outsider/insider, I hear about and see my patients being further oppressed by a system that provides them with no justice. The root causes contributing to criminal behaviour are constantly ignored.

First, let's talk about the police. I work with police and although there are some well-intentioned police officers who do great work, they will forever be attached to a historically racist and corrupt system. So, despite their good intentions, they won't gain the trust of the young men I work with. Too much has happened to them at the hands of police. Community officers, and "gang exit" programs are useless. In many ways they are retraumatizing individuals and communities, and creating further distrust and tensions within communities they say they help. Not one young man that I've worked with would associate himself with police, community officers, or their supposed gang exit programs.

I'll share some experiences these young men have had with police to illustrate my point. Countless numbers of them have talked about the physical abuse they have endured by police. Some have been beaten so badly that they've lost consciousness and suffered traumatic head injuries. Others have been kicked and punched and had bones broken. Several young men told me they have had police put a gun to their head when stopped but were later released and never charged. One young man who has lost several family members and friends to gun violence was picked up by the police, driven to a rival neighbourhood and told to get out of the car. They also stole his phone, so he had no way to contact anyone as he stood there feeling like "a walking target." This young man has severe complex post-traumatic stress disorder as a result of gun and street violence. He made it home safely, but the damage this did to his mental health was insurmountable. Many have lost family members and friends to police shootings. Some have had drugs, money, and other belongings stolen from them by police. Or they have been charged and convicted on the basis of perjured accounts and testimonies. It's not uncommon for these young men to have early memories of negative police experiences such as stopped and bullied by police, or seeing police arrest people close to them. A common narrative in the stories I have heard is that from a young age these men learned not to trust police, and as they grew up they lived through traumatic experiences with the police. It's unreasonable to believe that these same men would trust the police and engage in such "gang-exit" programs. Even if they didn't have such negative experiences with police, associating with the police could affect their safety and reputation in their community when the majority of community members do not trust the police. Two reports by the Ontario Human Rights Commission found that Black people are disproportionately arrested, charged, and subjected to use of force by Toronto police (Wortley and Jung 2020; Wortley, Laniyonu, and Laming 2020). It is unreasonable to continue to think that solutions will come from programs developed and run by police or other professionals working in the criminal justice system.

Although I have worked with many young men labelled "gang members, I don't know of any true gang exit program within the Greater Toronto Area, because not one of the men I've worked with has engaged in or benefited from such a program, despite really needing the help. The individuals that these gang-exit programs are supposedly helping should be questioned. They may be connecting with some community members, but not the ones who would benefit most from receiving support for exiting gangs, treating trauma, and reintegrating into society. The knowledge and work of insider/insider academics continue to be ignored because they don't fit with government agendas and police budgets. They also don't support the narratives constantly in the media about rising crime, increased gang violence, and dangers to communities. From my experience working with these young men, one of the most effective ways of helping ensure their safety temporarily is relocating them. However that's not a solution. Displacing them comes with isolation, further "othering" in a new community, potential for their mental health to decline, and lack of social and mental health supports. This also costs money, which they rarely have access to. Although this wouldn't be a solution I would propose, it has been the best temporary fix for young men who have had an immediate threat to their safety. This draws attention to the continued Band-Aid solutions our government and society applies to issues that continue to have their root causes ignored. The increased budgets of police and tough-on-crime programs continue to grow, whether or not there is evidence to support the need for or validity of these programs. The reasoning behind our government's decision to continually funnel money into police budgets instead of community organizations that can work towards addressing the socio-economic factors contributing to crime and violence needs to be seriously questioned. Prevention needs to outweigh enforcement but in order to do that, funding must be reallocated to appropriate prevention programs instead of the police. It's clear that not everyone wants a solution to problems of crime and violence because the solutions don't benefit them monetarily and may take power away from the people and institutions that benefit from the victimization of certain individuals and communities. These issues are often used as bargaining chips when elections roll around, but there is never any progress in working towards an effective solution.

The criminal justice system continues to use labels such as "gangs" and "gang members" to further stigmatize individuals as they move through "rehabilitation." For example, probation and parole Anti-Guns and Gangs units ensure that these labels stick with individuals throughout their time in the criminal justice system. I have been fortunate to work with a lot of probation officers throughout my career, the majority of whom care deeply about their clients and want the best for them. However, they are working in a system entrenched in racism and discrimination just like I am. This can make it difficult to successfully advocate for change. It's crucial to question who is developing the criteria to apply these labels and definitions. For example, what are the criteria for someone to be labelled a gang member? Do these criteria change over time? Are there biases in the way crimes are reported? If so, how do they affect the reliability of crime statistics and funding allocation? There have been times where crime prevention budgets have increased despite dropping crime rates. For example, a 2014 study by the Fraser Institute found that between 2001 and 2012, "police officers per 100,000 of population in Canada rose 8.7% while the crime rate declined by 26.3%" (Di Matteo 2014). The same study found that "real per capita police expenditures in Canada between 1986 and 2012 rose 45.5% while criminal code incidents per officer declined by 36.8%" (Di Matteo 2014). This promotes fear and anxiety among communities and misperceptions by the general public. A report by Westin (2021) examined data on reported crimes in Toronto. It found that crimes that had multiple subtypes were then included numerous times when collecting and analysing crime rates. The report found that "this can lead to an inflated estimation of the number of actual incidents which occur" (Westin 2021). This is concerning when crime statistics affect funding allocation and also the perception of crime amongst the general public.

I have worked with a lot of men who have been labelled as gang members when they view their associations as developing friendships/family and fostering safety within their own community. I have also worked with individuals convicted of firearm charges and were automatically labelled and associated with gangs through our system of control. One young man who was struggling with major depressive disorder and severe untreated post-traumatic stress disorder became suicidal. He had never been in conflict with the law before, he completed secondary school with good grades, and he was working to support himself. He wanted to ensure that his suicide would succeed, so he bought himself a gun. His loved ones learned of his plan and called 9-1-1 for help. Fortunately, he was taken to hospital for his own safety. However, once he was discharged, he was charged with possessing a firearm and subsequently convicted. He now has a criminal record and is followed up by the Anti-Guns and Gangs probation unit. I have worked with several young men who told similar stories. Few people hear their stories, but they see their labels and judge them on that basis. Their life stories are entrenched with themes of oppression, marginalization, and discrimination. Stories like these also speak to the need for funding in communities for affordable health care, housing, poverty alleviation, and much more. There was more money spent by the criminal justice system to persecute these young men, than the amount it would have cost to fund programs to help prevent them from choosing this path in the first place.

As time passes, the same discussions are had repeatedly. Our entire criminal justice system, including the police, is founded on and attempts to maintain white supremacy. We continue to invest in police rather than communities to fix our real and imagined problems. The public is continually fed false or misleading information through narratives put out in the media such as those in primetime news, newspapers, and social media. For many people this is their main source of education. The sensationalism of gangs, crime, and violence draw readers' attention, unfortunately. Although there are exceptional journalists doing very important work, others are irresponsible, including specific news outlets. We also must look at who has the power over the media and who continues to control these discourses in the media. People and institutions in power continue to control the narratives in a way that benefits them and keeps the power tilted in their favour.

Community Organizations: Turning Lemons into Lemonade?

I see the most passion, genuine care, and desire to help come from community and non-profit organizations, as well as the communities themselves. Despite the minuscule percentage of funding these organizations receive, they work tirelessly to provide support and positive change to their community. I have also seen the most creative and innovative approaches used in these organizations. They focus on providing culturally and socially relevant services to the individuals they are supporting. Art, music, theatre, fitness, and sports have been used to open up dialogues that remain closed in other settings. Through both employment and volunteer work I have worked within a few community and non-profit organizations that have made significant positive impacts on individuals' lives. Adam Ellis and I co-founded a therapeutic program called Hip Hop Healers and we recently completed a pilot project for the program. It uses hip hop and rap to provide clinical counselling and support to youth and young adults who are or at risk of coming into conflict with the law, have a history of trauma and other mental health struggles, including addictions. It fostered a sense of community and safety for the participants. It broke down hypermasculinity and created conversations about mental health, grief, substance use, racism, etc. These important conversations may have taken months to achieve in other settings. Participants also received professional support for their mental health, which had positive impacts on their level of functioning and well-being. This was all done within a community organizational setting with limited funding, donated equipment, and volunteered time from professionals. More programs with innovative approaches like this need to be developed. If these organizations were to receive more funding, they would be able to provide innovative programs like this and stay away from traditional medical model approaches that usually fail to resonate with the individuals they are supposed to be treating.

Community organizations are also more likely to work from a more holistic perspective, acknowledging and addressing social detriments to health that the health-care and criminal justice systems often fail to account for. Individuals also rarely connect these organizations with the systems that have oppressed them, which can have a positive effect on engagement because there is more trust. Throughout my career I have collaborated with community organizations that encouraged their clients to connect with the health-care system to receive further support for their mental health and addictions. I have worked with many individuals who had no trust in me at the beginning because of the system I was connected to. They agreed to see me only because their worker from a community agency vouched for me and/or went to their first few appointments until there was some trust built. This shows how important community partnerships are when we are trying to develop the most effective and strong circle of care for an individual.

Unfortunately, meagre funding for these organizations limits what they can do to help. Although well-intentioned, some community programs are running services that could have detrimental effects to the individuals they intend to support. Programs aimed at providing service to individuals with complex trauma must be careful in their approaches. An individual with complex trauma requires support from a professional with extensive training and education. Community organizations often can't afford to hire staff with these qualifications, therefore some staff may be underqualified for the services they are providing. For example, some peer programs state they are training youth to go out and speak to other youth in their communities about mental health and involvement in crime and gangs. Even if the aim is to just facilitate conversations about these topics, I cannot stress enough how dangerous this can be. Just talking about trauma can trigger people and cause them to experience flashbacks, panic attacks, hyper-vigilance, and depression, sometimes even leading to suicidal thoughts. If staff don't have the qualifications to treat complex trauma, they may leave individuals more vulnerable than before. Even if they do recognize that someone is being triggered, it is unlikely that they have the experience or training necessary to treat them. In my practice I routinely work with individuals living with complex trauma. Before opening trauma dialogues with them, I introduce mindfulness and distress tolerance skills before engaging people in trauma-focused therapy. Mindfulness techniques such as deep breathing, grounding, body scan, and meditation has helped people better manage distress caused by discussing their trauma. It also provides them with coping skills to manage distress on their own once they finish the counselling session. Crawford (2010) incorporates and adapts body mapping in her sessions for traumatized individuals who have trouble expressing their emotions and are more focused on their somatic symptoms. There is a lot of work required before discussions about trauma can take place, and some of these programs and services need to be reconsidered. Thankfully, not all organizations have issues such as this. Some have qualified professionals in their staff or as volunteers who can provide appropriate treatment. There needs to be more education about potential harms within the context of providing care. There also need to be more stringent evaluations of programs to determine what services are effective and what are not. This also applies to our government-funded programs through our health-care and criminal justice systems.

Reflection

As a health-care provider, I feel frustrated by the constant persecution and negative labels the individuals I work with are subjected to. Government policies are fixated on policing and controlling crime and gang violence, while politicians turn away and refuse to address the systemic, root causes for why these individuals end up living the life they do. Individuals I work with feel "othered" and labelled as "deviant," "no good," "a throwaway," "bad," and "a criminal." The lack of resources and attention to treating and rehabilitating them to be welcomed as a part of society speaks volumes about how broken our system is. Current resources are not focused on prevention, but instead are Band-Aid solutions to systemic problems. Until more attention is given to the systemic causes of inequality (poverty, discrimination, and marginalization) with this population, I feel as though I'm helping them put bandages over open wounds, only for them to be thrown back into the same system that created the wounds in the first place. In the end insiders are left with building a good life for themselves with roadblocks, buried paths, and powerful systems working against them. It's a constant struggle to choose a different path and rewrite a life story you feel has already been published and distributed to the masses.

REFERENCES

Crawford, A. 2010. "If 'The Body Keeps the Score': Mapping the Dissociated Body in Trauma Narrative, Intervention, and Theory." *University of Toronto Quarterly* 79 (2): 702–19. https://doi.org/10.1353/utq.2010.0231.

Cunningham, Michael, Dena Phillips Swanson, and DeMarquis M. Hayes. 2013. "School- and Community-Based Associations to Hypermasculine Attitudes in African American Adolescent Males." *American Journal of Orthopsychiatry* 83 (2–3): 244.

Di Matteo, Livio. 2014. *Police and Crime Rates in Canada: A Comparison of Resources and Outcomes.* Fraser Institute. https://www.fraserinstitute.org/sites/default/files/police-and-crime-rates-in-canada.pdf.

Ellis, A. 2017. "Memories of Urban Warfare: Trauma, PTSD and Gang Violence." *Journal of Community Corrections* 26 (2): 5–14.

Spencer, M., S. Fegley, V. Harpalani, and G. Seaton. 2004. "Understanding Hypermasculinity in Context: A Theory-Driven Analysis of Urban Adolescent Males' Coping Responses." *Research in Human Development* 1 (4): 229–57. https://doi.org/10.1207/s15427617rhd0104_2.

Sullivan, T. 2017. "Engaging in Effective Behavioral Health Treatment Methods: The Importance of Building Trust and Relationships with High and Proven Risk Men with a History of Childhood Trauma(s)." *International Development, Community and Environment.* 106. https://commons.clarku.edu/idce_masters_papers/106.

Westin, Morgaine. 2021. "Reported Crime Statistics in Toronto Can Be Misleading." https://tellingstorieswithdata.com/inputs/pdfs/paper_one-2021-Morgaine_Westin.pdf.

Wortley, S., and, M. Jung. 2020. "Racial Disparity in Arrests and Charges: An Analysis of Arrest and Charge Data from the Toronto Police Force." Ontario Human Rights Commission. https://www.ohrc.on.ca/sites/default/files/Racial%20Disparity%20in%20Arrests%20and%20Charges%20TPS.pdf.

Wortley, S., A. Laniyonu, and E. Laming. 2020. *Use of Force by the Toronto Police Service: Final Report.* Ontario Human Rights Commission. https://www.ohrc.on.ca/sites/default/files/Use%20of%20force%20by%20the%20Toronto%20Police%20Service%20Final%20report.pdf.

15 Fight Poverty, Fight Crime: A Justice-Focused Approach for Toronto/Canada

YAFET TEWELDE AND JULET ALLEN

Introduction

The Hate U (You) Gave Little Infants Fucks Everybody (THUG LIFE) was an exhortation from famed rapper Tupac Shakur. This acronym was (in)famously tied to Tupac because it was a predominant theme throughout his music while also tattooed on his abdomen. Although those close to Tupac debated the meaning of "THUG LIFE" (Westhoff 2014), for this chapter, the above definition provides a significant contextualization of how Black youth are labelled and mislabelled while simultaneously examining the way society uses stereotypes to justify violence and racism against Black people. THUG LIFE places the responsibility of how "thugs" are created onto the society "thugs" live in. For Black youth in America, thug life is American life. This is rooted in the understanding that the colonial history of Indigenous lands, enslavement of Black people, and subsequent legalization of the oppression of Black and Indigenous people is the original thug life. This understanding would also apply to Canada – another part of colonial North America. In this chapter, for Black youth in Toronto, thug life is Toronto (thus Canadian) life.

Depictions of Black people as thugs can be traced back to the early twentieth century when fear was reinforced through depictions of Black men as harmful and "brutish" (Smiley and Fakunle 2016). Blackness became closely linked with criminalization and allowed for white supremacy to scapegoat Black communities for all manner of societal problems, regardless of reality. Through criminalization and drawing on past racial stereotypes, the mythical brute became the realistic thug. The relationship between Black youth and the criminality that the "thug" label connotes is inextricably linked to understanding Canadian white supremacy. It is a label meant to underscore the impossibility for Blackness to exist within the white supremacist imagination that built the colonial entity that is Canada. Thug as crime-based terminology replaces racist slurs such as the n-word to justify anti-Black occupation-style policing. It underscores how racism, overtly and covertly, is directed at Black communities, providing police and white public with ammunition to justify mass incarceration and police brutality (Kitossa 2018).

Therefore, this chapter starts with the premise that the legal mechanisms used to address criminality, particularly amongst and within Black youth and their communities, such as police, courts, and prisons, are not addressing the root causes of criminality to eliminate it but are tools to maintain and reinforce white supremacist power structures within Canada. THUG LIFE is an entry point to addressing the root causes of criminality by rupturing the structures of colonialism, enslavement, and the legal entrenchment of inequality within Canadian society.

This chapter deploys thug criminology to discuss alternatives to address criminality amongst Black and other racially marginalized youth. It is necessary to begin with (and accept) the realities of Black youth in Canada, Ontario, and Toronto as shaped by the racist history of Canada. To understand this reality, and thus the need for this chapter, we need not look further than 2018 in Toronto, which has shown that the condition for Black youth is marred by a mix of violence, poverty, and targeted police abuse consistently marking them as outside the norms of supposed civilized society. Like previous years, there has been sensationalized media coverage of the record homicide rate reached in Toronto (MacLeod 2018; Gillis 2018; McLaughlin 2018). We have witnessed the ease with which Mayor John Tory and city councillors have used thug as coded language to describe Black youth to create fear in the populous and fuel anti-Black racism (Kitossa 2018). Beyond the high-profile killings that have contributed to the record numbers, the homicide rate in Toronto has remained steady over the last three decades (Tewelde and Olawoye 2013). For a large metropolitan city like Toronto to have homicide rates barely reaching a hundred, it would be easy to point out that public fears about safety and sensational media accounts of violence are exaggerated. However, the magnitude of the violence obscures the reality that the nature of violence in Toronto is concentrated among youth and within the most economically vulnerable areas of the city (Tewelde and Olawoye 2013; MacLeod 2018). The concentration of this violence within Black, racially, and economically marginalized communities points to a convergence of the roots of violence around alienation, economic inequality, and growing anger and resentment (Tewelde and Olawoye 2013; Galabuzzi, 2010). Indeed, Black communities are outsiders within Toronto's white imagination.

These fears were clear during Public Safety Canada's "guns and gangs" meeting in March 2018 of provincial and federal government, police, community, and Indigenous representatives to address gun violence and illegal gun ownership, and to "make vulnerable young people less susceptible to the 'insidious lure' of gang activity" (Bronskill 2018). However, the over-representation of law enforcement and academic institutions, along with the under-representation of youth-focused community and social services representatives (Bronskill 2018; Tewelde 2018), highlight a continuing rejection of the roots of youth involvement with guns, gangs, violence, and criminality more generally. This is particularly true for historically marginalized communities in Canada. The over-abundance of law enforcement is troubling, considering the December 2018 report from the Ontario Human Rights Commission, which found that a Black person was nearly twenty times more likely than a white person to be involved in a fatal shooting by Toronto police. Moreover, despite representing only 8.8 per cent of Toronto's population, Black people made up about 30 per cent of police use-of-force cases that resulted in serious injury or death, 60 per cent of deadly encounters with Toronto Police, and 70 per cent of fatal police shootings (Ontario Human Rights Commission 2018).

These events of 2018 point to a larger reality: there is a certain impossibility for Black communities to exist in white supremacist Canada because of the need to manage, contain, and surveil Black communities; it is the existence of Blackness that is the threat to white supremacist Canada that requires it to be "castrated" from the psyche (Tecle et al. 2017). It is important to note though that the federal government has tried to implement alternative mechanisms by looking at ways to ensure that young people charged under the Youth Criminal Justice Act are directed to specialized programs and services that provide comprehensive supports (Tewelde 2018; Winsa 2014). These supports were supposed to represent a collaborative approach among governmental and nonprofit community programs and services that provide educational assistance, employment, mental health services, familial supports, mentorship, and social isolation reduction. Even so, if there is continued reliance on the destructive nature of law enforcement, these efforts continue to be a one-step-forward-two-steps-back approach to addressing the realities and needs of Black communities in Toronto and Canada.

Thug criminology allows us to understand that Blackness is the threat to Toronto and Canada, making the existence of Black communities constantly in jeopardy. Therefore, this chapter argues that we need a justice focus that simultaneously understands how Canada has operated in unequal terms with Black youth, and that we need proactive solutions that reject the same unequal relations of "law and order," including prisons, police, and courts. These unequal relations operate like traditional criminology in that they reinforce white supremacy, thus marking Blackness as a threat. Our approach, built on THUG LIFE, uses Toronto as a case study to, first, provide an overview of how the inclusion of diversity, through Canada's multiculturalism legislation, is a "homegrown" example of how Toronto, and Canada, is built on white supremacist exclusion of Blackness. Second, through an analysis of racial profiling in Toronto over the last thirty years, we will argue that police and law enforcement are meant to maintain white supremacy in Toronto and not provide justice to Black communities. Third, a review of current youth justice and poverty-reduction strategies provide very preliminary entry points to begin steps towards a justice-based approach to criminality rooted in redressing the long history of white supremacist exclusion of Blackness in Toronto.

White Supremacy in Toronto/Canada

For this chapter, Canada's policy of multiculturalism typifies the ways white supremacy operates in Toronto, which acts as Canada's epicentre of the multicultural white supremacist project (Doucet 2001). Canadian multiculturalism needs to be understood alongside policing and other law enforcement entities as a form of surveillance "which exposes the underlying ugliness of multiculturalism as an oppressive act of governance over those deemed foreign" (Tecle et al. 2017, 189). The politics and history of Canada's own relationship to multiculturalism and Canadian citizenship can be best described as who does and does not belong (Abu-Laban and Gabriel 2002; Tewelde 2014). Canada's history has consistently been to deny and eliminate diversity attempting to circumvent the multicultural reality that existed before European contact and replace it with a white hegemonic order. Therefore, before discussing the ways multiculturalism is used in Toronto to reinforce white supremacy, it is necessary to understand its historical development.

Long before there was talk of multiculturalism, what we now call Canada was a vastly multicultural society. The Indigenous people of this country, as with other indigenous populations, were not a monolithic group but rather represented a collection of people made up of several ethnic groups and spoke several languages that spread across the land (Henry 2009, 120; Tewelde 2014). The arrival of the French, followed by the British from the sixteenth to eighteenth century, would underpin how Canada would come to determine who does not belong. While the ethnic diversity of the Indigenous populations was much greater than that of Europeans who had arrived, this settler group found it difficult and unnecessary to understand distinctions among the Indigenous people and referred to all Indigenous peoples as "Indians" (Henry 2009, 120–1; Tewelde 2014). This vulgarization of Indigenous peoples was not simply a misinformed view but rather rooted in ideas of Indigenous people as uncivilized and unable to govern the land and themselves (Henry 2009, 121; Tewelde 2014).

This theft of Indigenous land by the French and British settlers coincided with African slave labour, which was very much a part of the fabric of Canadian society. The existence of slavery in Canada is consistently downplayed because, in comparison, the slavery system in the United States was vast (Mensah 2002, 45; Tewelde 2014). However, this faulty logic ignores white hegemonic Canada's role in the larger global project of white supremacy and how its form of white supremacy has been carried out. So, while Canada may not have had a large plantation system, it maintained and benefitted from this construction of Blackness, even though it was a shelter for some enslaved Africans from the United States (Mensah 2002, 45; Tewelde 2014).

In the eighteenth century, Canada was no longer multicultural. Rather, it was further diversified beyond the widely varied Indigenous populations, who were joined by English, French, and enslaved Africans who came directly from Africa (and its vast diversity), the Caribbean, the United States, and Europe (Mensah 2002, 45; Tewelde 2014). Yet this multicultural reality was denied because the Indigenous peoples were viewed as "savages," despite their unique nomadic lifestyle, self-government, and religion (Henry 2009, 121; Tewelde 2014), while the Africans were not people either but labouring commodities to be bought and sold (Mensah 2002, 45; Tewelde 2014).

This exclusion forms the basis of the Royal Proclamation of 1763, which saw the defeat of the French at the hands of the British, leading to Canada becoming an Anglo nation. The proclamation also led to a mutual understanding that formed the basis of a binding relationship between whiteness and Canadian-ness. Since 1774, Canada has viewed itself as a two-nation state, when the French of Quebec were granted the right to maintain aspects of their social, legal, and religious particularity (Day 2000, 180; Tewelde 2014). And in 1791 Canada constructed itself as composed of "two founding races," leading to an Upper Canada for those who identified with "Britishness" and Lower Canada for those who preferred "Frenchness" (Day 2000, 107; Tewelde 2014). This explicit designation of what became Canada as belonging to the "founding races" and excluded the Indigenous inhabitants and African peoples also highlights the beginnings of how whiteness in Canada became synonymous with excluding non-whites. This exclusion was based on a definition of the "legitimate" citizens of Canada and not an exclusion of Indigenous and Black people's *labour*, which was equally important to maintain for the white settler society (Henry 2009; Tewelde 2014).

Canada's involvement and interest in controlling and expelling Black bodies has long been a part of its development and maintenance. Canada's history of colonial violence through the slaughter of Indigenous peoples and enslavement of African peoples was not an isolated moment in a time long past but a practice that is structurally ingrained in all aspects of Canadian society.

At the turn of the twentieth century, Canada's demand for labour stimulated the nation's need for immigration from previously defined "undesirables." The period of 1880 to the First World War introduced Canada to a host of diverse ethnicities, and "sociologically, this period is especially important, because it was during this time that the basic structure of ethnic stratification in Canada was established" (Isajiw and Stanley, 2000, p. 80; Tewelde, 2014). Directing immigration policy towards Anglo-Saxon people and the United States was not sufficient anymore and, with the completion of the railroad, Canada was opened to an influx of Eastern European and Asian immigrants. By 1921, Canadian society was different and resistance against Canada's bicultural (English and French) policies increased, as there were now many different races and ethnicities. Moreover, "these ethnicities did not represent isolated communities but were communities that became an essential part of the economy" (Isajiw and Stanley 2000, 81; Tewelde 2014).

The period after the Second World War marked another significant step in managing this house of difference (Mackey 1999; Tewelde 2014). During this time, public displays of racism became less acceptable to attract more immigrants to Canada whose numbers dwindled because of the war. Canada still wanted to limit immigration to "appropriate" individuals and nations through racist ideas such as climate suitability, which was a primary reason for excluding immigration to Africans and Caribbeans (Mackey 1999; Tewelde 2014). While the government made several attempts to give the perception that it was de-racializing immigration selection, it still maintained control and selectivity through such things as the points system (Mackey 1999; Tewelde 2014). Implicit discrimination still exists within the immigration policies because there are still hierarchies and assumptions about gender roles. The point system favours "high-skilled" work typically performed by men, reinforcing the public/private dichotomy where the male is the breadwinner and the female is dependent (Abu-Laban and Gabriel 2002; Tewelde 2014). Yet this could not stop the increased Third World migration of the 1960s, which caused fear that Canadian culture was dying (Mackey 1999; Abu-Laban and Gabriel 2002; Saloojee 2004; Austin 2013; Tewelde 2014). This period is typified by the Centennial celebration in 1967, where a strategy was announced to maintain a distinct Canadian culture built on ideas of cultural pluralism, tolerance, and biculturalism (Mackey 1999; Tewelde 2014). Against this backdrop Trudeau introduced Canada's multiculturalism policy in 1971 (Mackey 1999; Tewelde 2014).

It is evident that multiculturalism did not emerge despite Canada's history of colonialism, enslavement, and exclusion. Rather, this violent history of exclusion paved the way for the institutionalization of multiculturalism. Understanding Canada as a nation that has always been multicultural, which was consistently destabilized and undermined by white supremacy, challenges the myth of Canada as a peacekeeping nation with supposedly no history of colonialism, enslavement, and racism, that openly accepted its multicultural roots. It is more accurate to view multiculturalism as Canada's predominant method of propping up this mythology. By understanding Canada's historical relationship to exclusion, as Saloojee (2004) notes, it applies that "the development of social cohesion in Canada reflects the history of settler colonialism; as such, it is the product of the colonization of North America by the French and the British, with the latter establishing its political hegemony by the late

1700s. Subsequently the development of Canadian society, its governance, its bipolar national homogeneity and the resultant forms of Anglophone and Francophone social cohesion were all products of the particular form settler colonialism took in Canada. The modern state in Canada was born out of this history of colonialism and colonial settler violence" (413).

This argument sheds light on diversity discourses that do not stem from an enlightened perspective on how to best provide full citizenship to vulnerable populations. It is more useful to understand these internal debates amongst white supremacist colonial forces, such as the English and French, as grounded in who gets to control the land, the people who inhabit it, and through what mechanisms, as is most beneficial for the colonial forces. Therefore, non-whites are used as pawns in the Anglo-French rivalry, which is at the root of Canadian nation-building. The discourse of multiculturalism serves as a culmination of the ideological construction of Canada. The inscription of whiteness underwrites whatever may be called Englishness, Frenchness, and Europeanness, which spill over into each other, extending into the political, social, and economic (Bannerji 2000; Tewelde 2014). It is important to note that the multicultural policy, according to Pierre Trudeau, was meant to help in building Canadian unity and enlist ethnic groups as allies in the nation-building project (Mackey 1999; Tewelde 2014). The Black Canadian experience, though (like that of other non-white populations) points to a politics of fear within white supremacist Canada that configures Blackness as inherently outside the Canadian nation-building project. This fear of the potential of Blackness within white supremacist Canada has its own logic and methods distinct from the United States but similar in the white supremacist need to suppress Blackness.

The myth of Canadian multiculturalism has largely been sustained by Toronto and the assertion that it is the most multicultural city in the world. This claim was said to have been made by the United Nations Educational Scientific and Cultural Organization (UNESCO) during the late 1980s, and was often repeated by news media across Canada and the United States (Doucet 2001, 2). While UNESCO never made such a claim, it never stopped wilful ignorance of this fact by successive mayors, private businesses, and the media all wanting to project the image of a tolerant Toronto that supposedly entrenches its diversity in all aspects of Toronto life (Doucet 2001).

For example, in response to the 1988 police shootings of forty-four-year-old Lester Donaldson and seventeen-year-old Michael Wade Lawson, several social justice organizations emerged to push for change in policing and particularly to institute a civilian oversight body. The political organizing around the police shootings brought about immediate responses from the provincial government, which set up a task force to investigate police conduct, and charges were laid against the officer responsible for killing Donaldson (Moloney 1989; Tewelde 2014). However, the Toronto police became so enraged that they carried out their own protest, in which they did not carry weapons, only responded to emergency calls, and threatened to not respond to any crimes involving Black people (Moloney 1989; Tewelde 2014). To reduce this tension between Toronto's Black community and the police, Mayor Art Eggleton called for both sides to remember that "while [Toronto is] not free from its problems, it's one that's noted by the United Nations as being the most racially and culturally diverse city in the world. It's one where people can live together in peace and harmony and by and large do" (Moloney 1989, A8; Tewelde 2014).

This is the first reference in the mainstream media to the UN declaration of Toronto being the most multicultural city (Doucet 2001; Tewelde 2014). The invocation of Toronto's multiculturalism as an answer to the problem of police killings highlights how multicultural ideology must be used to pacify resistance. It is built on the erroneous assertion that diversity is equivalent to justice. More important, while Eggleton called for the Black community to reduce their political actions in the name of multiculturalism, the police were engaged in a secret campaign to monitor and infiltrate this very political organizing (Tewelde 2014).

Moreover, the reference to false reports of international recognition of Toronto and Canada's multicultural ranking ignores the use of police violence to destroy Blackness to maintain multiculturalism. The depiction of multiculturalism as Canada's shining example of a national integration policy highlights anti-Blackness sustained by surveillance (Tecle et al. 2017). As we will see in the next section, policing and its resultant racial profiling keep Black lives in a space of inferiority and oppression. The "surveillance of Blackness facilitates racial profiling resulting in the continued casting of Blackness, both historically and ontologically, as a problem" (189).

Racial Profiling as Surveillance

The policing of Black communities must be understood in the context of the colonial formation of Canada, and its historic roots in the earliest days of slavery. During this time plantation masters and slave patrollers monitored the movements of the enslaved and created rules to control and expel Black bodies, such as laws against vagrancy and loitering (Bass 2001). This early form of policing is located within a white supremacist mechanism to control Black populations. This type of social control is rooted in a pervasive notion that Black communities must be under constant surveillance because their humanity threatens white supremacist notions of nation-building. We must embrace, acknowledge, and understand the historical impact of racialization and how it has influenced the body politics of Black people (Smith 2007). Scholars have illustrated how race is monitored and negotiated in modern policing, showing that Black communities are over-represented in local police stops (Millar and

Owusu-Bempah 2011; Closs and McKenna 2006; Wortley and Tanner 2004; Wortley and Owusu-Bempah 2011). Therefore, to understand how the colonial and white supremacist nature of policing operates , this chapter will look at Toronto since the turn of the century. This focus will underscore how the criminalization of Black communities is tied to surveillance and control and not eradicating criminality.

Racial profiling in Toronto received mainstream attention in 2002 with the *Toronto Star*'s Race and Crime series, which found that Black people were taken into police stations more often than whites. The crime data also showed that a disproportionate number of Black drivers were frequently stopped, questioned, and searched by police for what became colloquially known as "Driving While Being Black Violations" (Wortley and Tanner 2004; Mastracci 2016; Canadian Civil Liberties Association 2015). Between 2008 and the middle of 2011 the *Star* reported that police stopped and detained Black youth at a rate 3.4 times greater than the city's population of young Black men. This report further highlighted that the number of young Black males aged fourteen to twenty-four stopped and detained in each of the city's seventy-two patrol zones was greater than white youth and the actual number of young Black males living in those areas (Rankin and Winsa 2013). This series highlighted how the use of national and racial characteristics to explain criminal behaviour characterized police carding and police violence directed against the Black community (Smith 2007; Bivens 2015). Racial profiling has emerged as one of the most important and contentious issues facing the City of Toronto, the Black community, and the Toronto Police Services. Racial profiling has been defined by the Ontario Human Rights Commission (2003) as "any action undertaken for reasons of safety, security or public protection that relies on stereotypes about race, colour, ethnicity, ancestry, religion, or place of origin rather than on reasonable suspicion, to single out an individual for greater scrutiny or different treatment" (6).

These studies underscored the ways in which racist acts are expressed –particularly that it is not in the form of abhorrent acts or expressions. Racism as white supremacy is particularly prevalent in "everyday racism," racist discourse being sophisticated, elusive, linguistically coded, and poorly understood (Henry and Tator 2003). Policing as an institution demonstrates how white supremacy is embedded in the operations of Canadian institutions and is concealed in system practices, policies, and laws that may seem neutral but have a serious detrimental effect on Black communities (Bass 2001; Bahdi, Parsons, and Sandborn 2009; Atkinson 1983).

Racial profiling is not only visible throughout the city and within certain communities. It replicates itself in every facet of life. So police officers begin to stereotype and behave in response to their pre-existing assumptions. It creates harm that reflects more than just racist attitudes, habits, and institutions in a society that is predisposed to favour white people's perspective on crime

(Lever 2005). The harmful effects of racial profiling far outweigh the benefits to law enforcement. The impact includes over-representation of Black youth in the criminal justice system and speaks to the extent to which Black bodies are scrutinized by police, social stigmatization, psychological harm, and negative attitudes to the criminal justice system (Tanovich 2002, 161).

Overrepresentation of Black youth in the criminal justice system is a direct consequence of how Black bodies are surveilled by police (Welch 2007; Owusu-Bempah and Wortley 2014). This is particularly evident in the ways in which Toronto neighbourhoods are used to control the movements of Black communities. The *Star*'s findings demonstrated that in each of the city's patrol zones, Black youth are more likely to be stopped and documented than whites, and those likelihoods increase in more affluent, predominantly white areas (Wortley and Tanner 2004; Rankin and Winsa 2013; Meng, Giwa, and Anucha 2015). A discursive Black criminality informs, reinforces, and inscribes the very strategies and goals of the police and state through the militarization of Black neighbourhoods (Bass 2001; Alagraa 2015). This view further perpetuates race-based territorial boundaries; in particular, spaces are inherently criminogenic when Black bodies are evident (Bass 2001; Tanovich 2002; Alagraa 2015). This draws our attention to power dynamics and the many settings in which it happens – it demonstrates the values of white supremacist Canada and the urgent need to protect the values of the nation state (Smith 2007). These values are simultaneously about maintaining white nationhood and surveilling, controlling, and expelling Black bodies, which are a threat to white nationhood (Tecle et al. 2017).

Still, Toronto Police Services has continued to resist the evidence in its reluctance to discuss race and racial difference. Canadian governments have instead chosen to use ethnic categories to measure race under the guise of multiculturalism. This only further victimizes Blacks, because the multicultural policy facilitates and accentuates the differences between Black communities and ignores the ways shared racial background consumes the practice of racial profiling (Wortley and Owusu-Bempah 2011). More accurately, the Toronto Police Service and those affiliated with the police structure have declared the Black community a threat to public safety if they continue to use a race-specific crime rate as evidence to support a race-specific stop rate in the absence of conclusive evidence of its efficacy to address crime (Meng, Giwa, and Anucha 2015; Goldsbie 2015). Therefore, the police practice of profiling which has harmed Black communities, is not about eradicating violence and other forms of criminality within Black communities (Brown 2004; Smith 2007; Tecle et al. 2017).

Racial profiling further underscores the fact that the colour of justice in Canada is white, creating greater risk for Black communities, and drawing the attention of law enforcement in public spaces. It is not the behaviour but the existence of Black communities that is the reason for surveillance (Tanovich 2002; Tecle et al. 2017). The Black criminal profile means that Black communities, regardless of age or location, are considered a potential threat (Bahdi, Parsons, and Sandborn 2009). The inherent criminality associated with Black bodies puts them on the front line of this assault, and spaces in which they socialize and live become the war zones where these actions play out (Alagraa 2015, 56). White supremacy in Canada implements state control over Black populations to restrict how and where they grow (Ruddell and Thomas 2015; Dollar 2014). Whiteness in Canada is intrinsically linked to a set of locations that are historically, politically, and culturally produced (Henry and Tator 2003). This allows for the production and reproduction of power dynamics that sustain institutional and society-wide oppression and reinforces superiority and subordination. Despite its elusiveness, most would agree that it is quietly involved with power and power differences.

It is time for Toronto Police Services and its governing bodies to devote significant resources and effort to address the allegations of racial profiling and racial bias in policing (Melchers 2003). This injustice reinforces the lack of confidence in the legitimacy and integrity of the criminal justice system. There is further harm because these feelings resurface during other interactions, even amongst police officers who are considerate, polite, and attempting to engage in equitable practices. It is the institution that is unjust, therefore the work of individuals is erased. Moreover, a cycle of reciprocal distrust is created when Black communities are reluctant to report crimes and cooperate with the police when they see crime taking place for fear of coming under suspicion. The profiled profile the profiling, creating a cycle of reciprocal distrust (Bahdi, Parsons, and Sandborn 2009). There is a presumption and expectation that Black communities should be loyal to the state, but the same state then rejects this presumption or expectation of loyalty with the underlying belief that Black communities cannot be trusted. This illustrates where Black communities suffer from the actions of white supremacy, which refuses to recognize the harassing and hierarchical nature of its action (Tewelde 2014).

This coded language is built into the discourse within the highest office of Toronto civic life. Consider the comments of Toronto Mayor Rob Ford after the infamous Danzig shooting in East Scarborough (a suburb east of Toronto), where shots were fired at a block party in a crowded neighbourhood, killing two young people and injuring several more:

> I'm going to hopefully meet with the Prime Minister to see if we can toughen our gun laws.... Once they're charged and they go to jail the most important thing is when they get out of jail. I don't want them living in the city. They can go anywhere else, but I don't want them in the city. I'm going to find out how our immigration laws work, whatever I can do to get them out of the city, I'm going to, regardless of whether they have family or friends. I don't want these people, if they're convicted to [of] a gun crime, to have anything to do with the City of Toronto. (Kuitenbrouwer 2012)

Ford's comments were made to news organizations two days after the shooting and before any suspects were announced. His statements were grounded in the assumption that the suspects were people of colour. Block party attendees were labelled in the media and by police as predominantly non-white, and this was read as a coded suggestion that they were Black. This discourse was coupled with the popular stereotype of the party's location. Danzig is considered one of Toronto's poverty-stricken areas, and the region is traditionally viewed as predominantly Black, riddled with gang violence and drug-related crimes (Kuitenbrouwer 2012). Ford's comments reified and supported the controversial police tactic of racial profiling in Toronto and reignited the discourse over this polarizing issue. This points to Blackness as a "problem" for white supremacist Canada that needs to be managed, controlled, and surveilled (Tecle et al. 2017).

Toronto Police Services have engaged in significant conversation on providing more effective services while managing ballooning policing budgets, abuse of vulnerable communities, and increased demands to do more community engagement and adapt to technological advancements. For example, in 2012, the Toronto Police Service responded to claims of racism and discrimination by developing the Police and Community Engagement Review (PACER). The result was a report that contained thirty-one recommendations on public accountability, governance, community consultation, professional standards, human resources, performance management, information management, operational improvements, intelligence-led policing, corporate communications, and project management (Toronto Police Service 2012). In 2017, Toronto police also developed the Transformational Taskforce, to better focus on what the public most needs from police, embrace partnerships to create safe communities, and better zero in on the complex needs of a large city (Toronto Police Service 2017).

Both initiatives underscore an understanding that traditional policing methods have been inefficient and unequal. The economics of these proposals would allow for a more efficient use of taxpayer dollars to enhance alternatives to fighting criminality through an equitable lens for Black communities. The savings that come from investing in social services and community work could be reinvested in further infrastructure to address the social, political, and economic inequalities that lead to youth criminality. There is a promising opportunity to open conversations about justice-focused mechanisms if these proposals provide an opportunity to go beyond arrests, convictions, and prisons, and rely on more community expertise.

This may allow for a move beyond merely discussing the systemic discourses of the practice of racial profiling. It can provide an opportunity to pay attention to the intersections of race, class, and gender and how they are inextricably linked to white supremacist power structures in Canada and the concentration of crime within Black communities in cities like Toronto. It is time to interrogate the silent discourse which takes whiteness for granted and equates whiteness with the norm (Yee and Dumbrill 2003) because of its connection to the perception and fear of the Blackness as a public enemy; this has served as the foundation for police racial profiling and the continued criminalization of Blackness.

Alternatives and Recommendations

As this chapter has laid out, the continued use of policing to address criminality, particularly within Black communities of Toronto, is part of the longer history of colonialism, slavery, and segregation in Canada. It is about surveillance for white supremacist state control. The language of "fighting guns and gangs" and "law and order" are code words in Canada that are politically expedient, allowing police, elected officials, and community members to identify who is desirable and undesirable. It does not offer success in eliminating crime.

For this chapter, a focus on justice for victims, perpetrators, and their communities are required so that a holistic approach is taken to support Black communities in preparing themselves for the future and give them real opportunity to experience their full potential. A justice focus for Black and marginalized communities requires an understanding that the Canadian legal system has operated on unequal terms. The racial and economic disparity between who is imprisoned and who is not is the most damning evidence against the reliance on police, courts, and prisons. This also means that for the Canadian government to consider itself concerned with justice, it is necessary to move away from policing, courts, and prisons as solutions to criminality and understand them as tools of a system that further marginalizes historically oppressed communities – particularly Indigenous and Black communities. A justice focus requires meaningfully investing in removing socioeconomic inequalities that have disproportionately affected Black communities.

Violence and criminality within marginalized communities, such as Black communities, points to the ways criminality is linked to alienation, economic inequality, and growing anger and resentment, especially among young, low-income, racially marginalized men. Consider that in 2012, forty-eight people – mostly young men – were victims of homicide in Toronto. Most were under the age of thirty, and disproportionately large numbers were young Black men and members of other racially marginalized communities. Black men under the age of thirty made up 33 per cent of the shooting homicide victims, even though the Black male youth under thirty years old make up 7 per cent of the male population under the age of thirty in Toronto (Tewelde and Olawoye 2013).

A deeper look highlights this point further by examining the community of York South Weston (YSW) in Toronto. YSW is in the west end of Toronto in the old city of York and contains 10 of the 140 official neighbourhoods. A staggering 6 out of 10 of these neighbourhoods (Rustic, Keelesdale–Eglinton

West, Rockcliffe-Smythe, Beechborough-Greenbrook, Weston, Mount Dennis) are designated by the city as Neighbourhood Improvement Areas (NIA) (City of Toronto 2014). NIAs are identified as "at risk" using socio-economic indicators, proximity to services, and the number of annual homicides; the city has identified 31 of the 140 official neighbourhoods as NIAs. YSW also has the third highest high school dropout rates within the Toronto District School Board (Brown and Marmureanu 2016) and some of the highest rates of child poverty in Canada (Family Service Toronto 2018).

Understanding the ways the legal system has operated unequally, and attempting to address the socioeconomic root causes is not only morally just, but also a more fiscally responsible path to reducing criminality and violence. The benefits are therefore potentially astronomical because there is an opportunity to better allocate the resources dedicated to police, courts, and prisons to include community and social service partners. This must be done if we are to shift the focus to justice, which is much more complex and requires the involvement of many partners beyond law enforcement.

Unjust treatment for Black communities points to factors that have a severe economic impact not only on the communities that experience the consequences of poverty but also on public institutions. The focus on policing and imprisonment places intense strain on our criminal justice system. For example, the Canadian Council on Learning shows that there are extreme costs that can be associated with dropping out of high school (Hankivsky 2008). The annual costs to the criminal justice system are estimated at over $220 per high school dropout, or $350 million per year. Furthermore, social determinants associated with crime are strongly correlated with dropping out. The average public cost of providing social assistance (e.g., benefits for food, fuel, shelter, clothing, and special needs, as well as work incentive programs) is estimated at over $4,000 per year per high school dropout, or $969 million per year (Tewelde and Olawoye 2013).

It is not hyperbole to consider the situation a crisis, considering that the over-policing of Black communities has led to the Canadian Black inmate over-representation to be similar to American data on Black inmates. For example, in Ontario, there are four times more Black boys in the young male jail population than there are in the general young male population (Tewelde 2018). Some estimates have conservatively estimated the cost of crime in Canada at $99.6 billion. Furthermore, Toronto's share of this cost can be conservatively estimated at $10.9 billion. This research points out that with previous "studies calculating that 4% of crime that can be attributed to poverty, we see that a total of $436 million of Toronto's crime-related costs are attributable to poverty" (Briggs, Lee, and Stapleton 2016).

We cannot continue to ignore that the concentration of violence and criminality within Black and low-income communities in Toronto is linked to alienation, economic inequality, and growing anger and resentment (Tewelde and

Olawoye 2013). The manner in which long-established inequalities are concentrated amongst Black and low-income communities in education, employment, income, housing, and health point to the oppressive relationship Black communities have with Canada (Tewelde Olawoye 2013). Therefore, it is time Canadian governments federally, provincially, and municipally put policies into practice that address the ways that the root causes of crime are in the colonial and racist history of Canada.

For some insight into how addressing root causes is a proven tactic, consider the work of one organization doing alternative justice work – For Youth Initiative (FYI). This organization received federal funds in 2014 for a three-year comprehensive gang intervention program that employs prosocial programs and services such as counselling, education re-engagement, and employment supports. The federal government recognized a need to find alternatives to the status quo. The success of the program can be seen in the partnerships developed with law enforcement agencies while still maintaining a community engagement focus. Out of the 100-plus young people who went through the program over the three-year period, fewer than 10 per cent reoffended; close to 90 per cent of participants in this program were Black. Furthermore, those who reoffended still received support and services from For Youth Initiative that mitigated any future criminal activity. At the close of the program, participants reported an increase in academic grades and ability, growing feelings of support and more networks for them to turn to, as well as a reduction in criminal engagement (Tewelde 2018).

However, even with success from FYI and similar programs, funding and government partnerships remain inconsistent and rarely move beyond the pilot phase. It is imperative that Canada increase its commitment to such programs to increase youth justice, because it's unsustainable to rely on non-profits using charitable dollars and other types of fundraising. Governments cannot continue to outsource this work to community and social service partners without properly resourcing and partnering with them. While this type of initiative is not the only solution to addressing racial and economic injustice, it is an example of how to deal with the systemic mechanisms that let them flourish. It is time for Canada to get behind a justice focus for youth. Therefore, this chapter proposes recommendations and questions to open a broader range of policy options to fight crime through direct intervention in the root causes.

Recommendations: Working towards a Justice Focus

Any discussion of a justice focus on crime must begin with an examination of the racialized pathologies that permeate the discourse of law and order. Canada operates with a legal system that focuses on maintaining the authority of the state and, therefore, white supremacy (Galabuzzi 2010). A justice system acknowledges the historical roots of inequality and seeks to correct them by acknowledging that the concentration of crime in Black, racially marginalized, low-income communities is inextricably linked to colonial white supremacy that founded Canada. To understand the increase and concentration of crime and violence in Toronto requires a focus on the high levels of poverty, marginalization, hopelessness, and powerlessness in these neighbourhoods subjected to the denial of government resources, and racial and class segregation.

A justice focus looks to developing a healthy community as the primary crime-fighting strategy. The elimination of poverty is tied to eradicating racism and how it operates within housing, education, health care, transportation, and the justice system (Tewelde and Olawoye 2013; Galabuzzi 2010; Tewelde 2018). This requires meaningful investments in all these areas, in order to make the social context work for everyone and move away from piecemeal and sporadic initiatives; otherwise we will continuously be taking one step forward and two steps backwards. The most disadvantaged must have access to excellent public service, which requires undoing the economic segregation that characterizes Canadian life in Toronto (Tewelde Olawoye 2013; Galabuzzi 2010; Tewelde 2018). As has been argued in this chapter, the high concentrations of disadvantaged communities creates huge long-term social costs and will require a sustained, steady accumulation of successes to reverse the current and very troubling trends. Therefore, this chapter proposes that federal, provincial, and municipal governments implement legislation that guarantees five poverty-elimination strategies as primary methods to fight crime in Canada, for every single person, regardless of income:

1. Quality housing
2. Pharmacare
3. Full mental health support
4. Affordable transportation
5. Access to quality food

Starting with poverty elimination as the primary crime-fighting strategy underscores the reality that traditional legal mechanisms such as police, courts, and prisons do not work. As has been argued throughout this chapter, they are costlier, do not address root causes, and are steeped in the colonial and racist history of Canada. Poverty elimination takes a preventive approach to crime fighting, which police, courts, and prisons do not and cannot accomplish. However, there also needs to be intervention to address criminality, which must happen simultaneously with the preventive approach of poverty eradication. The FYI program discussed earlier shows promising signs of what is possible if similar programs are more heavily implemented and scaled. They have proven successful and are far more cost effective but are not sustained because of inconsistent funding from all levels of government (Tewelde 2018). Therefore, this chapter proposes that all youth in conflict with the law be immediately directed to pro-social programs in three ways:

1. There needs to be a full redirecting of all youth detention facilities into education centres that are built into the communities where youth live. Every single Black youth who has committed a crime must be enrolled in and supported with counselling to complete a secondary and post-secondary education program.
2. Like the recommendation on education, all Black youth and young adults who have committed a crime must be directed to an employment training preparation program with a direct connection to employment.
3. There must be investment in education, social services, and opportunities for youth to prevent them from becoming involved in antisocial activities.

The identification of root causes that can lead to Black, racially marginalized, and low-income youth and communities to engage in criminality must be the primary focus. Policing operates as a form of surveillance, which is highlighted by the practice of racial profiling, which affects the life chances of Black, racially marginalized, poor populations; this (re)produces and reinforces the experiences of social exclusion and expulsion.

Going even further, refocusing policing, courts, and prisons as tools that support pro-social activities could be a mechanism to develop stronger collaborations between law enforcement and the wider community. It may allow for healthier interactions between police and Black, Indigenous, and other racially marginalized youth and their communities. Redirecting the focus of police away from arresting and processing youth through courts and prisons and towards mandating that all youth be directed to centres with emphasis on education and employment could be an opportunity to think of policing in different ways; in a community development approach the focus will be on the causes of criminality and the imprisonment of the vulnerable.

Restoration must be a goal of any justice focus in two ways: state to aggrieved communities to redress past wrong (i.e., reparations) and the offender to community (i.e., restorative justice). In restoration between the state and aggrieved communities, there needs to be development and implementation of a Restoration and Reparations plan that is specific to Black communities; the legalization of marijuana in Canada offers an opportunity to act. For example, Akwasi Owusu-Bempah (2017) has offered analysis that can be followed immediately:

1. Pardoning the convicted
2. Social reinvestment of tax revenue from legal sales
3. Incorporation of those affected by prohibition into the licit cannabis industry

There needs to be a full research project done on implementing a restorative justice mechanism that can replace prisons. Still, this chapter would argue for scaled-up programs like those at FYI. Angela Davis (2003) has provided similar alternatives which this chapter would further endorse.

Researchers have been limited to information on the race of people stopped and searched by police and therefore need to rely on qualitative information, which has been vigorously attacked as "anecdotal" or "junk science" by police officials and some academics (Wortley and Owusu-Bempah 2011). No matter the viewpoint, the research literature tends to ignore neighbourhood and socio-economic and political characteristics, and it is somewhat unrealistic to presume that researchers will have access to much of this research. The ambivalence to collecting data based on race makes it difficult for researchers to examine and question the disproportionate stop-and-searches and overrepresentation of Blacks within the criminal justice system and address racial discrimination. As a result, there needs to be an expansive analysis to determine the cost for governments to implement and stabilize funding for these initiatives. Direct costs to taxpayers must be outlined if we are to make the case for radically transforming to a justice approach.

Conclusion

This chapter has attempted to reclaim the language of "thug" by deepening the analysis for what constitutes violence. Particularly, in myriad ways systemic white supremacist violence in Canada has been directed towards Black communities to expose the ludicrous mainstream narrative of "Black-on-Black crime." Thugs focus on Black communities because anti-Blackness characterizes the policing of Black life, because anti-Blackness characterizes white supremacy. Canadian white supremacy attempts to fortify Canada's larger goal of controlling and expelling Black communities through illusory inclusivity and acceptance discourse alongside the disdain for thugs – code for eliminating Blackness. That any attempt to achieve a socially just Canada for all must eliminate anti-Blackness in order to eliminate white supremacy in all social, political, and economic relations. A thug approach is a justice-based approach.

So, to be thug is to be a real crime fighter, because thugs want to strike at the core of criminality. Thugs expose police, prison, and courts as feeble crime deterrents or suppressants. More important, thugs expose law enforcement as a tool for an oppressive colonial system built on the false superiority of whiteness and inferiority of Blackness. Thugs understand how crime is inextricably tied to the ways poverty is concentrated geographically and racially. To be thug is to understand the systemic nature of this violence towards Black communities in Canada. This includes over-incarceration, high rates of Black youth dropout (or rather push out) from school, how poverty operates in concentrated and generational ways, under-representation in political, social, and economic decision-making bodies, negative stereotyping for Black communities, and the constant ignorance to these facts within white supremacist Canada.

Thugs envision a liberated future that centralizes agency for Black communities, which simultaneously rejects white supremacy. To be thug is to acknowledge the pointlessness of seeking acceptance in white supremacist Canada. Black communities must strive for political, social, and economic autonomy for survival. Canada's myth of being a peaceful country socially, politically, and economically opens up larger questions about the futility of integrationist ideologies and the need for alternatives that affirm political, social, and economic autonomy for Black communities. To be thug is to ultimately support, reconceptualize, and develop Black communities' relationship to all of humanity, nature, and themselves.

REFERENCES

Abu-Laban, Y., and C. Gabriel. 2002. *Selling Diversity: Immigration, Multiculturalism, Employment Equity and Globalization*. Peterborough, ON: Broadview.

Alagraa, B. 2015. *Known to the Police: A Black Male Reflection on Police Violence in Toronto*. Toronto: Department of Geography, University of Toronto.

Atkinson, G.H. 1983. *Do No Further Harm: Becoming a White Ally in Child Welfare Work with Aboriginals*. School of Social Work, University of Victoria, BC.

Austin, D. 2013. *Fear of a Black Nation: Race, Sex and Security in Sixties Montreal*. Toronto: Between the Lines.

Bahdi, R., O. Parsons, and T. Sandborn. 2009. "Racial Profiling." BC Civil Liberties Association position paper submitted to the Board of the BCCLA.

Bannerji, H. 2000. "On the Dark Side of the Nation: Politics of Multiculturalism and the State of 'Canada.'" *Journal of Canadian Studies* 31 (3): 103–28. https://doi.org/10.3138/jcs.31.3.103.

Bass, S. 2001. "Policing Space, Policing Race: Social Control Imperatives and Police Discretionary Decisions." *Social Justice Journal* 28 (1): 156–76. www.jstor.org/stable/29768062

Bivens, F. 2015. "Ontario New Carding Policies Are Useless. We Need Real Conversations about Police Racism." *Globe and Mail*, 29 October. http://www.theglobeandmail.com/opinion/ontarios-new-carding-policies-are-useless-we-need-real-conversations-about-police-racism/article27028607/.

Briggs, A., C. Lee, and J. Stapleton. 2016. "The Cost of Poverty in Toronto November 2016." https://openpolicyontario.s3.amazonaws.com/uploads/2016/11/Cost-of-Poverty-R10-Final-forweb.pdf.

Bronskill, J. 2018. "Toronto Mayor Wants Tougher Gun Laws, Resources for Anti-Gang Efforts." CTV News, 7 March. https://www.ctvnews.ca/politics/toronto-mayor-wants-tougher-gun-laws-resources-for-anti-gang-efforts-1.3832144.

Brown, M. 2006. "In Their Own Voices: African Canadians in Toronto Share Experiences of Police Profiling." In *Racial Profiling in Canada: Challenging the Myth of a Few Bad Apples*, 151–83. Toronto: University of Toronto Press. https://doi.org/10.3138/9781442678972-009.

Brown, R.S., and C. Marmureanu. 2016. "Cohort Graduation Rates by Ward, 2010–15." Research report no. 15/16-19. Toronto: Toronto District School Board.

Canadian Civil Liberties Association. 2015. "A Recent History of Racial Profiling and Policing."

City of Toronto. 2014. "Neighbourhood Improvement Area Profiles."" https://www.toronto.ca/city-government/data-research-maps/neighbourhoods-communities/nia-profiles/.

Clarke, G.E. 2014. "An Anatomy of the Originality of African-Canadian Thought." *CLR James Journal* 20 (1–2): 65–82. https://doi.org/10.5840/clrjames2014983.

Closs, W.J., and P.F. McKenna. 2006. "Profiling a Problem in Canadian Police Leadership: The Kingston Police Data Collection Problem." *Canadian Public Administration* 49 (2): 143–60. https://doi.org/10.1111/j.1754-7121.2006.tb01976.x.

Davis, A.Y. 2003. *Are Prisons Obsolete?* New York: Seven Stories.

Day, R.J.F. 2000. *Multiculturalism and the History of Canadian Diversity.* Toronto: University of Toronto Press.

Dollar, C.B. 2014. "Racial Threat Theory: Assessing the Evidence, Requesting Redesign." *Journal of Criminology* 2014, Article ID 983026. https://doi.org/10.1155/2014/983026.

Doucet, M. 2001. "The Anatomy of an Urban Legend: Toronto's Multicultural Reputation." CERIS working paper no. 16. Toronto: Joint Centre of Excellence for Research on Immigration and Settlement.

Family Service of Toronto. 2018. "Riding by Riding Analysis Shows Child Poverty in Canada Knows No Boundaries." Campaign 2000. https://www.google.com/search?q=riding+by+analysis&rlz=1C5CHFA_enCA828CA828&oq=riding+by+analysis&aqs=chrome..69i57.6143j0j8&sourceid=chrome&ie=UTF-8.

Galabuzzi, G. 2010. "The Intersecting Experience of Racialized Poverty and the Criminalization of the Poor." In *Poverty, Regulation and Social Justice: Readings on the Criminalization of Poverty*, edited by D. Crocker & V.M. Johnson, 75–94. Black Point, NS: Fernwood Publishing.

Gillis, W. 2018. "With 90 Homicides in 2018, Toronto Marks Grim Record." *Toronto Star*, 18 November. https://www.thestar.com/news/gta/2018/11/18/with-90-homicides-in-2018-toronto-marks-grim-record.html.

Goldsbie, J. 2015. "Police Carding: Racist, Anti-Black and Useless." *Now Magazine*, 13 May. https://nowtoronto.com/news/police-carding-racist-anti-black-and-useless/.

Government of Canada. 2018. "Social Determinants of Health and Health Inequalities." https://www.canada.ca/en/public-health/services/health-promotion/population-health/what-determines-health.html.

Hankivsky, O. 2008. "Cost Estimates of Dropping Out of High School in Canada." Canadian Council on Learning.

Henry, F. 2009. "Racism and Aboriginal Peoples." In *The Colour of Democracy: Racism in Canadian Society*, edited by F. Henry and C. Tator. 4th ed. Toronto: Nelson Education.

Henry, F., and C. Tator. 2003. "Racial Profiling in Toronto: Discourses of Domination, Mediation and Opposition." Submitted to the Canadian Race Relations Foundation.

Isajiw, W.B., and S.R. Stanley. 2000. "Understanding Diversity: Ethnicity & Race in the Canadian Context." *Canadian Journal of Sociology* 25 (3): 405–8. https://doi.org/10.2307/3341653.

Kitossa, T. 2018. "'Thugs' Is a Race-Code Word That Fuels Anti-Black Racism." The Conversation, 17 October. https://theconversation.com/thugs-is-a-race-code-word-that-fuels-anti-black-racism-100312.

Kuitenbrouwer, P. 2012. "Life and Death on 'the Other Side of the Tracks.'" *National Post*, 17 July. https://nationalpost.com/news/danzig-street-shootings-even-shock-the-other-side-of-the-tracks.

Lever, A. 2005. "Why Racial Profiling Is Hard to Justify: A Response to Risse and Zeckhauser." *Philosophy & Public Affairs* 33 (1): 94–110. https://doi.org/10.1111/j.1088-4963.2005.00026.x

Mackey, E. 1999. *The House of Difference: Cultural Politics and National Identity in Canada*. London: Routledge.

MacLeod, M. 2018. "Stats Show Sharp Uptick in Toronto Shootings, but Murder Rate Still Below a Dozen Other Canadian Cities." *CTV News*, 21 December. https://www.ctvnews.ca/canada/stats-show-sharp-uptick-in-toronto-shootings-but-murder-rate-still-below-a-dozen-other-canadian-cities-1.4224142.

Mastracci, D. 2016. "Calling Out the Cops." *Ryerson Review of Journalism*, 12 April. http://rrj.ca/calling-out-the-cops/.

McLaughlin, A. 2018. "Toronto's Record Homicide Year Marked by 'Senseless' Violence, Top Investigator Says." CBC News, 20 December. https://www.cbc.ca/news/canada/toronto/hank-idsinga-toronto-homicide-record-1.4952952.

Melchers, R. 2003. "Do Toronto Police Engage in Racial Profiling?" *Canadian Journal of Criminology and Criminal Justice* 45 (3): 347–66. https://doi.org/10.3138/cjccj.45.3.347.

Meng, Y., S. Giwa, and U. Anucha. 2015. "Is There Racial Discrimination in Police Stop-and-Searches of Black Youth? A Toronto Case Study." *Canadian Journal of Family and Youth* 7 (1): 115–58. https://doi.org/10.29173/cjfy24301.

Mensah, J. 2002. *Black Canadians: History, Experiences, Social Conditions*. Halifax: Fernwood Publishing.

Millar, P., and A. Owusu-Bempah. 2011. "Whitewashing Criminal Justice in Canada: Preventing Research through Data Suppression." *Canadian Journal of Law and Society* 26 (3): 653–61. https://doi.org/10.3138/cjls.26.3.653.

Moloney, P. 1989. "Police Action Sparks Pleas to Cool Down." *Toronto Star*, 13 January.

Ontario Human Rights Commission. 2003. "Paying the Price: The Human Cost of Racial Profiling." http://www.ohrc.on.ca/en/resources/discussion_consultation/RacialProfileReportEN/pdf.

– 2018. "OHRC Interim Report on Toronto Police Service Inquiry Shows Disturbing Results." http://www.ohrc.on.ca/en/news_centre/ohrc-interim-report-toronto-police-service-inquiry-shows-disturbing-results.

Owusu-Bempah, A. 2017. "Let's Repair the Harms of Canada's War on Drugs." *Toronto Star*, 10 July.
Owusu-Bempah, A., and S. Wortley. 2014. "Race, Crime, and Criminal Justice in Canada." In *The Oxford Handbook on Race, Ethnicity, Crime, and Immigration*, edited by S. Bucerius and M. Tonry, 281–320. New York: Oxford University Press.
Public Safety Canada. 2018. "Building Safe and Resilient Canada." Summit on Gun and Gang Violence. http://video.isilive.ca/pssp/2018-03-07/Agenda.pdf.
Rankin, J., and P. Winsa. 2013. "Unequal Justice: Aboriginal and Black Inmates Disproportionately Fill Ontario Jails." *Toronto Star*, 1 March. https://www.thestar.com/news/insight/2013/03/01/unequal_justice_aboriginal_and_black_inmates_disproportionately_fill_ontario_jails.html.
Ruddell, R., and M. Thomas. 2015. "Determinants of Police Strength in Canadian Cities: Assessing the Impact of Minority Threat." *Canadian Journal of Criminology and Criminal Justice* 57 (2): 215–52. https://doi.org/10.3138/CJCCJ.2012.E17.
Saloojee, A. 2004. "Social Cohesion and the Limits of Multiculturalism in Canada." In *Racism Eh? A Critical Inter-disciplinary Anthology of Race and Racism in Canada*, edited by C.A. Nelson and C.A. Nelson, 410–28. Concord, ON: Captus.
Smiley, C.J., and D. Fakunle. 2016. "From 'Brute' to 'Thug': The Demonization and Criminalization of Unarmed Black Male Victims in America." *Journal of Human Behaviour Social Environment* 26 (3–4): 350–66. https://doi.org/10.1080/10911359.2015.1129256.
Smith, C. 2007. "Conflict, Crisis and Accountability: Racial Profiling and Law Enforcement in Canada." Canadian Centre for Policy Alternatives.
Tanovich, D. 2002. "Using the Charter to Stop Racial Profiling: The Development of an Equality-Based Conception of Arbitrary Detention." *Osgoode Hall Law Journal* 40 (2): 145–87. https://digitalcommons.osgoode.yorku.ca/ohlj/vol40/iss2/2/.
Tecle, S., T. Chimbganda, F. D'Amico, and Y. Tewelde. 2017. "Castrating Blackness: Surveillance, Profiling and Management in the Canadian Context." In Spaces of Surveillance: States and Selves, edited by S. Flynn and A. Mackay. Cham: Macmillan. https://doi.org/10.1007/978-3-319-49085-4_11.
Tewelde, Y. 2014. "Spooks, Spies, and Multicultural Lies: Surveillance and the Expulsion of Blackness in Canada." *Africalogical Perspectives* 10 (1): 209–40.
– 2018. "A Youth Justice System That's More Than Courts and Prisons." Policy Options Politiques, 20 April. http://policyoptions.irpp.org/magazines/april-2018/youth-justice-system-thats-courts-prisons/.
Tewelde, Y., and L. Olawoye. 2013. *From Analysis to Action: A Collective Approach to Eliminate Youth Violence*. Prepared for the Youth Anti-Violence Task Force.
Toronto Police Service. 2012. The Police and Community Engagement Review (PACER). https://tpsb.ca/The%20PACER%20Report.pdf.
– 2017. "The Way Forward: Modernizing Community Safety in Toronto."
Walker, B. 2010. *Race on Trial: Black Defendants in Ontario's Criminal Courts, 1858–1958*. Toronto: University of Toronto Press.

Welch, K. 2007. "Black Criminal Stereotypes and Racial Profiling." *Journal of Contemporary Criminal Justice* 23 (3): 276–88. https://doi.org/10.1177/1043986207306870.

Westhoff, B. 2014. "The Outlawz Speak on Tupac and His Ink, Dispute the Meaning of 'Thug Life.'" *LA Weekly*, 14 September. https://www.laweekly.com/music/the-outlawz-speak-on-tupac-and-his-ink-dispute-the-meaning-of-thug-life-2411036.

Winsa, P. 2014. "Federal Government Gives $500,000 to Weston–Mount Dennis Anti-Gang Program." *Toronto Star*, 27 March. https://www.thestar.com/news/gta/2014/03/27/federal_government_gives_500000_to_local_antigang_program.html#.

Wortley, S., and A. Owusu-Bempah. 2011. "The Usual Suspects: Police Stop and Search Practices in Canada." *Policing and Society* 21 (4): 395–407. https://doi.org/10.1080/10439463.2011.610198.

Wortley, S., and J. Tanner. 2004. "Discrimination or Good Policing? The Racial Profiling Debate in Canada." *Our Diverse Cities* 1: 197–201. https://www.yorku.ca/lfoster/2019-20/RESP%204052/lectures/Discrimination%20or%20Good%20Policing_WortleyTanner.pdf.

Yee, J.Y., and G. Dumbrill. 2003. "Whiteout: Looking for Race in Canadian Social Work Practice. In *Multicultural Social Work in Canada: Working with Diverse Ethno-Racial Communities*, 98–121. Don Mills, ON: Oxford University Press.

16 We Make the Path by Walking It: Repairing, Restoring, and Constructing Pathways

RICK KELLY

and tellin' those sweet lies and losin' again.
I was lookin' for love in all the wrong places,
Lookin' for love in too many faces,
searchin' their eyes and lookin' for traces

(Mallette, Morrison, and Ryan, 1980)

A Question of Perspective

What if our framing of the discussion about gangs and those involved in gangs mirrored the lines in this song? Are we looking in all the wrong places to understand gangs and gang involvement? What if, in some respects, the definitions and labels lead to a focus that was misleading? What would happen if definitions began with the views of those with lived experience? It would then be described as follows. "Gangs ... is used way to often ... too lightly ... gives negative power to those who are not gangs. Stick that label on .... then handled wrong versus a group of friends who hang out together ... because they are smoking weed together, stealing bikes. Then from a systems point of view they are surveyed by police ... like those in Jane Finch who then can't get jobs.... Cocktail for disaster" (Olumogba, personal interview, 8 November 2018). The label of gang does not reflect the underlying needs of the individuals who find themselves caught up in such activities.

What if we asked about the motivation for choices, not from a criminological perspective, but rather as the criminologist John Braithwaite suggests, from the standpoint of why people do the right thing (Braithwaite 1989)? He directs our attention to the fact that our connection to others is more often the motivation for actions and doing the right thing, even if there are disagreements over what is considered to be the right thing.

What if we directed our attention to where the problem does not yet exist and where individuals are not involved in gang activity? This would involve looking at people in their formative years, when they are young, before the intersecting forces propel some individuals into gang involvement.

The Discussion

This chapter builds on the voices and lived experiences of several individuals who have experienced, seen, or participated in violence in their communities, incarceration, weapons charges and/or tragically losing loved ones. They have also created different psychological and social spaces for those who may be or are on a path towards gang involvement.

It draws on the author's more than years as a youth worker, researcher, and educator which have included extensive work to create small- and large-scale opportunities for infants, children, youth and their families, and schools in those communities and neighbourhoods labelled as high priority or neighbourhood improvement areas. The author writes from the vantage point of being a cisgender male Caucasian, somewhat aware of his privilege and working to be a good ally. Throughout, the author applies a restorative lens that looks at the relational harm in events with a view to focusing on the reparative, restorative and preventive approaches that lead to transformation for individuals and their communities

The discussion draws from selected policy initiatives and frameworks used from the 1980s onward to frame action at a systemic or population level, in two approaches to child and youth development that aim to prevent high-risk involvement. Both are evidence based with more than twenty years of accumulated quantitative and qualitative data. One is an early intervention and health promotion model, the Better Beginnings, Better Futures demonstration project (Peters, Petrunka, and Arnold 2003) and the other is the model generated by Roca, Inc. (Baldwin and Zeira 2017) in the United States for high-risk youth. It uses current research on the racialization of individuals, groups, and communities, as well as current events and political responses. The attempt is to select salient moments and relevant perspectives that are representative and help us to answer the questions posed and move towards comprehensive solutions.

The Summer of 2018

It is the summer of the 2018. The City of Toronto and the GTA has been beset by gun- and knife-related violence that rivals and outstrips the experience of the infamously named "Summer of the Gun" in 2005 and approximates the number of deaths experienced in 1991. It is a reprise of a similar set of tragic and violent experiences, but with incidents and other features that have awakened the whole city as the violence moves into areas unaccustomed to seeing such events. Not all the events can be categorized in the same way. Some were singular acts intended to cause large-scale harm and havoc, by individuals perpetrating the violence that was refracted through the prism of mental illness. However, several events could be categorized as gang related and connected to retribution and turf wars as described by the chief of police for the City of Toronto, Mark Saunders (Mclaughlin 2018). All of these events have had, and continue to have, profound ripple effects as the impacts are felt by those directly harmed, their families, and the larger community.

As these events grabbed the headlines of local and national papers, the responses from all quarters covered the gamut of opinion from gun control from the mayor of Toronto (Robins-Early 2018) to a standard get-tough-on-crime from the leader of the federal Conservative party calling for increased policing and no gun control (Wright 2018), to a consistent set of insights that traced these events to dynamics anchored in communities, poverty, racial dynamics, and the opportunities thwarted for young racialized men. The headline responses and news reporting created a binary set of positions creating an either/or set of options. What is important is to take a nuanced and balanced approach to the issues. Any approach must consider and address the root causes of violence and gang involvement.

The Social Determinants of Health

The primary and social determinants of health – and in their absence, ill health – are the components of the foundation for the pathways and trajectories for young people, starting from their early years and moving into adulthood. The elements that comprise the social determinants of health exist through design or can be found to be absent through neglect and default. This way of thinking about health and development is a different paradigm. It moves away from individualizing experiences, and places events and social problems in a multi-factored context. It lends itself to more ecologically and integrated approaches. It sets the frame for public health responses to issues.

Pathways by Default

No infant comes into the world carrying a gun or wearing gang-coloured nappies. Social dynamics intersect and create the conditions for later development of young people that become problematic. One way of describing these determinants or their absence is captured in the words and reflections of a long-time resident, from the Jane Finch area in Toronto, Symone Walters.

Imagine to yourself an innocent child growing up laughing and playing, skipping in the yard, swinging in the park, and just steps away are the images of drug selling, brassy objects that stick out from under shirts that glisten as the sun shines down upon them, clusters of men dressed in all black huddle up in the corners and staircases of the high-rise buildings. What chance does this child have now? What influences will make this child who he or she will become? At a very tender age some of these children are recruited to do what they perceive as just a favour: "Bring this bag across the street and give it to the guy in the shiny, black car." No questions asked, the child does what he or she is told. One delivery becomes two, then three, then ten, and before that child realizes, he or she is sixteen and has become a permanent fixture on the street corner doing what was once an innocent delivery. The brandishes of silver and gold chains hanging from their necks, the $200 pair of shoes fastened to their feet, the $300 pair of jeans hanging off their hips. Unable to escape the life that was placed upon them, what chance does this child have now? (Walters, 15 October 2018)

A Wider Lens: The Ontario Child Health Study (OCHS, 1983)

There is no need to reinvent the wheel to understand the extent to which issues affect the population of children and youth. But there is room for improvement and advances in our understanding. There has been an evolving series of policy, research, and pilot initiatives that have brought us closer to a deeper understanding that more accurately captures the multiplicity of factors and suggests solutions.

In 1983 the Ontario government assessed the incidence and prevalence of mental health disorders in the child population, ages four to sixteen. This was a significant effort and advance in looking at individual issues through a broader and population-based lens. The findings revealed:

- 18 per cent of children in Ontario (one in six) were identified with a diagnosable psychiatric disorder
- Only 20 per cent of this group received appropriate mental health services
- There were identifiable contributing social factors that increased the likelihood of the presence of these disorders
- Some factors identified included such elements as early development, school performance, family income, and family size (Offord 1989),

The strength of the study was that it offered a broad picture of mental health for children in the province and associated risk factors. This created a way of targeting resources while expanding the focus to include associated social and family factors.

The limitation of this study was that there was no mention of race and the racialization of experience, and it did not embrace an explicit social determinants of health framework. Elements of some of the social determinants were identified but were not integrated as an all-encompassing framework. It was deficit focused, and when citing contributing factors such as "single led families" there was no alternative narrative to highlight the strength in such family configurations. The focus of the report and findings were expressed in and around diagnosable psychiatric terms and not in the voice or words of those who had lived experience.

Going Upstream: Better Beginnings, Better Futures (1989)

Early intervention is a model often cited and researched as one solution to the gang issue. Wendy Cukier, president of the Coalition for Gun Control and professor at Toronto Metropolitan University is quoted in a recent newspaper article making this very point. "If I were 'Queen of the World' in trying to find out systems that would drive change, there's no question that making sure kids have a chance to be successful is where you'd put your money. There's tonnes of evidence that early childhood intervention and supporting families, all those kind of things, can have a real impact" (Rankin 2018).

Based on the findings of the OCHS, the Ministry of Community and Social Services began to develop a model for programs and interventions that could address them. The Better Beginnings, Better Futures initiative was a tri-ministry model and policy demonstration project in eleven communities from around the province that aimed to investigate the cost benefits of a prevention approach to child maltreatment. The intent was to follow children ages from birth to four years and four to eight years old over a twenty-rive-year period to trace the trajectory of development that arose after laying a foundation of positive and comprehensive early years opportunities in the family, school, and community.

The goals were:

- For children: to prevent, by reducing emotional and behavioural problems and to promote social, emotional, behavioural, physical, and educational development
- For parents/family: to strengthen their abilities to respond effectively to the needs of their children
- For the neighbourhood/community:
  1. to develop high-quality programs responsive to local needs
  2. to encourage them and citizens to participate as equal partners with service providers in the planning, design, and implementation of programs and other activities
  3. to integrate services locally between service providers and education (Peters, Petrunka, and Arnold 2003)

The projects were integrated, grass-roots, community-driven efforts to develop and maintain programs to provide the best start for children in the zero-to-eight age range but would demonstrate the cost benefits of early investments.

Outcomes

Results from one location, the Highfield community in Rexdale, Toronto, are instructive, since this is an urban neighbourhood marked by a variety of factors associated with higher risk in a child's development as previously described in the Ontario Child Health Study and had many factors that paralleled the development of the Inner-City School models at the Toronto District School Board and subsequent neighbourhood improvement areas identified by the City of Toronto. This site undertook intentionally focused efforts in the classroom, in the school, and with the parents and community in the creation of a school as hub model (Kelly 2004). A comparative analysis of the other school-based sites (Sudbury and Cornwall) and with other non-program comparator sites indicated positive outcomes:

- Significant ratings by teachers and parents for improved social skills, pro-social behaviours, and decreases in emotional and behavioural problems (Peters, Petrunka, and Arnold 2003)
- Decrease in numbers of special education students while increasing in comparison sites (Peters, Petrunka, and Arnold 2003)
- "Improved parenting, decreased stress, improved marital, school and neighbourhood satisfaction and social support" (226)
- "Developed an organization characterized by significant and meaningful local resident involvement in all decisions" (226)

The last point needs to be juxtaposed against the "hostility, suspicion and mistrust" that the communities had towards government services and agencies such as school and the CAS in the years prior" (Peters, Petrunka, and Arnold 2003, 226).

Subsequent results based on the experiences from all eight remaining programs included the following outcomes:

- "Many of the outcomes that result in significant cost savings do not begin to occur until children are in their mid-to late teens" (Peters et al. 2010, 9)
- "Therefore, based on the average of $2,991 spent per family for participation in Better Beginnings programs, the government has saved approximately $4,569 per family by Grade 12 on other services, including education and social services" (12)
- "A close examination of statements by young people from the Better Beginnings communities suggested that they had participated more in community programs throughout their lives than had the youths from comparison communities, and that their participation had produced a greater impact in their lives in terms of prevention, by encouraging healthy behaviours and improvements in feelings of well-being" (8)
- "Overall, youth narratives supported the view that the Better Beginnings program created youths' positive sense of community" (8)

Strength of the Model

The strength of this model was that that it more explicitly addressed the social determinants of health. It was based on the voice and lived experience of community residents, families, and children. It worked across silos of service and across the formal and informal dimensions of community and services.

Limitations

In the model terms of reference, there was no explicit reference to race and racialized experience per se. It did not embrace a critical analysis of race. One must wonder if it also fallen victim to what has been described by Robyn Maynard (2017) and noted, with regard to Black individuals and communities that they remain "an absented presence always under erasure" (Walcott 2003, 27).

However, the choice of communities included five First Nations locations (four of which were defunded by the federal government early on), acknowledged the francophone focus for the Cornwall site, the predominance of French- and English-speaking residents in Sudbury, and forty language groups in the Highfield community in Rexdale for the Better Beginnings Better Futures initiative (Peters et al. 2010). At a community level an acute awareness of the ethnic diversity was a strength, a focus for programs, and source of community pride.

There was also no explicit analysis of the role of economics and poverty from a structural and systemic perspective. While awareness of the impact of poverty was implied by the selection of specific communities, the approach was to develop social programs that would compensate for the impact of poverty. At a community level there was an understanding of the structural aspect of, and inequity, that results in entrenched poverty and leads to a sense of false hope. Sara, twelve years old, presented to the newly formed City of Toronto council in April 1998 as part of a larger community deputation and said,

> I hear that many politicians and businessman would like me to be able to work in the global village where there is supposed to be a large and free market. I have three things to say to that. First of all, I am from the global village and so are my friends. They lived there and now they live here and there is quite a distance between here and there. Second of all I haven't found the free market yet.... Nothing seems to be free these days. Lastly if you want me to grow up capable, I learn all year long and all day long. (Dearing et al. 1999, 28)

In her prescient words she also identified the looming youth unemployment problem when funding for summer programs was to be eliminated and youth who were young leaders would not have the jobs they had counted on. As has been documented for years, youth unemployment persists at high levels and has to be seen as a condition and contributor to the economic possibilities that gang involvement can represent.

The challenge in the Better Beginnings model is whether it is sufficient to support development and the longer-term pathways needed to ensure safe passage through the ups and downs of adolescence into adulthood, especially for racialized youth. It poses the question of whether or not early prevention and promotion are enough to counteract the changing dynamics of adolescent development, while taking into account the dynamic interplay and practices found in schools, policing, and neighbourhoods.

In fact, the pattern of life in neighbourhoods and in the larger community for adolescents is very different from that for young children. Their movement, which entails where they live, learn, work, and play, finds them traversing multiple boundaries and locations (Rodricks et al. 2018).

The Underlying Roots: A Deep Dive

In 2005 violent events in the GTA led to the time being named "The Summer of the Gun." Then the Ministry of Children commissioned a study by Alvin Curling and Roy McMurtry in 2007–8.

It was called the Roots of Youth Violence (McMurty and Curling 2008) and created a benchmark in understanding the intersectional, underlying dynamics that come into play that lead to youth violence. The roots they describe include:

- Poverty
- Racism
- Community design
- Issues in the education system
- Family issues
- Health
- Lack of a youth voice
- Lack of economic opportunity for youth
- Issues in the justice system

While we discuss each root separately, many, if not all, of them frequently interconnect and intertwine to create devastating cumulative impacts for far too many of our youth. These interconnections must be recognized in long-range comprehensive strategies to address the roots of the serious violence that confronts us as a society (6).

A Matter of Race

It is important to view the evolution of youth violence through an intersectional lens. At the same time, given the overwhelming preponderance of research, writing, and testimonials to the facts of the inequity found in all systems towards Black individuals, their families, and communities, this requires a separate focus.

Carl James (2011, 10) writes, "As Zamudio, Russell, Rios, and Bridgeman ... wrote, 'Critical race theory focuses on the all-encompassing web of race to further our understanding of inequality.'" However, this analysis is not restricted to only Black males. It includes those of other races and ethnicities and identity groups where similar dynamics of exclusion and marginalization may occur, but with less of the inequitable experience that accompanies racialized experiences (Maynard 2017).

Black youth represent a significant portion of the population in the care and control systems found in child welfare (Maynard 2017), school discipline (Ontario Human Rights Commission 2004), and policing (Maynard 2017). What complements the aggregated numbers that show such a glaring inequity are the words of young people. The following was made by a recent participant in a focus group discussing the experience of living as a racialized person: "I was a racialized man simply because society told me I was a racialized man.... I'm an international student, I'm an immigrant in a sense, like in my home country, I wasn't a man of colour, I was simply just myself, I was me. And everyone looked like me ... and then I came here, and people are like 'oh yeah, you're a man of colour,' and I was like what does that even mean?" (Hyder 2018, 35).

This labelling is compounded by the absence of safe spaces (Hyder 2018), where individuals are welcomed, accepted, and embraced. "In a society overrun by commercialism, it becomes difficult to find those public spheres where young people can locate metaphors of hope" (Giroux 2012, xvii). The spaces that do exist, such as neighbourhoods, are marked by over-policing of neighbourhoods through carding (Cole 2015) and other measures that in many cases extend into schools. "Oversurveillance creates for black suspects a reality in which merely existing is treated as suspect" (Maynard 2017, 92).

In the words of another young person of colour and focus group participant, "To be considered guilty without committing a crime. To be considered inelegant, uncivilized or uneducated with nothing more than a glance. To be in constant defense of your existence to the rest of the world" (Hyder 2018, 35). As Giroux (2012) states, "Youth, particularly young people marginalized by class and colour, appear to live in a state of perpetual and unending emergency" (xv).

Stigmatization is compounded by the cumulative effects of marginalization, which takes forms of exclusion, streaming, push-out, and the inequitable application of school policies for codes of conduct and what was deemed acceptable (James OCHR). Maynard (2017) quotes from the Child Welfare Anti-Oppression Roundtable of 2009: "In both systems (school and child welfare) racialized children are negatively perceived and thus negatively impacted" (192).

Henry and Tator (as cited by James 2011, 468) state, "In 2007, Ontario Ministry of Education acknowledged that the zero tolerance policy 'could have a disproportionate impact on students from racialized communities,' and as a result, the policy was replaced with the 'progressive discipline' policy, which promotes 'in-school detentions, peer mediation, restorative practice, referrals for consultation, and/or transfer [to another school]."' This racialization expands beyond the home and school and manifests itself as the effective segregation of neighbourhoods through race and economics.

> "Observations fall in line with a map of Toronto put together by researchers led by University of Toronto professor David Hulchanski, that shows Black people living in clusters mainly outside the core – and very few downtown.... Hulchanski, also in attendance at the summit, said in an interview that he does indeed believe 'segregation' and discrimination are playing a role in the map's configuration" (Contenta, 30 September 2018). Using the 2016 census, Hulchanski's team calculated that 48 per cent of Toronto's census tracts are low-income neighbourhoods, where the average individual income is $32,000 before taxes. Fully 68 per cent of residents in these neighbourhoods are visible minorities, while 31 per cent are white. (Whites make up 49 per cent of Toronto's population [Contenta, 30 September 2018]).

Collective and cumulating impacts on young people of colour manifest in social presentations. Travis and Leetch (2013) describe the resulting presentation, seen in Black youth, which is described as putting on a suit of "cultural armour" in structural realities where the meaning of institutions has very different import for youth and do not represent hope or opportunity. They cite (Majors and Billson 1992, 8), who state, "Confidence and esteem strengthen from respect offered within a 'cool pose culture' where fearlessness, inhibited emotion, and creative posturing buffer against pain, marginality, and unstable confidence." As Symone Walters has observed through her own lived experience and observation of many young men, "Power is taken back in defiance of what young people are told not to do" (Walters, personal interview, 15 October 2018).

In this context the underlying needs for a sense of belonging, identity, power, and agency loom even larger and create the conditions for these needs, if not met, to be met through opportunities that can become precursors to gang involvement.

These environments leave a person isolated – in fact isolated from the self. Depending on what kind of early years and community experiences and supports the young person can take different pathways, adopting a protective cocoon around themselves (Walters, personal interview, 15 October 2018). The universal need for connection and belonging (Brendtro and Shahbazian 2003), which are the foundations for developing the competencies that support mastery and a sense of identity (Travis and Leetch 2013) are thwarted in many domains. Pride in history, a sense of connection, hope for a personal future, and the ability to have a sense of self are foundations that are relevant to everyone, regardless of race, ethnicity, or social identity (Talaga 2018). "If we are to fully understand and address the issues being investigated, then we need to take into account the cultural processes that underlie human interactions rather than merely focus on the individual" (James 2011, 467).

There Is Always Hope: Restoring Youth

While prevention is the ideal and most cost-effective approach to creating positive pathways for children moving into and traversing adolescence and then early adulthood, there are many established models of working with at-risk youth that support them and offer exits strategies from lives that have been subject to an absence of privilege and the impacts of oppressive structures and practices.

For the past thirty years, Roca has been working outside of Boston in five cities and has now expanded to twenty-one locations. They have generated a model described as achieving the status of evidence based. They have received a social impact bond for $21 million, which was granted on condition they for help "at risk" youth to achieve successful outcomes in educational attainment, employment, and economic sustainability (Baldwin and Zeira 2017). The overwhelming majority the youth they serve are racialized, live in poverty, and have experienced the effects of violence and trauma.

There are four phases in the model, each of which integrates a variety of evidence-based practices.

1. Outreach in which "youth workers are trained to be relentless, connecting and reconnecting with young people despite rejections" (Baldwin and Zeira, 10)
2. Transformational relationships, "where change process for participants is tightly connected to their relationship with their Youth Worker and other frontline staff" (10)
3. Stage-based programming, which is "is adapted for young people's stages of change … even if participants are not yet at a point where they actively choose to change their behavior" (11)
4. Engaged institutions using "a strategic method for this type of partnership: It applies the same techniques it uses to serve young men – relentless outreach and transformational relationships – to engage other organizations and systems" (13)

It is a model based on restorative, relational, and principles and practices of the peacemaking circle (Boyes-Watson 2008). The relational connection is provided by individuals who have lived experiences that mirror the lives of those young people, considered at risk, who are the focus of engagement.

It embraces the "circle of courage" (Brendtro and Shahbazian 2003,) which is built upon the universal needs for connection and supports the development of competencies that lead to a positive sense of self, which serves as the basis for giving back to the community. It offers intensive and case-managed supports over four years.

Roca's outcomes demonstrate that reducing recidivism and improving employment retention is possible, even for the highest-risk young people. They do not expect to see results until phase 3, years 3 and 4, of the program.

Outcomes for 2015 included:

- 93 per cent of participants in phase 3 were not rearrested and 88 per cent of those on probation complied with their conditions
- Phase 3 participants showed substantial employment gains
- 84 per cent of those enrolled for more than twenty-one months were placed in a job
- 92 per cent kept the job for more than three months, and 87 per cent kept it for six months or more (Baldwin and Zeira 2017, 22)

An Integrated Response: It Takes the Whole Damn Village

There are solutions to the interlocking nest of problems, as one author has asserted in the titles of two of her books *Within Our Reach* (Schorr and Schorr 1989) and a *Common Purpose* (Schorr 1998). The fact that these were written twenty-five and thirty-five years ago makes the point that the evidence and examples do exist. There is no need to invent the wheel or even reinvent it. It is stalled and trapped in the political machinations of ideology, which make funding and sustainability almost impossible. Those who control the levers of power, policy, and resources need to think beyond the short term, invest in the long term, and create solutions commensurate with the scope and demand of the problems (Rodricks et al. 2018).

Several best practice and evidence-based initiatives embrace a comprehensive approach to the development of pathways that support positive outcomes and can prevent involvement in gangs and the associated social problems. Two such approaches have been described in this chapter: one that begins with the early stages of life, and the other at the point when risks build up and are exacerbated by racist structures and practices.

The solutions involve a comprehensive approach to create pathways by design for young people across their life span into young adulthood. As the roots of youth violence have illustrated, by focusing on the intersectional dynamics of social forces and their impacts, they are, at the same time, also the roots of healthy development. The goals of the social and primary determinants of health culminate in education, viable jobs, and a decent living wage. Therefore, pathways need to be constructed and supported that lead towards that end. These are some of the elements that address the social and economic determinants of healthy child and youth development:

1. Use an overarching restorative framework that builds on relational engagement at all levels and is ecologically positioned on individual children and youth, families, schools, neighbourhoods, and agencies in order to build community and to repair, restore, and transform (Baldwin and Zeira 2017)
2. Begin with the voices of all participants and design, with them, the nature and focus of programs and initiatives (Peters, Petrunka, and Arnold 2003; Rodricks et al. 2018; Hyder 2018)
3. Use a systematic approach to engagement and development that includes relentless engagement, transformative relationships, peacemaking circles for leadership and skill development, and supported pathways in education and into good jobs (Boyes-Watson 2008)
4. Implement school-as-hub models for elementary and secondary schools based on shared power and decision making to ensure inclusive classrooms and community use of space (Kelly 2004; Chanicka 2018)
5. Provide spaces and places for youth that are accessible, "for them" and run by them, that are strength based and use language and art for expression (Hyder 2018)
6. Implement a comprehensive suite of poverty reduction and elimination strategies for youth employment, living wage, appropriate social assistance rates, basic income pilots, and adequate and accessible child care (Campaign 2000 2017)
7. Offer programs and mentoring support programs that foster positive alternative identities (Jivani 2018; James 2011; Hyder 2018)
8. Implement programs, supports and opportunities across the life span from prenatal to early adulthood that are both (Peters, Petrunka, and Arnold 2003) and targeted (Travis and Leetch 2013)
9. Provide stable long-term funding for programs and agencies to offer their services on a long-term basis (Rodricks et al. 2018)
10. Use a "fusion" model for policy development and integration of services and supports across silos and integrated with the community (Gaetz et al. 2018)

Reprise and Summary

As 2018 came to a close, and the city of Toronto hovered under the shadow of "The Summer of the Gun" for 2005, it approached new levels of lethal violence that may have this notorious label be placed on 2018. However, the discussions do not appear to have moved the responses any closer to, in a material form, embracing actions that address the roots and social determinants of violence. On the policing end there is ongoing distrust of the ability of the Toronto Police Services being able to provide an equitable application of their functions for the black community (Ontario Human Rights Commission 2018). In fact, from the vantage point of 2023 the same issues persist, accompanied by a continuing lack of a deeper analysis with real solutions from those who hold power. A case in point is that the budget for the police for 2023 includes a significant increase in the police force.

At a provincial level, funding for youth employment programs was also cut at this time in high-needs schools and communities. Despite the government's statement that the solution to poverty is a job, it is acting in ways that contradict that statement and fly in the face of perspectives on the benefits of youth employment and the economic drivers for gang involvement. It also mirrors austerity campaigns that have been found to exacerbate and contribute to escalating youth violence (Treadwell 2018).

However, there is hope in that there is no need to reinvent the wheel to find solutions. We know what works, have vigorously researched and evidence-based models of early and later forms of intervention. What is required is a dispassionate, logical, and long-term view of the issues and ways forward. The West Indian phrase that captures this sentiment is, "We make the path by walking it." Paraphrasing Travis and Leetch (2013), who quote the work of Flanagan and Levine, youth are immersed in a life world that, if it comprises a community that supports connection and belonging, furthers a sense of moral identity, enhances the ability to take responsibility and engage in civic matters, that can lead to "the kind of world they want to be a part of" (Travis and Leetch 2013, 108). This is a world of their own making. This needs to be surrounded by communities of care. In the words of Symone Walters, if the path we are walking is towards a higher journey, we need to remember this. All children have the ability to write their life story, but without members of the community who are committed to making a change, many of their stories will end in tragedy. Though we may not reach all youth, we are determined not to give up on any of them and will therefore continue our work (Walters, personal interview, 15 October 2018).

REFERENCES

Baldwin, M., and Y. Zeira. 2017. *From Evidence-Based Practices to a Comprehensive Intervention Model for High-Risk Young Men: The Story of Roca.* Boston: National Institute of Justice.

Boyes-Watson, C. 2008. *Peacemaking Circles and Urban Youth: Bringing Justice Home.* St. Paul, MN: Living Justice.

Braithwaite, J. 1989. *Crime, Shame and Reintegration.* New York: Cambridge University Press.

Brendtro, L., and M. Shahbazian. 2003. *Troubled Children and Youth: Turning Problems into Opportunities.* Champaign, IL: Research.

Campaign 2000. 2017. *Ending Child & Family Poverty Is Not Negotiable: Building Stronger Foundations for Ontario Families.* Toronto: Family Service Association.

Chanicka, J. 2018. "Inclusive Design: Students, Families and Staff Working Together." Huffpost, 20 February. https://www.huffpost.com/archive/ca/entry/inclusive-design-students-families-staff_ca_5cd5377ee4b07bc72975e549.

Cole, D. 2015. "The Skin I'm In: I've Been Interrogated by Police More Than 50 Times – All Because I'm Black." *Toronto Star*, 21 April. https://torontolife.com/life/skin-im-ive-interrogated-police-50-times-im-black/.

Contenta, S. 2018. "Toronto Is Segregated by Race and Income. And the Numbers Are Ugly." *Toronto Star*, 30 September. https://www.thestar.com/news/gta/2018/09/30/toronto-is-segregated-by-race-and-income-and-the-numbers-are-ugly.html?rf.

Dearing, B.G., M. Gohil, K. Hayward, R. Kelly, W. Maraboli, G. Nelson, ... J. Stevenson. 1999. *Building Rainbows: A Community of Hope and Diversity.* Toronto: Self-published.

Flanagan, C., and P. Levine. 2010. "Civic Engagement and the Transition to Adulthood." *Future of Children* 15: 139–54.

Gaetz, S., K. Schwan, M. Redman, D. French, and E. Dej. 2018. *The Roadmap for the Prevention of Youth Homelessness.* Toronto: Canadian Observatory on Homelessness.

Giroux, H. 2012. *Disposable Youth: Racialized Memories and the Culture of Cruelty.* New York: Routledge.

Hyder, S. 2018. "Competing Masculinities in North America: Providing an Alternative Approach." Unpublished.

James, C. 2011. "Students 'at Risk': Stereotypes and the Schooling of Black Boys." *Urban Education* 47 (2): 464–94. https://doi.org/10.1177/0042085911429084.

Jivani, J. 2018. *Why Young Men: Rage, Race and the Crisis of Identity.* New York: Harper Collins.

Kelly, R. 2004. "The School as a Hub: Best Practice Model for Child and Youth Work." *Journal of Child and Youth Care Work* 19: 141–7. https://cyc-net.org/cyc-online/cycol-0505-kelly.html.

Majors, R., and J. Billson. 1992. *Cool Pose: The Dilemmas of Black Manhood in America.* New York: Simon & Schuster.

Mallette, W, B. Morrison, and P. Ryan. 1980. *Lookin for Love* (recorded by J. Lee) on *Lookin' for Love* (album). Full Moon Label.

Maynard, R. 2017. *Policing Black Lives: State Violence in Canada from Slavery to the Present.* Halifax: Fernwood Publishing.

McLaughlin, A. 2018. "Police Chief Wants to Address 'Problem with Gunplay' as Toronto Exceeds Homicide Record." CBC, 18 November. https://www.cbc.ca/news/canada/toronto/mark-saunders-fatal-toronto-shootings-1.4911083.

McMurty, R., and A. Curling. 2008. *The Review of the Roots of Youth Violence*. Toronto: Queen's Printer.

Offord, D. 1989. *Ontario Child Health Study Findings*. Toronto: Queen's Printer for Ontario.

Ontario Human Rights Commission. 2004. *The Ontario Safe Schools Act: School Discipline and Discrimination*. Toronto: Queen's Printer.

Peters, R.P., K. Petrunka, and R. Arnold. 2003. "The Better Beginnings, Better Futures Project: A Universal, Comprehensive, Community-Based Prevention Approach for Primary School Children and Their Families." *Journal of Clinical Child and Adolescent Psychology* 32 (2): 215–27. https://doi.org/10.1207/S15374424JCCP3202_6.

Peters, R.D., K. Petrunka, M. Pancer, C. Loomis, J. Hasford, and R. Janzen. 2010. *Investing in Our Future: Highlights of Better Beginnings, Better Futures Research Findings at Grade 12*. Kingston, ON: Better Beginnings, Better Futures Research Coordination Unit, Queen's University.

Rankin, J. 2018. "What Toronto's Homicide Record Means and What We Can Do about It." *Toronto Star*, 18 November.

Robins-Early, R. 2018. "Toronto Votes for a Total Ban on Handgun Sales after Mass Shooting." *HuffPost*, 25 July. https://www.huffpost.com/entry/toronto-mayor-massshooting-n_n_5b58baf8e4b0de86f492c8bb

Rodricks, D.J., K. Gallagher, J. Haag, S. Wortley C. Fusco, A. DeLisio, ... L. McCready. 2018. *Crossing Places: A Review of Urban Youth Policy 1960s–2010s*. Toronto: University of Toronto Press.

Schorr, L. 1998. *Common Purpose: Strengthening Families and Neighbourhoods to Rebuild America*. New York: Anchor Books.

Schorr, L., and D. Schorr. 1989. *Within Our Reach: Breaking the Cycle of Disadvantage for Families and Communities*. New York: Anchor Books.

Talaga, T. 2018. *All Our Relations: Finding the Path Forward*. Toronto: House of Anansi.

Travis, R., and T. Leetch. 2013. "Empowerment-Based Positive Youth Development: A New Understanding of Healthy Development for African American Youth." *Journal of Adolescent Research* 24 (1): 93–116. https://doi.org/10.1111/jora.12062.

Treadwell, J. 2018. "Knife Crime and Homicide Figures Reveal the Violence of Austerity." *The Conversation*, 19 October. https://theconversation.com/knife-crime-and-homicide-figures-reveal-the-violence-of-austerity-104964.

Walcott, R. 2003. *Black Like Who? Writing Black Canada*. Toronto: Insomniac.

Wright, T. 2018. "Gun Violence a 'Significant Concern' for Canadians: Bill Blair." Canadian Press, 19 November. https://toronto.ctvnews.ca/gun-violence-a-significant-concern-for-canadians-bill-blair-1.4045887.

Epilogue: Reflection

ADAM ELLIS AND ANTHONY GUNTER

This book emerged out of dialectical conversations with fellow colleagues about the state of the art on gangs, who is privileged to construct this knowledge, and the impact that such knowledge may have on the communities who are the target of criminological (and more broadly sociological, anthropological, psychological) research. I (Adam Ellis) also had an alternative hidden agenda in developing this project. As the only former "gang member" turned academic in Canada (at least that I know of), I also learned that people like me are not supposed to make it into academia (as the result of historical oppression and marginalization). However, when we do reach the proverbial mountain top, we are often pushed aside by those who have not only proclaimed themselves to be experts of *our* worlds, but who have also monopolized the knowledge on crime in general, and gang in particular, as a means of self-advancement and monetary gain. Thus, it is on the icy fringes of academia where I felt the most isolated. I asked myself if there were others who felt the same as I do and whether they were experiencing similar oppression and isolation within the colonial-criminological project. Then I used the platform of thug criminology to find and network with people who came from similar criminalized backgrounds as I do (subsequently finding that this was a lot more difficult than it appeared). I also wanted to find these "insider/insider scholars" as a way to connect intellectually, where what and how I thought was not judged or dismissed, but instead embraced and understood. Along the intellectual journey of this book, I also learned dirty little secrets, including how orthodox criminology – and its research tentacles – have targeted people like me in their so-called campaign for truth and justice. However, and as highlighted through this text, this knowledge has been constructed primarily from one standpoint (that of the colonizers/traditional scholars), thus leading to a knowledge base that is dilute of counter-narratives that are more representative of what is actually happening in the street. Moreover, this hegemony of "gang/street" knowledge has also gone unchallenged and unchecked for nearly one hundred years, thus privileging not only the colonizers' voice, but also solidifying them as the experts on the – "others'" – criminalized world.

While the initial focus of this text was to use the voices of former "gang" members turned academics to challenge/disrupt the historical and contemporary discourses about "gangs", in hindsight that was only the beginning. As I developed this text with my colleagues (Drs. Gunter and Marques) it became apparent that this project was not just about "fixing" the colonial writing of the past. Rather, thug criminology became an intellectual exercise that seeks to transform how we – as insider/insider scholars – can change how knowledge is constructed and mobilized. In this context what has emerged is an intellectual platform that shifts how we think about "crime," removing knowledge construction from the hands of the colonizers, and placing it back in the hands of the community. Consequently, as thug criminologists we are not experts, but instead allies who seek to work in tandem with the communities we grew up in, elevating the voices of those who are not normally heard, integrating the community into the research process, and providing intellectual/financial opportunities for those who have been unable to access academia as a result of oppression, systemic racism, and marginalization. Considering all of this, I concede that it has been a messy process. I also recognize now that the enormous task to undo the harms of the colonial-criminological enterprise cannot be taken on by one individual or one project.

As such, this text is the start of what we hope to be several intellectual discussions and debates about how scholars, working across the social sciences, come to view, understand, and construct knowledge about crime and criminal behaviour. Having joined forces with intellectually driven – like-minded – people, we can see the future is bright. Many of us, while connected to mainstream institutions, are now willing to raise our fists, to scream from the mountain tops, and to draw attention to criminology and the academy in general – including its hegemonic gaze over those that they deem to be the "social problem."

Towards the Future

Thug criminology is the start of the social and intellectual project that looks to extend the counter-colonial critiques that have been levelled at criminology: to incorporate its love child conceived with law enforcement (alongside neoliberal policymakers and other state actors) – the gang industry. This book project is both a bold statement and a reflection of the stone-cold truth and reality of white-supremacist-capitalist-patriarchy. It has been very difficult, almost impossible task, to capture the voices and experiences of those criminalized as "thugs" and "gang members," as written in their own words and featured in this edited collection.

Most street-involved youth do not finish school and do not leave with any formal qualifications. More than likely, scholars working in academia sailed through the education system and were more comfortable reading books in their bedroom or school and university libraries, than they were "running the streets' and causing mayhem. It is not surprising then, that the bookworms become the academic experts, fascinated and obsessed by a life they themselves have never lived or directly experienced, on gangs and violence. They enter marginalized communities under the guise of doing research, spending a couple of years collecting field research data that they write up for their PhDs, books, and journals, and ultimately secure tenured academic faculty positions. Meanwhile, these neglected, maligned, and marginalized communities, from whom these professors have profited, receive no benefits from these new academic insights and knowledge production about violence and crime.

The mistake of thug criminology, which we look to rectify in future projects, is that we asked the community/the streets to come to us in the academy and write in the oppressor's language. This is not and cannot be emancipatory. It can never rectify the decades of wrongs and sins committed in the name of scientific fact. So thug criminology will be about agitating and educating from within the streets, in order to ensure that those "experts" in their ivory towers are critiqued and exposed for the harms they perpetuate, from the outside and below, and the solutions to the problems that were caused by external forces are created within the "hoods" by those who live and breathe it – or in the words of an Jamaican proverb, "The person who feels, it knows it."

Contributors

Julet Allen is a full-time faculty at Humber College in the Community and Justice Services Diploma Program, which focuses on the community and the institutional sectors of the justice system. She prepares students to work with individuals in conflict with the law, as well as marginalized communities, and she explores the development of community programs, restorative justice initiatives, and preventive measures through a social justice lens. She brings over twenty-five years of experience in the social service sector as a social worker, holds BSW and MSW degrees, and is registered with the College of Social Work and Social Service Practitioners. In 2019, she was recognized as one of the 100 Black Women to Watch by Canadian International Black Women.

When Julet is not teaching she provides therapeutic services to individuals and families. Her practice is culturally grounded, utilizing a framework that guides the client towards empowered self-determination. Julet integrates culturally appropriate techniques and utilizes traditional approaches that focus on traditional modalities such as culturally adapted cognitive behaviour therapy, family group conference, motivational interviewing, and narrative therapies. Her practice centres a methodology grounded in Blackness and its radically transformative potential. Julet is renowned for creating renewed family connections and creating spaces to heal from various traumas.

Stephanie Bélanger is the associate scientific director of the Canadian Institute for Military and Veteran Health Research, a unique consortium of forty-six Canadian universities dedicated to researching the health needs of military personnel, veterans, and their families. She is co-editor in chief of the *Journal of Military, Veteran and Family Health*. She is also co-founder of the New Directions in Foreign Policy, Military, and Security Studies Series (McGill-Queen's. She is the co-editor of *War Memories: Commemoration and Writings of War in the English-Speaking World* (McGill-Queen's 2017); *Beyond the Line: Military and Veteran Health Research* (McGill-Queen's 2013); *A New Coalition* *for a Challenging Battlefield* (CDA 2012); *Shaping the Future* (CDA 2011) and *Transforming Traditions: The Leadership of Women in the Canadian Navy* (CDA 2010). She is also author of "Guerre, sacrifices et persécutions" (L'Harmattan 2010). She co-chairs the CIMVHR annual forums, the biannual conferences on war memories (with Université de Rennes 2 and Paris VII), the annual conferences on military ethics, and she partners with many other institutes to co-host workshops. She is a board member of the North American chapter of the International Society for Military Ethics and the Center for International and Defence Policy. She was inducted as a member of the College of Young Scholars of the Royal Society of Canada in 2016. She is a professor in the Department of French Language, Literature, and Culture and the chair of the Master's of Public Administration program at the Royal Military College of Canada, where her research focuses on war testimony, soldier identity, and moral injuries. She specializes in military ethics and just war theories. She completed her PhD at the University of Toronto in 2003 and her MPA at RMC in 2013. She has served in the Royal Canadian Navy as a reservist since 2004.

Luca Berardi is an assistant professor of sociology and social psychology at McMaster University. His doctoral research, a five-year ethnographic "neighbourhood study," examined the impact of gun violence on residents of a Toronto social housing development. He is conducting research in Canadian provincial and federal prisons, studying the lived experiences of incarcerated individuals. Luca's research has been published in *City & Community*, *Qualitative Sociology*, and the *Canadian Journal of Sociology*. He is also co-editor of the *Oxford Handbook of Ethnographies of Crime and Criminal Justice* (Oxford University Press, 2022).

Gregory (Chris) Brown grew up in Los Angeles (Watts), and attended K–12 in the Compton Unified School District. He completed his undergraduate education at the University of California, Santa Cruz with a BA in sociology. He received his MA and PhD from the University of California, Irvine in social ecology, with an emphasis in criminology. Dr. Brown witnessed gang activity first-hand while growing up in Watts and Compton. He has been shot at and attended the funerals of many friends who were victims of gang violence. Growing up in a poor neighbourhood, he was subjected to police harassment and was beaten by the police on several occasions. These experiences had a powerful and lasting impact on his life and on the man he has become. He participates with Southern California Cease Fire to alleviate gang violence. Dr. Brown is an associate professor of criminal justice at California State University, Fullerton. His research, publications, and presentations have focused on crime, criminological theory, white-collar crime, prisons, and gangs. His most recent research has focused on original gangsters (OGs), the history of African

American Gangs in Los Angeles, civil gang injunctions, and gangs and the social media.

Clare Choak's career has followed the path of marginalized urban youth, with two decades of experience researching, consulting, and teaching about young people from a sociological perspective. As a youthologist she focuses primarily on three key intersecting identities: class, gender, and race. Her research on young women and road cultures, in London, built on Anthony Gunter's work exploring the experiences of Black youth. Recent research projects include digital poverty and university students, Black young Britons and COVID-19, and a youth violence intervention evaluation. In pedagogy, she has an interest in anti-racist teaching and culturally responsive curriculums.

Adam Ellis is an assistant professor in the Department of Sociology and Legal Studies at the University of Waterloo. Prior to being appointed in 2016, he was awarded the Vanier Canada Graduate Scholarship in support of his doctoral project "Reconceptualizing Urban Warfare in Canada: Exploring the Relationship between Trauma, PTSD and Gang Violence."

Overall, his research program seeks to humanize the "streets" in general, and the lives of "gang"-involved people more specifically. Dr. Ellis's interest in researching the streets is rooted in his own lived experience growing up on the margins, being involved in street subcultures, and having been harmed by the colonial systems of control.

His research program focuses on (1) exploring the streets, including the intersection between memory, trauma, and "crime," (2) shifting the lens and shedding light on the colonial institutions that harm and give rise to street groups as a means of protection/survival, and (3) exposing, challenging, and disrupting colonial and Eurocentric "truths" about the streets, including gangs.

In 2021 Dr. Ellis founded the Street Institute, an international collective of critical scholars and community activists – with direct knowledge and experiences of life on the "streets" – whose research interests and advocacy focuses on the structural factors that affect and manifest in the psycho-social harms and well-being of marginalized communities.

In 2022 Dr. Ellis also found the Urban Art(z) Lab at the University of Waterloo, where he uses urban art to transform research and pedagogy.

Lily Gonzalez is the re-entry coordinator for Project Rebound and the Insight Garden Program at California State University, Northridge. She is a co-founder of the Revolutionary Scholars student club at CSUN for formerly incarcerated and system affected students on campus. Lily graduated from CSUN with her BA in Chicanx Studies in 2017 and is working towards her MA in the same. Her thesis examines family separation as a result of women's incarceration. She is a former employee and graduate of Homeboy Industries as well. Lily is a formerly incarcerated student.

Anthony Gunter is an associate professor and program lead for Childhood and Youth Studies in the School of Education, Childhood, Youth, Sport, at the Open University (UK). Previously, he worked as an associate professor in criminology and criminal justice at the University of East London. His research interests and expertise are in Black young people, anti-Black racism, contemporary urban youth cultures and alternative transitions, urban violence and gangs, and policing multi-ethnic urban neighbourhoods. Recently he has been examining serious youth violence – in the United States, Jamaica, and the United Kingdom – regarding current policy, policing and preventive practice aimed at tackling "street gangs," and youth-led and community-based/-driven solutions and interventions. He is the author of *Growing Up Bad: Black Youth, Road Culture & Badness in an East London Neighbourhood* (Tufnell 2010), and *Race, Gangs and Youth Violence: Policy, Prevention and Policing* (Policy 2017). Before his career in academia, Anthony worked for over a decade as a detached community and youth practitioner and project/area manager.

Anthony Hutchinson is a doctor of psycho-social clinical practice in Ontario and a court-certified forensic examiner and case epidemiologist who works in and supports medical-legal capacities (including criminal law, family law, child welfare, child protection, personal injury law, and civil litigation). Dr. Hutchinson has been licensed to clinically practise in Ontario through the Ontario College of Social Workers and Social Service Workers since 2010. He is a clinician member of the Canadian Society of Medical Evaluators, an associate (medical) member of the Canadian Society of Forensic Science, and is a certified STATIC-99R sex offender assessor having completed training through the British Columbia Institute of Justice.

Ian Joseph is a research associate at the Open University and lecturer in criminology at the University of East London, where he is the module leader for research methods, criminological theory, and policing in modern society. He has over thirty years of policy/applied research experience that provides him with a grounded mix of practice-based teaching, policy-related scholarship, knowledge exchange, and co-production through collaborative partnerships. The focus of his work is in bringing academic scrutiny to local and central government policy research through a community-based approach. He has been the principal investigator and/or had a leading role on several large-scale research and evaluation projects that focus on policing, youth justice, and gang violence intervention. He is the principal investigator for the evaluation of a community-based public health approach focused on mitigating youth violence in

London, England. His career has an extensive body of qualitative and quantitative research covering a wide range of policy/applied issues, focusing specifically on race and inclusion. Much of this experience builds on ethnographic and participative action research methodologies for which he has a specialist interest in youth, harm, deviance, race, urban crime, and gangs.

Rick Kelly has been a child and youth practitioner since the mid-seventies. Starting from a mental health and clinical perspective, his focus widened to include innovative approaches to family engagement in their homes, to an ecological focus supporting the role of the community and "whole village" using a "school as a hub" model in Rexdale as part of a twenty-five-year policy research project. His last twenty years have been dedicated to knowledge mobilization and systemic change using a restorative lens for practice. He began this part of his career while teaching full time at George Brown College in the Child and Youth Worker program and was introduced to it through an indigenous and First Nations worldview. Since 2004, Rick has been a youth justice restorative conference facilitator and a trainer with the International Institute for Restorative Practices where he also completed his master's in 2014. He has since developed his own adaptations and model to decolonize and colourize the focus and the content.

He has expanded his focus on restorative practices to embrace peacemaking circles by studying with Kay Pranis at the Canadian School of Peacebuilding. Since 2012, Rick has continued this work and training through his own practice, Just Us: A Centre for Restorative Practices, and collaborates closely with YouthRex, a province-wide initiative based at York University, 360Kids, a youth shelter, housing and transitions organization for youth at risk, NextGen Builders, a community/labour/industry mentoring partnership for Black youth overseen by Toronto Community Benefits Network, and with Toronto Metropolitan University, George Brown, and Seneca College. He has written several publications using a restorative lens for youth work, pedagogy, and recovery from COVID.

He was presented with the OACYC Dennis McDermott Career Achievement Award in 2021.

Olga Marques is an associate professor in the Criminology and Justice Program at Ontario Tech University. Her teaching and research interests focus on the construction, policing, and regulation of sexed, gendered, and raced bodies, and the interrelationships between gendered/sexed social norms, social control, and resistance. As a critical criminologist, she also writes on the impacts of prisoning, critical re-articulations of "crime," anti-narratives, as well as Indigenous experiences of criminal (in)justice. Olga has previous employment experience in criminal justice, including victim support worker, program assistant in a social housing community, and behaviour counsellor in a women's federal correctional facility. She is working on several projects that relate to insider accounts of incarceration and prisonization. She earned her PhD in criminology from the University of Ottawa and her MA in sociology from the University of Windsor.

Melissa P. McLetchie is a PhD student in the Department of Sociology at York University. She grew up in Toronto and uses her experiences of being in a relationship with a man who has a history of imprisonment to guide her work. Melissa's research speaks to the collateral consequences of imprisonment, focusing on the experiences of Black families in Canada. As an insider/outsider to the "criminal punishment system" she offers a unique perspective that is often absent in academic spaces. To learn more about her research you can visit her website at www.melissamcletchie.com.

Jared Millican's formal education is in health and human services (Tyndale University) and industrial and organizational psychology (Adler University). Jared's research interests are in social division and moral foundations in psychology. Jared works in non-profit administration in higher education and as a research design and methods consultant.

Malte Riemann, PhD is a lecturer in international relations at the University of Glasgow. His research interests lie at the intersection of historical international relations, international political sociology, critical security studies, and global health. His work has been published in peer-reviewed journals including *Journal for Global Security Studies, Globalizations, Small Wars & Insurgencies, Defence Studies, Critical Public Health, RUSI Journal,* and *Peace Review*. He is co-editor of the book series Routledge Private Security Studies and Sandhurst Trends in International Affairs (Howgate). He won the International Studies Association's Historical International Relations Section's 2022 Merze Tate Prize for the best article in historical IR.

Javier Rodriguez is an adjunct faculty in the Los Angeles Community College District. He has a master's of social welfare from Luskin School of Public Affairs at the University of California in Los Angeles. His concentration is social and economic justice with an emphasis on dismantling institutional racism and systemic oppression. Co-founder of Underground Scholars Initiative at UCLA and recipient of the 2019 UCLA Charles E. Young Humanitarian Award, he is a radical activist scholar and aspiring licensed clinical social worker.

Yafet Tewelde is completing his PhD at York University looking at the history of policing and spying of Black social justice movements in Toronto. He is a research associate at SEIU Local 1 Canada and was the NDP candidate in York

South Weston for the 2019 federal election. For nearly twenty years, Yafet has been an advocate and educator for justice with and for Black communities.

Tammy Tinney is a clinical social worker working in forensic mental health. She completed a double-major Honours Bachelor of Arts degree from the University of Guelph in criminal justice & public policy, and sociology, followed by a master of social work degree from the University of Toronto. Tammy has worked in private practice, with non-profits, and in hospital settings. Hearing her patients' life experiences of discrimination, marginalization, and trauma inspired Tammy to advocate for systemic change by identifying and addressing barriers and gaps within the mental health and criminal justice sectors. Tammy is passionate about providing clinical counselling to individuals living with PTSD as a result of street and gang violence. She doesn't believe in a gold-standard approach to treatment and individualizes her treatment plans by finding creative ways to help her patients. When treating trauma Tammy emphasizes the importance of connecting the mind and body and draws heavily on mindfulness practices and the power of body movement. Throughout her clinical career she noticed a pattern of coping strategies among her patients – music, sports, fitness. In her clinical practice she has successfully incorporated hip hop and rap into therapy sessions to build rapport and introduce other treatment modalities. Tammy will be researching the benefits of using hip hop therapy and beat therapy when treating individuals with post-traumatic stress disorder as a result of street and "gang" violence.

Robert Weide is assistant professor of sociology at California State University, Los Angeles. He is the co-founder of and faculty advisor for Project Rebound and the Student Homie Union at Cal State LA. He graduated with a BA from UC Santa Barbara in 2001 and a PhD from New York University in 2015. His research and publications focus on the role of the state in exacerbating gang conflict on the streets of Los Angeles and in California's carceral institutions. Robert is a formerly incarcerated and gang-involved faculty.

Index

academia. *See* marginalization in academia
academics as gatekeepers, 59
academics as privileged: overview, 6, 23; and authenticity of research, 61; Choak's feelings, 43; co-option, 27–8; Ellis's experiences, 57–61; ethnographers, 64–5; reflection on, 50; and superficial scholarship, 66–9. *See also* traditional criminology
accountability, 18, 19
Ackerly, Brooke, 49–50
Adams, G.S., 19
administrative criminology, 34–5
African Americans. *See* Black men; Black people; Black women
Agnew, R., 113
Agozino, Biko, 16, 28
Alexander, Michelle, 35
Allison, P., 22
alternative criminology, 3, 18, 64. *See also* ethnography; thug criminology overview
alternative justice work, 226
American South, 30–1, 33, 147
anti-violence norm, 188–9
Asbury, B., 138
authority, 14, 17
auto-ethnography, 60–1, 92

Bacchi, Carol, 189
badness, 27, 44, 46, 47, 52n1, 52–3n3. *See also* women in gangs
banking system of education, 58
Baptist, E.E., 29
Barrios, L., 80
Barrows, Julie, 36
Beccaria, Cesare, 3, 112
Becker, Howard, 3
beliefs for injustice, 34
Bentham, Jeremy, 112
Bergin, T., 81
Better Beginnings, Better Futures, 239–41, 242
bias, 15, 49
Biden, Joe, 35
BIPOC (Black, Indigenous, People of Colour), 15, 29, 37, 78–9, 194, 244. *See also* Black, Asian, and Minority Ethnic; Black men; Black people; Black women; Indigenous Peoples
birth control, 148–9
Black, Asian, and Minority Ethnic (BAME), 173–5. *See also* BIPOC
Black British Caribbeans, 27–8, 85–92, 173–5
Black children, 149–50
Black feminist theory (BFT), 143–4
Black Gangster Disciples, 161–2

Black men: and homicides in Toronto, 224; and racial profiling, 220–1 (*see also* racial profiling); stereotypes of, 46, 150; and thug narrative, 15, 167. See also BIPOC; Black, Asian, and Minority Ethnic

Black P Stone Rangers, 161–2

Black people: children in child welfare, 243; crime and Emancipation, 30; crime and history, 212; crime and migration, 32–3; as CV clients, 193; and deindustrialization, 33–4; and early studies of crime, 30–3; and ghettos, 33; history in Canada, 215–16; life expectancy, 172; and police tactics, 36 (*see also* law enforcement); and poverty, 33; and racial profiling, 220–1 (*see also* racial profiling); and street gang definitions, 37; and trauma, 145; violence in Toronto, 213–14. See also BIPOC; Black, Asian, and Minority Ethnic

Black women, 51, 142–9, 150–1. *See also* BIPOC

Black-Canadian women, 143–4

Blackness, 212, 214, 218, 223, 224, 229

"Black-on-Black crime," 229

Bloom, S.L., 116

"Blue Wall of Silence," 136

body mapping, 210

book overview, 6–9, 251–2

Bourgois, P., 67, 81

Boyle, Gregory, 99

boyology, 45

Braithwaite, John, 229

Bridgeman, Jacquelyn L., 243

Brotherton, D.C., 79, 80, 81

Brown, Gregory, 75

Brown, W.B., 171

Burgess, Ernest, 113

Butts, J.A., 186, 188

California State University (CSU), 95–8, 100

California State University, Los Angeles (Cal State LA), 103

California State University, Northridge (CSUN), 99

Campbell, Anne, 47

cannabis, 228

capitalism, 29

carding, 174. *See also* racial profiling

Caribbean, 29

Carstensen-Egwuom, Inken, 49–50

Chabot, R., 78

Chambliss, William, 97

Cherry Beach, 123

Chicago, 31–2, 36, 161–2, 163

Chicago school, 32–3, 39n3, 45, 112–13

children, 120, 122, 123, 153, 237–43, 244, 246–8

Children's Aide, 142, 143, 145–6, 148–9, 150, 156, 243

Choak, Clare, 42, 43–5

choices, 19, 20

circle of courage, 246

citizens, 216

Civil War, 30

Clark, Doris J., 99

class, 43–4, 75, 77, 80, 150

Clinton, Bill, 35

Cloward, R.A., 81

code of silence, 66, 132–9

coercion, 47–8

Cohen, A.K., 75, 80

Cohn, E.G., 51

colonization: of British project, 28, 29; in Canada, 215–16, 217–18; and contagions, 194; as continuing, 38; and criminology, 28; and research, 16–17; in United States, 28, 29. *See also* slavery

Common Purpose (Schorr), 246

community organizations, 208–10, 226

community transformation, 70

complex trauma, 210. *See also* post-traumatic stress disorder; trauma
Comprehensive Crime Control Act, 35
Contreras, Randol, 60
convict criminology, 4
co-option, 27–8, 101–2, 107
Correctional Service of Canada, 19
Couture, Amanda, 44
cover-ups, 133
crack, 122, 123
Crawford, A., 210
crime (general): and Black people, 30–3; data as inflated, 207–8; designation of, 17; and gangs, 37; intellectual honesty about, 20; and justice focus, 226–9; and migrants, 32–3; and white people, 32–3. *See also* violent crime
Crime Bill, 35
crime prevention budgets, 207
criminal conspiracy, 137
criminal justice system: enforcement vs. rehabilitation, 205–6; and focus on drugs, 170; and high school dropout rates, 225; labeling defendants, 4–5; and violence, 174–5; and white supremacy, 208. *See also* law enforcement
criminal record stigma, 98, 99–100, 203
criminalization, 78–80, 93–4
criminology: overview, 3–4; administrative criminology, 34–5; alternative criminology, 3, 18, 64 (*see also* ethnography; thug criminology overview); and colonialism, 28; decolonizing, 51, 70; and free will concept, 112; and gender, 16, 48–52; and imperialism, 28; and incarceration, 4; and the "Other," 17; as reproducing systems, 13–14; silence on history of research, 16–17; strain theories, 113; and US focus, 5, 37. *See also* traditional criminology

Critical Criminology, 13–14
critical race theory, 243
Cukier, Wendy, 239
Cure Violence (CV) model, 185–95
Curling, Alvin, 242
Czifra, Steven, 101

Davis, Allen, 46, 47
Davis, Angela, 229
Defend Boyle Heights (DBH), 104
deindustrialization, 33–4
Delinquency Areas (Shaw), 32
democratizing knowledge, 21, 70
Densley, James, 46, 47, 68
Department of Defense, 35
Department of Education, 35
Deuchar, Ross, 50
devaluation, 21–3
Diagnostic and Statistical Manual of Mental Disorders (DSM-II), 144–5
Diagnostic and Statistical Manual of Mental Disorders (DSM-V), 115, 145–6
Dichiara, A., 78
discrimination, 89, 133, 145–6, 155, 217. *See also* racism
diseases, 169, 172
disrespect, 119
diversity points, 94, 97, 100, 106
doctors' code of silence, 134
Donaldson, Lester, 218
"Don't Ask Don't Tell" practice, 135, 136
Dorling, Danny, 34
Drill (music), 163
drugs: children selling, 120, 122, 123, 153; in communities, 111–12; and gang hysteria, 34; illicit drug policy, 170; victims and criminals, 15; War on Drugs, 35–6, 111–12, 173; and women in gangs, 48
Du Bois, W.E.B., 30–1, 32, 39n3
duping, 67

Durazo, Rojas, 190
Dying for Justice (Institute of Race Relations), 174

economic inequality, 171–2, 190–1, 192, 224, 225–6. *See also* poverty
education, 34, 228
Eggleton, Art, 219
Einwohner, Rachel L., 81
Ellis, Adam: overview, 111–12, 117–28; developing thug criminology, 21, 251; Hip Hop Healers, 209; and PTSD, 115–16, 119, 120–1, 124–7, 128; and traditional criminology, 57–61
Emancipation, 30–1
employment training, 228
"Ending Gang and Youth Violence" programs, 167
England, 167–8
England, P., 22
Enlightenment, 29
epistemic privilege/authority, 14–15
ethnography, 64–5, 66–8, 69, 78, 90–1
An Ethnography of Youth Violence (Densley), 68
eugenics, 148
exclusion, 89, 131, 216–17, 244–5
experts: overview, 253; and academic legitimacy, 4; conspirators of, 27; eschewing label of, 21, 23; and gang definitions, 81; vs. lived experience, 133; outsiders fighting for status, 66; as "parachuting in," 89; pathologizing vulnerable groups, 6; self-identified, 58–9, 60–1; and violence prevention programs, 155

facts, 14–15
Farrington, David, 51–2
fashion, 36
FBI, 35, 173
femininity, 43

feminism, 16
fight the power, 163
fights, 121, 124
Flanagan, C.A., 248
For Youth Initiative (FYI), 226, 227–8
Ford, Rob, 222–3
Forty-Ninth World Health Assembly, 168–9
Foucault, Michel, 185
free will, 112
Freire, Paulo, 58, 71n2
Freud, Sigmund, 144
Fricker, M., 15
Friedman, Milton, 192
FUBU, 70

The Gang (Thrasher), 68
Gang Leader for a Day (Venkatesh), 68
gangs: overview, 20–1, 32–3; academics connections to, 58–9; as balancing, 13; and crime, 37; definitions of, 24, 36–7, 63, 75–9, 80, 82, 170–1; Ellis's experiences, 117–20; exit programs, 206, 226; as families, 112; vs. groups, 77–8, 171; history of, 62–3; hysteria about, 34; laws against congregating, 36; members rejecting, 81; neighbourhoods and assumptions, 75, 77; numbers in 1996, 63; in other countries, 172; police identifying, 75; positive activities of, 78; and poverty, 34; preventing involvement in, 246–8; and prisons, 20; profiling, 36; as racialized, 34, 78–9, 243–4; "real recognize real," 65–9; as safer, 132; silence on, 18; as social reproduction, 80; as survival, 13; and violent crime, 4, 18; white people as, 37. *See also* street life stories; women in gangs; *various criminology entries*
gangs, scholarship on: in Canada, 16; ethnographers, 64–5, 66–8, 90–1; "experts," 66–7 (*see also* experts);

Miller, 62–3; monopolization of knowledge, 59–60 (*see also* academics as privileged); and power, 49–50; techniques, 66; US as focus, 5, 37
Gaventa, J., 3
g-checking, 118–19
gender, 16, 19, 22–3
ghettos, 33
Giordano, Peggy, 48
Giroux, H., 243
gladiator school, 118–22
globalization, 81, 194
good trouble, 93, 98, 108
Grandmaster Flash and the Furious Five, 161
Grekul, J., 20
guns: Ellis's first experience with, 118–19, 121, 122; Hutchison's first experiences with, 131, 132; and racial profiling, 222–3; responses in England, 167; and statistics in academic settings, 57–8; in Toronto 2018, 237–8; and Turk's friends, 154
Gunter, Anthony, 27, 52n1, 52–3n3
Gutierrez, Gabriel, 99

Hagedorn, John, 37
Haidt, Jonathan, 137
halfway houses, 199–200
Hallsworth, Simon, 50
Haraway, Donna, 193–4
Harding, Sandra, 50
Hardt, M., 194
health. *See* public health
health-care systems, 201–5, 209–10
healthy communities, 227, 239, 248
Henry, F., 243–4
Herman, J.L., 115, 116
high school dropout rates, 225
Hill, Robert, 93
Hill Collins, Patricia, 43, 49, 148
hip hop, 122–3, 126, 135, 161–4

Hip Hop Healers, 209
Hirschi, Travis, 52
Hispanics, 193. *See also* BIPOC; Latinos
Hoefnagels, G.P., 17, 23
Hogan, M.J., 171–2
Hollander, Jocelyn A., 81
Homeboy Industries, 98–9
homicide, 157–60, 163, 167–8, 171, 213, 224. *See also* violent crime
hooks, bell, 17
Hordge-Freeman, Elizabeth, 50
Howard, John, 112
Huff, Ronald, 36
Hulchanski, David, 244
Hutchison, Anthony, 131–2, 138
hyper-criminalization, 93–4
hypermasculinity, 203–4, 209

Ice T, 13
immigration, 32, 34, 75, 86, 216–17. *See also* Black British Caribbeans
imperialism, 28
In Search of Respect (Bourgois), 67
incarceration: and Black men, 225; and criminology, 4; deaths in detention, 174; and economic inequality, 224; funding for, 35; and gangs, 20; impacts of, 19, 20; numbers of people in, 35, 175
Indigenous Peoples, 19, 215–16, 241
individualism, 19–20
individuals and society, 19–20
industrialization, 29
injustice beliefs, 34
injustice victims, 34
insiders: auto-ethnography, 60; in ethnography, 64–5; as ignored, 206; insider/outsider binary, 44–5, 58; and mental health workers, 198–9; thug criminologists as, 4, 75, 251, 252
interpretations, 58
intersectionality, 51, 242

Iomos Marad (Singleton), 109
IRA, 86
Iratzoqui, A., 51–2
isolation, 27

Jackson-Jacobs, Curtis, 37
James, Carl, 243–4
Janack, M., 14
Javid, Sajid, 168
Jeru the Damja, 164
Jim Crow South, 147
jobs, 33–4
Joining the Gang and Becoming a Broder (Rodgers), 68
Joseph, Ian, 85–92
judges, 4–5
Just Culture festival, 102
justice focus on crime, 226–9
Justice LA, 104

Kane, C., 193
Katz, Jack, 37
Kelner, J., 134
Khan, Sadiq, 168
Klein, Malcolm, 35, 37
Klein, M.W., 77
knives, 121, 122
knowledge production, 3, 13, 14–15, 17, 69, 186, 189. *See also* democratizing knowledge
knowledge transmission, 71n2
Knox, G.W., 77
KRS-One, 163
Ku Klux Klan, 33

LaBoucane-Benson, P., 20
Lancaster State Prison, 103, 105–6
Latin Kings/Queens, 81
Latinos, 37. *See also* BIPOC; Hispanics
law enforcement: arbitrary gang labels, 75; and Black neighbourhoods, 36; budgets, 248; and code of silence, 136; and community development approach, 228; and gang definitions, 78; and "gang exit" programs, 206, 213–14; and gang history, 63; as increasing, 207; protests, 218–19; racial profiling, 174, 219–24; and racism in Britain, 173–4; raids, 142–3, 145–7; refusal to cooperate with, 137–8, 139; and snitching, 135; and Us vs. Them concept, 154; violence of, 123, 124, 174, 205–6, 214, 218–19; and War on Crime, 77; and War on Drugs, 35–6. *See also* code of silence
laws, 30–1, 35, 36, 63, 170
Lawson, Michael Wade, 218
Leetch, T., 244, 248
Legget, W., 192
letters from the streetz, 153–6
Levanon, A., 22
Lewis, John, 93
Liebling, A., 3
life expectancy, 172
lived experiences: in academia, 18, 57, 60–1, 133; Better Beginnings, Better Futures, 241; and Joseph's research, 91; in thug criminology, 6; and transformative programs, 23
local government research, 88–90
Lombroso, Cesare, 3, 46
London Campaign against Police and State Violence (LCAPSV), 174, 176
Lopez, Dennis, 99
Los Solidos, 78
loyalty, 137–9

macro-structural forces, 80
the Mafia, 134, 135
mainstream media, 208
mainstream politics, 88–90
mandated treatment, 201–2
marginalization in academia: overview, 94–5, 102–3, 106; and community

politics, 104–6; co-option, 101–2, 107; Ellis's experiences, 57–61; life after prison, 99–100; neoliberal universities, 95–8; posthumous degrees, 101; resistance to, 106–7; tuition fees, 95
Marques, Olga, 21
masculinity: and emotions, 156; hypermasculinity, 203–4, 209; testing in school, 117; toxic, 20; and victimhood, 46–7. *See also* badness
Matza, D., 80–1
Maynard, Robyn, 241
McKay, H.D., 3, 77, 113
Mcletchie, Melissa P., 142–7, 148, 150–1
McMurtry, Roy, 242
medicalization. *See* Cure Violence model; violence: as disease
mental illness, 203, 238–9. *See also* health-care systems
Merton, R.K., 3, 77, 113
"The Message" (song), 161
Metropolitan and West Midlands Police, 174
middle class, 43–4, 75, 77, 80
migrants, 32–3. *See also* immigration
military, 36, 77
Miller, Walter B., 62–3, 78
Mills, C. Wright, 60, 69
mindfulness, 210
misconceptions, 57–8, 59–60, 68–9, 79–80, 173
Mitchell, Koritha, 146–7
Moore, J.M., 20
Moore, J.W., 47
moral panic, 34, 173
moral taste receptors, 137
Morrison, Toni, 151n1
Morton, Brittany, 98–9
motherhood, 147–9
multiculturalism, 215–19, 221
multiple marginality, 80

murder, 157–60, 163, 167–8, 171, 213, 224
Murrillo, Danny, 101
music, 122–3, 126, 161–4

Nas, 163
National Front, 86
National Institute on Drug Abuse, 35
National Youth Gang Center, 63
Negi, A., 194
Negro Project, 147–8
Neighbourhood Improvement Areas (NIA), 225
neoliberalism, 19, 95–8, 170, 191–2
Netas, 81
Neutrons, 161
Nogueira, C., 15
non-disclosure agreements, 136–7

Office of Juvenile Justice and Delinquency Prevention (OJJDP), 62–3
official knowledge, 14–15, 17, 23
Ohlin, L., 81
omertà, 134
One Night in Miami (film), 164
Operation TIPS, 136
Opportunity Institute, 100, 103
Ortega, Daniel, 101
Ortega, Jose, 101
orthodox criminology. *See* traditional criminology
the "Other": overview, 6; and Black British Caribbeans, 27–8; and colonial hygiene, 194; criminology as science of, 17; as disembodied, 17; and experts, 6; fixing, 14; and health-care systems, 202; and privilege in knowledge production, 17, 27–8, 69; women as, 43. *See also* colonization; traditional criminology
outreach workers (OWs), 188, 192

outsiders: and Black women, 43; and gang definitions, 80, 81; insider/outsider binary, 44–5, 58; and mental health workers, 199; as threat, 75. *See also* academics as privileged
Owusu-Bempah, Akwasi, 228–9

pardons, 228
Parker, H., 48–9
Parmar, A., 51
paths, 198, 201, 237–8, 245, 246–7, 248
peer programs, 210
Penal Code 186.22, 79
personal/professional tensions, 90–2
Phillips, Coretta, 51
Pitts, John, 43–4
Planned Parenthood, 147–8
pocho, 107
police. *See* law enforcement
Police and Community Engagement Review (PACER), 223
police raids, 142–3, 145–7
policies as problems, 189–90
policy research, 88–90
poor laws, 149
positionality, 49–52
positive approach, 50, 60, 61
post-traumatic stress disorder (PTSD), 115–16, 119–21, 124–8, 144–6, 150–1, 210. *See also* trauma
Potter, Hilary, 51
poverty: and Better Beginnings, Better Futures, 241; elimination strategies, 227–8; and gangs, 18, 34; and ghettos, 33; and justice focus, 227; in NIAs, 225; and race, 33; as root of violence, 171–2, 190–1, 192, 242
power: defiance as, 244; in health-care systems, 201–2; and nothing to something, 13; and reflexivity, 49–50; and violent crime, 28; and whiteness, 222 (*see also* white supremacy);

Powers, Penny, 191
prisoners, 19, 20
privilege, 3–4, 14–15, 17, 27. *See also* academics as privileged
Project Rebound, 100, 103–6
property crime, 77
pseudo science, 29
psychology, 19
public health, 168–70, 172–3, 176, 185, 237. *See also* Cure Violence model
Public Safety Canada, 213

qualitative research, 49–52, 64–5
quantitative research, 60, 61–4, 190
Quinney, Richard, 97

race, 32–3, 35
race-based traumatic stress, 145–7, 150–1
Race-Based Traumatic Stress Symptom Scale (RBTSSS), 145
racial hierarchy, 29
racial profiling, 174, 219–24
racialization, 34, 78–9, 243–4
racism: in Britain, 86, 173–4; Children's Aid, 148–9; and Cure Violence, 193–4; and education, 202–3; everyday racism, 220; and gang involvement, 131–2; in health-care systems, 202–3; as ignored in explanations of gangs, 18; as individualism, 19; as ingrained in Canadian society, 216; and laws, 30–1; and pseudo science, 29, 38; as root of violence, 242; and War on Drugs, 35. *See also* discrimination; white supremacy
Ransford, C., 193
rap battles, 122
rape, 200
rastafarians, 86
rational choice theory, 112
Reagan, Ronald, 35, 95, 172–3

"real recognize real," 65–9
recidivism, 246
REDI project, 102
reformatories, 149–50
Reimann, Malte, 185
reflexivity, 49–52
religion, 86–7
relocation, 123, 206–7
rememory, 151n1
reproductive control, 147–8
resistance, 81
respect, 107, 120, 132
responsibility, 19
restoration, 228–9, 245–6, 247
Revolutionary Scholars, 100
Rexdale, Toronto, 240–1
Rice, Marcia, 51
Rios, Francisco, 243
Rios, Victor, 60
rites of passage, 45
road culture, 46, 47, 48, 52–3n3
robbery, 118–19
Roca, 245–6
Rodgers, D., 68
Roots of Youth Violence, 242
Royal Proclamation of 1763, 216
Russell, Christopher, 243

safe spaces, 243
Saloojee A., 217
San Francisco State University (SFSU), 103
Sara (community member), 241
Saunders, Mark, 237
"Saviour's Day" event, 162
schools, 118–22, 133, 247
Schuck, A.M., 171–2
science. *See* Cure Violence model
segregation, 33, 244
self-confidence, 107
Self-Help Graphics, 104
sexual exploitation, 42–3, 45–6

sexual violence, 20
Shakur, Tupac, 212
Shaw, C.R., 3, 32, 77, 113
Shelden, Randal, 37, 171
shootings, 174
silence/silencing, 16–17, 18
Singleton, Marcus, 109, 161–4
slavery, 29–30, 38, 146, 151n1, 215–16, 219
Slutkin, Gary, 185, 187, 190, 193. *See also* Cure Violence model
social control, 191
social disorganization theory, 32
social exclusion, 89, 131, 216–17, 244–5
society and individuals, 19–20
solidarity, 106–8
Spitzer, Steven, 94, 97
stereotypes: of Black men, 46, 150; of Black womanhood, 148, 150; and crime, 15; fighting, 86; and hypermasculinity, 203; and racial profiling, 220; and traditional criminology, 69–70; of women in gangs, 47
sterilization, 148
stigmatization, 98, 99–100, 243
"Stop Fuckin' Snitching" (DVD), 135
stop-and-search, 174. *See also* racial profiling
strain theories, 113
street life stories, 153–4, 155–6. *See also* Ellis, Adam
Street Terrorist Enforcement and Prevention (STEP) Act, 79
Stretesky, P.B., 171–2
subjectivity, 49–52
Sullivan, Mercer L., 37–8
Sultana, Farhana, 50
"Summer of the Gun," 242
surveillance, 192, 215, 219–24, 243
survivors, 127–8
survivor's guilt, 27

Sutherland, Edwin, 32, 77, 113
systems of repression, 13–14

Task Force on Black and Minority Health, 172–3
Tator, C., 243–4
Thrasher, Frederic, 32–3, 34, 45, 68, 75, 80
three strikes law, 35
thug criminology overview, 5–6, 22–3, 70, 82, 139, 229–30, 252–3
THUG LIFE, 212, 213, 214
thugs: as crime fighters, 229; as harmful label, 4–5, 94, 207; as term, 15, 212–13
Tinney, Tammy, 198–201, 204–5, 209
Tobin, K., 24
tokenization, 69
Toronto, Ontario, 213–14, 220–3, 224–5, 229, 240–2, 244
Tory, John, 213
Totten, M., 18, 20–1
Tracy, S.K., 171
traditional criminology: overview, 23, 69–70; barriers of, 61; challenging, 3–4 (see also thug criminology overview); Ellis's experience in, 57–61; and ethnography, 64–5, 66–7; as incomplete, 57–8; vs. lived experience, 57; quantitative research critique, 61–4; researchers getting duped, 65–9; and violence as disease, 176
Transformational Taskforce, 223
Trap, 163
trauma: overview, 20, 114; and Black women, 142–3; and careful approaches, 210; Ellis on, 126–8; re-enactment of, 116–17; studies on, 144; talking about, 198, 199, 210; and TG, 156. See also post-traumatic stress disorder
traumatic hysteria, 144
Travis, R., 244, 248

treatment approaches, 204–5
Trickett, Loretta, 48–9
Trudeau, Pierre, 218
True, Jacqui, 49–50
"truths," 58–60, 64–5. See also positive approach; "real recognize real"
tuition fees, 95
Turk, 153–4

Underground Scholars Initiative, 101–2
unemployment, 241–2
universities. See marginalization in academia
university administrators, 96–8
University of California, Los Angeles (UCLA), 101–2
University of California (UC), 95–8
University of Chicago, 31
urban violence. See violent crime
"us," 18. See also the "Other"
For Us By Us (FUBU), 70
US Department of Health and Human Services (USDHHS), 169–70, 173
US Naval Academy, 136
USI at UC Berkeley, 101, 102
USI at UCLA, 101

Valdez, A., 78
Van der Kolk, B.A., 116
Vargas, Jose Louis, 99
vengeance, 157–60, 188
Venkatesh, S., 68
vetting, 67–9
victims, 46–7
victims of injustice, 34
Vigil, James Diego, 80, 93
violence: and conscious hip hop, 163–4; as disease, 168–9, 171, 172, 176, 185–7 (see also Cure Violence model); Ellis's story, 117–28; in England, 167–76; by police, 123, 124, 174, 205–6, 214, 218–19; and political solutions, 190–1;

root causes of, 204, 225–6, 242; and trauma, 116; Vivar's story, 157–9; and white people in CV, 193–4. *See also* homicide; post-traumatic stress disorder
Violence by Youth Gangs and Youth Groups as a Crime Problem in Major American Cities (Miller), 62–3
violence interrupters (VIs), 188, 192
Violence Reduction Unit (LVRU), 168
violent crime: as abuse of power, 28; and economic inequality, 171–2, 190–1, 192; in England, 167–8; and gangs, 4, 18, 37–8; and gangs vs. groups, 77–8; scholarship on, 5; and wealthy nations, 172; and youth, 37–8. *See also* homicide
Vivar, Alejandro, 157–9
voyeurism, 6

Wacquant, Loic, 34
Walters, Symone, 237–8, 244, 248
war, 30, 114–15
war neurosis, 114
War on Crime, 77
War on Drugs, 35–6, 111–12, 173
War on Gangs, 78, 111
warriors, 114
Westin, Morgaine, 207–8
"What is the problem represented to be?" (WPR), 189–90
white children, 149
white men, 3, 50, 51–2. *See also* criminology; traditional criminology
white people: and crime, 32–3; and Cure Violence, 193; and gangs, 37, 75–6, 78, 79; law enforcement stop-searching, 174; and laws, 30–1; life expectancy, 172; as low income, 244; as minorities, 75; percentage of Toronto population, 244; police tactical teams, 146–7; and poverty, 33; vigilantes, 146–7

white supremacy: BIPOC as pawns, 218; and criminal justice system, 208; and eliminating Blackness, 229; and multiculturalism, 218–19; overview in Toronto/Canada, 215–19; and scapegoating, 212–13, 214, 218; in South, 33, 147; and surveillance, 219–24. *See also* racism
"whitemaleness," 51–2
whiteness, 222, 224
Windrush Generation, 85–8
Wise Intelligent, 162
Within Our Reach (Schorr and Schorr), 246
women: categories of young women, 45; sexual violence and incarceration, 20; as stabilizing, 46; as universities, 21–3; as victims, 47; as villains, 47; and work/education as devalued, 22. *See also* Black women
women in gangs: and agency, 47–8; and coercion, 47–8; as homogenous, 42, 48; research on, 45, 48–52; and respect, 47; as "at risk," 46; as sexual objects, 42–3, 45; as victims, 46; and violence, 43, 45
Work, Monroe, 31, 32, 39n3
working class, 43
World Health Organization, 168–9
WRP ("What is the problem represented to be?"), 189–90

"Ya Playin' Ya Self" (song), 164
Yablonsky, L., 77
York South Weston (YSW), 224–5
Young, Jock, 60, 61
Young, Tara, 48–9, 50
youth, study of, 45
youth detention facilities, 228
youth workers, 245

Zamudio, Margaret, 243